A Double Vision Hermeneutic

A Double Vision Hermeneutic

Interpreting a Chinese Pastor's Intersubjective Experience of Shi Engaging Yìzhuàn and Pauline Texts

SAMUEL HIO-KEE OOI
[HUÁNG HOÙJĪ]

PICKWICK Publications · Eugene, Oregon

A DOUBLE VISION HERMENEUTIC
Interpreting a Chinese Pastor's Intersubjective Experience of Shi Engaging Yìzhuàn and Pauline Texts

Copyright © 2014 Samuel Hio-Kee Ooi. All rights reserved. Except for brief quotations in critical publications or reviews, no part of this book may be reproduced in any manner without prior written permission from the publisher. Write: Permissions, Wipf and Stock Publishers, 199 W. 8th Ave., Suite 3, Eugene, OR 97401.

Pickwick Publications
An Imprint of Wipf and Stock Publishers
199 W. 8th Ave., Suite 3
Eugene, OR 97401

www.wipfandstock.com

ISBN 13: 978-1-62564-107-6

Cataloguing-in-Publication data:

Ooi, Samuel Hio-Kee [HUÁNG HOÙJĪ]

    A double vision hermeneutic : interpreting a chinese pastor's intersubjective experience of shi engaging Yìzhuàn and pauline texts / Samuel Hio-Kee Ooi.

    xvi + 276 pp. ; 23 cm. Includes bibliographical references and index.

    ISBN 13: 978-1-62564-107-6

    1. Bible. Epistles of Paul—Hermeneutics. 2. Philosophy, Chinese. I. Title.

BS2655 R35 O75 2014

Manufactured in the U.S.A.

I dedicate this thesis to my wife Yuen Shan and two daughters, Hiu Ching and Yan Kiu. During these five and a half years of research and writing, Yuen Shan had been a great support with her constructive comments and suggestions. Together we grew spiritually as the thesis gradually came into shape. Hiu Ching and Yan Kiu have both grown up. Over these years, they had heard many times: "Wait until daddy finishes this sentence, this section . . . the thesis" et cetera, yet never complained but rather, with love, encouragement, understanding, and prayer, offered their unfailing support.

The Master said,
"In ancient times, men learned with a view to their own improvement.
Nowadays, men learn with a view to the approbation of others."

"Xiàn Wèn," *Lúnyǔ*

The Master said,
"I will not be afflicted at men's not knowing me;
I will be afflicted that I do not know men."

"Xué Ěr," *Lúnyǔ*

But he said to me, "My grace is sufficient for you, for power is made perfect in weakness." So, I will boast all the more gladly of my weaknesses, so that the power of Christ may dwell in me. . . . for whenever I am weak, then I am strong.

2 Cor 12:9, 10b by Paul the Apostle

Contents

Acknowledgments   ix

Lists of Abbreviations   xi

Editorial Conventions, Use of Sources, and Research Matters   xiii

Abstract   xv

Introduction   1

1   Surveying Chinese Indigenous Theological Approaches   21

2   Constructing a Double Vision Hermeneutic   61

3   Text A1: *Shì* as a Cultural-linguistic and Traditionary Text   87

4   Interpreting Text A1: *Shì* with Text A2: *Yìzhuàn*   104

5   Text B1: Principalities and Powers: A Survey on Contemporary Discourse   137

6   Power in Text B2: Pauline Text I: Galatians   163

7   Power in Text B2: Pauline Text II: Corinthians   187

8   The Double Vision Hermeneutics of a Chinese Pastor's Intersubjective Experience of *Shì* Engaging *Yìzhuàn* and Pauline Texts   216

Appendix I: 64 Hexagrams   239

Appendix II: English Names of 64 Hexagrams   240

Glossary of Chinese Expressions   241

Selected Bibliography   247

Index   271

Acknowledgments

This thesis would not have been possible without the help from people near and afar. First of all, I am deeply grateful to my primary supervisor, Professor Dr Michael Northcott, professor of ethics of New College, School of Divinity, for his timely and constructive comments and support throughout the writing process, and most of all, during the post-viva period, his extra time and encouragement. I deeply appreciate the liberty he gave me in doing my research, which allowed me to pursue the methodology and knowledge that were most suitable for the formation of this thesis. I am also grateful to my secondary supervisor Prof Dr Joachim Gentz of Chinese Studies in the School of Literatures, Languages and Cultures, whose comments especially with regard to the studies of ancient China help me anchor my studies of *Yìzhuàn* in its historical contexts. His friendly conversational style had been an encouragement to me from time to time. I am, however, solely responsible for any mistakes that may remain.

My deep apprecation goes to Dr K. K. Yeo and Dr Elizabeth Koepping for their constructive comments and critiques in my viva. Unfortunately, Dr Yeo was unable to reexamine the revised thesis due to serious illness. My special thanks to Dr Victoria Harrison for whose prompt reply to be my new external examiner. While the post-viva rewriting experience felt like traveling through mountains and hills and crooked paths and rough places (Isa 40:4) to reach its final destination, it has been a spiritual character shaping experience for me.

I am indebted to Dr Thu En Yu, the principal of Sabah Theological Seminary, who had shown his support for my study in Edinburgh, and had made available the seminary's financial support for my tuition. My heartfelt thanks to Dr and Mrs Wong in Hong Kong, who generously suppport my family's living costs in Edinburgh. Bethel Chinese Church in Seria, Brunei has also been supporting us through these years. My hearty thanks to these brothers and sisters for their faithfulness.

Acknowledgments

My precious experience in serving in both Edinburgh Chinese Christian Church and Evangelical Chinese Church in Edinburgh over these years have not only enriched and transformed my view of pastoral ministry but also were important sources of insights and inspirations which contributed to the formation of my character and helped shape my thesis. I would also like to give special thanks to those in both churches who had faithfully offered financial supports and prayed for us.

To THECE (Theologically Hopeful Ethnic Chinese in Edinburgh), for your encouragement and support in times of frustration, thank you. My special thanks to Huáng Ēn-lín who had captured the essence of my thesis and suggested to me the idea of "shuāng tóng," i.e., "double vision." I hope our friendship will continue to grow beyond the academic boundary and touch our lives in a deeper and profound way.

Thank you Lord for your timely providence through Mrs Eleanor Perry, a colleague who came from England to Sabah in 2010, whose meticulousness, precision and sharpness in correcting my mistakes in English and suggestions for its style, and generosity to offer her precious time, to whom I am deeply indebted.

Thank you Lord for leading me all these years. Thank you for inspiration and all the hunches for discovering new materials, new ideas and for breakthroughs.

Thank you Lord for your abundant grace in life, the completion of this thesis and everything.

Abbreviations

Giles	Lionel Giles, *Art of War*.
Griffith	Sameul B. Griffith, *The Art of War*.
JCP	*Journal of Chinese Philosophy*
Legge	James Legge, *The Yî King*, Sacred Books of the East Vol. 16, The Sacred Books of China, vol. 2 of 6, Part II of The Texts of Confucianism, (Oxford, the Clarendon Press, 1882)
Louw & Nida	Louw & Nida, *Greek-English Lexicon of the New Testament Based on Semantic Domains*
Lynn	John Lynn, *The Classic of Changes: A New Translation of the "I Ching" as Interpreted by Wang Bi*
Minford	John Minford, *Sunzi, The Art of War*
Mair	Victor Mair, *The Art of War: Sun Zi's Military Methods*
NT	The New Testament
Nèizhuàn	Wáng Fūzhī, Zhoūyì nèizhuàn (Běijīng: Jiǔzhoū chūbǎn shè, 2004)
OT	The Old Testament
Rutt	Richard Rutt, *The Book of Changes (Zhoūyì): A Bronze Age Document.*
Shaughnessy	Edward Shaughnessy, *The I Ching (The Classic of Changes)*
Wàizhuàn	Wáng Fūzhī, Zhoūyì wàizhuàn (Běijīng: Jiǔzhoū chūbǎn shè, 2004)
Wilhelm/Baynes	Wilhelm/Baynes, I Ching.
Yulei	Zhū Xī, *Zhū Xī Yǔlei*, ed by Lí Jīngdé (Běijīng: Zhōnghuá shū jú, 1994)

xi

Abbreviations

Zhèngyì	Kǒng Yǐndá, *Zhoūyì zhèngyì* (Beǐjīng: Jiǔzhoū chūbǎn shè, 2004)

Yìzhuàn (Yìjīng and the Ten Wings)

Tuànzhuàn	The Tuàn Commentary or The Judgment (which contains two parts)
Dàxiàngzhuàn	The Dàxiàng Commentary or The Great Images
Xiǎoxiàngzhuàn	The Xiǎoxiàng Commentary or The Small Images
Wényán	Wényán or Commentary on the Words of the Text
Xìcí	Commentary on the Appended Phrases or Xìcízhuàn or Dàzhuàn (Great Commentary) (which contains two parts)
Shuōguà	Explaining the Trigrams (Shuōguà)
Xùguà	Providing the Sequence of the Hexagrams or Xùguà
Záguà	The Hexagrams in Irregular Order (Záguà)

Editoral Conventions, Use of Sources, and Research Matters

1. Confucian Sources and Transliteration

My primary source of *Yìzhuàn* is the received text, *chuán běn* 傳本 instead of the Mǎwángduī text. The Chinese version follows Kǒng Yǐndá edition included in which are Wáng Bì and Hán Kāngbó commentary and annotations, reproduced and published by Jiǔzhoū chūbǎn shè. I also rely and compare English versions by James Legge, Richard Wilhelm/Baynes, and John Lynn but always produce my own translations where I find them not satisfactory. Included in Lynn's translation are Wáng Bì and Hán Kāngbó commentaries. For James Legge's translation, I use *The I Ching* James Legge, tr. Sacred Books of the East, vol. 16 [1899], which is available at http://www.sacred-texts.com/ich/index.htm.

Other than these, I count *Zhū Zǐ Yǔlèi* and Wáng Fūzhī *Zhoūyì nèizhuàn* and *Zhoūyì wàizhuàn* reproduced and published by Jiǔzhoū chūbǎn shè as my primary sources. For *Yǔlèi*, the version is edited by Lí Jìngdé in eight volumes altogether with continual paging througout. For conveniency, I simply list the page numbers without mentioning which volume it is from for it is the *juàn* (book) and *zhāng* (chapter) which is more relevant for a Chinese classic text like this. Thus, *juàn yī* will be translated as Book One. It appears in footnotes as *Yǔlèi*, Book 1, 2, or 66 et cetera, sometimes followed by chapters or sections in Chinese characters.

Chinese transliterations instead of characters will be used. Original Chinese titles together with transliterations and English translation will appear in the bibliography. *Pīnyīn* system will be used with four tones. However, *qīngshēng* (light tone) will appear as without any tone signal and when *biàndiào* (changed tone) occurs, the original tone will be shown instead of the changed tone. This will apply even to cited texts but not original English titles that come with Chinese transliterated titles. I render

Editoral Conventions, Use of Sources, and Research Matters

Chinese compound terms for example as *zhéxué* instead of *zhé xué*. They appear in italic except when they appear as proper names including the tags of the hexagrams.

2. Christian Sources and Greek New Testemant

In terms of Christian texts, my primary source is Pauline texts, both in Greek, English and Chinese. I will not include post-New Testamental works from early church fathers to post-reformational periods; rather the effort will be dedicated in relying on the studies of Pauline scholars in recent decades both in terms of theological exegetical discussion in Pauline commentaries and theological hermeneutics of Pauline texts. The Greek New Testament I use is electronic version of *Novum Testamentum Graece* (*New Testament in Greek*), Nestle-Aland, 27th Edition, prepared by Institut für neutestamentliche Testforschung Münster/Westfalen, Barbara and Kurt Aland (Editors). Copyright © 1898 and 1993 by Deutsche Bibelgesellschaft, Stuttgart. Used by permission. Morphological tagging by William D. Mounce and Rex A. Koivisto. Copyright © 2003 William D. Mounce. Copyright © 2008 OakTree Software, Inc. All rights reserved. Version 3.6.

For the biblical texts, most English Bible verses are in NRSV unless otherwise noted. Chinese Union Version and New Version will be used where applicable.

Abstract

The aim of this thesis is to unfold the multilayered intersubjective experience of the author himself, a Chinese pastor. The author postulates himself as the subject in whom the said experience was evident, so that it can be analyzed and interpreted. The author argues for a cultural-linguistic experience of *shì* as the locus at which the intersubjective experience takes place. He then shows that such experience embodies a Chinese Christian's 'two texts' inheritance, and argues that it is through unfolding or revealing of such experience that the nature of his relationship with them can be demonstrated. The author will show that his relationship to these "two texts" is a continuing appropriation of them. The appropriation is not done through arbitrary readings of the texts, but careful exegetical study of both biblical and Chinese classic. The subjective appropriation will be studied by paying attention to the texts with their literary and historical contexts considered, not simply for the sake of reconstruction but for their relevancy to what the subject experiences. To unfold this experience, the author identifies five key texts that are found in his intersubjective experience: Text A1: *Shì*, Text A2: *Yìzhuàn*, Text B1: Pauline notion of principalities and powers, Text B2: Pauline Texts I and II: Galatians and 1 Corinthians, and Text 0 (zero), his *initial or seminal experience* of *shì*. The author provides the hermeneutical rationale in dialogue with Michael Polanyi and Hans Georg Gadamer, and proposes that a *double vision hermeneutic* will help interpret the multilayered intersubjective relationships between texts and the subject. The thesis will reveal, through the double vision hermeneutic, a unique way of conceiving Chinese Christian self that embodies fusion, intermingling and layers of understanding of texts and notions from the Bible and Chinese tradition. The author argues that study of this intersubjective experience reveals a vital facet of Chinese Christian self, and significantly enhances the study of Chinese theology. The author also hopes that the double vision hermeneutic as demonstrated will contribute to the understanding of a facet of Chinese Christian way of being.

Introduction

1. Background

This thesis arose from my personal experience as a Chinese Christian. Before the purpose of the thesis can be stated and appreciated, I will give a brief description of my background as a Chinese Christian and the formation of a Chinese Christian intersubjective experience of *shì*—with *yì* (grip or grasp) on the top and *lì* (power or force) the *radical*, a Chinese word implying not only power but also used to mean a situation, a circumstance, a tendency, and a tension that is about to be triggered off—and how it is related to my reading of *Yìzhuàn* and Pauline texts. The sections below aim to do that, followed by my statement of purpose and methodology, which will explain why *shì*, *Yìzhuàn* and Pauline texts are selected for my interpretation.

1.1: The Shaping of Chinese and Christian Identity in Early Years

I grew up in a Chinese cultural context. While my mother tongue is Fújiàn (Mǐnnán dialect), I learnt Mandarin from primary school. I went to one of the Chinese Independent High Schools (CIHS),[1] where I could learn more about Chinese language, literature and history. In high school years, influenced by my elder brothers, I also was attracted to Chinese martial-chivalry novels, among which were those written by Jīn Yōng (Zhā Liángyǒng), for example, *Shèdiāo yīngxióng zhuàn* or the *Legend of Condor Heroes*. Jīn Yōng's novels are among the best literary examples that embody Chinese

---

1. There are 60 Chinese Independent High Schools throughout Malaysia. According to the record of Dǒng Jiào Zhǒng (the Association of Chinese School Teachers and Trustees), there were 53,005 students studying in these schools in 2004. See http://www.djz.ed.my/djzong/djz3.hTM.

A Double Vision Hermeneutic

culture and the Three-Religion tradition (*Sānjiào*, namely, Confucianism, Daoism and Buddhism). It was in the *Legend of Condor Heroes* that I first encountered the following *Yìjīng* statements: *qiǎn lóng wù yòng* (Hidden dragon/Do not act) as in the first line of *Yìjīng* Qián hexagram, *jiàn lóng zài tián* (Dragon appearing in the field) as in the second line; *feīlóng zài tīan* (Flying dragon in the heavens) as in the fifth line, and *kànglóng yoǔ huǐ* (Arrogant dragon will have a cause to repent) as in the sixth line. While all these phrases may look meaningless and perhaps incomprehensible to non-native Chinese or people without a background knowledge of Chinese cultural-linguistic tradition, the dragon metaphor is obvious. Nevertheless, this dragon should not be understood as the dragon in the English Bible for example in Revelation 2:9, which indicates Satan. Rather it should be read based on its symbolism in *Yìjīng*.

Yìjīng is traditionally acclaimed as one of the Chinese *Five Classics*.[2] *Yìjīng* has shaped Chinese culture generation after generation. As Zhū Bólún states, "Although *Zhouyi* is a Confucian classic, its influence is not limited to Confucianism. Other philosophical systems have tapped into this same resource in their own way to enrich and fortify their philosophy."[3] According to Chung-ying Cheng, "the *Yijing* has functioned as the source of insight into reality from the time of Confucius continuously through Daoism, Neo-Daoism, Chinese Buddhism, and Neo-Confucianism to the present day."[4] Thus through Jīn Yōng's and many other martial-chivalry novels that I read, I had been immersed in many philosophical ideas as found in Chinese tradition in my youth.

I also grew up in a Christian family. Christian and Chinese identity were equally real to me. I was baptized at twelve. I attended Bible study classes, youth fellowship, evangelistic and revival meetings regularly, went to big and small retreats that lasted for five to six days every year in which I intensively learnt biblical teachings, and participated in the high school Christian fellowship. I read at least one chapter of the Bible in my daily personal devotion time. These had all established my Christian identity.

---

2. The received text that is widely referred to contains the *Ten Appendices* or the *Ten Commentaries*. Together it is called *Yìzhuàn*. In the following, I shall use *Yìzhuàn* when *Commentaries* are implied with no specific reference to any of them is necessary, and *Yìjīng* to refer to the text without the *Commentaries*.

3. Zhū, *Yi xué zhéxué shǐ*, 40. Translation mine.

4. Cheng, "Identity and Vision," 396. The Quánzhēn Daoist sect around the time of Jīn dynasty and Northern Sòng dynasty that often appears in Jīn Yōng's novels is one of the Neo-Daoist branches.

Introduction

Bearing both a Christian and a Chinese identity at the same time had never been an issue for me during those early years. Christian faith was more about my personal salvation than a matter for theological reflection. I was too young to start to think about the integration of both Chinese and Christian traditions. However, it was this unconscious adoption of two traditions and two identities at the same time without any feeling of conflict that had allowed the dual identity to fuse naturally in my life.

1.2: Starting to Reflect on Chinese Christian Identity

My personal interest in Chinese indigenous theology was kindled in the mid-1980s when I was introduced to *Huìtōng yǔ zhuǎnhuà* (Communication and Transformation), a book on Confucian-Christian dialog by Cài Rénhoù, Zhōu Liánhuá, and Liáng Yènchéng.[5] This interest in indigenous theology and Confucian-Christian dialog grew deeper over the years when I studied for my Master of Divinity (1994–1997) and Master of Theology (2000-2002) degrees. While studying in the seminary, I wrote a paper on Wáng Yángmíng (1472–1529 AD), a philosopher from the Míng dynasty, comparing his theory of *liángzhī*, innate knowledge or conscience with the "conscience" (συνειδήσεως) in the context of Romans 2:17–18.[6] The question of whether or not good Chinese common people, *laǒ baǐxìng*,[7] could be claimed righteous started to sink in my mind. From 1994 to 2002, with continued reading of books related to Chinese indigenous theology and Christian-Confucian dialogs, my eyes were opened to see many earlier Chinese Christian intellectuals who had wrestled with similar concerns.[8] In 2002, as a partial fulfilment for the degree of Master of Theology, I submitted a thesis on a study of the theological model of an indigenous Chinese theologian, Xiè Fúyǎ (Hsieh Nai-zen, 1892–1991).[9]

My pursuit during those years, like other Chinese Christian intellectuals, was not only an academic concern, but also a personal quest. As one

---

5. Cài, Zhōu, and Liáng, *Huìtōng yǔ Zhuǎnhuà*.

6. This was in 1995. Later I also wrote a paper, "Interpreting Zhū Xī's Ideas of Lǐ, Qì and Tàijí with Metaphorical/Symbolic Theology" in 2000.

7. Literally, *laǒ baǐxìng*, are made of *laǒ*, which means old, and *baǐ xìng*, which means a hundred surname, symbolizing all people under the heaven, *tiānxià* and also under the Son of Heaven, the Emperor.

8. For some of these people and their thoughts, see chapter 1.

9. Huáng, "Already But Not Yet." A brief review of the theology of Hsieh Nai-zen (Xiè Fúyǎ) with particular emphasis on his deliberation on *Yìjīng* philosophy will be provided in chapter 1.

Chinese theologian has recently confessed, "The more I study Christian theology, the more I have become convinced of how deeply Confucianism is embedded in my spirituality, my soul and my body. Subtly and powerfully, Confucianism works inside me." The Confucian-Christian dialog as personally experienced by him, he emphasizes, "is not a purely theoretical issue for me, it lives in me with tears and joy."[10]

The notion "works inside me" is worth pondering further. Even now as I reflect on my experience as a Chinese Christian, not only Confucianism but the entire Chinese tradition is working inside me. To use a metaphor, Chinese tradition is a lens through which I perceive the external world, and through which I interpret what happens to me. Yet on the other hand, it is equally correct to say that not only Chinese tradition, but also a Christian conscience is working inside me in many aspects. I will now refer to a personal experience of a power struggle during my years as a pastor, to show how these two traditions work in me at the same time.

1.3: A Narrative of My Double Vision Experience as a Chinese Pastor

I first became a pastor in 1997 in Hong Kong when I was 31 years old right after I graduated from a seminary. I started to serve in a Baptist church where there were six pastors in the pastoral team, including the senior pastor and me. I discovered later that there was some tension between the senior pastor and the board of deacons (all deacons are ordained, according to their tradition). I was the youngest in the pastoral team, and was much younger than the deacons, who were in their forties. They, the deacons, had grown up and served in that church since high school. Like a fool or as a Chinese idiom says, "Like a calf that had not yet learnt to fear a tiger," I trampled into a field where a power struggle was going on. One scenario will be sufficient here to illustrate such a situation.

During that time the church had three separate Sunday services. The senior pastor proposed a plan for three separate models to target three different groups. The deacons did not agree wholeheartedly to the plan but consented to the senior pastor trying it out. The senior pastor proposed to put me in charge of one model which targeted on young adults. I should have rejected this offer from my senior pastor, but could not and did not.

---

10. Huang, "Confronting Confucian," 10–11.

I was new and motivated by the opportunity to demonstrate my ability and talents.

However, as insensitive as I was initially, I became aware of the *shì*, a Chinese word loaded with cultural implication, which literally means the "disposition of the power dynamic." While the power struggle I experienced during that time is something one can find in all organizations across different cultures, as a Chinese, I quickly associated the situation with, and described it as *shì*. With this cultural lens, I understand and interpret what happens to me. This lens has given me a vision that is colored by Chinese culture. In other words, the phenomenon of power struggle described above was not anything particularly cultural that is worth singling out. What I want to emphasize is the perception and interpretation of such a phenomenon, which reflects a Chinese perspective. In other words, it was I, as a person rooted in Chinese culture who read what happened and interpreted it in terms of *shì*.

Nevertheless, as a Christian for many years, the Christian conscience has also been part of me. Serving as a pastor could only mean a stronger Christian conscience that sometimes worked more as an accusatory than a liberating power. During that time when I was caught in the church power struggle, I was myself at the same time wrestling with an internal struggle. On the surface, I was frustrated and angry about a church power struggle, which was beyond my personal control. However, what became inner turmoil was guilt and shame caused by my own lustful thoughts that were equally uncontrollable. The two struggles were not directly related. The one was about power structure, while the other about the bondage of sin as Paul describes in Romans 7. I felt the anguish of my heart, crying "Wretched man that I am! Who will rescue me from this body of death?"[11] For me, during that time, Paul's words were not so much addressing the power struggle within the church, as addressing the power of sin in my life.

The Double Vision

In the above example of my pastoral experience of power struggle, I have featured the Chinese cultural perception and the Christian conscience in two separate paragraphs. The one shows us a *Chinese vision*, while the other a *Christian vision*. Both of these work inside me, shaping my vision. I call this double vision. I am using "double vision" as a metaphor to capture

11. Rom 7:24.

these two visions. Although it is understood that "double vision" in English means "diplopia," a visual impairment, to me as a non-native speaker, its literal sense, which captured my attention more directly and instantly, can be used more freely. According to the *Oxford Advanced Learner's Dictionary*, it is defined that one who has double vision "can see two things when there is only one."[12] Thus with it I mean 1) being aware of two visions or two texts at the same time or seeing them both in one vision at the same time, 2) seeing one vision or text at the foreground but being aware of another text or vision in the background, or 3) two visions or two texts appearing sequentially and alternately.

With this basic assumption in mind, I started the hermeneutical project for this thesis. I am using the words hermeneutics and hermeneutical to indicate that which relates to the act and process of understanding. According to Paul Ricoeur, hermeneutics is about interpretation and explanation.[13] As this hermeneutics is about an interpretation and explanation of the double vision I claim I have due to my being at the same time both a Chinese and a Christian, it is in Richard Palmer's term, also a "hermeneutics in the phenomenology of *Dasein* and of existential understanding."[14] This thesis is thus firstly a hermeneutics of my existence with particular attention to my inheritance of two traditions.

Secondly, having wrestled with the double vision time after time in the process of writing, it has gradually become apparent that the double vision should describe not only the Chinese and Christian perceptions of the same scenario, but also the intersubjective relationships of Chinese and Christian texts. It is about a few texts with me, i.e., my intersubjective readings of 1) two Chinese texts, 2) two Christian texts, and 3) between the Chinese and Christian texts. What do I mean by intersubjective readings and intersubjective relationships?

---

12. Hornby, *Oxford Advanced Learner's Dictionary*, 458.

13. See Ricoeur, *Interpretation Theory*; Palmer, *Hermeneutics*, especially up to page 65.

14. Originally his definition of Martin Heidegger's hermeneutics in Palmer, *Hermeneutics*, 41–42. See also Gadamer, *Truth and Method*, 293; also idem, "On the Problem of Self Understanding (1962)," 49 where he says, "Even in *Being and Time* the real question is not in what way being can be understood but in what way understanding is being, for the understanding of being represents the existential distinction of Dasein."

1.4: An Intersubjective Reading of Shì and Yìjīng

It was a couple of years later as I read *Yìjīng*, that a new horizon of understanding opened up for me. Like many, I first approached *Yìjīng* by reading the first hexagram, Qián 乾 (The Creative, signifying Heaven) of the total sixty-four hexagrams. I was struck by what a revealing power the *Yìjīng* had to speak to a real situation of human affairs, and dynamism within an organization.

I started with the beginning of the *Yìjīng* text. There I found in the line statements attached to the first and second lines of the Qián hexagram:

> "Hidden dragon. Do not act."
> "Dragon appearing in the field. It furthers one to see the great man."[15]

As I said, I had come across the above statements in the *Legend of Condor Heroes*, one of Jīn Yōng's novels. However, this time they were no longer descriptions of martial arts movements found in the novel, but statements that spoke right into my situation. I felt that I was "the dragon" caught between the first *yáng* and second *yáng* situations, between being hidden and inactive, and appearing, at the opportune time, to take action. Although according to the tradition of *Yìjīng* interpretation, dragon has been applied to indicate a king or a nobleman (*jūnzǐ*) or someone with superior political and social status in ancient time, I could not resist associating myself analogously with the dragon and the poetic and metaphoric description of the dynamic relationship between "the dragon," "the field," and "the great man." The senior pastor to me was like the "great man" as mentioned above.

Had I known and been able to apply the philosophy of *Yìjīng* earlier, I would have been more prudent with regard to the power relations, I thought. Yet, insensitive to the complexity of the situation, unable to discern whether or not I had in fact encountered the "great man", and because of my ambition, I stumbled in bewilderment.

Such a reading of *Yìjīng*, relating it to power relations, revealed an understanding of *shì*, through the lens of *Yìjīng*. As I further meditated on the relationship between the *Yìjīng* text and *shì*, it became clear that every hexagram in the sixty-four hexagrams of the *Yìjīng* was about *yīn* power and *yáng* power. The two texts met in me, the subject. It was through me, the subject, that the *Yìjīng* text was being read into *shì* and vice versa. This kind of reading I call 'an intersubjective reading'. In a sense, I am seeing

---

15. See Wilhelm/Baynes, 5, 6.

power relations with the vision of *Yìjīng* as well as *shì*. This type of seeing is a double vision within one subject intersubjectively—*shì* in *Yìjīng* and *Yìjīng* in *shì*. However, this indicates only one layer of double vision. There are several layers, each forming a layer of intersubjective relationship of its own.

1.5: A Reading of Power in Pauline Texts

As I have mentioned earlier, Christian conscience had worked in me when I experienced the power struggle in the church. I was especially aware of Saint Paul's account of the power of sin. Believing that this should be how my Christian vision would be intermingling with my Chinese *Yìjīng*/*shì* reading of power relations, I started to engage with this in my reading of Pauline texts. The result has turned out to be that there is more in the Pauline texts about power relations than I initially thought. Moreover, having further studied the texts it dawned on me that my interpretation of Paul's understanding of power should include two perspectives: one that takes on the Pauline account of principalities and powers, and the other which unveils the power issues as found in the Galatian and the Corinthian churches. The two perspectives are interrelated, as when I read of the power issues in these two churches, I find myself thinking of the principalities and powers that are beyond the sociological and interpersonal dimension; that is to say, as I think of the power struggles as happened in Galatian and Corinthian churches and how they could be compared to the power struggle I experienced in Chinese churches, the theological aspect as expressed through the notion of the principalities and powers seems to provide an explanation more important than the sociological one. The comparison of the power struggles as happened in contexts of Pauline churches with that of mine is done through a "hermeneutics of application".[16] Moreover, the use of the Pauline notion of principalities and powers for the interpretation of the power struggles in respective contexts is done through me, the subject, in whom the fusion of various understandings has happened. This fusion happens because the subject has brought the different contexts of power struggles, and the understandings and interpretations of them into himself. This is made possible through my subjective appropriation[17] of them into me so that the power struggles can be interpreted through the notion of principalities and powers.

16. Gadamer, *Truth and Method*, 306–9. See my discussion in pages 101ff.
17. For "appropriation," see the next section.

Introduction

1.6: Double Vision of Chinese and Pauline Texts

The above introduces the four basic texts which I am going to engage with in this thesis: two from the Chinese tradition, and the other two from Paul. The first of these four is *shì*. It is the power dynamic I experienced in the church. By alluding to this word, I emphasize the Chinese cultural-linguistic perspective through which I understand power relations. The history of this word can be traced back more than two thousand years. The word itself is embodied in Chinese culture as part of the entire cultural-linguistic inheritance. I call *shì* with its cultural-linguistic implication Text A1.

The second text is Text A2: *Yìjīng* or *Yìzhuàn*. In the above, I refer to *Yìjīng* statements to interpret my own situation. Such a "hermeneutics of application" of a Chinese classical text to a real life situation reflects my situatedness in Chinese cultural and literary tradition.

As for the Pauline texts, I assign Paul's account of the principalities and powers as Text B1. While I referred earlier to the power of sin, I understand that to Paul, it only represents part of his theology of the principalities and powers. It will be read intersubjectively with my Text B2: Galatians and 1 Corinthians, i.e. the power struggles in these two churches.

2. Purpose of This Thesis

The purpose of this thesis is thus to *explain* the ontological manifestation of my double vision. In the above this double vision is shown in my intersubjective experience of *shì*. The experience embodies the double vision and the double vision embodies experience. The thesis is not a study of *shì* nor power per se. However, as my double vision is manifested in my intersubjective experience of *shì* and Pauline understanding of principalities and powers, it is inevitable that my discussion shall engage with both. In addition, my understanding of *shì* also embodies my understanding of *Yìjīng* and their intersubjective experience; I therefore need to engage *Yìjīng* in my discussion. However, the ultimate purpose is nonetheless to unfold the double vision that works in me, that is to say, how I understand and explain my reading and understanding of the texts. The purpose is to explain and to interpret, which is thus a hermeneutical one.[18]

---

18. See Ricoeur, *Interpretation Theory*.

A Double Vision Hermeneutic

Therefore, my task is to bring to light the various layers of intersubjective relationship between Texts A1, A2, B1, and B2. I assume that the texts themselves do not cause these relationships to exist. It is within and through the subject, myself, that such multilinear or multilayer relationships emerge. Nevertheless, the fact that the texts are within implies my appropriation of them into me. In his essay, "Appropriation," Paul Ricoeur deliberates on the meaning of appropriation in hermeneutics, i.e. on what happens between a reader and a text. "Appropriation" to him means "'to make one's own' of what was initially 'alien,'" originally from "the German term '*Aneignung*."[19] In terms of hermeneutics, this appropriation is "the counterpart of the timeless distanciation," which "struggle(s) against cultural distance and historical alienation." It "actualizes the meaning of the text to the present reader."[20] By appropriating them, I allow them to enter me. Thus, on the one hand I am reading them; on the other, they are changing me as they are entering me.

Ricoeur brings attention to another counterpart of the act of appropriation, a simultaneous "relinquishment," or a "letting-go," or a "divestiture," of one's own "*ego*". Instead of "taking possession" of what the ego has appropriated, Ricoeur emphasizes, "[i]t is in allowing itself to be carried off towards the reference of the text that the ego divests itself of itself,"[21] for he thinks "understanding is as much disappropriation as appropriation."[22] Thus, having presupposed my appropriation of Texts A1, A2, B1, and B2 as preceding the possibility of my intersubjective reading of them, I also observe the dialectic between the disappropriation and appropriation. This tension will be further elucidated below when I discuss Hans Georg Gadamer's hermeneutics in chapter 2.

In the process of "reading" and "entering," the intersubjective relationship is formed between me and the texts. However, the texts can only find those who read and appropriate them to be their hosts. Readers, hence interpreting subjects, are the primary creators of the intersubjective relationship. In this thesis, the intersubjective relationships between my texts are formed, and as such related within my perception or my vision.

As I have stated above, Texts A1 and A2 form one intersubjective relationship, Texts B1 and B2 another, and Texts A1 + A2 and Texts B1 and B2 another. I see in every layer a double vision. For example, in one layer,

19. Ricoeur, "Appropriation," 185.
20. Ricoeur, "Appropriation," 185.
21. Ricoeur, "Appropriation," 191. See also 192.
22. Ricoeur, "Hermeneutical Function of Distanciation," 144.

1) I am aware of Text A1 and A2 or see them both at the same time, 2) I see Text A1 at the foreground but am aware of Text A2 in the background, or 3) I see Texts A1 and A2 appear sequentially and alternately to me. Such a double vision is also found in the relationship between Texts B1 and B2, and between Texts A and B.

While power relations may seem to be the focus of this thesis, it is only so in the sense that it is the germinal experience whereby my understanding of my double vision has arisen and developed. In order to interpret my double vision, this germinal experience cannot be separated from my hermeneutics. However, the purpose of this thesis is not to solve the problem of power entailed in the issue of power relations per se; it is rather to unfold and to interpret the multi-layered intersubjective relationships as found within myself, the subject. It is also to show how the Chinese and Pauline texts are appropriated within me and how they form my double vision of/in the intersubjective experience of *shì*. The decision to focus on *shì* as a description of power or power relations is to reflect my rootedness in Chinese tradition, as it is through being embedded in this tradition that I perceive the power relations through the lens of *shì*. The decision is also engendered by the intersubjective experience itself. As was stated earlier, the experience embodies *shì* and power, and my interpretation or unfolding of the intersubjective experience will thus entail the discussion of *shì* and power.

Hence, the purpose of this thesis is to bring to light the various layers of intersubjective relationship between Texts A1, A2, B1, and B2 within my personal intersubjective experience and understanding of *shì*. My interest is not in deliberating on the intersubjective relationship of these texts in theory and in general, but to deliberate on them in relation to my *experience* of *shì*.

3. My Methodology and Texts for Interpretation

3.1 Methodology

The purpose of this thesis as stated above has determined my methodology. As the purpose is to *interpret* the *intersubjective* relationship between the various texts and between these texts with me, my approach will be *hermeneutical*. By hermeneutical, I imply to explain, to unfold and to understand not only texts, but also experiences and phenomena. Thus, texts may also imply nonliterary texts, for example, experience. To achieve this, I will explain the hermeneutical factors operating throughout the process of my hermeneutics. They will be set out in chapter 2.

3.2: My Selection of Texts: Shì, Yìzhuàn and Pauline Texts

As the above has shown, there are Texts A1, A2, B1 and B2. The basic texts I will be investigating will be *shì* as it appears in some pre-Qín texts (before 221 BC when Qín unified China), *Yìzhuàn* and Pauline texts.

Shì

For *shì*, I will focus on its appearances in *Sūnzǐ bīngfǎ* (*The Art of War*) by *Sūnzǐ* (sixth century BC), the militarist, *Hán Fēizǐ* by Hán Fēi (280–233 BC), a representative of the Legalist school, and *Xúnzǐ* by *Xúnzǐ* (c.310/2– 230 BC), a Confucian representative in the Warring States.

Yìzhuàn

The *Yìzhuàn* as I use it refers to *Yìjīng* and the *Shíyì* (the *Ten Appendices* or *Ten Commentaries*) in what is now called the received text of *Yìzhuàn*,[23] which I base for my study here. *Yìjīng* is the original main corpus that includes the sixty-four hexagrams and the statements attached to the hexagrams (the diagrams) and their respective six lines (see Diagram A below).

---

23. Two versions of the *Yìjīng*, the Book of Changes, are available to us: the received texts of *Yìjīng* and the *Mawangdui Yìjīng*. According to Chinese tradition, there were also *Guīcáng Yì(jīng)* (Return to the Hidden) and *Liánshān Yì(jīng)* (lit., Linked Mountains) which had been lost. See Smith, *Fathoming the Cosmos*, 18. *Mǎwángduī Yìjīng* was found in an excavation in 1973 near Chángshá, Húnán a Hàn tomb #3. See Shaughnessy, *I Ching*, 14. Since then a new area of study in relation to *Yìjīng* has started. For an introduction to the study of *Mǎwángduī Yìjīng* and its texts, see Shanghnessy, *I Ching*, 14–27.

Introduction

Diagram A

Studies have shown that *Yìjīng* is the first layer of the whole corpus, believed to be an edited text with collection of divination oracles from the Shāng Dynasty (c.1700 to 1100 BC), or from the ninth century BC or earlier.[24] The combined form, *Yìzhuàn*, existed at least from the Hàn dynasty (206 BC–8 AD for Western Hàn, 25–220 AD for Eastern Hàn, and 8–22 AD for Wàng Mǎng's Xīn Dynasty between them). Hereafter I will refer to the inclusive corpus with the *Ten Wings* as *Yìzhuàn*, and that without as *Yìjīng*.

INTERTEXTUALITY OF SHÌ AND YÌZHUÀN

In this thesis, my intention is to read *Yìzhuàn* through the lens of *shì* and vice versa. Being a collected corpus dating from pre-Chūnqiū (Autumn *and* Spring period) to the late Warring States (c.475–221 BC) or even early Hàn periods, *Yìzhuàn* reflects, in a nutshell, philosophical ideas from pre-Qín period including those of Confucianist, Daoist, Yīn-yáng, Fǎjiā (Legalist or Standardizer),[25] and probably Bīngjiā (Military Strategist) schools

---

24. For further argument of the dating of *Yìzhuàn*, see Lynn, "Introduction," 2. Liào Míngchūn argues for late Shāng or Early Zhōu Dynasty, see Liào, "Cóng yǔyán dé bǐjiàn lùn Zhōuyì běnjīng dè chéngshū niándài," 223. Based on his studies on H4 Mēng (Obscurity) and H7 Shī (Army), Marshall dates *Yìjīng* to Shāng Dynasty, see *Mandate*, 67–81, 96–97. He refuted Shaughnessy and Kunst who date *Yìjīng* to 800 BC, see *Mandate*, 46–47.

25. I follow the convention to call Fǎjiā as "Legalist." However, one should not think that "legal" as is found in here implies "law." More precisely, the *fǎ* as it is associated with the school with it as its name might probably mean "standard" according to the study of Chad Hansen who thus translates *Fǎjiā* as "Standardizers," see Hansen, *A Daoist Theory of Chinese Thought*, 347–50. Broadly speaking, *fǎ* probably is closer to what is meant by *lǐfǎ* "ritual-standard" or "ritual and standard" but does not exclude the narrower sense as to mean punishment. If one follows Cheng's argument, who groups the meaning of *fǎ* into two major categories, the one along the line of ritual, pattern, method, and principle, and the other of punishment and legislative law for the political convenience of the ruler to rule his people, then the *fǎ* as used in *fǎjiā*'s argument is closer to the latter. In that case, the conventional translation "legalist" is

with a predominantly Confucian philosophy. It reflects one significant form that shows an integrated grand system where its contemporary and preexisting ideas were assimilated and appropriated. It reflects a Confucian voice but is also able to reflect a rich pre-Qín context, where each different school articulated its own unique interpretation of many of the key ideas, such as *daò, shì, tiān* et cetera.

As Johanna Liu comments on the intertextuality between Chinese classics,

> a text is never a solitary work done by an isolated writer, but a network of writings by quoting one text from another, or by alluding one text to another, through and by which a continual deferment of an idea or a meaning in a particular culture would be able to continue.[26]

Liu expounds the cross-temporal appearance of texts by defining it as "a continual deferment." She contends that, "In view of literary texts in Chinese classics, this type of intertextuality could be found everywhere since the time of Confucius, who claimed that: 'I transmit but do not innovate' (Analects, 7:1)."[27] Likewise, the intertextuality between *Yìzhuàn* and texts by other thinkers from Chūnqiū to Qín does exist. As Richard Smith succinctly puts it when commenting on a famous thinker from the Qín dynasty, Dǒng Zhòngshū (179–104 BC), whose thoughts reflect a combination of ideas across different schools,

> Although committed to moral values consistent with Confucian tradition broadly defined, early Han thinkers like Dong drew upon a variety of philosophical and religious traditions, including "the way of the Yellow Emperor and Laozi" (Huang-Lao dao) an outlook devoted to Daoist practices of physical and spiritual cultivation as well as ways of ruling often characterized as Legalist (Fajia).[28]

What is meant is that Dǒng integrated Confucian, Daoist, and Legalist tradition. Thus, I assume the intertextuality of *shì* in the Confucian as well as in the works of the Legalists and Military Strategists. With this assumption in mind, I will discuss *shì* in more detail later as it appears in the works of different writers Sūnzǐ, Hán Feīzǐ, and Xúnzǐ whose works

not too far from what it implied. See Cheng, "Legalism versus Confucianism," 311-38.

26. Liu, "Music [yue] in Classical Confucianism," 63.
27. Liu, "Music [yue] in Classical Confucianism," 63.
28. Smith, *Fathoming the Cosmos*, 32.

Introduction

appeared from the sixth to the third century BC, roughly contemporary to *Yìzhuàn*. I assume that the final form of *Yìzhuàn* can be traced back to before the time of Dǒng, and therefore, believe that the combination and integration of ideas and interpretations across the pre-existing schools is found in *Yìzhuàn* as it is in Dǒng's work. Thus, I also assume an intertextuality between *Yìzhuàn* and *shī*.

Pauline Texts

Modern Scholars have divided the Pauline epistles[29] into two groups: the undisputed letters,[30] and the disputed letters.[31] In this thesis, a differentiation is not needed. While my focus will be Galatians and 1 Corinthians, I will take the stance that all thirteen letters are Paul's, which allows me to discuss different letters intertextually. To me, most relevant of all, are the situational issues, which probably also determine the styles found in different letters.[32]

I hold the view that, if we treat them all as Pauline, his letters were written within the dates ranging from the early forties to the late sixties of the first century.[33] Thus, although not all canonized Pauline texts will be

---

29. In this thesis, the terms epistle and letter are interchangeable. For an explanation of differentiation, see Beker, *Paul the Apostle*, 23–24.

30. Though the issue is controversial, to the first group are ascribed seven letters: Romans, 1 and 2 Corinthians, Galatians, Philippians, 1 Thessalonians, and Philemon. For a brief discussions on this, see Carlson, "The Disputed Letters of Paul," 110–20; Porter, ed.,*The Pauline Canon*; Gorman, *Apostle of the Crucified Lord*, 41–42, 88, 91; Wright, *Paul*, 18–20 or more recently in *Justification*, 26–28.

31. More recently, Luke Johnson also challenges the wide consensus concerning the pseudepigraphical nature of Pastoral Epistles, as Childs points out (Childs, *Reading Paul*, 46; Johnson, *The First and Second Letters to Timothy*, 55–97). Another concise argument for Pauline authorship is seen in Knight, *The Pastoral Epistles*, 13–52. Childs himself, with his canonical approach, attributes pastoral epistles to a "passive Paul" in contrast to the "active Paul" that is found in the authentic epistles. The "passive Paul" reflects Pauline legacy which testifies to a canonization process of Pauline corpus and the circulation of his earlier letters. It is a transition from Paul as teacher to Paul "as the model by which sound doctrine is measured" (Childs, *Reading Paul*, 73, see all through 69–75).

32. Murphy-O'Connor, *Paul: A Critical Life*, 1–31; Gorman, *Apostle*, 44–45; Bruce, *The New Testament Documents*, 8. This book was first published in 1943 as *Are the New Testament Documents Reliable?* and later as *New Testament Documents: Are They Reliable?* (Downers Grove, IL: InterVarsity Press, 1981). For Pauline authorship of pastoral epistles, see Bruce, *The New Testament Documents*, 8. This date is still validated by Murphy-O'Connor, see *Paul*, 31.

33. Bruce accepts all thirteen letters as Pauline in his 1943 monograph, see Bruce,

15

treated in this thesis, I have presupposed that they are a unitive whole,[34] written within two decades and by a mature Christian, Paul, who came to an understanding that he was meant to be an apostle to the Gentiles.[35]

With the above presuppositions, I intend to treat Paul, the person, as the hermeneutical pivot of different issues that appeared in different churches.[36] Paul as who he was, and his understanding of what the gospel meant would take precedence and determine what he would say in all situations. Socio-rhetorically, he might have said what he did on different occasions, but he would not have said it if he was not who he was. In other words, there is a continuity between Paul's character and his words and deeds.

4. Chapters Overview

My plan for this thesis is as follows. First of all, it is important to set my thesis in a context. The concern of this thesis is to attempt an interpretation of my experience as a Chinese Christian, and I understand that I am not alone in this regard but in line with others who share this dual identity. There have been many in the past whose works have expressed

---

The New Testament Documents, 8. This book was first published in 1943 as *Are the New Testament Documents Reliable?* and later as *New Testament Documents*. He argues in a later work that even if they were not composed by Paul, they "represent *desiecta membra* of Paul's correspondence and instruction, collected by one or more of his friends and disciples, and given a continuous form by the provision of editorial transitions," or penned by his amanuensis, Luke, one of his most inner circle co-workers with the evidence that the style and vocabulary do reflect a homogeneity with the Books of Acts, see Bruce, *Paul, Apostle of the Heart Set Free*, 442–44.

34. In this regard, I handle Pauline texts somewhat like Horrell, Hays, and Gorman. See Horrell, *Solidarity and Difference*; Hays, *The Moral Vision* under the section on Paul, and Gorman, *Cruciformity* in one way or another although they differ from one another. What I mean is that they all construct Paul under certain encompassing thematic structure to make their case.

35. Watson argues that Paul did not start off preaching to the Gentiles but to the Jews. The turn to the Gentiles was a gradual development, partly due to his coming to understand the mystery of the gospel (see *Paul, Judaism, and the Gentiles*, 70–82), which is the righteousness of God to include the Gentiles into the covenant (I borrow Wright's language).

36. Horrell has acknowledged a similar concern in the field that "it is important that we gain some appreciation of the distinctive character of each individual letter," while proceeding to "examine various areas in the study of Paul, and draw evidence from all of his letters." See Horrell, *Introduction*, 44–45.

Introduction

such a concern in various ways. In chapter 1, I will review some of these approaches, focusing mainly on three models: 1) the doctrinal, 2) the two-text, and 3) the cultural-linguistic models. I will argue the need for the value of the second and third models and suggest that in this thesis, I wish to show an experience embodying the two texts as well as the Chinese cultural-linguistic tradition. To explain such an experience, I am proposing a double vision hermeneutics, which I will explicate in chapter 2.

Having delineated the guiding principle for the hermeneutics of intersubjective readings of the four texts, and emphasized their relationship to the subject into which these four texts are appropriated in chapter 2, in chapter 3, I will first introduce *shì*, i.e., Text A1. The procedure of discussion will be first to introduce and analyze the meaning of *shì* in its historical and various literary contexts, and follow this with an interpretation from the perspective of the double vision hermeneutics.

Chapter 4 will focus on introducing the *Yìzhuàn* philosophy and the dynamic view of change and timeliness, or timing. *Yìzhuàn*'s *yīn-yáng* dynamic nature and idea of change and timeliness will be introduced to interpret *shì*. Various hexagrams will be explicated to show how *Yìzhuàn* is being employed in interpreting the dynamistic relation between various players in the scenario, as was experienced by a Chinese pastor. The chapter aims also to demonstrate in what sense does the intersubjectivity between Texts A1 and A2 are taking place.

Chapter 5 serves as an interval chapter. Having discussed Text A1 and A2, the next step is to ready myself to enter Texts B1 and B2. I shall in this chapter briefly survey some key discussions on Pauline studies on power, tracing their turn from biblical-theological to sociological, and their returning to biblical-theological. I will suggest that the Pauline notion of "principalities and powers" should be made a hermeneutical motif for an understanding of power, in addition to the sociological perspective.

Chapters 6 and 7 form a pair, which aim at showing the intersubjective relationship of Text B1, the Pauline theology of "principalities and powers" to Text B2, Galatians and 1 Corinthians. The purpose mainly through a survey of Galatians and 1 Corinthians is to identify various power symbols that seemed to form the power relations therein and the contesting arguments Paul offered. The sociological analysis, and reconstruction of the two respective communities behind these two texts, will be attempted. Attention shall be paid to the στοιχεῖα and the law in Galatians, and to wisdom and pneumatics, patronage and position, and eloquence in 1 Corinthians. All these were important power symbols within the two respective communities.

The conclusion will show a theological hermeneutical construction of a constellation of power symbols. I will show how Texts A1 + A2 and Texts B1 + B2 are appropriated by me and how such appropriations have formed the double vision hermeneutics I am claiming.

5. The Significance and Limitations of This Thesis

This thesis arose from my personal experience as a Chinese Christian. I do not claim such an experience to be universal. Nevertheless many Chinese Christians have indicated that they have experienced something analogous to my double vision experience. Indeed from earliest origins of Christian mission in China there was an effort to incorporate elements of a deep cultural interpenetration in the writings and ritual practices by both Jesuit missionary Matteo Ricci (1552-1610) and his converts Xǔ Guāngqǐ (1562-1633), Lǐ Zhīzǎo (1565-1630), and Yáng Tíngyún (1557-1627) in Míng dynasty. In early twentieth century there was another major thrust for cross-cultural interpretation by Zhaò Zǐchén [T. C. Chao] (1888-1979) and his contemporary Christian literati. The same double or cross-cultural dynamic is evident in the writings of contemporary Chinese-Christian scholars such as Archie C. C. Lee and K. K. Yeo.[37] In attempting an interpretation of my experience as a Chinese Christian and of how Chinese tradition and Christian scripture have shaped me, I hope to demonstrate one way in which Chinese Christians may engage in indigenous theological reflection. The emphasis this thesis will put, on engaging personal cultural-linguistic experience, and on the intersubjective experience of "traditional texts" is intended as my contribution to the Chinese Christian theological interpretation.

Having thus positioned myself, I also understand that this thesis is a multi-disciplinary project. Therefore, I do not seek a breakthrough in terms of sociological, historical and textual aspects in either *Yìzhuàn* or Pauline texts, but rely on other scholars' discoveries to consolidate my own discussion. Likewise, the thesis does not focus on power in its own right, although the discussion inevitably involves power discourse. Power, or more precisely *shì*, is an inextricable and essential ingredient of my double

---

37. Zhaò Zǐchén, Archie C. C. Lee, and K. K. Yeo will be reviewed in chapter 1.

vision hermeneutics, so cannot be avoided as I unfold the multilayered intersubjective experience I claim. The purpose of this thesis is to explicate the latter rather than power per se.

1

Surveying Chinese Indigenous Theological Approaches

The story told in the introduction shows an indigenous Christian experience that invites further theological reflection. It involves a self, the subject, within which the Chinese culture and tradition and biblical teachings both form their respective effects. In terms of my double identity, as a Chinese Christian who has inherited Chinese tradition as well as Judaic-Christian tradition, I have many predecessors who have reflected on the dialog and integration of two traditions and two texts. This chapter intends to provide a context within which my own double vision hermeneutics will be compared.

The earliest and most remarkable attempts in this regard are still found in the writings of the Confucian Christian literati in the Míng dynasty, such as Xǔ Guāngqǐ (1562–1633), Lǐ Zhīzaǒ (1565–1630), and Yáng Tíngyún (1557–1627),[1] which show early attempts of Chinese Christian interpretation and "appropriation"[2] of Christian and Chinese classics.

The next prominent group of works are those written by Christian literati from the 1920s such as T. C. Chao [Zhaò Zǐchén] (1888–1979),

---

1. For Yáng, see Standaert, "Xu Guangqi's Conversion as a Multifaceted Process," 170–85; Gernet, "A Not on the Context of Xu Guangqi's Conversion," 186–90. There are earlier important studies on Xu in non-English European languages, see Standaert, op. cit., 170–71. Around the same period were converts *Li Zhīcao* and *Yáng Tíngyún*, who were also *jìnshì*, or a "presented scholars" qualified in the national imperial examination for recruits serving in government administration, typical degree holders who were literally "soaked in" and familiar with Chinese classics. Together they are called the "Three Pillars" (*sān zhù shí*). For a brief summary of their relation to Matteo Ricci and Christian faith see, Lǐ, *Kuà wénhuà quánshì*, 12–13.

2. Borrowed from Ricoeur. See my discussion of this earlier.

A Double Vision Hermeneutic

Wu Yao Tsong [Wú Yaòzhōng] (1893–1979), Xǔ Baǒqiān, and Wú Leíchuān,[3] and those who moved to Hong Kong when a Communist government took over China in 1949 including Zhoū Yìfú, Hú Zānyún, Fēng Shànglǐ, Xiè Fúyǎ who continued the integration of Christian and Confucian classics.[4] Their legacy has become an important source for the further development of Chinese indigenous theology.[5]

This concern regarding double identity has recently been addressed by some as the "hyphenated identity,"[6] or of the "hybrid identity."[7] Both try to express a doubleness within one single individual. Nevertheless, while all who carry this doubleness may carry a concern for the relationship between their two identities and two traditions, having gone through a different process in wrestling the issue, they have given birth to different models of integration.[8]

---

3. See Wú, *Jīdūtú yǔ Zhōngguó shèhuì biànqiān*.

4. Many of their works can be found in Chinese *Ching Feng*. Lee, "Preparation for Christian-Confucian Encounter," 19; also see Yeung, *Fùhé shénxué yǔ jiàohuì gēngxīn*. Sītú Zuózhèng describes the indigenous theology of this period as "expatriate period" and names six representatives, namely Zhoū Yìfú, *Xiè Fúyǎ*, Zhoū Liánhuá, Zhāng Lìshēng, Wú Míngjié, and Wú Sōngshí, see Sītú, "*Yǐ běntǔ* wénhuà weí biāozhì dè bēnsè shénxué," 205–27.

5. I have in other place discussed Chinese indigenous and contextual theologies from 1950s–90s. See my unpublished MTheol thesis, Ooi, "Already But Not Yet."

6. See Lee, "New Route in Christian-Confucian Dialogue." Regarding "hyphenated Christian" and discussion of double identity, see also Berthrong, *All Under Heaven*, 165–87; much earlier than both Lee and Berthrong was Julia Ching who had made a similar notion. See Ching, *Confucianism and Christianity*, 5.

7. K. K. Yeo describes it as hybrid identity, see his *Musing With Confucius and Paul*.

8. I am aware of recent attempts by Asian American Christian scholars to address the issue of hybrid identity. However, the hermeneutical approach they take is different from mine. To take Phan, for example, in "Betwixt and Between: Doing Theology with Memory and Imagination," 113 where he says, "To be betwixt and between is to be neither here nor there, to be neither this thing nor that. Spatially, it is to dwell at the periphery or at the boundaries. Politically, it means not residing at the centers of power of the two intersecting worlds but occupying the precarious and narrow margins where the two dominant groups meet and clash, and denied the opportunity to wield power in matters of public interest. Socially, to be betwixt and between is to be part of a minority, a member of a marginal(ized) group. Culturally, it means not being fully integrated into and accepted by either cultural system, being a *mestizo*, a person of mixed race. Linguistically, the betwixt-and-between person is bilingual but may not achieve a mastery of both languages and often speaks them with a distinct accent. Psychologically and spiritually, the person does not possess a well-defined and secure self-identity and is often marked with excessive impression-albinos, rootlessness, and an inordinate desire for belonging." As shall be clear, the identity crisis addressed by Phan is about a longing for a sense of belonging one does not possess, about two

Surveying Chinese Indigenous Theological Approaches

In the following examples I will show seven attempts, all Chinese individuals except one and all Christians except one unclear, which share the common concern of dual identity and two texts, mainly Christian and Confucian. My focus lies in showing how in their works, they have struggled to make sense of their dual identity and inheritance of two traditions.[9] As my concern is more on these writers' engagement in their reflection on the pre-Qín classical texts rather than later ones, my selection will not include those using modern theologians and later Confucian figures as their sources.[10] These seven attempts will be presented under three models. The first is the doctrinal model which focuses on Confucian-Christian dialog. Four efforts will be discussed with two of which particularly engage with *Yìzhuàn*. Confucian-Christian dialog has been one of the most popular approaches, and two selections, *Confucianism and Christianity* by Julia Ching and *Father and Son in Confucianism and Christianity* by Zhaò Yànxiá, represent an earlier contemporary attempt (1977) and a more recent attempt (2007).[11] The latter is also selected for its Pauline analysis. The two remaining examples of the first model, while sharing a similar doctrinal approach, are reviewed especially for having engaged *Yìzhuàn* in their theologizing. Lee Yung Young and Xiè Fúyǎ will serve as examples.[12] I will demonstrate through this thesis how my approach differs from theirs.

The second model is what I call the "two-text model." This model is particularly important for the attention it pays to neither reading biblical texts out of context nor using the doctrinal approach, which represents a

---

languages, and about marginality and liminality. Mine is about integration rather than disintegration, about a dialectic both-and rather than a "betwixt and between." For a similar concern, see also Wan, "Betwixt and Between," 137–51.

9. Neville, *Behind the Masks of God*, however includes both Confucianist and Daoist ideas; idem., "The 'Puritan Ethic' in Confucianism and Christianity," 100–103; Berthrong, *All Under Heaven*. I especially recommend Lauren Pfister's approach, see Pfister, "Re-Examining Whole Person Cultivation," 69–96.

10. Some examples of recent discussions along this line include: Kwok, "The Christological Doctrine of Reconciliation," 233–48; Kim, *Wang Yang-ming and Karl Barth*; Zhèng Shùnjiā, *Táng Jūnyì yǔ Bātè*; Lai, "Puritanism and Neo-Confucianism," 149–72; Tang, "Confucianism and Bonhoeffer," 97–103.

11. Ching, *Confucianism and Christianity*; Zhao, *Father and Son*.

12. Their works will be referred to later. Another theologian who has engaged *Yìjīng* theologically is Peter K. H. Lee. See for example his article, "The *I Ching*'s Cosmology of Changes in Christian Perspective," 92–127. While in this article he introduces the basic philosophy (cosmology) of changes as found in *Yìjīng*, his discussion is limited. As will be shown, his approach is close to Yung Young Lee and Xiè Fúyǎ, it is suffice to only focus on the latter two.

response to the lack of serious engagement with biblical theological exegesis as detected in earlier Chinese theological attempts, as has been recently summarized by Lai Pan-chiu.[13] I have selected Archie C. C. Lee and K. K. Yeo as examples of this model.

The third model is one which reflects a Chinese cultural-linguistic concern. I have made *shì* the locus for my double vision hermeneutics. The experience of *shì* is a cultural-linguistic experience. I will present various voices arguing for the need to engage the cultural-linguistic dimension followed by an example, a work of Zhaò Zǐchén, to show his embeddedness in Chinese language and culture, and a further theoretical framework by Anthony Gittens. All of the above shall serve as the research background and rationale for the double vision hermeneutics through which the two texts and the Chinese cultural-linguistic dimension can be integrated, to articulate my Chinese Christian experience.

1. Confucian Christian Integration

1.1 Julia Ching's Comparative Study: Inheriting and Integrating Two Heritages

Julia Ching's *Confucianism and Christianity*, first published in 1977, is still a classic text in the field of Confucian-Christian dialog. She is ethnically a Chinese, and the book was produced out of her concern to integrate the two heritages that she inherits, which she calls her "dual background":

> I believe also that I have pondered many times over the questions discussed in this book, and always as a Chinese with a non-Christian background, who considers herself both Christian and non-Christian, and attempts a dialectical integration of the double heritage.[14]

She admits that her "main focus remains Confucianism" and aims to "present a comparative study." She regards herself "as doing the work here of a comparative historian of ideas and doctrines—with the understanding of the word *doctrina* in the broad sense of 'teaching' . . . with the aim of initiating religious dialog between the two living traditions."[15] As she says, her "priority is always placed upon a clearer exposition of Confucianism

---

13. See Pan-Chiu Lai, "Sino-Theology, Bible and the Christian Tradition," 266–81.
14. Ching, *Confucianism and Christianity*, xix.
15. Ching, *Confucianism and Christianity*, xvii.

with reference to certain themes common to itself and Christianity."[16] Thus, for example, she devotes a major portion of a chapter on the idea of man to bring out "the Confucian man" that leads to the crux of the problem of evil, so that the doctrine of sin according to Christian tradition, can be brought into discourse "correlatively."[17] She also devotes another chapter to dealing with whether or not there is a concept of a personal God in Confucianism. Her answer is an affirmative one, i.e., by demonstrating that there is a "correlation" between Confucian and Christian idea of God. Again this time, she firstly refers to the biblical narrative of God in general way rather than through detailed exegesis of the text,[18] although she says, "I consider exegesis to be crucial to a correct understanding of Christianity as well as the common themes in the two traditions while contributing to a broader, hermeneutical task of rendering meaningful the work of exposition and interpretation."[19]

In spite of this deficiency in her generalization, her comprehensive knowledge, shown especially in her summary of the history of Confucian-Christian dialog, philosophical development in both Confucian and Christian doctrines, and not least Confucianism itself, make this work a signal contribution to Confucian-Christian dialog.

1.2 Zhào Yànxiá's Comparative Study of Xúnzǐ and Paul

Zhào Yánxiá writes not out of a concern for dual identity, nor claiming that she inherits "two texts," but simply for the sake of comparing two great traditions. Strictly speaking, hers represents what Lee defines as a "luxury" for those who struggle to find an integrated identity.[20] Nevertheless, as her *Father and Son* focuses on Xúnzǐ and Pauline,[21] and thus represents

---

16. Ching, *Confucianism and Christianity*, xix.

17. Ching, *Confucianism and Christianity*, 68–79. I am using this word following Paul Tillich's theological "method of correlation" as demonstrated in his three-volume *Systematic Theology*.

18. Ching, *Confucianism and Christianity*, 112–23.

19. Ching, *Confucianism and Christianity*, xviii.

20. Lee, "Cross-Textual Interpretation and Its Implication," 249.

21. For a review of this monograph, see Jonathan Tan's review "Father and Son," 205–6 in which he criticizes vehemently, among other points, her "sweeping generalizations and uncritical contemporary extensions of the oppressive status quo" through asserting the hierarchy ideology. He accuses Zhào for reading Xúnzǐ "in isolation from the long history of oppressive patriarchy and misogyny, and also in isolation from the writings of contemporary Confucian scholars who challenge and reinterpret the

a contemporary attempt at a comparative approach to Confucianism and Christianity. Moreover, hers engages with Pauline texts, which is related to my project. Let us first look at her intention.

Zhào deems that

> comparison between Chinese culture and Western culture is necessary and has great significance in terms of developing dialogue as shared values. Since Confucianism is the mainstream of Chinese culture and Christianity is the cornerstone of Western culture, then Chinese culture cannot be understood without understanding Confucianism, and nor can the Western spirit be interpreted without interpreting the spirit of Christianity.[22]

Zhào argues that "father and son" (F-S) is a prominent and long standing motif in both "Confucian thinking" and "Christian consideration."[23] Hence, her discussion is one about Xúnzǐ's (c. 312–230 BC in the Warring States) "secular-ethical" F-S relationship[24] and St Paul's "ethical divine"[25] F-S relationship. She acknowledges the importance of Xúnzǐ in drawing a parallel between the natural F-S relationship and the ruler-ruled relationship which was later developed by Han scholars to fortify the status of the ruler of a state.[26]

I shall leave aside her rationale for juxtaposing Xúnzǐ and Paul, and will not deal with her discussion of Xúnzǐ. My main interest is to point out a flaw found in her engagement with Pauline texts. Like many comparative studies of Confucianism and Christianity, scholars tend to enter into both traditions by selecting from both one or more key ideas or doctrines.[27] The seemingly unavoidable deductive method these scholars adopt sometimes lead them into eisegeses. The following will serve as examples.

In her discussion of Paul's discourse on wisdom in comparison to Xúnzǐ, she claims that "Paul regards wisdom as the endowed nature of

---

classical Confucian tradition in favor of gender equality." I agree with most of what Tan's criticism. However, in spite of Tan's assertion that Zhaò's work is "not yet a major resource for Christian-Confucian dialogues," my review is driven by the need to include an overview of cross-textual readings.

22. Zhao, *Xunzi and Paul*, 1.
23. Zhao, *Xunzi and Paul*, 1.
24. Zhao, *Xunzi and Paul*, 5.
25. For a concise comparison of these two paradigms, see the charts in Zhao, *Xunzi and Paul*, 85–86, for detailed elaboration, see 93–121 for Paul and 122–48 for Xúnzǐ respectively.
26. Zhao, *Xunzi and Paul*, 6.
27. For example, Yao, *Jen and Agape*.

humans, which comes from humans' imitation of God. God is full of wisdom; although human beings as imitators of God cannot have the same wisdom as God and, compared to God's supreme wisdom, theirs is always inferior and inefficient, humans certainly possess some kind of wisdom."[28] There is no indication as to where she deduces this idea from, but based on her following allusion to 1 Corinthians 1 and 3, my assumption is that she makes her comparison of God's wisdom and human wisdom based on 1 Corinthians 1–4. Her argument thus makes the presupposition of "the distinction between God's supreme and humans' inferior wisdom" as her premise.[29] She also explains, "As Paul indicated, Man, although created in the image of God, does not possess the same full and perfect wisdom as God."[30] Here the flaw of her approach is even more obvious.

As I shall show in chapter 7, the centre thrust about wisdom in 1 Corinthians is not about human wisdom in comparison to God's wisdom, but about a potential crisis, namely, the tendency of members of the church to boast about and ultimatize certain church member's wisdom, which to Paul will blur the message of the gospel of Jesus Christ and His cross, the seeming foolishness of God. The key issue is boasting, which may lead the Corinthians to follow a way antithetical to the true spirit of the gospel.

We can conclude that she probably takes such an approach to the text due to her presumption of Pauline texts, like other biblical texts, as moral teaching.[31] Her attempt is close to the doctrinal approach, which does not take seriously the textual and socio-historical background into its interpretation of the text. I therefore find Zhaò treatment to Pauline texts does not do justice to them and her approach to the two texts, cannot fully address the concern of a Chinese Christian looking for an integration of his dual identity.

The following two examples are similar to the aforementioned two. However, while I am drawn to Zhaò Zǐchén and Zhaò Yànxià because of their engagement with Paul, my interest in the following two lies primarily in their engagement with *Yìzhuàn*.

---

28. Zhao, *Xunzi and Paul*, 155–56.
29. Zhao, *Xunzi and Paul*, 155–56.
30. Zhao, *Xunzi and Paul*, 156.
31. See, for example, her discussion in Zhao, *Xunzi and Paul*, 162–70.

1.3: Jung Young Lee's Doctrinal Approach to Yìjīng

In the twentieth century, there is only one theologian in the English-speaking world who incorporates *Yìzhuàn* concepts in his theological construction, namely Jung Young Lee. Although he is not, by ethnicity, Chinese, I include him because he identifies himself as a Confucian and that he engages a study of *Yìzhuàn* as a Christian theological concern. However, his approach to *Yìzhuàn*, which is basically doctrine, is different from mine. As my thesis also engages *Yìzhuàn* for interpretation, which takes serious account of the pre-Qín cultural and historical context behind the *Yìzhuàn* text, and attempts at an intersubjective reading. He first wrote *The Theology of Change: A Christian Concept of God in an Eastern perspective* in 1979.[32] Then in 1996 he worked *Yìzhuàn* into his trinitarian reformulation in *The Trinity in Asian Perspective*.[33] My focus will be on the second book.

Jung Young Lee's *Trinity* is rooted in a concern to de-Westernize the theology of the Trinity. He begins by addressing this need and ends with a conclusion which readdress his dissatisfaction with early church fathers' formulations of trinitarian theology. He thinks that they have difficulty in grasping the mystery. The reason for this lies in that "they used substantial thinking, which is more individualistic than communal and more divisive than unitive."[34] This has motivated him as a theologian with an East Asian cultural background, to delve into *Yìjīng*'s paradigm, which provides him with the *yīn-yáng* symbols. He commends the *yīn-yáng* model, arguing that they, *yīn* and *yáng*, are more "mutually complementary" and more "relative and inclusive of each other." Moreover, it is a "holistic" model.[35]

Yīn-yáng model symbolizes a both/and paradigm, for *yīn* and *yáng* include each other. For *yīn* is in *yáng* and *yáng* is in *yīn*. He calls this codependency the inner connecting principle. Applying this principle to the Father-Son relationship, he says, "The Father and the Son are one in their 'both/and,' but also at the same time, they are three because 'in' represents the Spirit, the inner connecting principle which cannot exist itself. In the inclusive relationship, two relational symbols such as *yīn* and *yáng* are trinitarian because of 'in,' which not only unites them but also completes

---

32. Lee, *The Theology of Change*.
33. Lee, *Trinity*.
34. Lee, *Trinity*, 213.
35. Lee, *Trinity*, 213.

them."³⁶ *Yīn* and *yáng* are relational; they are "harmony of opposites" they represent "complementary relationship." They are "the opposites but also fulfill each other." Their relationship is "not conflicting dualism but complementary dualism."³⁷ Moreover, the "inness" of one in the other also represents the unitive and integrative principle of the Spirit.³⁸

Yīn and *yáng* reflect both the masculinity and femininity of God, with God the Father as the masculine principle, the Holy Spirit as the feminine member of the trinity,³⁹ and the Son as both male and female representing "individuality and communality."⁴⁰

Lee also postulates the cosmo-anthropological assumption. He bases this on Zhāng Zǎi's *Xī Mín* (960-1127 AD) in the Sòng dynasty, arguing for Heaven as the father, Earth as the mother, and human beings as their children.⁴¹ Obviously, he also bases this on a preliminary notion of the Qián and Kūn hexagrams which represent heaven and earth.⁴² One notices that in *Shuōguà*, the father-mother designations already appear. He also alludes to *sāncái*, heaven, earth and man, and asserts that the three lines in a trigram (e.g. ☰) represent heaven (upper line), earth (lower line), and humanity (middle line) respectively.⁴³

Lee alludes to Qián (Heaven) as he speaks of moral and spiritual principles. He associates Qián to God the Father, and uses the four virtues in *Wényán*: *yuán*, *hēng*, *lì*, *zhēn*, i.e., heaven as originating, successful, advantageous, and correct (not much different from Legge's translation), to argue that these represent the attributes of God the Father.⁴⁴

His references to particular hexagrams are uncommon and unclear. Hexagrams that he refers to include: Yì, Jiàn, Fēng, Tài, Xián, Jié. The way he uses them is first to adopt the principle of *sāncái*. Then he assigns the two old *yáng* lines to the Father, the two old *yīn* lines to the Mother (Spirit), and a *yīn* on top of a *yáng* to the Son. He then looks for the meaning in the interplay between the *yáng* and *yīn* symbolism and argues for a

---

36. Lee, *Trinity*, 58.
37. Lee, *Trinity*, 30–31.
38. Lee, *Trinity*, 107–11.
39. Lee, *Trinity*, 102–7, 136–40.
40. For this and more detailed explication of Jesus encompassing maleness and femaleness in his divinity and humanity, see Lee, *Trinity*, 78 then 77–79.
41. Lee, *Trinity*, 76, 214.
42. Lee, *Trinity*, 75.
43. Lee, *Trinity*, 195.
44. Lee, *Trinity*, 131–35.

proper order of mother and father. He shows how different orders could create different effects, endorsing his argument by using the hexagram statements as his proof texts.

Thus his attempt starts from a concern to solve trinitarian language. His approach, therefore, starts from a doctrinal concern and does not engage with any biblical text systematically and exegetically. Likewise, his use of hexagrams does not consider the historical allusions or layers of meaning that might lie behind each hexagram. In other words, his doctrinal concern dictates his reading of *Yìjīng*. As shall be seen in the next chapter where I delineate my hermeneutics, and in chapters 4, 6, and 7, my approach to both *Yìjīng* (*Yìzhuàn*) and Pauline texts will take the historical and textual contexts much more seriously.

1.4: Xiè Fúyǎ's Theological Integration of Zhoūyì (Yìzhuàn)[45]

Our fourth candidate is Xiè Fúyǎ (1892–1991). He inherits the Confucian-Christian integration of earlier generations. That he stands out and is reviewed here is due to his theological construction engaging *Yìzhuàn*. His effort displays an integration of process theology and *Zhoūyì*'s metaphysics.[46]

First of all, based on his theological interpretation of *Yìjīng*, he constructs a doctrine of God which he calls "God in two modes" or "God who is of *yì tǐ liǎng tài*, one substance in two modes—God in Himself and God for Himself (bipolarity of God)."[47] With "God-in-Himself," Xiè asserts that God is the absolute unmoved (*jìng*, tranquility) and ineffable One (*wú*, nothingness). Here Xiè reflects Daoist idea. As is said in Daò Dé Jīng, "He is the *Dao* that cannot be named." Daò, and therefore God, transcends time and space. To Him there is no difference to say if there is history or not; the infinite past and the infinite future are all here and now. He is the unchanged eternity.

---

45. I use *Zhoūyì* instead of *Yìzhuàn* here to be in consistent with Xie's own preference.

46. For my discussion of his theology to process theology, see my unpublished MTheol thesis, Ooi, "Already But Not Yet." His construction probably precedes Ching's reference to the commensurability of Confucianism and process thought, particularly of the idea of "The Absolute as Becoming," see Ching, *Confucianism and Christianity*, 128–34 published in 1977.

47. Ooi, "Already But Not Yet."

In contrast to God-in-Himself is the God-for-Himself which implies a dynamic God in motion. To use the Wújí (Without Ultimate) and Tàijí (Great or Supreme Ultimate) paradigm as Zhōu Dūnyí (1017–1073), a Confucian from the Northern Sòng, has constructed, God-in-Himself is the Wújí while God-for-Himself the Tàijí. The latter refers to God who does not cease to create, or as we may say, with Him it is *creatio continua*. He does not stop evolving and changing.[48]

In other words, with this paradigm, the doctrine of creation can be understood with the Daoist statements: "Dao generates 'one', 'one' generates 'two', 'two' generates 'three', while 'three' generates the ten-thousand natural kinds."[49] The 'one' who generates is the dynamic God, who generates into 'two' that is the Father and the Son, and into 'three' that is the trinity.[50] This forms his theology of the bipolarity—God-in-Himself and God-for-Himself. While the Daoist philosophy is not exactly the same as the *Yìzhuàn* philosophy, *Yìzhuàn* may already have incorporated the Dào Dé Jīng philosophy which came before it in pre-Qín times. Anyway, this is not of Xiè's concern. Xiè considers the paradigm of bipolarity more compatible with the Chinese *yīn-yáng* dynamic philosophy.[51]

The *Zhōuyì* metaphysics provides Xiè the freedom to use some of *Yìjīng*'s hexagrams to restructure Christian theology. He considers the Christian notion—"in the beginning God created the world"—to be symbolized by the first and second hexagrams of *Zhōuyì*, Heaven (Qián ☰) and Earth (Kūn ☷), which say, "In change there is the great ultimate; this is what generates the two modes."[52] As Wáng Fūzhī (1619–1692 AD) emphasizes, Qián and Kūn symbolize the great beginning (*tàishǐ*) that governs all the other changes implied in the remaining sixty-two hexagrams.[53] In *Yìjīng*, it is said: "How great is the fundamental nature of Qián! The myriad things are provided their beginnings by it."[54] Likewise, "how great is the fundamental nature of Kūn! The myriad things are provided their births by it."[55] It seems that Xiè has extracted the symbolic

---

48. Xie, "Píng xiānggǎng shèngjīng gōnghuì xīnjìn biānyìn de 'lìshǐ de gǎizaò zěh,'" 272.

49. Laozi, *Dào Dé Jīng*, chapter 42.

50. Xiè, "Zhōuyì xīntàn," 278.

51. The *yīn-yáng* dynamism is the basis of *Zhōuyì* or *Yìjīng* philosophy. See my discussion in chapter 4.

52. This he quotes from *Xici* I.11; see Lynn, *Changes*, 65.

53. Wáng, *Zhouyi neizhuan*, 9.

54. See Tuànzhuàn of Qián, in Lynn, *Changes*, 129.

55. See *Tuànzhuàn* of Kún, in Lynn, *Changes*, 143.

A Double Vision Hermeneutic

meaning of Qián and Kūn to combine it with the Daoist statements: "Daò generates 'one', 'one' generates 'two', 'two' generates 'three', while 'three' generates the ten-thousand natural kinds."[56]

Not only does he apply a *Yìjīng* interpretation to the doctrine of creation, he also derives from *Yìjīng* a theological interpretation of sin and salvation. He interprets the fallen situation of human kind with the hexagram Bó ䷖, (H23: Falling Apart),[57] and the restoration or salvation with Fù ䷗ (H24: Returning). According to the paradigm of "Twelve Hexagrams of increase and decrease" (*shí èr xiāo xí guà*) derived by Mèng Xǐ (90 BC-?) in the Hàn dynasty,[58] Bó symbolizes the ninth month of the year in the Autumn according to Chinese lunar calendar. In such a time, the leaves of the tree are withering. The lonely top *yáng* line in the hexagram ䷖ reflects the dim sunlight the earth is receiving at this time of the year. On the other hand, Fù symbolizes the opposite phenomenon. While it is used to indicate the eleventh month of the year, it is actually in the Winter when the earth is covered with snow. However, ancient Chinese, like Mèng Xǐ, interpret the eleventh month as the time when the *yáng* force begins to grow. This can be seen in the hexagram ䷗ in which shown a *yáng* begins to appear in the first line. It appears that Xiè understands this symbolism and uses the Bó hexagram to interpret the world and humanity which have fallen apart and are without hope because of sin, and uses Fù to signify the coming of Christ who brings salvation and hope.

In a similar way, Xiè uses Jìjì ䷾ (H63: Ferrying Complete) to interpret the completion of the work on the cross, and Wèijì ䷿ (H64: Ferrying Incomplete) to interpret that which has not been completed, i.e., the incomplete awaiting more work to be done through Christians in the world.[59] In other words, he is using these two hexagrams to explain the eschatological notion of the already-but-not-yet.[60]

Regarding *Xìcí*'s explanation that, "The two basic modes generate the four basic images; while the four basic images generate the eight trigrams," he contends that it is about the creational dimension.[61] Once again, he

---

56. Laozi, *Daò Dé Jīng*, chapter 42.

57. H23 indicates Hexagram No. 23. This implies to all hexagrams mentioned in this thesis.

58. The depiction of the increase and the decrease is first seen in *Tuànzhuàn* of Hexagram 23: Bo (Peeling or falling apart): "*Jūnzǐ* takes heed of the alternation of increase and decrease, fullness and emptiness," modified from Wilhelm, *I Ching*, 501.

59. See Ooi, "Already But Not Yet," chapter 3, 4, and 7.

60. Xiè, "*Zhoūyì dė zhōngjiaò jiàzhí*," 89.

61. Xiè, "*Zhoūyì xīn tàn*," 278.

32

does not provide an exegesis of the texts, as if what is stated in the texts is as clear to others as it is to him. According to the traditional interpretation, the "two basic modes" denote the *yīn* and *yáng*, while the "four basic images" denote the greater *yáng* ⚌, the lesser *yīn* ⚎, the lesser *yáng* ⚍, and the greater *yīn* ⚏, which may symbolize the four seasons. From these four were generated the eight natural phenomena.[62] He argues that the statements "The eight trigrams determine good fortune and misfortune, and the good fortune and misfortune generate the great enterprise,"[63] may be used to expound a philosophy of history. He assumes that the good fortune and misfortune are what are found in human affairs. Thus, to him, the generation of "the great enterprise" from the fortune and misfortune, probably of the human affairs, could imply all the works in this world humanity has to complete before the kingdom of God is consummated. Thus, the philosophy epitomized by this statement, while originally revealing the cosmogony, or primordial beginning of this world, could be used by Xiè to correlate with Christian theology.[64]

This brief review has shown Xiè's attempt to construct a systematic theology employing the *Yì* paradigm which includes the Trinity, eschatology, Christology, and other areas in line with Christian tradition. In spite of his insights in finding commensurability of *Yì* philosophy through a theological lens, he reads into *Yì* symbolism most of the times by resorting to an intuition interpretation or correlating his Confucian heritage to Christian theology. What is lacking is a more careful exegetical analysis of either *Yìzhuàn* or biblical passages.

Xiè's theological interpretation of *Yìjīng* may seem unrestrained and arbitrary, and irritating to Confucian scholars. The weakness of his interpretation is that he shows no interest in digging into the literary and historical context of the various hexagrams he refers to. His interest in finding compatibility from a Christian doctrinal perspective has led him into a quick association. Judged from the tradition of *Yìzhuàn* interpretation, his is not too far removed from the long tradition of diversified interpretations of *Yìzhuàn*. In every generation from the Hàn to Míng dynasties, from Wáng Bì to Wáng Fūzhī, each individual interpreter had tried to apply *Yìzhuàn* to his own particular situation and time.[65] As we

---

62. For the eight trigrams, see chapter 4.
63. For this statement that he cites, see Lynn, *Changes*, 65–66.
64. Xiè, "Zhoūyì xīn tàn," 278.
65. For examples Wáng Bì, Kǒng Yǐndá, Zhāng Zaǐ, Chéng Yǐ, and Shū Shì, et cetera. For a concise discussion of *Zhoūyì*'s succession and diversification of interpretation in

shall see later, a text can have multiple meanings with multiple interpretations. Having said that, Xiè has not argued for his legitimacy but assumed it. While his double identity and double inheritance may have dictated his undertaking and reading of the texts, he may also have seen the correlation as the result of a 'double vision', i.e. that these texts had formed an intersubjective relationship with him. Nevertheless, resources for biblical exegesis and Chinese texts are now made more available to Chinese theologians, which at the same time have posed a challenge to them, that their reading and interpretation needs to be more nuanced.

2. Two Texts Approaches

A dissatisfaction among Chinese theologians has been articulated since the latter quarter of the twentieth century criticizing earlier Chinese theology for its lack of serious engagement with biblical theological exegesis, as Lai Pan-chiu has recently summarized.[66] This is a concern which anyone who takes up Chinese Christian theological construction with the intention of engaging Confucian ideas has to take into account.

In responding to this dissatisfaction, two recent attempts are more prominent: Archie C. C. Lee's cross-textual interpretation and Khiok-Khnn Yeo's cross-cultural interpretation, which show a true concern for Chinese tradition and biblical hermeneutics by Chinese Christian scholars who exhibit the spirit of dual identity.[67]

2.1: Archie C. C. Lee: Cross-textual Reading

Lǐ Chìchāng [Archie C. C. Lee], a professor in Old Testament and Asian Hermeneutics at the Chinese University of Hong Kong,[68] is sensitive to

---

these figures, see Hon, *The Yijing and Chinese Politics*; also Smith, *Fathoming*.

66. See for example, Pan-Chiu Lai, "Sino-Theology," 266–81.

67. In his review, "Biblical Scholarship in Hong Kong," Craig Y. S. Ho has particularly singled out three prominent biblical scholars: Ronald Y. K. Fung (*The Epistle to the Galatians* (NICNT) in 1988), Archie C. C. Lee, and K. K. Yeo. Unlike the latter two, Fung's works do not show any interest in an interpretation of the Bible from a Chinese cultural perspective.

68. See Archie Lee, "Kuà yǔ wén běn yuè dú de fāng fǎ: yǐ Shīpiān yǔ Shījīng weí lì," 27–49; idem, "Lamentations in the Hebrew Psalter and in the Chinese *Shijing*," 249–73; idem, "Cross-Textual Interpretation and Its Implication for Biblical Studies," 247–54; idem, "Cross-Textual Hermeneutics," 60–62.

Surveying Chinese Indigenous Theological Approaches

Asian Christians who inherit "the legacy of biblical faith" and live within pluralistic social, as well as religious, realities.[69] He designates this double legacy as 'two worlds', 'two stories' and 'two texts', and is concerned about how these might split the Asian Christian "self." Hence he urges Asian biblical scholars "to take equally seriously both cultural and religious heritage," to avoid "subjugating one 'text' to the other or making one of these 'texts' the absolute norm." He continues, "Both Text A and Text B must be held in creative dialogue and interaction. One text has to be open to the claims and challenges of the other text in order for transformation to take place in a meaningful way."[70] The very nub of his concern is the dual identity he sees in Asian Christians. He argues that, "[u]nless genuine crossings take place between these two texts within the self of Asian Christians, the self will remain disintegrated—self torn between two worlds."[71] He thus declares one of most fundamental arguments for a "cross-textual interpretation," that it is "not simply to engage in the luxury of doing comparative studies, but rather to bring about an integrated self."[72]

The very notion of "the luxury of doing comparative studies" articulates the core ethos of all Chinese Christian theological attempts, which is a "genuine" attempt to be true to oneself. Comparative though it may seem, the spirit is entirely different. The concern is deeper than simply to compare.[73] Thus, looking into the "two texts" is not an "option" nor is it an "intellectual game."[74]

Lee points out that in the West, the relationship of Chrisitan faith to the Western history and civilisation is closely interwoven. They mutually inherit each other's richness, interpret and appropriate one another.[75] He welcomes Asian theologians who have made use of Asian resources to engage in theological reflection. He believes this is a path Asian theology should tread, which nonetheless is only in its infancy and in need of much revision, reflection, critique, and improvement.

Looking at Chinese culture which he himself inherits, he points out that the influences of Confucianism, Daoism and Buddhism are deeply

---

69. Lee, "Cross-Textual Interpretation and Its Implication," 248.
70. Lee, "Cross-Textual Interpretation and Its Implication," 249.
71. Lee, "Cross-Textual Interpretation and Its Implication," 249.
72. Lee, "Cross-Textual Interpretation and Its Implication," 249.
73. I support this ethos. I thus see the attempts of Yao, *Confucianism and Christianity*; Zhao, *Father and Son* as inadequate in this regard.
74. Lee, "Cross-Textual Interpretation and Its Implication," 249.
75. Lǐ, *Yàzhōu chǔjìng yǔ shèngjīng quánshì*, 4.

embedded in its tradition and history. The moral teachings are infused into its "literatures, languages, idioms, customs, festivals, mythologies, legends, stories, and folk beliefs."[76] For him, texts refer not only to "written texts", but also to "non-written texts—such as orally transmitted scriptural traditions as well as social contexts, economic and political experiences, and life experiences."[77] This understanding of "texts" perpetuates on the cross-textual hermeneutics that he proposes.

What he means by cross-textual is the crossing of two texts, two traditions, and two worlds, as we have noted. He further delineates, that for some, one text may be more important, take precedent, take higher position, be more privileged than the other. For others the Bible or Christian faith is more important, or alternatively the Asian religious classics or social-political texts. For himself, Lee identifies the Asian Text as his Text A and Biblical Text as Text B.[78]

As a Chinese, he acknowleges the two worlds that belong to a Chinese Christian. He admits "the Christian text and the Chinese text are unrelated from a historical point of view, growing as they did out very different cultural and historical contexts of their own." Refering to Zhāng Lóngxī's comparative literary theory, he defines his approach as one that wishes "to transcend that limitation of a narrowly defined perspective and to expand our horizon by assimilating as much as possible what appears to be alien and belonging to the Other," or to what Hans-Georg Gadamer calls the "fusion of horizons."[79] Lee's intention is to "go beyond a mono-scriptural hermeneutics" and "enter into dialogue" with other religious traditions not only "of the Ancient Near East and the Bible," but also "our own religious heritage and cultural traditions" for mutual illuminations.[80] One thus sees his undaunting efforts in writing and promoting such a reading.[81]

---

76. Lee, *Yàzhoū chǔjìng yǔ shèngjīng quánshì*, 5.

77. Lee, "Cross-Textual Interpretation and Its Implication," 250. He makes it clear that it is also not "intertextual" as used to refer to reading or cross referencing the one text with another within the Bible, see 254 footnote 17. See also, idem, *Yàzhoū chǔjìng yǔ shèngjīng quánshì*, 6.

78. Lee, *Yàzhoū chǔjìng yǔ shèngjīng quánshì*, 6.

79. Lee, "Cross-Textual Interpretation and Its Implication," 250. He cites Zhang, *The Tao and the Logos*, xiv.

80. Lee, "Cross-Textual Interpretation and Its Implication," 252.

81. See earlier footnote.

He makes a distinction between his cross-textual hermeneutics and intertextual hermeneutics.[82] He understands intertextual as to refer to the Rabbinic hermeneutic tradition that aims to see the relationship a textual passage has with others, for rabbis see the Hebrew canon as one "organic whole." They believe that the Bible itself is consistant from beginning to end. Passages and texts within the Bible are mutually englightening and interpretative. One does not need an extra-biblical reference to understand what it says.[83]

His most finely articulated definition of cross-textual hermeneutics is as follows: Taking "cross" to imply crossing over to the other shore, he emphasizes the meaning of "to encounter"and "to interact" (with the other), so that new meaning can be discovered. It is to put two texts together, or side by side, so that "Text A" can shed light on "Text B" and vice versa.[84] Moreover, the "crossing" is not a once-and-for-all experience. There can be many "crossings" and from different "texts." The purpose of crossing to and fro is not to undertake comparative study but to reach "transformation" and "enrichedness." The crossing entails the participatory presence of one's entire being, that leads toward a life-uplifting experience and a process of self-discovery, which ultimately brings one to an "enriched-transformed existence."[85]

To summarize, Lee's cross-cultural hermeneutics, as a concern of one's identity, is about a congruity and integration of one's very being that embraces two traditions. It is about a self which is not being torn apart by two texts. The purpose of the interpretative process is a life-long process, for the "crossing" is not a once-and-for-all experience. It aims at self-transformation.

---

82. "Intertextual" or "intertextuality" as referred here is different from Johanna Liu's reference, and the discussion that follows in the introduction, in terms of that the one refers to the Rabbinic tradition, the other, Chinese classics. However, the concern regarding how a certain "passage" or "text" appears in different texts within a tradition across generations is the same.

83. See Lee, *Yàzhoū chǔjìng yǔ shèngjīng quánshì*, 6. He points out that, a contemporary theorist and biblical scholar, Michael Fishbane, also works on this approach.

84. Lee, *Yàzhoū chǔjìng yǔ shèngjīng quánshì*, 6-7.

85. Lee, *Yàzhoū chǔjìng yǔ shèngjīng quánshì*, 7. He remarks that he borrows the notion "transformed existence" from Richard Wentz's *The contemplation of Otherness*, 13.

2.2: Khiok-khng Yeo: Cross-Cultural Hermeneutics and Intersubjective Readings

Khiok-khng Yeo, a professor of New Testament studies and hermeneutics at Garrett Evangelical Theological Seminary,[86] is studied for his continual contribution to bringing Confucianism into dialog with various Pauline theological motifs. Yeo's academic contribution in cross-cultural interpretation first appears in his dissertation on cross-cultural interpretation applying a rhetorical approach.[87]

Two features are worth drawing attention to: cross-cultural hermeneutics and intersubjective readings.

2.2.1: Cross-Cultural Hermeneutics

Yeo's cross-cultural hermeneutics arises from his identity as a Chinese Christian. He considers that the Chinese cultural heritage he inherits must somehow integrate with his Christian experience. He acknowledges that the concern of a person's cultural being is also what contextual theology tries to address. Such a notion first appeared as a rationale for embarking on the cross-cultural hermeneutics described in his doctorate thesis: *Rhetorical Interpretation*:

> Contextual theology is particular and culturally oriented theology that acknowledges humans as cultural beings. We can only interpret the world as we perceive it from the given situation. Contextual theology seeks to name the presence and love of God in a particular culture. Cross-cultural hermeneutics is related to the universal, cosmic unity through diverse and ambiguous contexts.[88]

The language used above shows not only a contextual theological concern but also reveals his indebtedness to the hermeneutical theories he elaborates on and discusses in chapter 2 of his thesis monograph.[89] By emphasizing a contextual concern, he addresses how a given situation, and particular culture, can precondition one's hermeneutics. Thus, his cross-

---

86. His monographs include: *Rhetorical Interaction in 1 Corinthians 8 and 10*; *What Has Jerusalem to do with Beijing?*; *Chairman Mao Meets the Apostle Paul*; *Cross-Cultural Rhetorical Hermeneutics*; *Musing With Confucius and Paul*.
87. Yeo, *Rhetorical Interaction*.
88. Yeo, *Rhetorical Interaction*, 24.
89. Yeo, *Rhetorical Interaction*, 15–49.

cultural hermeneutics addresses diversity of contexts. To him, "different cultures have different relations between the communicative system and their experienced world," which affect the very act of understanding.[90] He thus concludes, "Hermeneutics is therefore a process of understanding a text through similarities in differences and through the interpreters' contexts."[91] Differences always lie between different cultures; to acknowledge cultural differences, therefore, is the preliminary and primary assumption for cross-cultural hermeneutics.

Among many theories Yeo elaborates on and appropriates, Gadamer's idea of *Horizontsverschmeltzung* ('fusion of horizons') is a key one.[92] Appropriating Gadamer, Yeo contends that cross-cultural hermeneutics is a process of the fusion of horizons. He sees the crossing and the fusion of horizons as a process of dialog. He highlights, "we ought to participate creatively and actively in the dialogical process of *Horizontsverschmeltzung* ('fusion of horizons')."[93] Here he cites Gadamer who addresses interpretation as the "interplay of the movement of tradition and the movement of the interpreter."[94] To express his agreement with Gadamer, he also emphasizes, "horizons will and can be expanded only in the *dialogical* process."[95] Elaborating on Gadamer's notion of horizons and historical consciousness, Yeo furthers explains:

> A text speaks without denying the truth of its tradition; but interpreters can hardly objectify the tradition since the text itself is in a closed horizon. However, horizon of the past is formed, reformed and transformed within the "historical consciousness." Therefore, the dialogical process is an attempt to overcome the gulf between the interpreter and the tradition.[96]

Being open for reformation, tradition as "horizon of the past" can, through a dialogical process, enter into the horizon of the interpreter. Thus being dialogical, the cross-cultural hermeneutics anticipates a transcendency of the tradition, as Gadamer calls it,[97] in "a closed horizon," and

90. Yeo, *Rhetorical Interaction*, 31.

91. Yeo, *Rhetorical Interaction*, 37.

92. Theorists such as Julia Kristeva's and Roland Barthes' ideas of intertextuality and intersubjectivity are also important, especially to his later works.

93. Yeo, *Rhetorical Interaction*, 41. Italic his.

94. For Gadamer, see *Truth and Method*, 293.

95. Yeo, *Rhetorical Interaction*, 41 n. 117. Italic mine.

96. Yeo, *Rhetorical Interaction*, 41.

97. The "traditionary texts" or "*Überlieferung*," literally "tradition," which means

its transformation towards a present where our "historical consciousness" is situated.

To Yeo, to successfully achieve a cross-cultural hermeneutics, Gadamer's emphasis on two horizons—that of the tradition in the past and that of the interpreter—seems to be not sufficient. Developing from there, Yeo suggests the possibility of and elaborates on the idea of a "confluence of traditions," which is "a process that *increasingly differentiates the uniqueness and affirms the diversity* of various traditions."[98] I believe that for Yeo, such a confluence is made possible because "the gulf" is to be bridged not only between "the interpreter" and one tradition, but also across different cultural traditions.

Yeo thus further suggests that his cross-cultural hermeneutics is also a "trans-spatiotemporal process" that seeks "communication, identification, differentiation, and transformation" of cultures and traditions.[99] For him, simply acknowledging one's inheritance of cultural tradition, and unveiling the traditional text, are not enough; the text has to be reinvigorated and resurrected.[100]

Being aware of one's cultural embeddedness helps one appreciate others as well. This prevents one from taking a too sentimental approach to one's own cultural inheritance that creates a pseudo-fideism of it. This also calls for a critical assessment of one's own cultural tradition. As he says, "the cross-cultural hermeneutic is a socio-critical enterprise which allows *one* to maintain the tension of being both certain (trustful) and unsure (doubtful) of *our* theologizing."[101] His use of "certain" and "unsure" is less helpful than "trustful" and "doubtful." According to his elaboration in the statements that follow, what he wants to highlight is the necessity for critical acumen from a distance to allow interpreters to "appreciate the past traditions and at the same time socially and critically question *these traditions* for the sake of clarification and appropriation."[102] Yeo's cross-cultural hermeneutics opens up another dimension to the originally proposed fusion of horizons between the past and the present by Gadamer. In Yeo, the fusion is a fusion between different traditions.

"what comes down to us from the past" or "handed down from the past." See "Translator's Preface," in *Truth and Method*, xvi.

98. Yeo, *Rhetorical Interaction*, 42. Italic his.
99. Yeo, *Rhetorical Interaction*, 43.
100. Yeo, *Rhetorical Interaction*, 49.
101. Yeo, *Rhetorical Interaction*, 43. Italic his.
102. Yeo, *Rhetorical Interaction*, 43. Italic mine.

Surveying Chinese Indigenous Theological Approaches

Nevertheless, I see a need for further deliberation on this notion by emphasizing it in terms of 'subject'. I will elaborate on this by engaging Yeo's notion of "dialogue" with reference to Ricoeur. My interest in Ricoeur is to relate him to Yeo's notion of dialog.

In "What is a Text?," Ricoeur discusses the similarity and difference between a text and a speech. He defines a text as "any discourse fixed by writing." However, "an event of discourse" is primarily something in which "the realization of language [*langue*]" or "the production of an individual utterance by an individual speaker" takes place. Saying that a text is a "discourse" is to compare it to a speech. However, a text as a "writing" is somehow a delayed speech, what he calls a "late appearance." As Ricoeur explains, "writing as an institution is subsequent to speech, and seems merely to fix in linear script all the articulations which have already appeared orally." Thus, in a sense, a writing is an "inscription of speech."[103] It is similar to a speech, but only in the sense that it occurs "at the site" where a "speech could have emerged."[104] Such a delay in time, and a replacement of the what "could have" been mark the difference between a text and a speech.

Regarding this difference, Ricoeur directs attention to the difference between the interlocutor-speaker and the "writing-reading" relationship. The former is a direct "speaking-answering relation" between two persons in conversation. However, one cannot say that there is a direct "speaking-answering relation" thus "dialogue" between the author through his work with the reader.[105] Ricoeur argues that "[d]ialogue is an exchange of questions and answers," and "there is no exchange of this sort between the writer and the reader." He contends, "The writer does not respond to the reader." Moreover, between them "there is no communication."[106]

If, as Ricoeur contests, there is no "dialogue" between the writer and the reader, comparable to that found between the speaker and the interlocutor, how can a cross-cultural interpretation be done by an interpreter within one cultural tradition on another cultural tradition? Communication by the text is not possible by itself if the "author is dead."[107] Yet communication is opened up by the reading of the text. Instead of saying that

---

103. Ricoeur, "What is a Text?," 145–46.

104. Ricoeur, "What is a Text?," 146.

105. Ricoeur, "What is a Text?," 146.

106. Ricoeur, "What is a Text?," 146. He calls this a "double eclipse." which means: "The reader is absent form the act of writing; the writer is absent from the act of reading."

107. Ricoeur, "What is a Text?," 147.

a text (of a given tradition) is itself communicating cross-culturally to a recipient (of another tradition), it is the reader, the reading subject, who is bringing the text into his own horizon. In other words, the reading subject is bringing the text, and the tradition within which he is embedded into dialog. The role of the interpreter, or the reading subject, in bringing different texts and contexts into dialog, rather than the texts having dialog between themselves is more clearly articulated in Yeo's more recent article, as shown below.

2.2.2: Intersubjective Readings

In an article published in 2004, "Culture and Intersubjectivity as Criteria of Negotiating Meanings in Cross-cultural Interpretations,"[108] he addresses the hermeneutical focus of the intersubjectivity which had not been fully developed in *Rhetorical Interaction*. The focus in the *Rhetorical Interaction* was "an interactive model in biblical reading and cross-cultural hermeneutics based on rhetorical theories."[109] In "Culture and Intersubjectivity," his aim is a "further explication" of "the rhetorical nature of the reading process."[110]

By intersubjectivity, Yeo emphasizes "the dialogues between the writers and the readers" in the process of the readings of the texts. He contends that the encounter of a reader and a text written by a certain writer is also a process of meaning-production or reproduction.[111] He claims,

> This reproductive and productive process of reading allows and requires text/writer and reader/interpretation to be intersubjective. A text not only carries meaning but allows readers to create meanings. Similarly, readers not only interpret texts, they are being "read" by texts, that is, their stories are made meaningful by the texts. Because understanding and reading processes are reproductive and productive, a writer cannot control the meaning of a text and limit that meaning to just his or her own "original" intention.[112]

Here Yeo's attention is on the meaning-producing process of an ancient text. He argues that for a text to be a living text, it has to interact "with

---

108. Yeo, "Culture and Intersubjectivity," 81–100.
109. Yeo, "Culture and Intersubjectivity," 82.
110. Yeo, "Culture and Intersubjectivity," 83.
111. Yeo, "Culture and Intersubjectivity," 86.
112. Yeo, "Culture and Intersubjectivity," 87.

Surveying Chinese Indigenous Theological Approaches

its successive audiences, from ancient to modern times."[113] A text passing down through ages can have multiple interpreters, multiple interpretations and meanings.[114] This is especially so when the reading process is taking place in "a real-life setting" as an interpreter is communicating a particular text "to different audiences." Such is a "meaning-producing process."[115] He emphasizes that in such a process one sees the *rhetorical interaction*, "a complex interaction between the text, the writer and the readers/audience."[116] However, one question remains: how then can a writer interact with the readers/audience if he or she cannot convey or control his or her meaning to the readers/audience? Perhaps here Yeo has an imagined open text that has left the author. One wonders how he applies this theory to a classic for example *Lúnyǔ* in his *Musing With Confucius and Paul: Toward a Chinese Christian Theology*.[117] This could mean that a classic which contains "communal wisdom" and has "stood the test of time" is an open text.[118] Its author cannot control the meanings of the text. There is plurality and ambiguity in the understanding of any text.

Yeo names the complex factors entailed in the reading process: "the physical situation, the subject of the discourse, the intention of the speaker (psychological context), the participants' social context, the linguistic code, the rhetorical techniques, the genre of the message of text and the complex horizons of the readers."[119] This list covers facets of the attention paid to a reading process that can be likened to speech. As Ricoeur says, "reading becomes like speech," but not "becomes speech." He insists "reading is never equivalent to a spoken exchange, a dialogue."[120] What Yeo delineates reflects a reading scenario in which the life of the reader is concretely encountering the text. While Ricoeur thinks that a text is like a postponed speech which should have been uttered but never was,[121] Yeo's bringing alive of the context of the reader has made the encounter of the reader and the text similar to that of a speaker and his audience.

---

113. Yeo, "Culture and Intersubjectivity," 84.
114. Yeo, "Culture and Intersubjectivity," 85.
115. Yeo, "Culture and Intersubjectivity," 85.
116. Yeo, "Culture and Intersubjectivity," 85.
117. Yeo, *Musing With Confucius and Paul*.
118. Yeo, *Musing*, 55.
119. Yeo, "Culture and Intersubjectivity," 85.
120. Ricoeur, "What is a Text?," 159, cf. 146.
121. Ricoeur, "What is a Text?," 146–47.

With multiple factors affecting the reading process, one has to agree that "a purely objective reading of Confucius and Paul that transcends culture is unrealizable."[122] This is why "every reading process is intersubjective,"[123] as Yeo claims. He emphasizes that such a reading process is "a constant shifting of images between the writer and the reader."[124] However, a nuanced differentiation has to be remarked upon. Whereas Yeo here emphasizes an interchange, or in another place a dialog, between the writer and the reader,[125] he also says that the writer has no control over the meanings of the text.[126] The contradiction between these statements can be resolved by emphasizing the role of the subject/reader who appropriates the texts and who, as Yeo has already pointed out, produces/reproduces the meanings rather than the relationship between the writer and the reader. This is a strategy in which I will differ from Yeo.

As the reading of a text is an act of communication, it is thus interactive; as it is rhetorical, it aims at persuasion. He emphasizes that in addition to these two dimensions, a biblical text is also hermeneutical and theological, for it is meaningful and carries theological content.[127] In other words, it has something to communicate, the writer or the speaker finds ways to deliver and persuade his reader to enter his "worlds-of-meaning."[128] Here his discussion is more nuanced and elaborate than that in *Rhetorical Interaction*.

Yeo further develops an intertextual and intersubjective reading in his interpretation of the *Analects* (*Lúnyǔ*) and Galatians in *Musing With Confucius and Paul*. He says, "I am honored when I can read Galatians and *Analects* as a Chinese Christian, creating a Confucius and a Paul in my image."[129] The reading of "two texts" as the concern of a Chinese Christian is very much evident in *Musing*, which crystalizes, at least twenty years' effort preceding this publication,[130] and furthers his cross-cultural hermeneutics, which aims to articulate the inheritance of two texts.

---

122. Yeo, *Musing*, 54.
123. Yeo, *Musing*, 54.
124. Yeo, *Musing*, 54.
125. See also Yeo, "Culture and Intersubjectivity," 86–87.
126. Yeo, "Culture and Intersubjectivity," 87.
127. Yeo, "Culture and Intersubjectivity," 86–87.
128. Gittens, *Gifts and Strangers*, 12. See section 1.
129. Yeo, *Musing*, 54.
130. As he himself acclaims in an article in 2004 (compared to *Musing* which was published in 2010), "Over the last fifteen years I have done extensive cross-cultural reading of the Pauline epistles." See "Culture and Intersubjectivity," 82. More evidence

In it, he clearly describes his hybrid identity as a diasporic Chinese Christian who originated from Malaysia and has embraced a mixture of Malaysian, Hong Kong, Taiwanese, and American experience over many years. This unique background has indeed created for him a unique hermeneutical angle in reading classics, rather than a culturally neutral one.[131] It is interesting to observe that I have lived in Malaysia, Taiwan, Hong Kong, and Scotland and as such have reflected on my Chinese Christian identity. While in *Musing* Yeo has focused on *Lúnyǔ* and Paul, I am focusing on *Yìzhuàn* and Paul. I am reading *Yìzhuàn* mainly as a text produced in the hands of pre-Qín Confucians, and thus finding an integration of Confucian and Christian heritage as Yeo does in *Musing*. This coincidence is a herald of resonance, perhaps of Chinese Christians of similar backgrounds.

In one layer of the discussion, he introduces the literary and historical worlds to which each classic belongs, while on another he highlights the mutuality between the Confucian ideas of harmony, mutuality, community and his personal hybrid background.[132] He acknowledges the major differences between two ethical systems: for Paul it is the "historicizing apocalyptic interpretation," Christo-centric "cosmological and apocalyptic eschatology" and sin; for the Confucian, it is the natural process of creation and redemption and the emphasis of *dé* (moral excellence)[133] which is already endowed by Heaven in man.[134] While he takes enough

---

can be found in his published articles over these years: "The Intertextual Reading of Pauline Theology and Confucian Political Ethics," 141–65; "The Debate in Galatians on Culture and Theology," 43–62; "On Confucian Xin and Pauline Pistis," 25–51; "System of Harmony According to Confucius and Paul," 37–51; "Musical Harmony According to Confucius and Paul," 163–89; "Political Theology of Paul in a World of Violence," 99–127; "The Law of Love According to Confucius and Paul," 203–22; "Li and Law in the Analects and Galatians: A Chinese Christian Understanding of Ritual and Propriety," 309–32.

131. Yeo, *Musing*, 3–13. He relies on Homi K. Bhabha's construct of "a process of hybridity" in Bhabha, *Nation and Narration*. The ideas highlighted are the "in-betweenness" and the "liminality," see op. cit., 1–4. For this in Yeo's reference to Bhabha, see *Musing*, 12.

132. This paragraph is excerpted from my review of this book published in Ooi, review of *Musing With Confucius and Paul*, 276–77.

133. He uses "virtue" instead.

134. See Yeo, "Paul's Theological Ethic," 120–27. And it is quite evident as well that though Yeo does differentiate Daoist and Confucian sources, but to him both traditions form a common Chinese way of living and the difference is of no importance. For his earlier notion of Gadamer's "fusion of horizons," see idem, *Rhetorical Interaction*, 1. However, there he did not have space to really show such a fusion in a supposedly

care not to blur the difference between the two texts, throughout his writing, he deliberately creates as much fusion between Paul and Confucius as he deems possible.[135]

My review of Yeo is necessarily and purposefully much longer than the previous reviews. As I will show in the next chapter, while I develop from Gadamer some of his key hermeneutical concepts, Yeo's and Gadamer's notion of intersubjectivity will both form one of the guiding principles for my double vision hermeneutics. Nevertheless, although they form a partial theoretical background for my hermeneutics, my thesis will show how I rely on, but differ from them.

3. Cultural Linguistic Factor

The need to construct theology which is cultural-linguistically relevant to Chinese language and tradition has not been left in the dark. Even in the case of Yeo, who did not particularly aim to articulate the cultural-linguistic aspect in his works, the Confucian doctrines that he studies, like *yì* (righteousness), *rén* (benevolent love), and *lǐ* (propriety),[136] are all words that carry cultural implications which help pass down the tradition. Tradition and language cannot be separated. Hendriks Kraemer, in his reflection on Christian mission to China three quarters of a century ago, pointed out the key principle for "all adaptation and indigenization," i.e. to see to it that the "new religious insights and attitudes" may find "characteristic expression."[137] He emphasized that such expression would carry "the flavour of their own environment" and be rooted "fully and wholeheartedly both in Christianity and in the Chinese world."[138] The core idea of his argument was that the real character of Christian revelation should

---

"Chinese" "life-world," except in the final chapter, as was pointed out earlier.

135. See, for example, his theological creativity in weaving the idea of *rénrén* and the love for one's neighbor, and a Pauline-Confucian integration as cruciform *rén* and love for one's enemies, in *Musing*, 291–303. He devotes at least one section in every chapter to an interpretation from a "Chinese Christian" perspective. For this see op. cit., 50–52, 80–109, 173–76, 240–52, 261–91, 333–51, 370–98, and the entire epilogue. We however cannot engage in detailed discussion in these various areas.

136. Yeo, "Paul's Theological Ethic," 127–37.

137. Kraemer, *Christian Message*, 324. Kraemer differentiates intellectual and cultural syntheses in the indigenization process, recommending the latter's "long and living development" as a better model than the former that "are thought out without being related to an actual development of the spiritual life."

138. Kraemer, *Christian Message*, 324, 379.

Surveying Chinese Indigenous Theological Approaches

penetrate the core of Chinese culture and be expressed in unique Chinese ways.

The reason for the former underdevelopment of Chinese theology was partly due to the Western theological hegemony which dominates what and how theology should be discussed. What C. S. Song, the author of *Third-Eye Theology*, is rejecting is the theological hegemony of the West first "imposed on" Asian Christians by the West and then by Asians themselves. He points out,

> We were always many steps behind the schools and systems of theological thoughts established by our theological mentors in the West. We held onto the space vacated by them or the space superceded by those who came after them. If we were not preoccupied with "perpetuating old theological traditions," then we were busy learning to "sing new theological tunes" that reached our shores from beyond the Pacific. Sadly, this is still the state of most Christian churches and theological schools in Asia even at the present time.[139]

He describes this kind of theology as "beating the air," signifying a theological space that does not contain the stories, histories and cultures of Asia. What he is calling for is an "authentic theological voice" and a theology that takes Asia's "own cultures, religions, and histories" seriously.[140] Hence, Asian theologians should compose their own "theological symphony."[141] To him, this is a theological awakening, "that we cannot continue to perpetuate someone else's confessional tradition and sing somebody else's theological tune."[142] He contends that,

> The basic thrust of theological reconstruction in Asia is not just to give an "Asian color" to Christian theology. It is not a matter of sprinkling traditional theology with oriental perfume. It has little to do with adding Asian trappings to the systems of Christian truth developed in the history of Western Christianity. Nor is it a variation of current theological trends in the rest of the world outside Asia.[143]

Perhaps there is more awareness in the West of the continuing hegemony Song describes. As Andrew Walls recently expresses, "The

139. Song, *Third-Eye Theology*, 5.
140. Song, *Third-Eye Theology*, 2, 6.
141. Song, *Third-Eye Theology*, 8.
142. Song, *Third-Eye Theology*, 6.
143. Song, *Third-Eye Theology*, 6.

emergence of Christianity as a non-Western religion provides both a new story and new means of understanding the old story. The story of non-Western Christianity, with all its new elements, is continuous with earlier Christian history."[144] This means that the non-Western Christian stories cannot be "simply a source of interesting additional options in the curriculum. Still less does it mean that these histories can simply be appended to existing syllabuses as though they were an updating supplement."[145] In academic settings, he is concerned that sometimes,

> respectable and respected biblical scholars or dogmaticians assume that the task can be done with a chapter at the end of the dissertation "relating the topic to Africa." Strong-minded students sometimes meet frustration in the face of conventional selection or formulations of topics.[146]

What Song and Walls have said above may not be directly related to the incorporating of Chinese tradition, culture and language into theological construction. However, such an incorporation can only be taken as legitimate in the West, and globally, when the said hegemony is avoided. With such a freedom, perhaps Chinese theologians can embrace what Alister McGrath has recently underlined:

> Calvin was interested in—and, to some extent, influenced by—the language and concepts of the classical Roman philosophical and rhetorical tradition. China has an older philosophical and rhetorical tradition. Why should Asian Christians use the same ideas that Calvin borrowed when they have a distinguished heritage of their own from which to draw?[147]

What McGrath calls attention to is Chinese tradition through which a unique expression of Christian faith, as Kraemer earlier called for, can be produced.

Chinese theologians themselves, in addition to Song, Yeo, and Archie Lee mentioned above, are not silent on this concern. Nevertheless, Peter K. H. Lee asserted that a pivotal factor for constructing a relevant

---

144. Walls, "In Quest of the Father of Mission Studies," 98.

145. Walls, "Structural Problems," 146.

146. Walls, "Structural Problems," 152.

147. McGrath, "Evangelical Theological Method," 36–37. In a slightly different way, Jung Young Lee, a Korean theologian, has boldly pointed out that non-Western perspectives on Christianity should not be regarded as subsidiaries to the Western perspectives, see Lee, *Trinity*, 11–12. Lee is not alone on this perspective. Now even much of the West has echoed such a valid call. See Jenkins, *The Next Christendom*.

Surveying Chinese Indigenous Theological Approaches

indigenous theology lies in finding a correct theological method, with the cultural-linguistic aspect being emphasized. He proposes what he calls the New Hermeneutic, with which he emphasizes:

- a hermeneutic that recognizes the importance of historical existence in the process of history. He argues that Chinese theology should be able to show its recognition of and response to its Chinese past and present.
- an acknowledgement of the influence of interpreters on the texts they interpret, who are themselves determined by the ideology of the local context in which he reads the text.
- an emphasis on the importance of linguistic or literary characteristics, for a language represents its cultural background and the Chinese language carries with it its own uniqueness.

Thus, the "past and present," "the ideology of the local context," and "the language or literary characteristics" of the Chinese language should all be seriously considered as one constructs a Chinese theology. A theologian who takes this approach hopes to reflect the indigenous elements of Chinese culture.[148] The following will show how I incorporate these into my hermeneutics.

Liú Xiǎofēng, who represents a voice from the contemporary Chinese literati and is the initiator of the recent *Hànyǔ shénxué* or Sino-Theology (theology constructed in the Hàn language) in the 1990s, provides another observation:

> In the development of its linguistic experiences throughout the last two millennia, Chinese thinking has amassed an extremely rich reservoir of linguistic experiences. By far, these linguistic experiences have not been dedicated to the discourse of the intellectual experiences of the Christian faith, as it had been in the case of the ancient Greek and Latin linguistic experiences.[149]

Liú therefore also encourages theologians to tap into poems, lyrics, prose, and all other literary expression in popular literature that belong to the Chinese people to express the new experiential structure of Christian faith.[150] As Gadamer describes,

---

148. Lǐ (Lee), "Běnshè shénxué—Jiùgēng hé xīnkěn," 7–15.
149. Liú, "Sino-Christian Theology," 76–77.
150. Liú, "Xiàndài yǔjìng," 46.

49

> Linguistic tradition is tradition in the proper sense of the word—i.e., something handed down. It is not just something left over, to be investigated and interpreted as a remnant of the past. What has come down to us by way of verbal tradition is not left over but given to us, told us—whether through direct retelling, in which myth, legend, and custom have their life, or through written tradition, whose signs are, as it were, immediately clear to every reader who can read them.[151]

Gadamer's idea of tradition or "traditionary texts" will be deliberated in the subsequent chapter. "Traditionary texts" is a neologism the English translator creates for *Überlieferung*, literally "tradition," which means "what comes down to us from the past" or "handed down from the past."[152] From the above, we can infer that for Gadamer, linguistic tradition is also part of the "traditionary texts" that "has come down to us."

Returning to Liú's argument, there is, already, a great reservoir of ideas and thoughts within the Chinese language. He suggests that the development of Sino-Christian theology could either of two models: one is to develop Christian theology using the existing ideological system and linguistic conception, and the other is to develop it using the living experience and its language. The first model will use the Confucian, Daoist, and Buddhist ideological systems to express the Christian faith by integrating existing Christian theological literary heritage written in Western languages. The second model is to develop from the daily language used by today's Chinese living in real life in various regions experience into a Christian theology, but to reject the use of any ideological system embedded in any particular region to interpret the Christ event.[153]

Liu's proposal is not one that aims to engage Chinese classical texts in theological reflection. However, as far as Liù may want to distantiate himself from the traditional indigenous theological approach, he seems not to have walked far enough. Rather than proposing to engage Chinese classics, Liú promotes the use of *Hànyǔ*—Hàn or Chinese language—to do theology, thus Sino-theology, and emphasizes that a Sino-theology as such, has to take Chinese cultural and linguistic distinctiveness seriously into account.

However, as is said, to do theology with *Hànyǔ* means to do it with the Chinese *language*. One wonders how one could tap into a

---

151. Gadamer, *Truth and Method*, 391.
152. "Translator's Preface," in Gadamer, *Truth and Method*, xvi.
153. Liú, "Xiàndài yǔjìng," 45.

cultural-linguistic reservoir without also, inevitably, engaging the tradition in which the language itself, and the ideology embedded in it, is so deeply rooted. He has acknowledged that the two thousand year reservoir of Chinese linguistic experiences "[has] not been dedicated to the discourse of the intellectual experiences of the Christian faith;" thus rather than avoiding the classical texts, it investigates how many Chinese words have appeared, reinterpreted, or been appropriated as intertexts in many works throughout the centuries. There is no way to avoid the classics and the tradition, nor to split them. A Chinese theologian today can consider himself not limited the study of a key Chinese word in a Chinese Classic per se, but to expand it into an intertextual study by taking Johanna Liu's and Richard Smith's arguments into account.[154] As this thesis will show, an intersubjective reading of the texts will be emphasized in the double vision hermeneutics, which also acknowledges the intertextual relationship between different Chinese texts as *shì* and *Yìzhuàn*.

In this section I have argued for the significance of the Chinese cultural-linguistic dimension in constructing a Chinese theology. In the following, I will give one example showing a work which reveals the embeddedness of a Chinese theologian in the Chinese cultural-linguistic heritage.

3.1: *Zhào Zǐchén's Shèng Baǒluó zhuàn (The Biography of St Paul)*

A growing number of studies have been published over the past two decades regarding Zhaò Zǐchén's theology and writings,[155] but less attention has been paid to the Chinese cultural-linguistic background reflected in his writings. His *Shèng Baǒluó zhuàn* (The Biography of St Paul) is a biography of Paul crafted with Zhaò' theological interpretation based on Pauline texts and the *Book of Acts*. While his book aims not to show the Chinese cultural-linguistic background but to faithfully tell the story of Paul, the text frequently betrays the author's rootedness in such a background. As Hans-Georg Gadamer says, "It is true that those who are

---

154. See pages 19–20 in the introduction of this thesis.

155. For studies on Zhaò Zǐchén, see Lam, *Qǔ gaō hé guǎ* and Gluer, *Zhaò Zǐchén dè shénxué sīxiǎng*; Xíng, *Xúnqiú jīdūjiào dè dútèxìng*; idem, "Zhaò Zǐchén de zhōngjiào jīngyèn." Also Lín, "Zhaò Zǐchín yú xīn Zhōngguó chénglì qián dè běnshè jiaòhuì lǐlùn yú shíjiàn,"141–56; Wan, "Poised Between Grace and Moral Responsibility," 39–68; idem, "The Emerging Hermeneutics of the Chinese Church," 351–82.

brought up in a particular linguistic and cultural tradition see the world in a different way from those who belong to other traditions."[156] I will point out a few significant examples.

The first is his interpretation of *yōngshēng* (eternal life). He says, "The life after death is not another kind of new life, but the continuation of one's life in Christ; what is different is its mode of existence, *qíngjìng*. Thus, in our life, there are two worlds that mutually penetrate one another. The mode (*jìngjiè*) of immortality is already found within the moral experience."[157] It is hard to translate *qíngjìng* here. *Qíng* literally denotes 'feeling related to emotion, affection, and passion'; *jìng* denotes 'dimension or horizon', as seen in *jìngjiè*. Combined, they could mean circumstance or situation. Be that as it may, a characteristic of Chinese language, the symbiosis of the subjective (*qíng*) and the objective (*jìng*), is evident.

Even more unique is his translation of "justification by faith" as *yǐ xìn wéi zhí*, originally translated as *yǐ xìn chēng yì* (*yīn* instead of *yǐ* in the Chinese Union Version). He argues,

> It is more appropriate to translate it as *yǐ xìn wéi zhí*. *Zhí* is the *zhí* as seen in *qūzhí*, crooked and straight, which is also the *zhí* as in "repay hatred with uprightness."[158] . . . God sees the faith of man, and reckons such as uprightness. For instance, it is said in the Bible, "Abraham has faith in God; this faith is reckoned as his uprightness." Because Abraham believes, God takes his faith as his uprightness; he is thus straight and upright, instead of crooked and sinful. A man of "uprightness" of course is an upright man. However, "uprightness" and "righteousness" are two different words, although their meanings seem to be similar. *Zhí* is a forensic (*fǎlǜ*) noun, while "*yì*" is a moral vocabulary.[159]

What is surprising in his argument is his differentiation of the moral and forensic connotations of these two words, which are found, in Greek, with the same root δικαιο. As Jewett and others have pointed out, "advocates of a forensic doctrine of justification point to the frequent use of δικαιόω and its Hebrew equivalent in the sense of 'acquit, justify, declare right, vindicate'" which "usually appears in the context of social justice

---

156. Gadamer, *Truth and Method*, 447.
157. Zhào, *Shèng Baŏluó zhuàn*, 154.
158. It says *Lúnyǔ* (in chapter *Xiànwèn*) 14:36, "(The Master says) Rather, repay hatred with uprightness and repay virtue with virtue," cited from Chan, *Source*, 42.
159. Zhào, *Shèng Baŏluó zhuàn*, 49. Translation mine.

where God or the judge takes the side of the weak" (see Ps 81.1–3).[160] My point is to show how his Chinese linguistic background, and a familiarity with Chinese classic texts, have given Zhaò a special sensitivity to rooting the language of Christian faith in the soil of a Chinese cultural linguistic context.[161]

Other unique arguments, which probably also reflect a tendency for flexibility within Chinese culture[162] can be found in the introduction of *Shèng Baŏluó zhuàn*. For instance, in arguing for the credibility of the records of miracles in the Book of Acts, he says,

> Since St Paul himself has said that he had performed miracles, for example, "The signs of a true apostle were performed among you with utmost patience, signs and wonders and mighty works" (2 Cor 12:12), how could scholars simply discredit that? The records of miracles and of other events in Acts are intermingled in the narrative. If these had indeed happened, one cannot argue that they have not based on the premise that does not see such things happen today. . . . Each ear has its own expectation and each generation has its own wonders; how could one be sure that the wheel of the universe would turn this way but not the other? Moreover, could God with his almighty power not work in all sorts of opportunities and turning points? With such a person, such a faith, such a mentality, as long as it is in accordance with the will of God, there is nothing that is impossible.[163]

By this logic he criticizes some scholars for their artificial and meaningless decisions as to what, in Acts, is acceptable and what is not.[164]

This argument appears in one of his twelve self-designed principles in writing history: an awareness of the animation of life (*wù shēngjī*).[165] He contends that life is full of changes. Thus the study of history should not follow a mechanistic methodology. He observes a younger, middle-aged Paul who was domineering and less patient, who had quarrelled with

---

160. Jewett, *Romans*, 281. It also relates to the faithfulness of God. For this, see my discussion in chapter 6.

161. For the relationship between language and belief system in terms of acculturation of Christian faith, see Gitten, *Gifts and Strangers*, 15.

162. I am saying this based on the flexibility of and multifarious perspectives on interpretation as seen in *Yìjīng* interpretation and the effect it has injected through ages, into the vein of Chinese culture. For this aspect, see Smith, *Fathoming*; Zhū, *Yìxué zhéxué shǐ*.

163. Zhào, *Shèng Baŏluó zhuàn*, 4.

164. Zhào, *Shèng Baŏluó zhuàn*, 4.

165. I take *shēngjī* here as in *shēngjī bóbó*.

Barnabas over Mark's leaving in the middle of their mission trip; who, when he grew older, became more accepting and forgiving and was no longer bothered by the earlier incidence.[166] Zhaò also makes a similar imaginative deduction, built first upon Acts 17, to show Paul's effort in resorting to philosophical argument with those who were merely interested in arguments following the fashion of the time. Such effort, Zhaò argues, ended up winning no one to Christ. Zhaò concludes that Paul, therefore, later determined not to use such an approach, but to preach Christ and his cross, as seen in 1 Corinthians. He cites 1 Corinthians 1:20–21 saying, "Where is the one who is wise? Where is the scribe? Where is the debater of this age? Has not God made foolish the wisdom of the world? For since, in the wisdom of God, the world did not know God through wisdom, God decided, through the foolishness of our proclamation, to save those who believe."[167] Thus he claims that this was Paul's new approach: instead of adapting himself and resorting to the rhetoric and philosophy of the time, he simply proclaims the "foolishness" of the "cross." Pauline scholars may still find that Zhaò's interpretation in this regard does not take account of the Corinthian social context and the situation the church faced. What Paul said in 1 Cor 1:20–21 was nothing less than rhetoric which could be understood only if one understood the social and philosophical trends of the time. Moreover, as I will argue later, Paul had a theological concern, which was that the Corinthians might deviate from the gospel if they followed the wisdom of the time. Such a theological concern was what Zhaò had pointed to but not precisely articulated.

To sum up, what is found in Zhaò's biography of Paul is not an overt and unreserved intentional embracing of the Confucian ethos but an attempt towards careful and scholarly discussion of Paul. What stands out in this work is his, perhaps less intentional, use of Chinese expression and literary ability, which have indeed helped him superbly create the first Pauline studies in the Chinese language. His theological nuances stand out, by weaving the Chinese cultural-linguistic into his narrative. His insights on Paul emerge from his cultural-linguistic sensitivity but, surprisingly coincide with recent interpretations of some Pauline texts. The two texts—Chinese and Pauline—may have been two separate texts, but they are found in fusion within the subject, Zhaò Zǐchén. It is more conducive to assume that the result is a natural outcome emerging from

---

166. Zhào, *Shèng Baǒluó zhuàn*, 4.

167. Zhào, *Shèng Baǒluó zhuàn*, 90. Zhào might also have known that some issues surrounding the Corinthians were related to the Stoics, but there is no evidence that he was aware of Sophist issues. See op. cit., 5–8.

Zhao's Chinese background than an intentional attempt by him to see Paul through a Chinese eye. Nevertheless, in spite of his self restriction and his, probably, intentional avoidance of the Confucian belief he once strongly held, one sees in this work a, possibly, more mature critical integration of Pauline and Confucian thoughts.

Thus far, in this section, I have explained that many have argued for a Chinese theology that is rooted in Chinese cultural-linguistic experience, and shown an example of such rootedness, exhibited in a Chinese theologian's work. I will assume the above as the background for my own incorporation of *shì* as a key text in this thesis. My discussion and interaction with the theoretical framework of Anthony Gittens in the subsequent section will further clarify the difference between my undertaking and those derived from Christian mission as implied in Gittens' discussion.

3.2: A Cultural-linguistic Aspect of Anthony Gitttens

With regard to cultural-linguistic aspect, several ideas articulated by Anthony Gittens: cultural "deep structure," "faith-intuitions" of native speakers, "belief systems," and "worlds-of-meanings," are worth studied. While I find they are, in general, relevant to my assumption of engaging Chinese cultural-linguistic aspects into a Chinese theological attempt, the difference between his and my concern has to be noted. He writes from a Western background and to those mostly coming from a similar background. The majority of his audience are those who have participated in Christian mission, and thus have experienced cross-cultural communication. Although also concerned with this cultural and linguistic dimension, I am more interested in Gitten's ideas which enable me to respond as a native Chinese speaker. Thus, my discussion of the ideas below starts with the feeling of empathized with and move further on towards my response and revision.

First of all, he argues that there is a cultural "deep structure" in the kernel of a tradition.[168] Borrowing a linguistic idea, he refers to the "*base-component*," i.e., the "syntactic *deep structure*,"[169] found within a given sentence that is only accessible or can be appreciated and understood by

---

168. This somewhat reflects the "kernel and husk" model, see Schreiter, *Constructing Local Theologies*, 7.

169. Gittens, "Beyond Liturgical Inculturation," 51. He defines: "The *deep structure* is an abstract underlying structure 'that incorporates all the syntactic information required for the interpretation of given sentence.'" Italic here and above are all his.

either a linguist or a native speaker. For a native speaker, such an ability comes in the form of intuition. In other words, it is because he or she is born into that particular linguistic environment that the language becomes part of him or her.[170] Assuming the existence of a deep structure within a receiving culture, Gittens contends that it is at this level that Christian faith and other traditions encountering one another. He states,

> we must discover how to generate, in cultural practices, ways to embody and incarnate the faith that make (new) sense to native speakers of the language of faith, in terms of their (enhanced) intuitions about behaviourally acceptable and theologically meaningful expressions of Christianity.[171]

In other words, the native speakers of a certain culture should be able to express themselves out of their "faith-intuitions,"[172] which means the authentic Christian message born out of their soul. For him a true inculturation should allow the Christian message to be found expressed through the "faith-intuitions" of a native speaker.[173] An inculturation, as he argues, is "an embodiment, an incarnation of the faith."[174] What Gittens argues coincides with what the missiologist Kraemer has already pointed out to let indigenous Christians find expression that is meaningful to them. Hence, in reflecting cross-cultural mission from a linguistic perspective, Gittens claims that it is

> virtually impossible to understand belief systems at first hand unless we know the language. For language and behavior and belief are all intimately related. A cultural heritage is transmitted through language.[175]

Thus a Chinese Christian reflecting on his own experience in Chinese would naturally reflect on his cultural heritage, and the belief system found within it. Beliefs are "obligatory," and they actually "existed before

---

170. For a linguist expert, it is through training that he or she can enter into this "deep structure." When it comes to communication, Gittens emphasizes that a willingness between the two speakers must be present to appreciate what the sentence is actually meant to convey. See Gittens, "Beyond Liturgical Inculturation," 51.

171. Gittens, "Beyond Liturgical Inculturation," 50.

172. Gittens, "Beyond Liturgical Inculturation," 53.

173. He refers to inculturation as a process. Implied here are at least two belief systems involved in the inculturation process. See Gittens, "Beyond Liturgical Inculturation," 70.

174. Gittens, "Beyond Liturgical Inculturation," 56ff.

175. Gittens, *Gifts and Strangers*, 15.

we did, and we are not really free to switch."[176] And a "belief system" according to him "is a scheme into which people are born (or, more rarely, construct), which helps to make sense of their own experience and to order the universe."[177] Moreover, people of a particular cultural-linguistic background root their belief system within the "worlds-of-meanings" of that particular system.[178] The cultural and linguistic conditions not only reflect the cultural "deep structure," but also reflect the "worlds-of-meanings" whereby any meaning is to be understood.

An understanding of the culture of the people receiving the gospel is crucial if an authentic inculturation is to be achieved. As Gittens argues, to be able to see true inculturation actualized, "People of faith and people of culture must encounter each other, and so must the core values of Christians and the core values of a culture: each must give and receive life."[179] However, this cannot imply that the gospel can be sacrificed to accommodate itself to the receiving culture. Gittens stresses, "No culture may ever be allowed to compromise or domesticate the Christian faith, but nor must people of faith ever overlook or trivialize human culture."[180] His point is very clear: any emphasis on gospel and the culture should never mutually sacrifice the uniqueness of the other.

The weakness of applying this type of theory to a Chinese Christian reflection lies in the presupposition of an antithesis of culture and gospel. Gittens' argument may demonstrate a consideration of Christian mission which sees the relationship between the gospel and the culture in terms of one which sends and the other which receives. Gittens is correct in pointing out that both the gospel and the receiving culture have their own "deep structures."[181] It is correct to warn against the gospel being compromised and diluted in the process of communication and inculturation. However, as a Chinese Christian who grew up inheriting and integrating the biblical message and Chinese culture synchronically, what Gittens has contributed still falls short of articulating the symbiotic relationship of the doubleness of such an identity. What I face is not faith/gospel against or versus culture. In such a case, the meeting of two deep, cultural structures goes

176. Gittens, *Gifts and Strangers*, 13. As we shall look at later in chapter 2, what Gittens points out here is similar to what Gadamer says about tradition.

177. Gittens, *Gifts and Strangers*, 12. He quotes from Frank Manning "The Case of the Healthy Hindu."

178. Gittens, *Gifts and Strangers*, 12.

179. Gittens, "Beyond Liturgical Inculturation," 71.

180. Gittens, "Beyond Liturgical Inculturation," 71–72.

181. Gittens, "Beyond Liturgical Inculturation," 70.

further than designating culture as the receiving partner as if the gospel is the only seed while the culture is the soil in which the seed will germinate and grow. To interpret the interwoven relationship of gospel and Chinese culture found within me for example, the "seed" and "soil" model seems inadequate.

As a Chinese Christian, I do not only reflect on one cultural heritage and belief system. The situation is somewhat embarrassing. I am not a Jew who speaks Hebrew as my mother tongue nor was I born into its culture and heritage. While Paul, when he referred to the gentile Christians as the "wild olive shoot" and the covenant of God to be his people (as the Jews who was first made His people), he was speaking from a Jewish perspective (Rom 11:17). From this perspective, I, like many other Christians, am "a wild olive shoot" who is "grafted" onto the "olive tree." I do not experience the Hebrew language and cultural heritage first hand, nor am I able to truly experience the effect of the Hebrew belief system as a Jew. Now the Hebrew cultural and faith traditions had also gone through cultural exchange and assimilation, as found in the time of the New Testament. The reinterpretation of the Old Testament heritage into a new era was a big challenge, and the new expression of faith, in a language other than Hebrew and Aramaic was an ingenious invention.

Having said that, I have pointed out the complexity found in the transmission vis-à-vis the subjective experience of faith. Encountering the biblical text, I face a cultural-linguistic barrier which, according to Gittens, I am not able to cross over unless I know the language. In contrast, I inherit a Chinese cultural-linguistic heritage, which I find diffusing many aspects in my life. Yet as a Chinese Christian, even as I claim I inherit two heritages, this double inheritance can only be understood as a limited inheritance. At least according to a Jew, I never can understand his or her culture and heritage as he or she does. Thus, I am not claiming a double cultural inheritance in a strict sense according to Gittens. What I claim is a subjective appropriation of two inheritances. In other words, I do inherit both texts, but in terms of the Judaic-Christian text, I inherit it through a life-time of reading of it in its translated version. It is experienced as the text of my faith experience rather than as a cultural heritage. The Chinese cultural-linguistic heritage I inherit is different experience. However, such an experience may differ from that of a Chinese growing up in Taiwan, Hong Kong, or America.

The cultural-linguistic dimension should be taken into account in the construction of a Chinese theology. However, as has been pointed out, a different hermeneutical framework has to be used to express the double identity vis-à-vis the double inheritance of a Chinese Christian. This means that, on the one hand, I shall incorporate Chinese cultural linguistic heritage in my hermeneutics, but in a manner different from Gittens; on the other I have to embrace the concern of "two texts" articulated by Archie Lee and the intersubjective relationship between two texts as pointed out by K. K. Yeo.

4. Overall Remarks to the above Seven Attempts

Let me summarize the above and reiterate some key contributions as well as some underdeveloped or unsatisfactory areas found in the respective approaches. The first model has covered Julia Ching, Lee Yung Young, Xiè Fúyǎ, and Zhaò Yànxiá who take a doctrinal approach in one way or another. Julia Ching's knowledge of Chinese classics and tradition is undeniably admirable, but her treatment of Paul does not fulfill what she herself requires, the demand for exegesis. Lee and Xiè, by using Christian doctrines as a framework for constructing a theology with *Yìzhuàn's* philosophy, commit the fallacy Samuel Sandmel warned against, which he calls "parallelomania" and defines as "that extravagance among scholars which first overdoes the supposed similarity in passages and then proceeds to describe source and derivation as if implying literary connection flowing in an inevitable or predetermined direction."[182] They nevertheless do not engage serious exegesis with the biblical texts and *Yìzhuàn*, having undertaken a doctrinal approach.

A dissatisfaction among Chinese theologians has been voiced since the last quarter of the twentieth century, criticizing earlier Chinese theology for the lack of serious engagement with biblical theological exegesis, as Lai Pan-chiu has recently summarized.[183] In view of this, my objective is to avoid "making Paul's context conform to the content of the alleged parallels" which Sandmel "cautions against."[184] Instead, the literary and historical contexts of the texts shall be considered, while the subjective

---

182. Cited from Lee, *Paul, the Stoics, and the Body of Christ*, 12. For Sandmel, see "Parallelomania," 1.

183. See Pan-Chiu Lai, "Sino-Theology."

184. For Sandmel, see "Parallelomania," 1. He emphasizes, "it is critical to evaluate the significance of the parallels rather than simply list excerpts since two passages may sound the same in isolation, but their contexts may reveal their differences rather than their similarities."

aspect of the readings will be emphasized. This will be revealed in the next chapter.

In comparison, Archie Lee's approach which enables us to maneuver Asian cum Chinese Christian theological hermeneutics into clear focus by taking up the reality of the "two texts." While Yeo's and Archie Lee's approaches may look different, the emphasis on the Chinese Christian self is the same. Yeo emphasizes the reading and appropriation of texts (or as he puts it, 'read by texts'), the intersubjectivity, the dialog between the reader and the writer/text, and his hybrid identity which influences his reading. Lee puts much emphasis on the Asian or Chinese context, his Text A, in which an Asian or a Chinese is situated, and the many crossings between Text A and Text B. In one way or another, one sees the influence of hermeneutical insights provided mainly by Gadamer and Ricoeur, among other theorists, in Yeo's and Lee's proposals.

My review has also brought attention to the necessity of taking the Chinese cultural-linguistic aspect as an indispensable component in constructing a Chinese theology. The argument is supported by looking at the example of Zhaò Zǐchén, who was deeply rooted in the Chinese cultural-linguistic background, which he has projected into his theological reflection on Paul's life and theology. Gittens was expounded, to provide a theoretical framework for the argument. As shall be seen in the next chapter, this cultural-linguistic dimension will be considered under various Gadamerian accounts.

Both the call to more exegetical and expositional interpretation of biblical texts, and to the inclusion of a cultural-linguistic dimension will be responded to in this thesis. Moreover, although the former refers to the interpretation of biblical texts, I shall apply the same principle to my reading of *Yìzhuàn*.

In the next chapter, to prepare for the hermeneutical attempt to unfold and interpret the intersubjective relationship of the various texts, I will propose a double vision hermeneutics. This is in preparation for an exploration of the relationships between Text A1 + A2 and Text B1 + B2.

2

Constructing a Double Vision Hermeneutic

In the introduction, I have proffered myself and my experience as the locus of my double vision hermeneutics. In chapter 1, dissatisfaction was expressed with the doctrinal approach and interest shown in developing Archie Lee's "Two Texts" concern and K. K. Yeo's cross-cultural and intersubjective hermeneutics. I accept the call for an exegesis that seriously considers both the literary and historical context of the texts seriously and will apply this exegetical principle to my study of *Yìzhuàn* and Pauline texts. I find the reflection of my personal experience to be in line with Chinese Christians who wrestle with their inheritance of a dual identity and double tradition. I embrace the ethos articulated by Archie Lee: the need to engage in a reflection of two texts not for the sake of comparison but to find an integrated self. I am eager to take my Chinese cultural-linguistic inheritance seriously in my reflection, and put in place a hermeneutics that helps elucidate self-understanding of my Chinese Christian experience.

The aforementioned conditions are all taken into account as I delineate the four texts (Text A1 + A2 and Text B1 + B2) be involved in my double vision hermeneutics. These four texts can stand alone outside my experience; they can also be subjectively experienced and appropriated by me. I am suggesting that this kind of double existence, both outside and inside of me, as intersubjective.

Thus, as the title of this thesis—"A Double Vision Hermeneutics of a Chinese Pastor's Intersubjective Experience of *Shì* Engaging *Yìzhuàn* and Pauline Texts"—indicates, a double vision hermeneutics, the intersubjective experience of *shì*, *Yìzhuàn* and Pauline texts will be dealt with. To restate briefly: by double vision, I mean 1) being aware of two visions, or two texts, at the same time or seeing them both in single vision, 2) seeing one vision, or text, at the foreground but being aware of another text, or vision, in the background, or 3) two visions, or two texts, appear sequentially and alternately. Hence, the double vision hermeneutics will be the apparatus that demonstrates how *shì*, *Yìzhuàn* and Pauline texts are interrelated, and also be the interpretation premise on which the intersubjective relationships of these texts will be displayed.

The purpose of this chapter is to deliberate the hermeneutics involved in the unfolding of the various layers of the intersubjective relationship between Texts A1 and A2, B1 and B2 and between these texts with me. As has been presented in the introduction, Texts A1 and A2 form one intersubjective relationship, Texts B1 and B2 another, and Texts A1 + A2 and Texts B1 + B2 another. I see, in every layer, a double vision. Given that these are all function, in the hermeneutical process, between the mind of the subject and the texts, how do they operate? This should become clear by the end of this chapter.

1. Oppose Objectivism and Retrieve Tradition: Gadamer and Polanyi

I will derive hermeneutical principles which will operate in my double vision hermeneutics from Hans-Georg Gadamer's *Truth and Method* and Michael Polanyi's *Personal Knowledge*,[1] however these will not be investigated further than is necessary for the purpose of this hermeneutic. In terms of publication, the two works appeared around the same time, 1960 [German first edition] and 1958 [first edition] respectively. Both challenged the scientism and objectivism,[2] but on different premises. Gadamer is concerned with the throwing away of (Christian) tradition with the rise of post-Enlightenment scientism and with it the objectivism. He pinpoints this problem:

> It is the general tendency of the enlightenment not to accept any authority and to decide everything before the judgment seat of reason. Thus the written tradition of scripture, like any other historical document, cannot claim any absolute validity, but the possible truth of the tradition depends on the credibility that

---

1. For Polanyi, see Polanyi, *Personal Knowledge*.
2. Polanyi, *Personal Knowledge*, 3–17.

Constructing a Double Vision Hermeneutic

is assigned to it by reason. It is not tradition, but reason that constitutes the ultimate source of all authority.[3]

Thus in advancing his philosophy of hermeneutics, he clears up the premises by which "the experiences of philosophy, of art, and of history" can be understood. These experiences reflect spheres of life the narrow scientism has excluded from its epistemology based on its objectivistic definition of science. As David Linge says, "it is Gadamer's contention that this (epistemological) preoccupation has distorted the hermeneutical phenomenon in its universality by isolating the kind of methodical understanding that goes on in the *Geisteswissenschaften* from the broader processes of understanding that occur every where in human life beyond the pale of critical interpretation and scientific self-control."[4] In *Truth and Method*, he deliberates,

> The phenomenon of understanding not only pervades all human relations to the world. It also has an independent validity within science, and it resists any attempt to reinterpret it in terms of scientific method. The following investigations start with the resistance in modern science itself to the universal claim of scientific method. They are concerned to seek the experience of truth that transcends the domain of scientific method wherever that experience is to be found, and to inquire into its legitimacy. Hence the human sciences are connected to modes of experience that lie outside science: with the experiences of philosophy, of art, and of history itself. These are all modes of experience in which a truth is communicated that cannot be verified by the methodological means proper to science.[5]

Having thus argued, Gadamer intends to retrieve the abandoned tradition but not without redefining the meaning of "'human sciences' (*Geisteswissenschaften*)"[6] as one who has been a child of the post-Enlightenment, the age of reason. He thus retrieves the place for authority by emphasizing an authority based on knowledge. He argues,

> It is true that it is primarily persons that have authority; but the authority of persons is based ultimately, not on the subjection and abdication of reason, but on recognition and

---

3. Gadamer, "The Historicity of Understanding," 257.
4. Linge, "Editor's Introduction," xi.
5. Gadamer, *Truth and Method*, xx–xxi.
6. See Weinsheimer and Marshall, "Translator's Preface," in Gadamer, *Truth and Method*, xviii.

knowledge—knowledge, namely, that the other is superior to oneself in judgment and insight and that for this reason his judgment takes precedence, i.e. it has priority over one's own. This is connected with the fact that authority cannot actually be bestowed, but is acquired and must be acquired, if someone is to lay claim to it. It rests on recognition and hence on an act of reason itself which, aware of its own limitations, accepts that others have better understanding. Authority in this sense, properly understood, has nothing to do with blind obedience to a command. Indeed, authority has nothing to do with obedience, but rather with knowledge.[7]

Similar remarks on tradition, to our surprise, are unexpectedly found in Michael Polanyi, who as a scientist is situated in a very different scholarly context. As Zhenhua Yu points out, "Michael Polanyi, with his intimate knowledge of the practice of science, advocates something like a rehabilitation of tradition in the natural sciences, similar to what Gadamer does with respect to the human sciences. At this point, philosophy of science and hermeneutics converge."[8] Polanyi, from his post-critical philosophical perspective, "argues that critical philosophy's overestimation of critical reason and its blindness to the positive role played by the uncritical elements, such as belief, trust and the acceptance of tradition and authority in the shaping and holding of knowledge is untenable."[9] Under the section "Tradition" in chapter 4 of *Personal Knowledge*, Polanyi deliberates on the meaning of tradition and authority, saying,

> To learn by example is to submit to authority. You follow your master because you trust his manner of doing things even when you cannot analyse and account in detail for its effectiveness. By watching the master and emulating his efforts in the presence of his example, the apprentice unconsciously picks up the rules of the art, including those which are not explicitly known to the master himself. These hidden rules can be assimilated only by a person who surrenders himself to that extent uncritically to the limitation of another. A society which wants to preserve a fund of personal knowledge must submit to tradition.[10]

---

7. Gadamer, "The Historicity of Understanding," 263.
8. Yu, "Tradition, Authority and Originality," 41.
9. Yu, "Tradition, Authority and Originality," 40.
10. Polanyi, *Personal Knowledge*, 53. His idea of authority is related to his idea of "connoisseurship," a section he devotes attention to after "tradition," see 54–55.

Constructing a Double Vision Hermeneutic

These two philosophers, writing around the same time yet coming from different backgrounds, both stress tradition, and call for an epistemology that must take account of the tradition in which one is rooted.

In the light of the Gadamer's and Polanyi's retrieval of tradition, and their objection to objectivism, this thesis also rejects the objectivism. As the following discussion will reveal, in rejecting the objectivism, I am moving toward an intersubjective interpretation that will consider both the text and myself, the interpreting subject. The discussion of Polanyi and Gadamer is as much an unfolding of their ideas, as it is a construction of my double vision hermeneutics.

2. The "Traditionary Texts" and the "Historically Effected Consciousness"

My fundamental experience of *shì* first arose from my rootedness in Chinese cultural-linguistic tradition. Nonetheless as my reflection has led me further and deeper, such an experience was not an experience enclosed within itself, but had revealed multilayered intersubjective experiences of various texts, inter-textually and between the texts and me. As has already been referred to, the texts—*shì*, *Yìjīng*, Pauline texts—with which I have the intersubjective relationships are classics passed down through the tradition. To unfold the intersubjective relationships therein, and to undergird my interpretation towards better comprehension, some ideas derived from Gadamer alongside my concerns will be deliberated below.

2.1: Traditionary Texts

"Traditionary texts" is a neologism Joel Weinsheimer and Donald G. Marshall, the English translator for *Truth and Method*, have created for *Überlieferung*: literally "tradition," which means "what comes down to us from the past" or "handed down from the past."[11] In this thesis, "traditionary texts" will be used for the convenience of juxtaposing them with other texts. Besides that, the phrase also implies tradition in a more generic sense.

One major concept behind this idea is the transcendent nature of the text. As Gadamer claims, there is, in the traditional texts, i.e. the

---

11. Weinsheimer and Marshall, "Translator's Preface," in Gadamer, *Truth and Method*, xvi.

classics, "a consciousness of something enduring, of significance that cannot be lost and that is independent of all circumstances of time—a time of timeless present that is contemporary with every other present."[12] Thus, the classics are a body of works that transcends time, and "precedes all historical reflection and continues in it."[13] In other words, the classics or traditionary texts, are larger than any individual or the sum of individuals of any given time within a cultural context.

As David Tracy remarks, "classics are those texts that bear an excess and permanence of meaning, yet always resist definitive interpretation."[14] Tracy's notion of "permanence" and "excess" is indebted to Gadamer's idea of "traditionary texts" and "excess of meanings."[15] In his words, the dialectic lies in that a classic's "permanence . . . can quickly become excess."[16] Consequently, the excess can "yield to a radical insatiability of different receptions that defy any definitive interpretation."[17] Thus, to Tracy, the classic represents "an example of both radical stability become permanence and radical instability become excess of meaning through ever-changing receptions."[18] Hence every reception is a new reading with new meaning. The "permanence" and the "excess" stand against each other in tension similar to that which I find between the subjective reading of a text against its "transcendency." While a traditionary text may seem transcendent and carries permanent meaning, the possibility of multiple meanings always lies behind the invitation for interpretation.

To put it in another way, as Tracy interprets it, "we allow the text to have some claim upon our attention," as that, "we are never pure creators of meanings. In conversation we find ourselves by losing ourselves in the questioning provoked by the text."[19] Thus, we enter the text with our subjective inquiry, but in the process of doing so, we are addressed, provoked, and enriched by the text. Tracy thus enriches our understanding of what Gadamer implies by traditionary texts. The intersubjective relationship of the interpreter and the traditionary texts will be further discussed at a later stage.

12. Gadamer, *Truth and Method*, 288.
13. Gadamer, *Truth and Method*, 288.
14. Tracy, *Plurality and Ambiguity*, 12.
15. See Linge, "Editor's Introduction," xxv.
16. Tracy, *Plurality and Ambiguity*, 14.
17. Tracy, *Plurality and Ambiguity*, 14.
18. Tracy, *Plurality and Ambiguity*, 14.
19. Tracy, *Plurality and Ambiguity*, 19.

2.2: Gadamer's Notion of Tradition Criticized

Gadamer's claim regarding tradition (and the ontology of language) did not escape the scrutiny of critics. The classic critique is found in the "Gadamer-Habermas debate."[20] Matthew Robert Foster succinctly encapsulates one key concern of Habermas, i.e., "[w]hen the immanent tradition is taken as the scope of all possible understanding . . . then there is no objective knowledge or means by which to identify and uncover the ideological elements of that tradition."[21] Foster's concern is that the tradition and language are so tied up,[22] with Gadamer's ontological hermeneutics of language itself,[23] i.e., to see language as being, the danger is that one speaks and lives the language but cannot stand outside the language even when the whole tradition embodied in the language itself is a distorted one. The distortion has prevented the one who lives the language from perceiving reality, as the only reality that is being communicated to him/her is through language and tradition which are already distorted, or even dominated by the so-called traditional authority. As Ingrid Scheibler points out, Habermas sees the danger of "unexamined prejudices" serving as "the standard of judgment, the source of normatively" being "inculcated through systematic distortion passed on through dogmatic authorities and traditions."[24] Habermas himself also expresses his own doubt "that the background consensus of established traditions and language games can be a consciousness forged of compulsion, a result of pseudocommunication," which can infiltrate the "entire social systems."[25] While "it is impossible" for Gadamer to wholly "escape the influence of language and tradition," says Scheibler, in his defense, "[t]his does not mean that the potential for critical engagement and interrogation of existing traditions and one's own prejudgments and prejudices . . . is precluded."[26] In other words,

---

20. See a summary of Habermas–Gadamer debate in Foster, *Gadamer and Practical Philosophy*, 121–79; Scheibler, *Gadamer*, 9–70; Negro, "Gadamer-Habermas Debate," 113–19.

21. Foster, "Habermas and Gadamer," 124.

22. Cf. Scheibler, *Gadamer*, 40.

23. On the ontology of language, see for example in Gadamer, *Truth and Method*, 391 where he states, "The essential relation between language and understanding is seen primarily in the fact that the essence of tradition is to exist in the medium of language."

24. Scheibler, *Gadamer*, 60.

25. Habermas, "On Hermeneutics' Claim," 317.

26. Scheibler, *Gadamer*, 39.

while Gadamer may have wanted to salvage the position of tradition from being eclipsed by the modern world, he did not treat it uncritically.

2.3: Two Traditions

We need not pursue the debate at length here. My interest in the traditionary text or tradition is that I am situated in Chinese cultural linguistic tradition on the one hand, but on the other, have also inherited Christian scripture through reading its Chinese version since I was very young. My inheritance of Christian tradition does not fundamentally arise from reading Christian classics of a Western Christian tradition. Nevertheless, two texts—one from Chinese cultural-linguistic tradition and the other from the Christian Bible—have been with me for decades. How have these two texts been influencing me and interacting in my life? Do they enjoy equal status? Does one override the other only intermittently or does it do so over a longer period of time? With the double vision hermeneutics I propose here, I hope to answer these questions and unfold the intersubjective relationship between the various texts delineated earlier. I aim to do so as faithfully and truly as possible. And if the truth is that one tradition does penetrate and dissolve the other, then so be it, and I will reveal it as such. Alasdair MacIntyre points out, dealing with the translatability of ideas from one language into another, that there will always be the possibility for a tradition to be open to enrichment. He argues that it is in encountering another tradition that one may discover the inadequacy and limitations of one's own tradition, beliefs, and language and comprehend and translate the ideas and meanings in the other tradition one encounters. He asserts,

> The only rational way for the adherent of any tradition to approach intellectually, culturally, and linguistically alien rivals is one that allows for the possibility that in one or more areas the other may be rationally superior to it in respect precisely of that in the other tradition which it cannot as yet comprehend.[27]

It is impossible to gauge how true MacIntyre's assertion is until this thesis is finished. As I have stated in the introductory chapter, my interpretation of *shì* will be a critical one; it will thus intend to be corrective.

---

27. MacIntyre, *Whose Justice? Which Rationality?*, 387–88. Scheibler makes a similar comment with reference to Gadamer: "A point that Gadamer does not adequately address is, Are there cases in which, once one does begin to view the relation to tradition as a living one . . . One would 'reflectively'—that is, actively—opt out of the 'living relation' to tradition?" (Scheibler, *Gadamer*, 68 n. 86).

2.4: History of Effect

Previously I pointed out that as the "traditionary texts" transcend and precede every historical time, they can never be understood unless within a given historical time. In the opinion of Hyun Höchsmann, the underlying principle of "Gadamer's hermeneutical epistemology is that understanding is always from within a lived human context, both individual and social."[28] Every lived human context is linked with a given historical time.

In this thesis, my task is to understand my personal experience, i.e. the intersubjective relationship between Texts A1, A2, B1 and B2 and of them within me. All things that happen within time and space are not neutral but laden with previous history. Previous history thus has an effect on the present and its efficacy to shape reality. When Gadamer deals with the problem of hermeneutics, he cannot see it other than as an understanding that happens within "the reality and efficacy of history."[29] For him, history is always a "'history of effect' [*Wirkungsgeschichte*]."[30] By this he means an understanding as an activity that cannot happen in a vacuum.

In the process of understanding a text, an intertwined relationship between history and self-in-understanding is thus involved. To further deliberate the notion of "history of effect," it would be more specific to say 'a particular history of effect within a history of a particular culture, or nation, or civilization'. According to Gadamer, "self" is not an independent individual understanding "through the process of self-examination." This understanding can only happen in the context of "family, society, and state in which" one lives. These entities exist long before any individual, just as history pre-exists every individual. Thus he claims "history does not belong to us;" on the contrary, "we belong to it."[31] As long as it is correct to say we belong to the history, it lives in us and affects us from inside out. Likewise, tradition does not belong to us, but we belong to it.

Being embedded in the effects of Chinese cultural and linguistic tradition and history, I experience the intertwined relationship between inherited tradition and history, and myself-in-understanding. It manifests itself in how I understand my self, the reality, and the texts I inherit, read, and appropriate.

---

28. Höchsmann, "Foreseeing a Fusion of Horizon," 128.
29. Gadamer, *Truth and Method*, 299.
30. Gadamer, *Truth and Method*, 299.
31. Gadamer, *Truth and Method*, 278.

2.5: Historically Effected Consciousness

The above reflects exactly how Gadamer understands a "self" within effective history. He calls this "self" or subject "*wirkungsgeschichtliches Bewußtsein*" or "historically effected consciousness." Gadamer explains it by defining what we normally call "situation" with the understanding of "effective history." He says,

> The very idea of a situation means that we are not standing outside it and hence are unable to have any objective knowledge of it. We always find ourselves within a situation, and throwing light on it is a task that is never entirely finished. This is also true of the hermeneutic situation—i.e., the situation in which we find ourselves with regard to the tradition that we are trying to understand. The illumination of this situation—reflection on effective history—can never be completely achieved; yet the fact that it cannot be completed is due not to a deficiency in reflection but to the essence of the historical being that we are. *To be historically means that knowledge of oneself can never be complete.*[32]

Here we find several implications. First, this consciousness is always the consciousness of an historical being within the flow of history, which it cannot elude. Second, the self as consciousness is always an historical being within a situation from which one understands oneself. Third, being an historical consciousness within a situation of effected history, one can never have a complete knowledge of oneself. The whole process of understanding is thus "essentially, a historically effected event."[33] Through this process, Gadamer says, the historical consciousness "understands itself in terms of its own history;" it "is a mode of self-knowledge."[34]

2.6: Cultural-Linguistic Context and Text

As is articulated in chapter 1, the cultural-linguistic aspect is indispensable in Chinese theological reflection. To be situated in one's cultural linguistic context can be understood as being situated within the flow of that particular cultural linguistic history. "We are who we are because of the traditions that form us. Our lives are shaped by the preconscious effects

---

32. Gadamer, *Truth and Method*, 301. Italics his.
33. Gadamer, *Truth and Method*, 299.
34. Gadamer, *Truth and Method*, 228.

Constructing a Double Vision Hermeneutic

of all the traditions whose narratives and ways of envisioning the world have forged our memories and consequently our actions."[35] Such a preconscious effects of tradition, as I have already shown in the introduction, had manifested itself in my intersubjective experience of *shì* when I perceived the power relations at the church where I pastored.

Shì is found in many pre-Qín texts which are still being read today. It is a word of high cultural currency and appears in many *cíyǔ*, coined-word phrases that are currently in use. This will be discussed in detail in the next chapter. Here my focus is on interpreting its effect in me. Being a word of more than two thousand years old, the idea of *shì* precedes any individuals who now interpret it. As a word that carries many shades of meanings in its historical literary contexts and has been absorbed into the cultural-linguistic tradition, it precedes my existence and is transcendent. Thus I have before me a word rooted in its historical literary and cultural linguistic contexts, with its meanings I have inherited.

Words are intermingled with the tradition and cultural values in which they are employed. For me whose first language is Chinese, this is especially true as I reflect my personal experience. I find any further inquiry into my use of the language leads to larger historical and traditional texts, teachings, and lore which are sedimented in layers. Thus, to interpret *shì*, I find myself already first exist within the scope of its effect. In other words, *shì* is within me, as my way of being and my understanding of what has happened, and might happen, around me are all affected by this effect. In other words, it owns me cultural-linguistically and resides in me rather than being owned by me. This can be further illustrated applying the idea of historically effected consciousness introduced above. What does he mean by that? It shows that I am always a consciousness situated within an "effected" historical moment in the living Chinese tradition. I was affected by its "effect" in the first place. Having said that, this is only a partial truth. The fact is, that even if I do not own it, I have appropriated it. It, at least what I have appropriated, is in me but still remains outside of me. It can reside in me because I first allow it to enter. In this kind of relationship both I as one subject, and the text as another, are being maintained. To enter into me, the text, metaphorically speaking, has to acknowledge a 'me' in front of it; likewise, to appropriate the text, I have to know that I do not possess the text, and that the text has its own subsistence and can exist alone, independently of me. The relationship is one of intersubjectivity.

---

35. Tracy, *Plurality and Ambiguity*, 37.

3. Intersubjective Readings

In the previous section, I emphasized the self as an "historically effected consciousness" where personal experience is deemed significant in the act of understanding and interpretation. To highlight historical condition is to emphasize the subjectivity in each situation that differs from one another, and the conditioned self whose perception changes from time to time.

3.1: Subjectivity versus Objectivity

By subjectivity, in other parts of this thesis, I mean that which belongs to the subject, and thus everything seen, understood, and interpreted from the perspective of the subject who is situated within a certain context. As I said earlier, the approach of this thesis emphasizes the "personal" aspect. Besides emphasizing that my experience is personal, I wanted to highlight the concept that it is also subjective, in the sense as above defined, rather than stating it in contrast to the concept of objectivity. Nevertheless, an explanation is due to clarify the earlier mentioned personal quest for a solution relevant to my research to emerge, which may appear subjective and arbitrary.

Polanyi in defining *personal* as "neither subjective nor objective," elaborates that "in so far as the personal submits to requirements acknowledged by itself as independent of itself, it is not subjective; but in so far as it is an action guided by individual passions, it is not objective either. It transcends the disjunction between subjective and objective." Thus what he understands as "subjective" are the states "in which we merely endure our feelings" without the active participation through our commitment that is characterized by what he assigns as personal.[36] In other words, being subjective is an indulgence in feelings, which is entirely different from an active "commitment" which is highly demanding of one's concentration, intellect and energy.[37]

Polanyi, aiming to bridge "the disjunction between subjectivity and objectivity,"[38] acclaims,

---

36. Polanyi, *Personal Knowledge*, 300.
37. Polanyi, *Personal Knowledge*, 61.
38. Polanyi, *Personal Knowledge*, 17. Polanyi describes, "This reliance is a personal commitment which is involved in all acts of intelligence by which we integrate some things *subsidiarily* to the centre of our focal attention" (italics mine). I will explain his idea of "focal awareness" and *subsidiary* awareness later.

Constructing a Double Vision Hermeneutic

> Yet the prevailing conception of science, based on the disjunction of subjectivity and objectivity, seeks—and must seek at all costs—to eliminate from science such passionate, personal, human appraisals of theories, or at least to minimize their function to that of a negligible by-play. For modern man has set up as the ideal of knowledge the conception of natural science as a set of statements which is "objective" in the sense that its substance is entirely determined by observation, even while its presentation may be shaped by convention. This conception, stemming from a craving rooted in the very depths of our culture, would be shattered if *the intuition of rationality in nature* had to be acknowledged as a justifiable and indeed essential part of scientific theory.[39]

Not only does Polanyi point to the cause of the objectivism of then his age, but his prognosis aims further to retrieve *"the intuition of rationality"* and to return it to its place in scientific theory.

While Polanyi works on the post-critical philosophy of science, Gadamer works on hermeneutics and is also concerned with the falsely established antithesis between subjectivity and objectivity. He disagrees with "dividing the hermeneutic problem" into two sides: one "the subjectivity of the interpreter," and the other "the objectivity of the meaning." He opposes basing an "understanding of a text" on the finding of a "con-geniality," a happy unity of "the creator and the interpreter of a work."[40] Thus, in his view, if hermeneutics is an event, and if every interpretation starts from the "life-world" and aims to be applicable to the "life-world," the goal of interpretation is not only to treat the text as something objective with a meaning to be understood, but also to allow it to mean what it means to the interpreter in his context.

3.2: *Intersubjectivity*

As I intend to show in this thesis, the engagement with traditionary texts, be it *Yìzhuàn* or Pauline texts, will take the objective side into account. By saying objective, I do not mean that I can exhaust the meaning of the text as if this were the only goal of the interpretation of a text.[41] Neither do I mean that one can actually understand an historical situation as it was

---

39. Polanyi, *Personal Knowledge*, 15–16. Italics mine.
40. Gadamer, *Truth and Method*, 309.
41. See my earlier discussion on Gadamer's interpretation of objectivity.

then or a text as what it had originally meant per se. What I assume is the historical reconstruction of the socio-historical world and the audience the text is meant to address. This may imply the more specific context we find in Pauline texts[42] or a more loose designation, the various layers of context behind individual *Yìjīng* passages and *Yìzhuàn*.

As I have referred to earlier, according to Gadamer, a traditionary text transcends us and exists far earlier than we did. Thus, as a traditionary text pre-exists its readers and is not possessed by any single reader, it invites multiple readings. That readers can produce and reproduce multiple meanings[43] from a text does not imply that a text can be anything other than itself. Analogically, we can read a person's work at different times. Each reading may leave us with a new impression and understanding of the person. However, that does not mean that this person is not a self-embodied person independent of our readings. The transcendent nature of the traditionary text thus prevents it from having fallen prey to arbitrary reading. With the understanding of a text as a traditionary text, we can transcend the traditional differentiation of subjectivity and objectivity.

As we have shown, the understanding of traditionary texts happens within an effected history. To the interpreter the understanding does not happen in isolation from the context and the "life-world" in which he is situated,[44] and for which the hermeneutics of application is done.

According to Gadamer, "understanding always involves something like applying the text to be understood to the interpreter's present situation."[45] He regards hermeneutics as an activity that includes "not only understanding and interpretation, but also application as comprising one unified process."[46] Thus, he considers "application to be just as integral a part of the hermeneutical process as are understanding and interpretation."[47]

Taking a legal text as an example of his hermeneutics of application to illustrate his idea of understanding, he says, "The split runs through

---

42. For example, the reconstruction as seen in Meeks, *The First Urban Christians* which takes the sociological world where the text first appears to be its primary research concern.

43. Yeo, "Culture and Intersubjectivity," 86, 87.

44. See below for Gadamer's idea of "life-world" (*Lebenswelt*). For the use of this term in *Truth and Method*, see 239ff. "Life-world" will be used in accordance to the English version throughout this thesis when it refers to Gadamer's usage.

45. Gadamer, *Truth and Method*, 306–7.

46. Gadamer, *Truth and Method*, 307.

47. Gadamer, *Truth and Method*, 307.

legal interpretation also, in that discovering the meaning of a legal text and discovering how to apply it in a particular legal instance are not two separate actions, but one unitary process."[48] In other words, the process is not first-theory-then-practice. Gadamer further explains, bringing in the idea of understanding as event:

> We showed that understanding is not a method which the inquiring consciousness applies to an object it chooses and so turns it into objective knowledge; rather, being situated within an event of tradition, a process of handing down, is a prior condition of understanding. Understanding proves to be an event, and the task of hermeneutics, seen philosophically, consists in asking what kind of understanding, what kind of science it is, that is itself advanced by historical change.[49]

It is the "life-world" within which the event of understanding happens and the fusion of the traditionary texts and the historically effected consciousness takes place.

Thus, instead of setting up an antithesis between an objective text and a passive and detached interpreter, Gadamer argues instead for intersubjectivity, pre-understanding, and effected history at play. He deliberates that,

> The interpreter dealing with a traditionary text tries to apply it to himself. But this does not mean that the text is given for him as something universal, that he first understands it per se, and then afterward uses it for particular applications. Rather, the interpreter seeks no more than to understand this universal, the text—i.e., to understand what it says, what constitutes the text's meaning and significance. In order to understand that, he must not try to disregard himself and his particular hermeneutical situation. He must relate the text to this situation if he wants to understand at all.[50]

That is to say the text the interpreter finds relevant to his own context is also the text he finds understandable. In other words, the context and situation help him to bring the text to life. Having said so, being in a particular situation and context of his own, the interpreter does not enjoy the total freedom to carry out an interpretation in total isolation from the

---

48. Gadamer, *Truth and Method*, 309. Another example he uses for illustration is "preaching" (306).
49. Gadamer, *Truth and Method*, 308.
50. Gadamer, *Truth and Method*, 324.

text. What Gadamer emphasizes is not only the intersubjectivity between the text and the interpreter, but also the dialectic relationship between the subjectivity and objectivity of the text. The subjectivity is not defended at the expense of objectivity. Gadamer respects the objectivity of the text but emphasizes the situatedness and subjective aspect of the interpreter.

4. From Experience to Self-Understanding

I have argued in the above, for Gadamer, understanding happens in the "life-world" of the interpreter. For him, while the hermeneutical experience is concerned with the understanding of a text, it is also an understanding with its applicability in mind, which is thus a "hermeneutics of application."

My concern is about understanding as not only the understanding of a text, but also as self-understanding, i.e. not only to understand and interpret the text, but also to *apply* it to my "situation."[51] It lies in how to bring my experience into the hermeneutics as an essential element of the hermeneutics itself. This means that the understanding I am concerned with is one that helps reveal what is embodied in and signified by the experience I refer to. Does Gadamer's idea of understanding support understanding for the sake of self-understanding?

One should, however, be wary of what Gadamer means by understanding. As is shown above, as much as Gadamer emphasizes the effect of tradition on individuals, it is better here to assume that he will put self-understanding in relation to the tradition in which one is rooted. He believes, "understanding involves a moment of 'loss of self' that is relevant to theological hermeneutics and should be investigated in terms of the structure of the game."[52] As Joel Weinsheimer and Donald G. Marshall explain, "In play, we do not express ourselves, but rather the game itself 'presents itself.'"[53] In a game, one is required to play according to the rules. While the goal for the players into the game is to win the game, it requires that

---

51. Gadamer, *Truth and Method*, 307.

52. Gadamer, "On the Problem of Self Understanding," 51, and fuller discussion from 49–55. See the "Translator's Preface," in *Truth and Method*, ix which states, "In a preparatory analysis of 'play,' Gadamer shows that play is not a subjective attitude of the player, but rather the players are caught up in the shaped activity of the game itself. Where this activity takes on enduring form, it becomes 'structure,' *Gebilde*." For other discussion of his idea of game and play, see especially, *Truth and Method*, 102–10.

53. Weinsheimer and Marshall, "Translator's Preface," in *Truth and Method*, ix.

Constructing a Double Vision Hermeneutic

they throw themselves totally in the game to the extent that they forgot themselves other than as the ones who are playing.[54] Gadamer contends, "the actual subject of play is obviously not the subjectivity of an individual who, among other activities, also plays but is instead the play itself."[55] In other words, one "loses oneself" in the game.

His hermeneutics of game is not unrelated to his idea of one's experience of a work of art. Developing from W. Dilthey's idea of *Erlebnis* (experience), Gadamer defines *Erlebnis* as "something that flows past quickly in the stream of conscious life" but has formed "a unity" between the person and that which is experienced that signifies "a new mode of being one."[56] He thinks that *Erlebnis* should be understood from an aesthetic perspective. He argues that this term, which has now been used for aesthetics, was originally adopted and fashioned in biographical and autobiographical works. His intention is to argue that everyone's interpretation of a text is as subjective as one's experience of a work of art. According to him,

> the work of art is not an object that stands over against a subject for itself. Instead the work of art has its true being in the fact that it becomes an experience that changes the person who experiences it. The "subject" of the experience of art, that which remains and endures, is not the subjectivity of the person who experiences it but the work itself.[57]

Thus there is no antithesis between the work of art as an object and the interpreter as a subject. For the work of art itself is also a subject that can change the person, the interpreting subject, who experiences it. He emphasizes that "the 'subject' of the experience of art," having been experienced, is "that which remains and endures" in the person. The "work itself" rather than "the subjectivity of the person who experiences it" is the subject within the person when the experience happens. In other words, the work of art is no longer an object standing against the experiencing subject, and there is no longer an antithetical role between subject and object, but an intersubjective relationship.

How does this intersubjectivity relate to the self-understanding I am aiming for? By arguing for his idea of intersubjectivity, which emphasizes the situatedness of a hermeneutics as an "event" that happens

---

54. Gadamer, *Truth and Method*, 105ff.
55. Gadamer, *Truth and Method*, 104.
56. Gadamer, *Truth and Method*, 53, 58. See Ricoeur, "Appropriation," 192.
57. Gadamer, *Truth and Method*, 103.

A Double Vision Hermeneutic

in a "life-world," Gadamer removes the dialectic of objectivity and subjectivity.[58] Gadamer does this through bringing *Erlebnis* back to what it originally wants to invest into itself: "life-world". This means that, *Erlebnis* as happening as an event, does not isolate itself as an experience of understanding an artwork or a text. The happening itself is embedded in the "life-world". Thus the experience has become *Erfahrung*.[59] *Erfahrung*, according to him, is something one undergoes, through or after which "subjectivity is overcome and drawn into an 'event' (*Geschehen*) of meaning."[60] Hermeneutics, in his view, implies that "the experience (*Erfahrung*) of meaning that takes place in understanding always includes application."[61] Every application happens in the life-world of the interpreting subject, for every understanding is a hermeneutics of application that is meaningful for this subject in whom is found another subject, the text, the work of art, or that which one experiences. Thus whether it is in his hermeneutics of one's experience of a work of art, hermeneutics of game, or his account of event, it is not an antithesis of a subject with an object. Hermeneutics is thus not about exhausting the meaning of a text. It is an event that happens in the "life-world".

In other words, the subjective and objective aspects are not mutually exclusive but exist concomitantly. Thus, an interpreter of traditional texts does not simply indulge in subjectivity, but takes the texts into *unity* with his or her inner world and gazes into the texts-in-experience and experience-in-texts. As *Erfahrung*, the *unity* is also found in the interpreter's own "life-world", a fusion between the traditional texts and the interpreting subject in his "life-world".

That having been said, can I then assume that this fusion will lead to a self-understanding? As has been pointed out, Gadamer emphasizes a "loss of self"[62] in a hermeneutic experience. This "loss of self" for Gadamer is equivalent to one's experience in "the realm of language"[63] as one interprets the text. It is in the language and understanding itself that the *being* comes into being (*Dasein*). The primacy he has of language and understanding

---

58. Cf. Gadamer, *Truth and Method*, 240.
59. Gadamer, *Truth and Method*, 84–86.
60. Weinsheimer and Marshall, "Translator's Preface," in *Truth and Method*, xiii.
61. Gadamer, *Truth and Method*, 385.
62. Gadamer does not uses this expression, but the meaning, as I have elaborated on earlier (104), is clear a loss of self in a hermeneutic experience as in a game.
63. Gadamer, "On the Problem of Self Understanding," 50.

Constructing a Double Vision Hermeneutic

is evident.[64] As he explains, understanding "cannot be grasped as a simple activity of the consciousness that understands, but is itself a mode of the event of being."[65] What he emphasizes is the "dynamic process" found in "the relation between the understanding and what is understood."[66] In that sense, the *self* in the understanding seems not to be the focus of the understanding itself. In such a thought, neither the self-understanding, according to the idealist "self-evident certainty" of consciousness or the post-Cartesian emphasis on the "authentic self," is important anymore.[67]

Having said that, does Gadamer's rejection of self-understanding of the said two modes mean that there is no self-understanding on the interpreter's side, gained through reading the texts. I will use Gadamer's own idea of "a new mode of being one,"[68] by which he means the subject and the work of art as being one. It is not only that understanding happens as an event, but also that the new mode of being one is always a being one in relation to an historical time, never what simply happens in one's mind. Taking his explanation of understanding in terms of relation, the being-oneness is found in the relationship that exists between the subject and the artwork. It is new because there has never previously been such a relationship between them.

However, if there is now a preliminary relationship, what if there are multiple readings after the initial reading? Is the relationship found in the preliminary reading the same as those that will come after? If not, the multiple readings would not create more new modes of being one. If it is, whether it may be because the historical times and the situations where the other readings are being done vary, or the reading and interpreting subject is changed after the preliminary reading and each subsequent reading. As much as situations may change and "life-world" contexts may vary, the being of the reading subject may also change after the emergence of each "new mode of being one" which he experiences. Upholding the idea of "new mode of being one" should encourage the seeking of self-understanding rather than discouraging it.

As I have referred to in the introduction, "appropriation" means "'to make one's own' of what was initially 'alien,'" (originally from "the German

---

64. Gadamer, "On the Problem of Self Understanding," 50.
65. Gadamer, "On the Problem of Self Understanding," 50.
66. Gadamer, "On the Problem of Self Understanding," 50.
67. Gadamer, "On the Problem of Self Understanding," 50.
68. Gadamer, *Truth and Method*, 53, 58. See Ricoeur, "Appropriation," 192.

term '*Aneignung*").[69] Personal knowledge, according to Polanyi, is foremost "the personal participation of the knower in all acts of understanding," through which knowledge is acquired.[70] Combining Ricoeur, Polanyi and Gadamer's insights, we can say this: an understanding of a thing involves the participation of the very subject who experiences and knows, without which no understanding can be claimed; and in so doing the understanding involves an appropriation of the meaning which was originally alien to the one reading the text. In other words, what is truly understood is truly experienced and truly known. What is already understood, experienced and known shall no longer be merely something 'out there', but will also become something which stays within the interpreting subject. Therefore, because every mode of being one is not static but ongoing, there is an ongoing process of understanding, experiencing, and knowing that creates sequential modes of being, one after another,[71] as new beings in historical time and "life-world", not isolated from the influence of traditionary texts. These new modes of being, not new modes of being one, must embody the self-understanding of the being.

To return to where I began, my initial, personal, intersubjective experience of *shì*, as retold in the introduction, is first a personal experience. By personal experience, I mean something I have experienced, appropriated, owned, and is now inside of me as something I can gaze upon and draw out as material that I can further contemplate, reflect on, analyze, and interpret. The hermeneutical methodology undertaken in this thesis, as developed and revised from Gadamer, allows me to include all the texts. I, therefore, also assume that in the process of research I, as a subject, never stop experiencing the hermeneutical circle between myself and the various material I am working with. New experiences, however, are acquired from the research materials as well as from life experience and come into my hermeneutical horizon. If I call my initial state of being, *'me': the subject, who had the intersubjective experience of shì* as Text 0 (zero), the modes of being subsequently growing out of new experiences of reading, understanding and interpretation will then be Text 1, Text 2, Text 3, Text 4 etc.

---

69. Ricoeur, "Appropriation," 185.
70. Polanyi, *Personal Knowledge*, vii.
71. See also Ricoeur, "Appropriation," 192.

5. Double Awareness

In *Personal Knowledge*, Polanyi constructs the idea of "focal awareness" and "subsidiary awareness,"[72] which is best captured by his 'hammer and nail' illustration:

> When we use a hammer do drive in a nail, we attend to both nail and hammer, *but in a different way*. We *watch* the effect of our strokes on the nail and try to wield the hammer so as to hit the nail most effectively. When we bring down the hammer we do not feel that its handle has struck our palm but that its head has struck the nail. Yet in a sense we are certainly alert to the feelings in our palm and the fingers that hold the hammer. They guide us in handling it effectively, and the degree of attention that we give to the nail is given to the same extent but in a different way to these feelings. The difference may be stated by saying that the latter are not, like the nail, objects of our attention, but instruments of it. They are not watched in themselves; we watch something else while keeping intensely aware of them. I have a *subsidiary awareness* of the feeling in the palm of my hand which is merged into my *focal awareness* of my driving in the nail.[73] (Italics his)

In other words, in the process of hammering in the nail, the two awarenesses are simultaneously and constantly present. I may have been focusing on driving in the nail in one my hands, but there has not been a moment I am not aware of the act of hitting which comes from my other hand. The constant and the simultaneous, as found in this hammer and nail illustration, also appear in my double vision of Texts A1 and A2 or Texts B1 and B2 or Texts A and B or other hermeneutical moments, which address two things at the same time.

Polanyi also elaborates on this interplay in terms of the relationship between parts and wholes. He says, "[w]hen focusing on a whole, we are subsidiarily aware of its parts, while there is no difference in the intensity of the two kinds of awareness."[74] This means that the subsidiary is no less important than the focal. Moreover, the subsidiary can be equally strong in terms of determining the meaning forming in the mind. In other words,

---

72. See Polanyi, *Personal Knowledge*, 55–65 for his discussion.
73. Polanyi, *Personal Knowledge*, 55.
74. Polanyi, *Personal Knowledge*, 57.

A Double Vision Hermeneutic

"when something is seen as subsidiary to a whole," it also "participates in sustaining the whole."[75] The whole cannot exist without the parts.

The reference to Polanyi's "parts and wholes" is used to describe the integrative process of parts and wholes, not within the texts themselves, but as they are integrated in me, the subject, and in its written form, the formation of this thesis. It is not the texts that are interpreted, but the new text vis-à-vis the new mode of being which will be "realized."[76]

As stated earlier, I see the socio-historical and literary contexts of the texts as an indispensable factor in my interpretation. This exegetical concern is necessarily a hermeneutical one, as well as a response to the dissatisfaction Lai Pan-chiu has voiced out, which has been pointed out earlier.[77] This implies that when I interpret a particular passage whether in *Yìjīng* or Pauline texts, I take the meaning(s) within the literary context and possible background into account. Every passage exegeted, which is considered a *part*, will be brought into my concern only if it helps to reveal the problem of *shì*, which is the *whole*. As attention is paid to an individual *part*, that it is occupying my focal awareness while the *whole* is occupying my subsidiary awareness; this is reversed, for example when I am *focusing* on the cohesiveness of the *whole* of the *Yìjīng* interpretation of *shì*, when my *subsidiary* awareness will be on the individual passages on which I have done an exegesis.

Let us say that the two sides of the pole are X and Y. X takes up my focal awareness when Y takes up my subsidiary awareness; but when Y takes up my focal awareness, X takes up my subsidiary awareness. The following are some examples of double awareness interplay between X and Y.

---

75. Polanyi, *Personal Knowledge*, 57.

76. Gadamer, *Truth and Method*, 293. Referring to Heidegger's view, he says, "The circle of whole and part is not dissolved in perfect understanding but, on the contrary, is most fully realized."

77. Pan-Chiu Lai, "Sino-Theology."

Constructing a Double Vision Hermeneutic

X	Y
A particular Pauline passage	Its historical and social background
The cohesive understanding of the historical and social background as revealed in a particular scriptural passage	The fiduciary search aiming at solving the problem of *shi*
My personal experiences of *shi*	*Shi* as texts in their respective literary contexts and pre-Qín background
Shi as a cultural-linguistic experience	*Shi* interpreted through the *Yìjīng* hexagramic paradigm
The *Yìjīng* hexagramic paradigm	A particular Pauline text

In short, in these examples, the focal awareness and subsidiary awareness work alternately depending on which is the focus at any particular moment. The interplay between the focal and the subsidiary is not based on the objectivist agenda but presupposes the "intuition of rationality,"[78] or the "fiduciary principle" Polanyi argues.[79]

Furthermore, this double awareness can also be used to explain the interplay between my awareness of myself being as an "historically effected consciousness" and the "traditional texts"; or between the socio-historical and literary context(s) of the text(s) and of the texts appropriated in me. It also implies the interchange of subsidiary and focal awareness of the Chinese and Christian eye. The eyesight, or vision, is not fixed but is adjusting from time to time, with new experiences and corrective lens added through numerous readings of Chinese Classics and Christian Scripture.

6. A Double Vision Hermeneutic of Multilayered Intersubjectivity

The double vision hermeneutics I propose includes all the above factors. As defined earlier, by double vision, I mean 1) being aware of two visions or two texts at the same time or seeing them both in one vision at the same time, 2) seeing one vision or text in the foreground but being

---

78. Polanyi, *Personal Knowledge*, 55.
79. Polanyi, *Personal Knowledge*, 301.

A Double Vision Hermeneutic

aware of another text or vision in the background, or 3) two visions or two texts appear sequentially and alternately. I now incorporate Polanyi's double awareness to further explain the mechanism of this double vision hermeneutics.

I have mentioned that there are several layers of intersubjective relationship between Texts A1, A2, B1 and B2. With Polanyi's double awareness incorporated into the double vision hermeneutics, the latter can be elaborated as: 1) being aware of or seeing Texts A1 and A2 at the same time, 2) seeing Text A1 at the foreground while aware of Text A2 in the background, or 3) seeing Texts A1 and A2 appearing sequentially and alternately. Such a double vision and awareness is found in the relationship between Texts B1 and B2, and between Texts A (1 + 2) and B (1 + 2).

Multiple Texts		
	Text 0	My Pastoral Experience of *Shì* (the narrative)
Chinese Tradition	Text A1	*Shì* as a cultural linguistic text or a tradionary text
	Text A2	*Yìzhuàn* (*Yìjīng* and the *Ten Wings*)
Pauline Christian Tradition	Text B1	Pauline notion of Principalities and Powers as a Theological Focus
	Text B2	Pauline Texts: Galatians and 1 Corinthians

I will follow the sequence of the chart above to restate the relationship between these texts.

Firstly, in this hermeneutics, I judge that my experience count. My personal experience, as described in the introduction formed the launching point for the hermeneutical activities which follow. It is therefore treated as Text 0. As an experience, it is not an experience of something abstract which exists in a vacuum, but an experience of a cultural-linguistic text within a condition which I call *shì*.

To be able to call it an experience of *shì*, I must have an idea of what *shì* is. This I call my appropriation of what is implied by this Chinese word which is itself embedded in a larger cultural-linguistic tradition. Originating from the pre-Qín period or earlier, and has been transmitted through history. It has then become what Gadamer calls a traditionary text which lives through history to the present day. This is Text A1. We now have are Text 0 and Text A1. Between them is an intersubjective relationship:

Constructing a Double Vision Hermeneutic

the subject who owns the experience of *shì* (as narrated in Text 0) as appropriated from Text A1. The latter is the text through which the subject interprets the world he is experiencing.

I started reading *Yìzhuàn* (Text A2) as an attempt to understand my situation as a young pastor. I was within a tradition and came to be "confronted" by it as I tried to understand myself. Being Chinese, I could not resist interpreting my context by applying the revealing insights I gained through reading *Yìzhuàn* to my situation. I had already acquired a degree of familiarity with the text from my wider cultural context. There was a hermeneutic interplay between "the traditionary text's strangeness and familiarity" or between "being a historically intended, distanced object and belonging to a tradition."[80]

The Pauline notion of sin emerged in my experience (Text 0) as an appropriated consciousness of my sinful nature. In this appropriation, the intersubjectivity of Pauline texts and my experience of power and *shì* is evident. Such an awareness has led me to engage myself with further interpretation of Pauline texts, for within them one finds warnings, as well as examples, of how power is at play within Christian communities.

A double awareness, hence a double vision needs to be present to pay simultaneous attention to these two intersubjective relationships: one between *shì* and *Yìzhuàn*, and the other between the Pauline notion of *principalities and powers* and *Pauline texts: Galatians and Corinthians*. Thus when I *see* or pay attention to *shì*, *Yìzhuàn* is always there in the background, and vice versa; when I interpret the letter of Paul to the Galatians or Corinthians, I am always thinking of the presence of principalities and powers. That the two texts (Text A1 with A2, and Text B1 with B2) can be mutually interpreted is due to one always being present in the other. Texts A1 and A2 can operate in a similar way because they are appropriated within me where they meet and are present within each other, as are Texts B1 and B2. This is intersubjectivity.

On the one hand, there is a transcendent aspect to *Yìzhuàn* and the Pauline texts as traditionary texts. In other words, this is the objective aspect of the hermeneutical circle. In approaching them, I must keep a certain distance from them, to respect their respective historical and situational contexts, i.e. the objective aspect, to which they belong and in which they were first composed.

On the other, the intersubjective experience of *shì* with the subject is brought into these texts through my reading and interpretation; having

---

80. Gadamer, *Truth and Method*, 295.

thus brought this particular 'cultural-linguistically-effected' consciousness of *shì* when I experience and see the *shì* manifest itself in a situation, I have also penetrated the texts with something that was originally alien to them. The objective or transcendent and subjective aspects have to be kept in balance, but allow the intersubjective experience to occur.

Theoretically, we have to maintain the transcendent texts as transcendent with their socio-historical backgrounds not at our disposal. However, once become part of the subject through reading as appropriation, these texts may remain transcendent but are no longer strangers. Between the texts and *the subject,* a dynamic intersubjective relationship forms.

As Gadamer has remarked, "Every experience has implicit horizons of before and after, and finally fuses with the continuum of the experiences present in the before and after to form a unified flow of experience."[81] Hence, all Texts A1 + A2 and Texts B1+ B2 are reproduced in me not once but as a continuing influence, a process through which an ever-ongoing new self is coming into being.

In the following, while acknowledging the continuum of my experiences of these texts before and during the process of reading, understanding, and appropriating them, my immediate task is to reveal 1) the individual texts, 2) the various layers of intersubjective relationship in relation to *shì* and power both in *Yìjīng* and from the Pauline perspective. In the next chapter, I will first deal with Text A1, *shì* in its pre-Qín literary context and explain its treatment as a cultural-linguistic tradition vis-à-vis traditionary texts.

---

81. Gadamer, *Truth and Method,* 237.

3

Text A1: *Shì* as a Cultural-linguistic and Traditionary Text

The word *shì* appears frequently in current Chinese terms, for example: *xíngshì*, the propensity (tendency) or dynamic of the situation; *shìlì*, to judge someone's status based on one's power (*shì*); *caíshì*, the power of the wealthy; *dìshì*, the terrain or geographical area judged to be advantageous or disadvantageous; or as *shì zaì bì xíng*, to say that something to be done is imperative (as being forced). Without exception, the key word that determines the meanings reflected in these various combinations is *shì* which first became widely used in pre-Qín China.

It has been noted that *shì* (tendency) was a popular idea in all pre-Qín schools,[1] which appeared around the sixth to the third centuries BC. It has continuously appeared in later writings down the centuries. For example, in a text from the Jìn Dynasty (266–420 AD), we already see *shì rú pòzhú*, which first appeared in the "Xíshū" chapter of *Dù Yù zhùan* which describes that "(a military action) as like the splitting of a bamboo culm; once the knife is carried down several nodes of the culm, the bamboo will be split into half smoothly," i.e., "once the strength of the army has successfully manifested itself."[2]

---

1. In late *Chūnqiū*, in Sun Wu's *The Art of War*, one finds a description of *shì* as a crossbow stretched to its maximum, *shì rú zhāng nú*, which appeared in "*Shì Biān*," in *The Art of War* by Sun Wu in late *Chūnqiū*. In another chapter in the same book it also says, *bīng wú cháng shì, shuǐ wú cháng xíng*, that the array of troops follows no constant disposition, just like water flows in no fixed form, see Sun Wu, "*Xūshí*," in *The Art of War*.

2. Translated by me. In Chinese it says, "*Jīn bīng wēi yǐ zhèn, shì rú pò zhú, pì rú pò zhú, shù jié yǐ hoù, jiē yǐn rèn eŕ jěi.*" (See "Xí shū," in *Dù Yù zhùan*.)

A Double Vision Hermeneutic

Shì, implying timeliness and tendency, is used in a coined phrase, *shíshì*. This meaning is best elaborated on in the works of Wáng Fūzhī in the Late Ming dynasty. In his interpretation of *Yìzhuàn*, he creatively combines his idea of *shì* with *Yìzhuàn* philosophy. In his writing, we can see how time and tendency, or propensity, are related. For example, he says, "If the moments differ, the *tendencies* differ, the logics which govern the processes also differ."[3] And "the *tendency* depends on the opportunity of the *moment* just as the internal logic depends on the *tendency*."[4] Also "(o)ne must appraise the *moment* in such a way as to detect its *tendency* and, consequently, seek to conform with its coherence."[5]

I do not intend to trace the etymology of *shì*. In this chapter the survey of *shì* will be limited to some seminal texts from pre-Qín China, the purpose of which is to construct the semantic scope for *shì* as a text. I have, in the introduction, explained the idea of text, intertext, intertextuality, and text within texts. In this chapter, I will treat *shì* as a cultural-linguistic text, and see it through Gadamer's lens as a traditionary text, which means that it has its *effect* in contemporary oral and written texts, with its meanings born far earlier, and have been passed down through generations.[6] I also see it as a text appropriated by various thinkers who used it in distinctive ways. While each may contribute to one or more of the facets of meaning, the fluidity between different shades of meaning is maintained. Where it appears in the texts of these thinkers, it appears as a text within each individual text. The maintenance of fluidity between texts will allow us to preserve as many aspects as possible of the ways power had been defined in these early texts.

These inclusive meanings, as will be understood later in this chapter, will be Text A1. In the introduction I designate my initial intersubjective experience of *shì* as Text 0. Text A1 will serve as a motif that is to be read into Text 0, as well as into Text A2, *Yìzhuàn*. The integrated Texts A1 and A2 will be the Text A that will form a Chinese Christian double vision hermeneutics with Text B (the Pauline Texts B1 + B2).

---

3. Wáng, *Sònglùn*, ch. 15, 260, cited from Jullien, *Propensity*, 209. In Chinese, it says, "*Shì yì ér shì yì, shì yì ér lǐ yì.*"

4. Wáng, from one section of *Dútōngjiànlùn*, ch. 12, "Mǐndì," 386, cited from Jullien, *The Propensity of Things*, 209. In Chinese it says, "*Shì yīn hū shí, lǐ yīn hū shì.*" This section argues about the unavoidable fall of King Mǐn.

5. Wáng, *Sònglùn*, ch. 4, 106, cited from Jullien, *Propensity*, 209. In Chinese it says, "*Zhī shí yǐ shěn shì* (*shì* as an event or a thing), *yīn shì* (propensity or circumstance) *ér qiú hé yú lǐ.*" Here and the above, italic mine.

6. With "effect," I am inferring from Gadamer's "historically effected consciousness."

Text A1

1. To Survey Shì in Early Literary Contexts

As stated in the introductory chapter, *Yìzhuàn* reflects an integration of philosophical ideas from the pre-Qín period, including those of Confucianism, Daoism, the Yīn-yángjiā, Fǎjiā (Legalist or standardizer), and probably Bīngjiā (military strategist) schools with a predominantly Confucian philosophy. The division of different schools has been a convention in the study of pre-Qín philosophy. This has been recently rejected, for example by Michael Puett, who argues that it is unhelpful and often misleading to categorize pre-Qín texts according to schools.[7] However, to help us appreciate the dialectic tension between the Confucian and other schools especially Fǎjiā, the legalist or standardizer, it is better to retain the conventional classification. As François Jullien points out, there had been opposition between the Confucians or the "moralists" represented by Mèngzǐ and those he called the "realists" and "legalists."[8] For Confucians, what was important was "personal merit," while for the realists, it was "the occupation" of the "position of authority."[9] The study of *shì* here takes this division for granted so that the distinctive use of the word *shì* in the texts as shown in the following can be better appreciated.

Viewing the popularity of *shì* among these different schools, one wonders what was the socio-political background—the Warring States— they shared. The Warring States era reflected a time of social turmoil and political instability in early China. It was also one of the most dynamic and vibrant periods for philosophical debate, from the perspective of politics or virtue. It continued and reflected what had already been chaotic in the Chūnqiū period. According to Xúnzǐ's record, in the early Chūnqiū period, there were known to be seventy-one states, each with a designated feudal-lord.[10] By the time of Qín's conquest the other states, only six states remained, namely, Yān, Qí, Chǔ, Hán, Wèi and Zhào. To use Victor H. Mair's words, the Chūnqiū and the Warring States periods were marked by "an intensification of interstate rivalry and a growing tendency to use

---

7. Puett, *To Become a God*, 25 n. 44. He contends that many of the so-called "schools" only "first appeared in our received texts in the essay of 'Yaozhi,' by Sima Tan (d. 110 BC)." Thus, he argues that "our concern should be to explicate the claims of each text within the debates of the time. Discussion of these claims in terms of a 'school' is seldom helpful." "Yaozhi" should be "Lùn liùjiā yàozhǐ"; see also Hansen, *A Daoist Theory of Chinese Thought*, 345–46.

8. Jullien, *Efficacy*, ix, 30–31.

9. Jullien, *Efficacy*, 31.

10. See Xúnzǐ, "Rú Xiào: 1."

military force to achieve domination, rather than relying on diplomacy and relatively small-scale armed conflicts to maintain the alliances and balances that had characterized the Spring and Autumn period."[11] In other words, during that period, it was normal that a king would measure his own power by the display of power, i.e. *shì* among neighboring states.

Under such political circumstances, the relationship between "a ruler and the feudal lords" was inevitably "ambivalent."[12] One could imagine that the king of Zhōu competed with feudal lords and the feudal lords with one another for power and domination in terms of how big a territory they owned and how strong a military power they were able to deploy. The concern of the weaker states, however, was how to avoid confronting the greater powers.

In that context, the political philosophers engaged themselves in debate about the merits of 'the kingly way' (*wáng dào*) and the abusiveness of 'the autocratic way' (*bà dào*), the use of moral power and the power of authoritative position and influence (*quán shì*).[13] The autocratic and authoritative ways are always associated with *shì*. As Jullien points out, a prince who manipulates his subjects is like the spirits that haunt the human world. He "never has to 'make an effort,' since his subjects," as if being haunted, "feel themselves to be determined, not by some external causality, but simply by their own spontaneity."[14] Thus, one sees similar domination, which is invisible but is infused in one's body and soul.[15] To make use of a *shì*, as "[t]he art of a ruler," is to "[get] everyone else to contribute toward the maintenance of his own position."[16] Such was the background where *shì* appeared.

This brief depiction of the socio-political environment of that period can at least allow us to have a basic awareness of the nuances of the word *shì* as used in the works reviewed below. I will limit myself to reviewing the work of Sūn Wǔ (sixth century BC), Hán Fēi or Hán Fēizǐ (280–233 BC),[17] and Xúnzǐ (c.310/2–230 BC). Sūn Wǔ represents the militarist, Hán Fēi the Legalist, and Xúnzǐ the major post-Mencius Confucianist schools

 11. Mair, 23.

 12. Mair, 23–24.

 13. For an early discussion of this, see Xúnzǐ, "Wáng Bà", check online the Chinese Text Project at http://ctext.org/xunzi/wang-ba. John Knoblock translates bà as "lord-protector." For his, see Knoblock, *Xunzi: Book 7–12*, 140.

 14. Jullien, *Propensity*, 51.

 15. For this aspect of power, see my discussion of Pierre Bourdieu below.

 16. He refers to a passage in *Huáinánzǐ*, chapter 9. See Jullien, *Propensity*, 49.

 17. For the dating of *Sūn Wǔ*, see the following.

Text A1

during the Warring States period.[18] I will try to reveal how this word was used by them. At the same time, the tug-of-war between the Legalist or Standardizers' and Confucian political ideologies will be hinted at.[19]

The dialectic relationship between a Chinese pastor's preoccupation with *shì* and Confucian way of life based on moral excellence (*dé*) that permeates the Chinese psyche in general as a cultural moral ethos will be at the background of the discussion of *shì* vis-à-vis the Confucian-Legalist dialectic ideological relationship.

1.1: Sūn Wǔ

The authorship of *Sūnzǐ Bīngfǎ*, *The Art of War* is conventionally attributed to Sūn Wú. The dating for Sūn Wǔ himself, and the evidence of his existence are hard to ascertain, as is argued by Mair. Nevertheless, "[t]he conventional view is that the author was a man named Sun Wu who was a great military theorist and who allegedly lived around the end of the Spring and Autumn period, making him a contemporary of Confucius."[20] According to John Minford, he was possibly alive roughly a hundred years before Sūn Bìn (380-316 BC), a contemporary of Mèngzǐ (371-289).[21] As for the dating of the book, Mair argues "the pattern of war, battle tactics, the conduct of armies, strategic planning, and weaponry" are irrelevant to the Spring and Autumn period but perfectly compatible with the Warring States period.[22] What matters here is that the book and its author were contemporary with *Yìzhuàn*, around the time of the Warring States. For the purpose of this thesis, these texts will be attributed to the pre-Qín period to match with the presupposition that philosophers during that

---

18. Other major theorists who had discussed *shì* include Shèn Daò (350-275? BC), Guǎn Zhòng (685-645 BC), Guǐgǔzǐ (475-221 BC), Lǚ Bùweǐ (290?-235 BC), to Hàn dynasty in Huáinánzǐ (206 BC- AD 9) and Wáng Chōng (AD 27-97?). Ames' work (*The Art of Rulership*) does not cover Guǐgǔzǐ and Wáng Chōng. See also Jullien, *Efficacy*.

19. That the Legalism and Confucianism represent rival voices in many ideas in pre-Qín is a basic assumption among scholars, see Cheng's discussion in "Legalism versus Confucianism."

20. Mair, 12.

21. See Minford, xx.

22. He thus rules out any date that is before the Warring States. He believes the whole corpus "was not all written by the same person." Thus no single date can be attributed to it. See Mair, 27-28.

time had a variety of philosophical and political ideas at their disposal to develop individual standpoints and arguments.

Sūn Wǔ's *Sūnzǐ bīngfǎ* (*The Art of War*), chapter 1, "Shǐjì," refers to *shì* as follows: "when an advantageous assessment has been heeded, one must create for it a favorable configuration (*shì*) to assist the war effort externally. A favorable configuration (*shì*) is one that signifies the creation of power (*quán*) in accordance with advantage."[23] As was noted earlier, it is hard to translate *shì* because of its multivalent meanings. The above is the first evidence of *shì* rendered as "configuration." The same word in the same section is understood by Minford as "dynamic potential energy of the situation,"[24] also abbreviated to "dynamic." Lionel Giles translates it as "circumstances."[25] Given the above translations, we might summarize *shì* as 'power which is dynamic and implies potential'. It is related not so much as a self-contained object but as a factor working within a situation, and is better understood not as an idea that stands independently, but in relation to other factors that form its "configuration." Thus, in considering *shì*, there is a tendency to take account of what is advantageous.

In other words, the tendency (*shì*) normally tilts towards or favors what one finds advantageous. Here one finds the "subjective" factor at work. By believing that something is advantageous, one has already made a judgement. A judgement that it is a *shì* includes a judgement of its tendency towards what it judges to be advantageous. The knowledge of such a *shì* is based on a pre-knowledge of what makes a *shì*. Here we have an external circumstance or situation which is not entirely external; rather it is the subjective judgement of it that we have. This two-in-one external/subjective dimension, can be called the intersubjective aspect, as previously illustrated in the double vision hermeneutic methodology.

---

23. Mair, 78. In Chinese, it says, "*Jì lì yǐ tīng, naǐ yǐ wéi shì, yǐ zǒu qí wài; shì zěh, yīn lì ér zhì quán yě*." For other references, see Giles, *The Art of War*, 56. Giles' translation is among the earliest, but is worth referring to. Minford renders it as "settle on the best plan / Exploit the dynamic within / Develop it without. Follow the advantage / And master opportunity: This is the dynamic" (6, 111–12). Minford's consideration of the economy of words in accordance with the Chinese text leaves too much space to guess what it means. See also Samuel Girffith, 66. For *quán*, Mair renders it as "power," Minford as "opportunity," Giles uses "plans," and Griffith as "balance." In this regard, Minford, Giles, and Griffith all try to reflect *quán* as in *quányí*, to get the best decision by calculating the pros and cons. By reading *quán* as "power, Mair however associates *shì* with power, probably of a political kind. Both of these readings capture the nuances in one sense or another.

24. Minford, 111.

25. See note 181.

The next noteworthy feature is that a judgement of *shì* is based on calculation. The emphasis is on the measuring of circumstances, i.e., advantageous, favorable, or beneficial. Its focus is not about one's *dé* (virtue or moral power) or character, but one's ability to calculate and fathom the internal dynamic of the situation. As Jullien describes, it is a "[C]alculation of the relation between the forces in play," thus an expert should know how to take account of "a series of factors" in a situation to come up with the best calculation.[26]

Thirdly, related to a calculation is the timing, which is also found in Sūnzǐ's use of *shì*. Chapter 5, "Bīngshì," states,

> The raging torrent can by its gushes float the boulders along its course; this is due to its *shì*; by one shot a swooping falcon breaks the back of its prey; this is due to its precision. Therefore, a good warrior makes good use of a risky *shì* (circumstance) and a blinking moment (*jié*); such a *shì* is likened to the bending crossbow, such a timing (*jié*) the releasing of the trigger (*shì rú zhāng nǔ, jié rú jī fā*).[27]

Besides speed, it is the precise use of force in combination with good timing that should be taken into account when measuring a *shì*. To be able to estimate the "raging torrent" is about knowing the movement of the force and allowing oneself to follow it.[28] Thus, the ability to grasp the exact moment should be acquired by a good general or a leader. Moreover, being a leader, one "does not only make his subordinates be accountable for (the result of a battle)," but rather "makes use of the dynamic propensity of the circumstances ("*gù shàn zhàn zhě, qiú zhī yú shì, bù zhé yú rén.*"[29]

26. Jullien, *Efficacy*, 24.

27. Cf. the translation of Lionel Giles, 56. Mair, 92–93; Minford, 169–70, and Griffith, 92. Mair's and Minford's translations are both closer to Griffith. A few words on translation are needed. This section examines the translators' adoption of freedom of expression in the Chinese language, afforded by its use of metaphor and metonymy. For example, the literal translation of *shì rú zhāng nǔ* should be: power is like a bending crossbow. The simile "bending crossbow" is the power, the *shì*. How can it be rendered this way? What is assumed is "the tension found within the bending crossbow." The metonymic twist is assisted by the word "*rú*". Therefore, a more complete translation should be: "power is something like the tension one may find in the bending crossbow." But to translate a poetic prose in this fashion would be to sacrifice all the beauty and rhythm of the original work.

28. For the implication of "to allow," see Jullien, *Efficacy*, vii. The way of "allow" things to grow, a *shì* to grow, or a result to show, without interrupting or forcing the process, according to Jullien, reflects a Daoist philosophy, see *Efficacy*, 89–91.

29. Cf. Giles, 57. The *shì* in parenthesis is mine. Mair renders *rén* (men) in these

A Double Vision Hermeneutic

To be able to make use of the efficacy of *shì* depends on the judgement of timing, force and movement, based on one's intuitive calculation, a judgement which appears to emerge naturally from one's inner being.

In *The Art of War* chapter 6: "Xūshí (The Void and the Concrete)" it also says, "as the water has no constant form, so the array of troops has no constant disposition" (*bīng wú cháng shì, shuǐ wú cháng xíng*).[30] Because an army is like water, therefore a general should learn to deploy his troops according to the strength and weakness of the enemy as much as the water conforms to the highs and lows of the land.[31]

One wonders what is comparable between water and an army. Water belongs to nature, while an army is made of people, thus they belong to different categories. However, here again one has to go deeper to find the subtle, almost obscure link the language itself never finds necessary to clarify. As much as clarity seems to be lacking, it expects the reader to look for compatibility beneath the surface, i.e. not from their shape but their disposition. The key to their compatibility is thus the "*wú cháng*," the non-regular, non-constant factor as the essence of these two things. Hence one sees *shì* being used as "disposition" to resemble the potential of the water to produce different forms, adjusting according to external factors. In other words, it is the continuous "changes" one should pay attention to. Thus, besides calculating and fathoming the internal dynamic of the situation and grasping the proper timing, *shì* involves one's act in accordance with the disposition and form of external factors, like water follows the form of the land.

If Mair's dating of Sūn Zǐ to the Warring States period is correct, it is revealing to see in *Yìzhuàn*, as I will show in chapter 4, similar images carrying a Confucian tone, in contrast to those in *Sūnzǐ Bīngfǎ*. This again reflects an ideological rivalry: as much as Sūn Zǐ's idea of *shì* is compatible with *Yìzhuàn* in terms of judging proper time and propensity, it is *shì* as interpreted through the lens of the *Yìzhuàn* hexagramic system, that will be adopted to contrast with the *Yìzhuàn* moral vision. We will provide further evidence in what follows from Hán Fēi, before examining an integrated effort as demonstrated by Xúnzǐ.

---

instances as "subordinates", and renders "*qiú zhī yú shì*" as "looking the effect of combined energy," see Mair, 93. See also Jullien's interpretation in *Propensity*, 29–30.

30. My translation.

31. See Sun Wu, "Xūshí (The Void and the Concrete)" in *The Art of War*.

Text A1

1.2: Hán Fēi

Hán Fēi probably synthesized Shang Yāng's (d. 338 BC) idea of *fǎ* (law or standard), Shēn Búhaì's (d. 337) idea of *shù* (statecraft, techniques, methods and the like) and Shèn Daò's (ca. 395–315 BC) idea of *shì*.[32] Interestingly, although known as a legalist, he was a student of Xúnzǐ, a Confucian.[33] Thus, it is very interesting to observe how his idea differs from the Confucians in terms of their focus on the ideal state as built on a leader's moral character, i.e. his humaneness, and his on *shì*.

In "Nánshì," *Hán Fēi Zi*, Hán Fēi debated the determining power of *shì*. He argued against contemporary or earlier Confucians, who thought a ruler could gain the trust of his people by virtue of his humane-righteousness, *rényì*, and instead postulated that they secured their rule through succumbing to *shì*. For example, he argued, that though already known as a sage in his time, cultivating and manifesting the Daò, and sojourning from one state to another teaching the way of *rényì*, humaneness and righteousness, Zòngní (Confucius) failed to convince even one state ruler to adopt his way of *rényì*. The reason, according to Hán Fēi, was that those who valued benevolent love were rare, and those who were able to practice righteousness were hard to find.[34]

He further alluded to the case of former sage kings (Yaó and Shùn) and villain kings (Jié of Xià dynasty and Zhoù of Shāng dynasty) to advance his argument. Contrary to the contemporary assertion that the state could be ruled in an orderly fashion if it had a sage-ruler, he argued the determinant was not the sagacity of the person who ruled the state, but his use of *shì*. Similarly, if a villain successfully usurped a state and created disorder, it was not because of who he was, but his ability in using *shì*. Hán Fēi thus contended that *shì* can be used by either a virtuous or villainous person, the difference being simply that: villainous people are many, while virtuous people few.[35]

A second point to be made is that although Hán Fēi seems to have been influenced by Shèn Dào, he criticized him for interpreting *shì* as an internal natural law who argued that the water goes down stream due to its *shì* of going down, rather than being due to a situation caused by human

---

32. See Chan, *Source Book*, 252.

33. For one recent argument against the idea that Xúnzǐ was probably not a Confucian but rather a philosopher whose ideas are closer to the Legalist, see Cheng, "Legalism versus Confucianism."

34. Hán Fēi, "Wǔ dú," in *Hánfēizǐ*, chapter 5.

35. Hán Fēi, "Nanshì," in Chén, *Hánfēizǐ jiàoshì*, 73–87.

effort.³⁶ Contrary to Shèn Daò, Hán Fēi argues that in as much as how things change, human factors in power dynamism are as determinative in human affairs as in human history. Thus Hán Fēi goes beyond the mechanistic idea of power by emphasizing the importance of human factors in power relation as well as historical propensity. Nevertheless, there is no evidence as to whether Hán Feī has elaborated on the psychological factors at work in human affairs or networks, or on a moral judgement of power. What is lacking, however, can be found in Xúnzǐ's work.

1.3 Xúnzǐ

Living after the Daoist-legalist Shāng Yāng and Shèn Dào and Confucianist Mèngzǐ, and having the advantage of exposure to The Scholars' Palace at Jīxià, the centre of academic studies and philosophical debates for different schools of his time,³⁷ Xúnzǐ was aware of Confucianism's idealization of people's ability to achieve personal good and the state's welfare. He was also aware of the argument between Confucians and Legalists.³⁸ He did not totally reject the interpretation of *shì* according to the Legalists and had appropriated some of it into his own thinking. He was concerned that the use of manipulative and autocratic power had become common. It had jeopardized the ideal of humane-righteousness as the core value a ruler should possess. As in "Wáng Bà: 1–2," Xúnzǐ argued that even if one may have secured power thanks to the efficacy of *shì*, one needed to consider three conditions of becoming a ruler. The first was a ruler whose rule was based on his "righteousness," who will be called "a king;" the second by "his credit" to be called "a lord-protector (*bà*)"; and the third by "his manipulation of power (*quánmoŭ*)." The one who uses *quán moŭ* "is doomed to fall."³⁹

Being aware of the legalist's emphasis, he placed more emphasis than his Confucian predecessors on how to order the state with *lǐ* (propriety or rite) and law (*fǎ*), not in the manner of a Legalist per se, but as a realist Confucian.⁴⁰ In *Xúnzǐ*, chapter 16: "Jiāngguó piān" (On Strengthening

36. For the relationship between Shèndào and Hán Fēi, see Wáng, "Shèn Dào sīxiǎng zhī fēnxī," 251.

37. See Yan-qin Peng et al., "Bridging Confucianism and Legalism," 51.

38. In this respect, he was close to his own student Hán Fēi. For Hán Fēi's argument, see "The Synthesis of Legalistic Doctrine" in Chan, *Source Book*, 252–60.

39. See Xúnzǐ, "Wáng Bà: 2," translation mine.

40. I adopt this designation from Rickett, who uses it to describe Guǎn Zhòng and

the State) he declares, "To obtain a position of power that allows one to dominate others (*chǔ shèng rén zhī yì*) and so to carry out the way of domination that no one in the whole worlds feels resentment—such were Tang and Wu."[41] Here *yì* (grip or grasp) is understood as *shì*,[42] without the *radical lì* (power or force) of the latter. Both convey a comprehensible meaning on their own.[43]

It is known that Tang, as referred to above, was the founding king of the Shāng dynasty, who seized power from the last king of the Xià dynasty, King Jié, and Wu was King Wǔ of Zhoū, the founder of the Zhoū dynasty who conquered King Zhoù of Shāng, a king as equally villainous and immoral as King Jié. Xúnzǐ did not avoid acknowledging that it was Tàng's and Wú's domination (*yì*) that allowed them to obtain power, yet no one showed resentment of their doing so.

In a debate between Xúnzǐ and the Lord of Línwǔ, the latter argued, "In warfare what should be most prized is the power inherent in advantageous circumstances (*bīng zhī gùi zhě yì lì yě*),"[44] to which Xúnzǐ objected, who instead proposed the way of a humane king which was based on his humaneness and will-spirit (*zhì*).[45] Although he also referred to *shì*, his argument was different. In other words, a humane king should not focus only on *shì* but cultivate his moral character. The sage-king model provides a Chinese pastor with a model he or she can emulate, rather than following the propensities of *shì*.

2. Interpreting *Shì*

We have discussed *shì* as it appeared accordingly in three thinkers' works. I do not however assume that by referring to three thinkers' usage of this word, I have thus gathered three clear cut meanings of this word, nor have I exhausted its meanings. Rather, the background is more a political and

---

also Xúnzǐ, see Rickett, "Introduction," 13.

41. Knoblock, *Xunzi*, 241, 343, n. 26

42. Or *yì* as "art."

43. For the Chinese linguistic terminologies here and a study of semantic radicals and phonetic radicals or components of Chinese characters, see Reldman and Siok, "Semantic Radicals in Phonetic Compounds," 19–35; Zhou and Marslen-Wilson, "Sublexical Processing in Reading Chinese," 37–63. Yì appears in Xunzi in 49 paragraphs, search http://ctext.org/xunzi?searchu=%E5%9F%B6. It seems that this word is used by him in multifarious ways, with meanings differing from *shì*.

44. Here *yì* means *shì*, which Knoblock translates as "circumstances."

45. Knoblock, *Xunzi*, 218.

military context, while the style of communication in conveying the idea is more flexible. The earlier the text, the less moralizing is the use of *shì*. In the case of Sūnzǐ, *shì* is more a term to depict geographical and natural phenomena as well as including military dispositions, military weaponries or tools. The purpose is to depict the power, the speed, the flow, and the inner force deposited within the *shì* as dispensable for those who know how to make use of them. Likewise, a general makes judgement and takes advantage of the *shì* in the formation and deployment of his troops in order to win a victory in battle. The judgment of a circumstance is compared to an estimation of how strong and fast a raging torrent may be, or how swiftly a falcon may capture its prey. *Shi* is related to timing and speed. Thus if *shì* is interpreted as power, it is not about a certain A exercising his or her power over or dominating a certain B.[46]

2.1: Redefining Power

A brief reference to Steven Lukes' and Pierre Bourdieu's definition of power will help show the distinctiveness of *shì* as described above.[47] The purpose here, however, is not to do a comparison or a detailed discussion of power per se, but to integrate Lukes' and Bourdieu's ideas into our understanding of *shì* as gathered above.

According to Steven Lukes' summary, the exercise of power is often found in the manner of exerting power especially where decision making is called for in a given situation. Based on such an understanding, behind any power which is exercised must be a certain intention by the one who activates it. The result of the decision being made will determine which of the parties will be the winner in that power struggle. The one who wins may imply that his power prevails.[48] What is depicted above as *shì* in terms of power, speed and flow of a given geographical and natural *shì* is not so much of power relations between A and B, but between various factors.

Thus there are situations in which no decision is explicitly made, such as where one is disabled psychologically or loses the power to make any decision. A person may be incapacitated from having been dominated by certain people exerting a strong influence over them for a long period. This again reflects "binary power relations."[49]

---

46. See Lukes, *Power*, 109.
47. See Lukes, *Power*; Bourdieu, *Masculine Domination*.
48. Lukes, *Power*, 5.
49. Lukes, *Power*, 108–9.

2.2: Power that Dictates One's Nature

Attempting to define power beyond this "binary" formula, Lukes redefines power as "a capacity" rather than "the exercise of that capacity," because a power "may never be, and never need to be, exercised."[50] Rather power can be found where "the securing of compliance to domination,"[51] i.e., the securing of "the consent to domination of willing subjects" is manifested.[52] Domination is therefore an imposition or "significant constraint upon an agent or agents' desires, purposes or interests, which it frustrates prevents from fulfillment or even from being formulated."[53] It is that which "dictates of one's judgment" or "one's nature."[54]

Accordingly, "those subject to it (power) are rendered less free."[55] Lying behind this notion is the idea of freedom of choice, i.e., the freedom to choose one's preference and ability to judge what should be preferred. However, now as one's "nature" is controlled over or dominated, it is somehow less able to function or "to use reason correctly."[56] Because of the "sustaining" influence of power that can stunt and blunt the subject's "capacity for rational judgment," the subject can be misled into having an illusion "of what is 'natural' and what sort of life their instinctive 'nature' dictates".[57] In other words, the "natural" is not natural at all. The nature that they believe they possess still possessing is but an illusion.

This power as domination or which dictates "one's nature" is well interpreted by Bourdieu in his notion of "symbolic violence," by which he means "a gentle violence, imperceptible and invisible even to its victims," and its effect,[58] that shapes the "*habitus*" i.e., "the embodied dispositions which yield 'practical sense' and organize actors' visions of the world

---

50. Lukes, *Power*, 12.

51. Lukes, *Power*, 108–9.

52. Lukes, *Power*, 109. However, one should understand that the "'willing' and 'unwilling' compliance to domination are" not necessarily "mutually exclusive," meaning "one can *consent* to power and resent the mode of its exercise" (italics his). See Lukes, *Power*, 150.

53. Lukes, *Power*, 113, also 85.

54. Lukes, *Power*, 116–17.

55. Lukes, *Power*, 114.

56. Lukes, *Power*, 115.

57. Lukes, *Power*, 115.

58. Lukes is referring to "[t]he effect of symbolic domination (whether ethnic, gender, cultural or linguistic, etc.)" in Bourdieu, *Masculine Domination*, 37, cited in Lukes, *Power*, 140.

A Double Vision Hermeneutic

below the level of consciousness in a way that is resistant to articulation, critical reflection and conscious manipulation."[59] Such effect is "durably and deeply embedded in the body in the form of dispositions."[60]

Moreover, with regard to the *habitus*, one has to understand how it is created by "the durable effects" of the "social order" of the said social or cultural group exerted on the effected one.[61] According to Bourdieu, social agents are "endowed with *habitus*, inscribed in their bodies by past experience."[62] He argues that the *habitus* is "a product of history," which

> produces individual and collective practices—more history—in accordance with the schemes generated by history. It ensures the active presence of past experiences, which, deposited in each organism in the form of schemes of perception, thought and action, tend to guarantee the "correctness" of practices and their constancy over time, more reliably than all formal rules and explicit norms.[63]

Elaborating on Bourdieu, Lukes argues, "social norms and conventions of the various fields are 'incorporated', or 'inscribed', into their bodies, thereby generating 'a permanent disposition, a durable way of standing, speaking, walking, and thereby of feeling and thinking.'"[64] This process can also be described as the internalization of the social and traditional norms. As Bourdieu describes, "the internal dispositions—the internalization of externality—enable the external forces to exert themselves, but

---

59. Bourdieu, *Masculine Domination*, 1–2 which is based on his study focusing on male domination over female and of the notion of *habitus*. For the former, for example he says, "Being included, as man or woman, in the object that we are trying to comprehend, we have embodied the historical structures of the masculine order in the form of unconscious schemes of perception and appreciation. When we try to understand masculine domination we are therefore likely to resort to modes of thought that are the product of domination" (*Masculine Domination*, 5). For the latter, for example he says, see Lukes, *Power*, 140.

60. See Bourdieu, see *Masculine Domination*, 39, 41; also Lukes, *Power*, 141.

61. Lukes, *Power*, 140. For Bourdieu, see *Masculine Domination*, 41.

62. See Bourdieu, *The Logic of Practice*, 70, cited in Lukes, *Power*, 141.

63. Bourdieu, *The Logic of Practice*, 54.

64. Lukes, *Power*, 141. For Bourdieu, see *The Logic of Practice*, 70. This is similar to Lukes' earlier notion about those who look for "conformity," "public self-ascription" and "solidarity" i.e., for cultural or group-related identity when they are dominated by the culturally defined values which have been infused in their being. See Lukes, *Power*, 119.

in accordance with the specific logic of the organisms in which they are incorporated, i.e., in a durable, systematic and non-mechanical way."[65]

2.3: Multivalent Meanings of Shì: Political Power, Political Propensity, Moral Excellence

To return to our discussion of *shì*, in Hán Feī, one sees that for him *shì* is used in relation to political power. Instead of emphasizing that the ruler or the king himself has the power to dominate his subjects, Hán Feī's discussion reveals that attention is paid to the circumstances and political affairs that help shape a *shì*, a political propensity which the ruler can take advantage of. What he needs to do to rule is simply to follow the *shì*. Or perhaps the submission of the people is due to power having infused the blood and body of the people to such an extent that they are unable to do anything other than submit to the rule of these rulers.[66] Alternatively it is merely the result of the kings' moral excellence rather than coercion that people feel compelled to follow them.

A preferable reading might be that the focus is not so much on a ruler's overpowering (A = king overpowers B = people)[67] but on the nature of the circumstances and propensity he is making use of. Perhaps, it is also not largely focused on how the dominated people are affected and exploited. People are not important in this regard. Rather, of primary importance is that through the teaching of the art of rulership, a king may know how to make use of a *shì*.

To sum up, the idea of juxtaposing moral excellence with *shì* is seen in Shèn Daò and Hán Feī, but it is in Xúnzǐ that the significance of moral excellence overtakes that of *shì*. In Xúnzǐ, the manipulation of power (*quánmoú*) to establish the ruler's advantage to rule over his subjects by overpowering them, is rejected. In Xúnzǐ, the discussion of *shì* has turned into a moral philosophy rather than simply a political philosophy. While moral philosophy cannot be fully explored in this thesis, the underlying implication is implied.

---

65. Bourdieu, *The Logic of Practice*, 55.
66. For the allusion to "the body and blood," see Bourdieu, *The Logic of Practice*, 70.
67. See the discussion above.

3. Relating *Shì* to Double Vision Hermeneutics

Shì has travelled down through the centuries and survived longer than any individual or generation since its early inception. In Gadamer's word, with its rich gamut of ideas reverberating with each use, *shì* is a "traditionary text". Having been transmitted as part and parcel of the tradition, it will exist in Chinese culture for as long as the Chinese language is being used and taught alongside its literary and historical background. As individuals learn to use this word, they appropriate the whole package of meaning and implication together with its efficacy in the history and society. Individuals are *as much cultural-linguistically effected as historically effected*.[68]

Shì as shown in the various texts discussed above is a text within texts. I have assumed that it is also a traditionary text as well as a text that carries high cultural linguistic currency. As a Chinese, knowing instinctively when to use this word, *shì*, as a text, has been from the first learnt as a traditionary text in its linguistic form as well as its cultural implications. By this I mean the range of meanings as defined within the various literary contexts I have discussed above which have been infused into daily usage by those who use the word. Thus what happens is "a continual deferment of an idea or a meaning" in Chinese culture through the passing down of a text in "a network of writings," as Johanne Liu interprets it.[69]

Moreover, as Gadamer has defined, in one's experience of an art, there is "a unity" between the person and that which is experienced which constitutes "a new mode of being one."[70] According to him, the work of art is not an object that stands over against a subject in its own right. The work of art as the subject changes the person who experiences it.[71]

Thus, having been learnt, *shì* as a traditionary text has been appropriated. It has become part of me. Having been appropriated, *shì* remains in me who experiences it, and becomes part of me. The text is no longer an object out there but exists intersubjectively in me, as well as remaining a traditionary text independently of me. Such an intersubjective relationship with *shì* is thus not merely the dialog between the writers and the readers as asserted by Yeo.[72] What needs to be underlined is an under-

---

68. See chapter 2.

69. Liu, "Music [*yue*] in Classical Confucianism," 63. Liu discusses about intertextuality, see the introduction of this thesis.

70. Gadamer, *Truth and Method*, 53, 58.

71. Gadamer, *Truth and Method*, 103.

72. Yeo, "Culture and Intersubjectivity," 86.

standing of *shì* as a cultural-linguistic inheritance that has already made me an *effected consciousness*. It has its effect on me before any conscious dialog with it takes place.

Having thus interpreted my intersubjective relationship with *shì*, two further dimensions of intertextual and intersubjective relationship require explication: the one found between *shì* and *Yìzhuàn* and the other between *shì* and "principalities and powers." These two dimensions are currently suspended and kept within my subsidiary awareness. While I focus on deliberating on *shì*, my focal awareness has been active in explaining what it means in the pre-Qín text as well as its cultural significance. I thus highlight it as a traditionary text. However, in the existential dimension, my understanding of *shì* through the lens of Pauline understanding of "principalities and powers," albeit existing in my subsidiary awareness, never ceases to exist. These dimensions coexist synchronically.

In the next chapter, the intersubjective relationship between *shì* and *Yìzhuàn* will be first elucidated.

4

Interpreting Text A1: *Shì* with Text A2: *Yìzhuàn*

> Confucius says, "He who knows the *daò* of change and transformation may be said to know what is done by that of spiritual (power)."
>
> —*Xici* I:9[1]

In the double vision hermeneutic I delineated in chapter 3, I had emphasized the intersubjective factor, i.e. the intersubjective experience of *shì*. Developing from the hermeneutic of Gadamer, I have drawn attention to the cultural-linguistic effect of *shì* as part of the larger body of Chinese traditionary texts, and *shì* as culturally inborn and subjectively experienced within myself, which together form an intersubjective experience. Thus, *shì* is something that is external to me, the interpreting subject but yet simultaneously exists as an intrinsic element in me. In other words, with *shì* as part of my inner world acting as a lens, I see and interpret the outside world when its effect is activated. *Shì* as we have said is a cognate of *power* with particular Chinese nuances.

Though *shì* appears in several pre-Qín texts, the word itself is not found in *Yìjīng*. However, as I have mentioned earlier these two texts share a contemporaneous context; to analyze one with the other is an appropriate approach. Moreover, if *shì* is understood in terms of the understanding of a group of powers in constellation, or through the lens of the *Yìjīng* hexagramic system, there is much potential in interpreting one through

---

1. Modified from Legge, 366.

the lens of the other, and the possibility of discovering another layer of intertextual fusion of horizons.

Chapter 3 reviewed the multifarious aspects of *shì*. By the end of this chapter those aspects will be highlighted to show a particular understanding of *shì* as power, through the lens of the *Yìjīng* system, a system with sixty-four hexagrams. Each of the sixty-four hexagrams, as shall be introduced in more detail, is an ancient diagram formed with six lines. Each is correlated with the others.

The efficacy of the hexagramic system is best demonstrated by giving attention to two of its unique concepts: changes and timing. In order to understand how the concept of change and timeliness is embedded in the *yīn-yáng* elements, we have to briefly, but meticulously, explain its basic formation and mechanism. This interpretation aims to show how these two motifs are related to power. It will also attempt to show that knowing of change and time was deemed as inseparable from the moral power of ancient sages, as a certain esoteric knowledge was from special wisdom power.

In this chapter, my aim is to interpret *shì* within the *Yìjīng* hexagramic system. I will first explain how hexagramic system works, followed by an hexagramic-*shì* integrative interpretation of a pastor, Pastor Y's situation, and hence demonstrate the intersubjective relationship between Texts A1 and A2.

1. Encountering the Dynamism of Unlimited Change

1.1: From Yīn-Yáng to Ten Thousand Things

This study of *Yìjīng* aims to use it as an interpreting lens to show powers displayed in constellation as well as their respective dynamic potencies, determined by the *yīn* and *yáng* factors. To allow us to understand the *Yìjīng* hexagramic system on its own terms, the following will be more expositional. Nevertheless, it will be helpful to think of *yīn yáng* as *yīn* power and *yáng* power.

The *yīn* and *yáng* lines are the most fundamental units in the *Yìjīng* hexagramic system. The eight fundamental trigrams are derived from these two lines. It is hard to judge when the idea of *yīn* and *yáng* was first conceived, probably before the third century BC.[2] Graham's, Major's, and Blanc's studies of *yīn-yáng* basically based on a second century BC Text: *Huáinánzi*.[3] Blanc traces the notion of *gǎnyìng* ("resonance") back to *Yìjīng*,[4] which was "formulated in a systematic way" in *Huáinánzi*.[5] These all are proven to be works later than *Yìjīng*.

Therefore, it is at least correct to say that the *yīn-yáng* concept might have been developed at an early date not later than late Zhōu and became popular in the Warring States (475–221 BC) or more so in the Hàn period (206 BC–220 AD).[6] This thesis has adopted the view that many of the *zhuàn* of *Yìzhuàn* should be dated to the Warring States period, the time when the *yīn-yáng* concept had become popular.

Yīn and *yáng* are the basic units of a hexagram. There are old and young *yīn* and *yáng* with 7 (*yīn*) and 8 (*yáng*) being young and 6 (*yīn*) and 9 (*yáng*) being old. According to *Yìzhuàn*, the numbers were first inscribed in *Hétú* (Yellow River Chart of the dragon) and *Luòshū* (Luo

    2. No evidence of date is given in in the entry under "*Yin and Yang*" in Cua ed., *Encyclopedia of Chinese Philosophy*, or under key term entry "*yīn/yáng*: Five Phases correlative theory" in Nylan, *Classics*, 369–71. Richard Rutt notes that *yīn-yáng* theory and the *taìjí* emblem "were as yet unknown in *Zhōuyì*," see Rutt, 10. Harper locates the emergence of *yīn-yáng* idea in the third century BC, which means it might have been there before that. See Donald Harper, "Warring States Natural Philosophy and Occult Thought," in Loewe and Shaughnessy ed., *The Cambridge History of Ancient China*, 809–10, 823–24.

    3. Graham, *Yīn-yáng and the Nature of Correlative Thinking*; Major, *Heaven and Earth*; Blanc, *Huai-nan Tzu: Philosophical Synthesis*. See particularly *Huáinánzī*, chapter 3: Tiānwènxùn, section 2: "Yīn and Yáng," in Major, op. cit., 64–65. Puett's discussion of the origin of the cosmos in Chinese tradition begins with a paragraph in *Huáinánzi*, "Jīngshén," 7.1a. Viewing that *yīn-yáng* was often associated with cosmogenesis in early texts, *Huáinánzī* is one of the best texts to investigate for traces for the dating of *yīn-yáng* idea, see Puett, *To Become a God*.

    4. In H31 Xián (it may also have been pronounced as *hàn* as shown in *Shūo wén jiě zhì*), it says, "Xián, gǎn yě. Roú shàng ér gāng xià, èr qì xiāng yìng yǐ xiāng yǔ." Lynn translates, "Reciprocity is a matter of stimulation. Here the soft and yielding is above, and the hard and strong is below. The two kinds of material force [*qì*] stimulate and respond and join together." See Lynn, 329. Rutt translates *qì* as "energies," see Rutt, 377. The two *qi* (material forces) can be understood as *yin* and *yang*. It is very common in *Yìjīng* to say for example, the first yin has *gānyìng* with the fourth *yáng*, or the second *yang* has *gǎnyìng* with the fifth *yīn*, et cetera. Kǒng Yǐndá elaborates that this helps to explain *rénshì*, human affairs, for example the *gǎnyìng* of man and woman, husband and wife.

    5. Blanc, *Huani-nan Tze*, 9; see also the postface of *Huáinánzī*, cited from Hall and Ames, *Anticipating China*, 262.

    6. Gernet has traced the idea of *yīn-yáng* and *wǔxíng*, five elements, to Hàn dynasty, see Gernet, *Chinese Civilization*, 158.

Interpreting Text A1

River Writings of the tortoise),[7] out of which Fúxī, the sage, derived the eight primordial trigrams.[8] There is no need to speculate on how these two charts were conceived.

Hétú 河圖

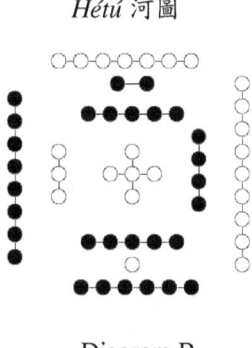

Diagram B

Yìzhuàn explains how the Number of *Dayan*, or *Dàyān zhī shù*, 55, can be derived from *Hétú*. As shown in the chart there are numbers of dots from one to ten. The sum of all the numbers between one and ten is 55. Those on the perimeter are 6, 7, 8, and 9. Those four numbers symbolize the four *xiàng* (images),[9] which in turn symbolizes the four *shí* (seasons).[10]

The Number of *Dàyān* also represents the total number of yellow stalks the ancient diviners used for divination. With each four-fold random division of the yellow stalks, a diviner would yield a remainder. The

---

7. *Xìcí* testifies that the sages (Fúxī and Yú) who had received *Hétú* (Yellow River Chart of the dragon) and *Luòshū* (Luo River Writings of the tortoise) had also received "meaning signs" and conceptualized them "as ruling principles." For the origins of Hétú and Luòshū, see discussion in Gāo Huáimín, *Sòng Yuán Míng Yìxué shǐ*, 168–82. More classic discussion in found in Zhū Xī, *Yìxué qíméng*, see Adler, *Introduction*, 1–14. See also *Xìcí* I: 11 in Lynn, 66. Lynn explains: "The Yellow River chart Hétú) is supposed to have been inscribed on the back of a dragon-horse (*lóngmǎ*) that emerged from the Yellow River at the time of thy mythical sage-king Fuxi, who modelled the eight trigrams on it. The Luo River diagram (Luòshū) was the design on the back of the spirit-tortoise (*shéngui*) that appeared when the later sage-king Yu was controlling the flood and that Yu used as a model for the ninefold division of ancient China, see Lynn, 74. See also Smith et al., *Sung Dynasty Uses*, 175–76.

8. I have briefly introduced the eight trigrams in chapter 1 so will restate them at this point.

9. This I follow Kǒng Yǐndá, see Kǒng, 650. For English resources that explain meticulously of how the mechanism of Dàyān functions and about Hétú, see Rutt, *Zhouyi*, 158–66.

10. See *Xìcí* I:9.

A Double Vision Hermeneutic

remainder would either be a 6, 7, 8, or 9, which determined a line to be an old or young *yīn* or an old or young *yáng*. The old have a higher propensity for change, i.e., from *yīn* to *yáng* or *yáng* to *yīn*. The diviner repeated this six times to form a six-line hexagram with a mixture of different possibilities of old or young lines. *Yīn* and *yáng* are taken here as symbols for power. In other words, in a hexagram with six old or young lines, there are different combinations with various power levels.

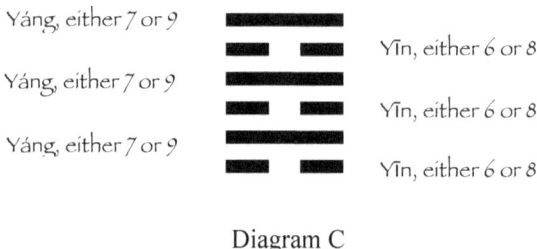

Diagram C

To further explain the formation of 64 hexagrams and their ability to form a symbolic world of "myriad things": Firstly, the possible combinations of *yīn* and *yáng* over six lines are $2^6=64$, thus sixty-four hexagrams. The total lines for each of *yīn* and *yáng* lines is 192.

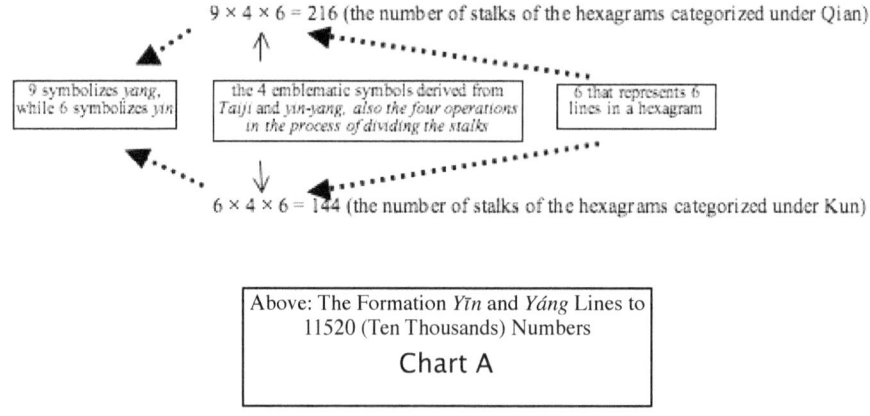

Above: The Formation *Yīn* and *Yáng* Lines to 11520 (Ten Thousands) Numbers

Chart A

Interpreting Text A1

Rutt gives a very clear illustration of this:

(a) . . . 216 wands (stalks) had to be counted out in order to generate a hexagram of six whole lines; and 144 for a hexagram of six broke lines. (b) 11,520 wands had to be counted out to generate every hexagram in the book, which includes 192 whole lines and 192 broken lines.

These figures make it clear that 216/6 = 36 wands were counter out for a whole line and 144/6 = 24 for a broken line.[11]

The calculation can be broken down as follows:

6 × 64 ÷ 2 = 192 the total number of *yīn* or *yáng* lines respectively

9 × 4 × 192 = 6912 the total number of stalks of *yáng* lines

6 × 4 × 192 = 4608 the total number of stalks of *yīn* lines

6912 + 4608 = 11520 the total number of stalks of 384 lines

Chart B

Therefore, it declares in *Xìcí* I:9, "The stalks in the two parts [of the Changes] number 11,520 and correspond [roughly] to the number of the ten thousand [i.e., "myriad"] things."[12]

Thus every *yīn* could be a *yīn* with six or eight (stalks), representing old or young *yīn*, while every *yáng* could be a seven (young) or nine (old). When a *yīn* is old, it tends to change into *yáng*, and vice versa. As has been shown above, each of the 192 *yáng* lines holds within itself nine possibilities. For example consider that the line is an old *yáng* (the stalks' remainders total 36, divided by four yielding the old *yáng for* a line), which can be understood as nine stalks. Similarly, each of 192 *yīn* lines consists of six possibilities. If that line is an old *yīn* (the stalks' remainders total 24, divided by four that yields the old *yīn for* a line). Whether it is a nine or a six is determined by the four operations, which implies different probabilities to produce a six, a seven, an eight, or a nine. Therefore, the calculation is

---

11. Rutt, 160. Word in bracket is mine. See also Wáng Bì's comment in Lynn, 61 and Lynn's explanation, see 19 and also 72 n. 39 which also includes Kǒng Yǐndá's explanation.

12. Lynn, 61.

192 x 4 x 9 or 192 x 4 x 6 which yields 6912 and 4608 respectively, which produce a total of 11520.

Now if we apply all these probabilities as "ten thousand things" (hence 11520), everything, including the categories of time, social position, and event, can be categorized as a "thing."[13] By inference, an action or a move symbolized in one *yīn* or *yáng* line will affect other lines in the same hexagram and the symbolism of the hexagram, which will then affect other hexagrams. To change a line is to change a hexagram. See the surrounding world through the lens of dynamism created by change, or the increase and decrease of *yīn* and *yáng*, is thus a way of looking at life situations.[14] If we say each of the "ten thousand things" symbolizes one situation or one human affair, a change of personnel in an organization or the change of power relationship caused by this, we can further infer that each of these things represents a *shì*.

Furthermore, *yīn* and *yáng* imply power. These "ten thousands" thus imply changes of situations, personnel, power relations in their very minute ways. Scrutinizing thousands of possibilities allows us to capture the microscopic, dynamistic nature of power. This is the primary reward of reading power as *shì* through a hexagramic, microscopic, dynamistic lens.

The implication of this can be extended further by retrieving what was emphasized regarding the intrinsic and subjective nature of *shì* inhibiting a subject, and its intersubjective nature, i.e., *shì* being something outside that we judge as *shì* but also something affecting our being internally, or as Gadamer might define, "effected" in our being, acting as a lens through which we see many situations and power relationships, whereby we always understand that things or powers, with thousands of possibilities, inevitably cause us to ponder all these powers in a continuous momentum of change, which affects our way of being.

The systemic structure formed by sixty-four hexagrams, the six lines, and the unlimited changes or "myriad things" encrypted in its symbolic system with layers of meanings embedded within have been explained briefly. The changes can be understood from the perspective of the

---

13. *Yǔleì*, Book 66, "Yì sān. Gāng lǐng xià. Zhǒng lùn guà tuàn yaó," 1666.

14. This principle is explained in *Xìcí* I:12, in which it says, "*Tuī ér xíng zhī wèi zhī tōng, jǔ ér cuò zhī tiān xià zhī mín, wèi zhī shìyeì.*" For English see Lynn, 67, which says, "By extending this to practical action, one may be said to achieve complete success. To take up this [the Dao of change] and integrate it into the lives of the common folk of the world, this we call all 'the great task of life.'"

Interpreting Text A1

mechanism of various *biànguà*,[15] the changing of hexagrams. A description of how these changes work will follow.

1.2: Introducing Hexagramic Change

As previously stated, there are sixty-four hexagrams in the *Yìjīng* system. The method by which each of these may turn into another within the system, can be worked out in several different ways. It will suffice to introduce two major categories of *biànguà* (hexagram-change): "counter-changed hexagrams" (*cuòguà*) and "inverted hexagrams" (*zòngguà*) as found in a Chinese idiom, *cuò zòng fù zá*, very complex and complicated. What is a *zòngguà*? To put it simply, when the hexagram is also inverted, it means the situation symbolized therein also *inverted*. A *zòngguà* happens when a hexagram is flipped upside down, as is H3 Zhūn ䷂ (Difficulty at the Beginning) *and* H4 Měng ䷃ (Youth Folly/Juvenile Ignorance).[16] A *cuòguà* happens when all the *yáng* or *yīn* lines changed into their opposites, for examples H27 Yí ䷚ and H28 Dàguò ䷛.[17]

---

15. One early *biànguà* is called *zhīguà*. For an English explanation of this mechanism and the meaning of *zhīguà*, changing from one to another hexagram with a flip of *yáng* to *yīn* or *yīn* to *yáng* in a "changeable line," see Rutt, 154–55. *Zhīguà* appear in an early text, *Zuǒzhuàn*, an annotated commentary to *Chūnqiū*, the *Spring and Autumn*, one of the *Five Classics*, and one of the earliest documents that contain numerous records of the use of *Yìjīng* that could illustrate this dynamism and fluidity of meanings. According to Rutt, nineteen stories related to *Zhōuyì* (*Yìjīng*) are told in *Zuǒzhuàn* (173) which he translate all except one. As Rutt points out, both tortoise shells and yarrow milfoils were being used in divination, see Rutt, 149. who dates them between 671 and 487 BC, see 173–97. For example, in Year 22 of Zuānggōng (Duke Zuāng) of Lǔ, Duke Chén divined and received Guān zhī Pǐ (Hexagram 20 ䷓: Viewing changed to Hexagram 12 ䷋: Obstruction), in which one finds the old *yīn* in line four of Guān is changed into a *yáng* line forming Pǐ; in Year 12 of Xuāngōng (Duke Xuān) recorded Shī *zhī* Lín, which means H7 ䷆ Shī (The Army) is changed into H19 ䷒ Lín (Overseeing), in which old *yīn* in line one of Shī (The Army) is changed into a *yáng* line forming Lín (Overseeing). For one brief discussion of *zhīguà* in *Zuǒzhuàn* other than Rutt's, see Zhū, *Yùxué zhéxué sǐ*, 25–26

16. There are eight hexagrams: H1 Qián ䷀, H2 Kūn ䷁, H27 Yí ䷚, H28 Dàguò ䷛, H29 Kǎn ䷜, H30 Lí ䷝, H61 Zhōngfú ䷼, and H62 Xiǎoguò ䷽ in and with which *cuòguà* can be formed but not *zòngguà*.

17. And there are eight hexagrams—two pairs—which are counter-changed at the same time inverted: Tài ䷊ and Pǐ ䷋, Suí ䷐ and Gǔ ䷑, Jiàn ䷴ and Guīmèi ䷵, Jìjì ䷾ and Wèijì ䷿. These are Hexagrams 11, 12, 17, 18, 53, 54, 63, and 64. There are twenty inverted pairs (which are not counter-changed), forty-eight which are counter-changed (which are not inverted). See Wáng, *Nèizhuàn*, 454.

A Double Vision Hermeneutic

The purpose of the following demonstration is to show how change in a hexagram implies a change of time and situation, especially apparent when examining four interrelated hexagrams with either a *cuòguà* or a *zòngguà* relationship.

1.3: Demonstrating Changes: Zhūn and Mēng, Gé and Dǐng

1.3.1: Understanding H3 Zhūn ䷂ and H4 Mēng ䷃

The reason Zhūn and Gé are chosen here is because they are the most relevant to situations Chinese pastors may encounter. This will become clearer in a later section. While Mēng is Zhūn's inverted hexagram, H49 Gé ䷰ (Revolution) is the inverted hexagram of H50 Dǐng ䷱ (The Caldron). Referring to one of the earliest commentaries, *Xùguà*, which states how these two hexagrams relate with one another:

> *Zhun* [Birth Throes, Hexagram 3] here signifies repletion. *Zhun* is when things are first born. When things begin life, they are sure to be covered. This is why *Zhun* is followed by *Meng* [Juvenile Ignorance, Hexagram 4]. *Meng* here indicates juvenile ignorance, that is, the immature state of things. When things are in their immature state, one cannot fail to nourish them. This is why *Meng* is followed by *Xu* [Waiting, Hexagram 5].[18]

Signifying "repletion," Zhūn is indeed a time that is "full" of *dynamic*. It is "dynamic", for the author of *Tuànzhuàn* interprets it as a time when *gāng* (the strong *yáng*) and *róu* (the weak *yīn*) begin "their intercourse,"[19] in which *yīn* and *yáng* are *active* and in the state of *continuing exchange*. However, as it is *dynamic*, it is also unstable and full of danger. Note that *yīn* and *yáng* are to be understood as *yīn* power and *yáng* power. This hexagram (Zhūn) or image or situation could imply that it is full of energy and opportunity for the *yīn* and *yáng* to change as they are both active and dynamic.

To extend this implication: whether in nature, or human affairs or power structures, it is unstable, full of possibility for eruption and chaos, but yet also full of the opportunity to change into what is better. It is advised that at this particular time symbolized by Mēng, one should only

---

18. Lynn, 103, 109.
19. See Legge, 62.

wait and take no action to execute any scheme other than to *jūzhēn*, "to abide correct and firm"[20] and to build up and consolidate one's support from marquis and lords.

The impact of the effect of hexagramic change's amazing power to embody the dynamism and complexity of human affairs may be better appreciated, if H3 Zhūn ䷂ is changed into H4 Méng ䷃ by simply inverting the hexagram. Having inverted, the first *yáng* has moved to the second line and the fifth *yáng* to the top.

Two Possibilities—Both/And—This change can be understood by examining how the trigrams within each hexagram change, i.e., Kǎn ☵ (the top trigram) and Leí ☳ (the bottom trigram) in Zhūn ䷂ have changed into Gěn ☶ (at the top) and Kǎn ☵ (at the bottom) in Méng ䷃. Leí ☳, according to *Shuōguà* and *Xùguà*, symbolizes movement and dynamic.[21] When the hexagram is inverted, Leí ☳ becomes Gěn ☶.[22] Gěn, according to *Xùguà* means stop.[23] What needs to be remembered is that H51 (Leí) Zhèn ䷲ means active; H52 Gěn ䷳ means stop, despite all meticulous mechanisms which have been demonstrated.

Thus, while Zhūn signifies "repletion" and "dynamic," once it becomes Méng, it means "juvenile ignorance, i.e. the immature state of things," for in Méng ䷃ it is not the Leí ☳ but Gěn ☶ (as the top trigram) that determines the situation. The hexagram thus teaches *when one is too young or while the states of affairs are immature, it is wise to stop*. That is perhaps why *Xùguà* says, "This is why Zhūn is followed by Méng," and interprets their correlative relationship by saying, "[w]hen things begin life,[24] they are sure to be covered [the literal meaning of *méng*—i.e., encapsulated in membranes, eggs, or seeds]."[25]

Hence the basic implication of the mechanism shown in hexagramic inversion is that being able to be mutually inverted, they show two opposite aspects at the same time. The two aspects could represent two

---

20. Legge, 62.
21. Lynn, 121.
22. It is interesting that the sequence of hexagrams also has H51 (Leí) Zhèn ([Thunder] Quake) followed by H52 Gěn (Restraint).
23. Lynn, 109.
24. This refers to Zhūn.
25. *Xùguà*, Lynn, 103. Comments in parathesis are Wáng Bì's.

situations. Thus, it shows a two-way or both/and thinking pattern. Such is the way of the wise.[26]

Four Possibilities—Multiple Perspective—The change with inversion that signifies a change of situation may be further applied further by looking at the *Tuànzhuàn* of both hexagrams. In Mēng, according to *Tuànzhuàn*, the mountain is on top of the water. It symbolizes the natural phenomenon of a mountain which curbs water within a safe boundary. However, there is no danger, even though water (☵) may also signify danger.[27] *Tuànzhuàn* thus comments, "Mēng consists of a dangerous place below a mountain. In danger and brought to a halt: this is Mēng."[28]

In contrast to this phenomenon, it is said, in *Tuànzhuàn*, that Zhūn refers to "one who takes action in the midst of danger"[29] ("*dòng hū xiǎn zhōng*"). Thus, each teaches a way to face a dangerous situation. It may not be that one is less dangerous than the other; rather it is one's ability to cope within the situation. Thus, although there is danger, "if one perseveres there is a prospect of great success in spite of the existing danger."[30] The timing is important, as well as holding onto one's strength of rectitude.[31]

Thus, with regard to the relationship between these two hexagrams, one could possibly find at least two sets of four conditions could be viewed:

1. One is aware of one's own Mēng state; or perhaps Zhūn state;

2. One knows that obstacles/dangers are unavoidable, thus stop in time; or take action even if one faces dangers.

3. One's ability and moral power are not ready yet; it is advantageous to hold firm and keep to the middle path (*gāngzhōng*).

4. One's time, which is still Mēng, is unclear,[32] but with persevere one can proceed; or because it is full of dynamic, there is no danger in moving forward.

---

26. As it says, "the reciprocal process of *yīn* and *yáng* is called the Dao." Yet "the benevolent see it and call it benevolence, and the wise [*zhì*] see it and call it wisdom." See *Xici* I:5, in Lynn, 53.

27. Nevertheless, mountains can sometimes signify obstacles, things that stop one from advancing. In the above, it is the alternate meaning which is more appropriate.

28. Lynn, 159.

29. Lynn, 152.

30. Wilhelm/Baynes, 16.

31. "Rectitude" is taken from what is signified by "*gāngzhōng*". For detailed discussion of this, see chapter 6.

32. Wáng Fūzhī defines Mēng: "*Chaǒ huì cóng shēng zhī weì, hue yì ér weì yoǔ biàn*

Interpreting Text A1

The above are simply a few of the possibilities. As with all possibilities, it is hard for one to determine which is the most likely outcome or best step to take. However, the underlying meaning of the advice of both hexagrams—Zhūn and Méng—is that whether something is an opportunity or would bring danger is most probably due to being young or inexperienced, i.e. ignorant. In either case, if one is too preoccupied with coding and decoding life situations, i.e. paying too much attention to the dynamic momentum of change, or powers in constellation, propensity and potential momentum hidden behind all situations, one is obsessed with the *shì*-orientated way.

Meanwhile, H49 Gé ䷰ (Revolution) and H50 Dǐng ䷱ (The Caldron) should further demonstrate the change of hexagrams that connote changes of situation.

1.3.2 Incorporating H49 Gé ䷰ and H50 Dǐng ䷱

Having understood the basic implication of Zhūn and Méng, we now further incorporated two other hexagrams to understand a more complex four-hexagram cluster. This begs the question: What kind of relationship do these four hexagrams have? Note that H49 Gé ䷰ is the complete opposite of H3 Zhūn ䷂ by a double change, i.e, through both inversion (*zòngguà*) and counter-change (*cuòguà*), while H50 Dǐng ䷱ is also the complete opposite of H4 Méng ䷃ by inversion and counter-change. In addition, H49 Gé ䷰ is a counter-change of H4 Méng ䷃, and H50 Dǐng ䷱ is a counter-change of H3 Zhūn ䷂.

While contra Zhūn and Méng advise that time is still immature, both Dǐng and Gé are hexagrams that signify time for change and taking action. Wáng Fūzhī (1619–1692) also shows that these are two correlative pairs by using Qián and Kūn which symbolize pure *yáng* and pure *yīn* as a hermeneutic principle. The *yīn-yáng* principle Wáng applies is derived from Zhōu Dūnyí's (1017–1073 AD) Tàijí-Wújí symbiosis and the *cuòzòng* (inverted-counter change) correlative changes, with which he argues that for all the six lines in every hexagram, there are always the *xiǎn yǐn míng àn*, the manifest-hidden and the conspicuous/inconspicuous aspects. If *yīn* is the one that manifests conspicuously, the one hidden will be *yáng*.

---

yě." It describes the sprouting of grass and flowers, and that it is unclear and hidden, hardly recognized. *huì* means "dark, unclear, obscure; night" while *yì* means "shade, screen; to hide, screen," cited from Website of *Chinese Text Project*, http://chinese.dsturgeon.net/dictionary.pl?if=en&char=晦翳.

A Double Vision Hermeneutic

Thus, if Zhūn and Mèng are in the manifesting state, Dǐng and Gé will be the ones hiding.³³ In other words, while one is heeding the first two hexagrams, one should not leave the latter two out of one's mind.

An attempt has been made to illustrate the problems that may arise as one enters a classical text. There are layers of meanings, and possible allusions to historical events that are ingrained in the symbolic and ideological system. Each layer is coupled with historical study of possible allusions to earlier historical events and commentaries that help us to understand the meaning of the texts across different times. In what follows, by attending to H50 Dǐng ䷱ and H49 Gé ䷰ to show the effect of hexagramic changes, it will be shown how this can be further complicated by considering historical allusions in the interpretation.³⁴

It is understood that *dǐng* (caldron) as a vessel was an important utensil not only for everyday cooking functions but also serving as an utensil in sacrificial ceremonies.³⁵ The *Dàxiàngzhuàn* of the Dǐng hexagram states that it symbolizes the *jūnzǐ* (noble person) who is readying himself for assignment.³⁶ How does this "assignment" relate to the image of a *dǐng*?

In his study Shaughnessy is able to reconstruct and transcribe a problematic seven-graph Shāng Bronze inscription, which says, "(King Wǔ) *suì*³⁷ and *dǐng* (caldron)-sacrificed and was able to make known that he had routed the Shāng."³⁸ He thus infers that since "it is well known that caldrons have long represented a dynasty's legitimacy, a symbolism that was particularly strong during the Zhōu dynasty," it is therefore possible

---

33. Wang, *Zhoūyì neìzhuàn fǎlì*, chapter 7, in *Waìzhuàn*, 354–55.

34. Early commentators might be more accessible to these allusions perhaps through oral transmission.

35. For some evidences, see Shaughnessy, *Sources*, 100–101.

36. Here again Wilhelm's translation of *"jūnzǐ yǐ zhèng wei níng mìng"* as "the superior man consolidates his fate by making his position correct" (194) is probably wrong by especially using "fate" to translate *"mìng"* whereas Legge's is preferable, by translating it as "the appointment (of Heaven)" (329). Nevertheless, both do not convey correctly the implication of "readiness." Neither is Rutt's "making his orders hold" (387) satisfactory.

37. Against a possible transcription of *suì* as year, Shaughnessy argues its probable meaning as related to sacrifice, and thus also to *Lì guǐ*, a certain tureen especially used in sacrifice. He asserts, ". . . The evidence seems to show that originally the word *suì* connoted a type of sacrifice (probably to the ancestors); yet by at least the middle of the Western Zhou, a second meaning, 'year,' had come to be associated with the word" (99). Therefore *suì* would imply a type of sacrifice. For his discussion of *suì* and *Lì guǐ*, see *Sources*, 95–100, for *guǐ* (tureen) and *Lì guǐ*, 128–32, and for *dǐng*, 100–101.

38. Shaughnessy, *Sources*, 104. For his detailed reconstruction of these seven characters, see 92–104.

that it is through "the *dǐng* sacrifice" as "a significant rite" that a king establishes his government,[39] which legitimized King Wǔ's replacement of the Shāng king's rulership.[40]

Note that H49 Gé ䷰ (Revolution) is the inverted hexagram of H50 Dǐng ䷱ (Caldrons symbolising legitimate reign) or vice versa. One can derive from cauldron (*dǐng*), a symbolism for legitimization, a potential revolution by using the logic of inversion—a bringing in of a new claimed mandated change, because a *dǐng* that symbolizes the establishment of a government is brought about through a revolution (Gé ䷰). A Dǐng can always be turned upside down (inversion), which brings in Gé; the image changes from fire ☲ on top of wood ☴ into fire ☲ burning water ☱. When fire is on the top, wood symbolizes the people who are supporting the fire. Thus, Dǐng symbolizes the one who has secured the reign, who should also be administering according to Heaven's mandate. However, Gé also symbolizes one who has yet to secure his reign, but who, having followed the great timing the Heaven has sanctioned by heaven, can launch a revolution.[41] This following of the mandate of Heaven and the aspiration of the people is taught in *Tuànzhuàn* through the allusion to the revolutions carried out by King Tāng of Shāng who overthrew King Jié of the Xià dynasty and later King Wǔ of Zhoū who overthrew King Zhoù of Shāng.

Shaughnessy argues that the *dǐng* reflects King Wǔ's expedition to Shāng, although there is no direct mention of King Wǔ in either its hexagram or line statements, nor Shaughnessy argues, does this apply exactly to the Dǐng hexagram. Nevertheless, I find this historical interpretation aids and enriches my own understanding of the Dǐng hexagram and what it might have meant at the time. As I have explained in chapter 2, 'what it might have meant' in a text forms the objective side of the hermeneutic, but the purpose of gathering further objective discoveries is to help arrive at an understanding that is meaningful for integration without falling into an arbitrary subjective interpretation.

Having thus understood Dǐng, I would suggest that Gé might be alluding to King Wǔ's revolution. Here timeliness for revolution is probably the emphasis of this hexagram, not simply that in *Tuànzhuàn*, one sees in *Dàxiàngzhuàn* a precept given for *jūnzǐ* based on the principle of

39. Shaughnessy, *Sources*, 105–6.

40. Shaughnessy marks that "both *dǐng* and *zhèng* 政, 'to govern; government,' were closely homophonous and certainly belong to the same family of words." Shaughnessy, *Sources*, 106.

41. See *Tuànzhuàn* of both hexagrams.

timeliness. Moreover, the line statement of the second *yīn* also refers to a time, i.e., *jǐrì*.⁴² However, there is no need to know the exact date.⁴³

Thus in this section H3 Zhún ䷂, H4 Méng ䷃, H49 Gé ䷰, and H50 Dǐng ䷱ have been used to demonstrate change. It will be repetitious to reiterate the multi-layered and complex meanings as explicated above, but the above should help to appreciate *Yìzhuàn*'s teaching on timeliness through the juxtaposing of Zhūn and Méng with Gé and Dǐng. The Zhūn/Méng pair shows us a time full of exuberance and a time to wait; the Gé/Dǐng pair, however, reveals a time that is ripe, a time to act and to execute ministrations.

Throughout the history of *Yìzhuàn* hermeneutics, alternative patterns have been developed, such as *hùyì guà* (the exchange of positions of the upper and the lower trigrams in the same hexagram) and *jiāohù guà* (using lines 2 to 4 as the lower trigram and lines 3 to 5 as the upper to form a new hexagram). These all help capture as many as possible of the changes developed by later innovators and interpreters as they observed the world. As each hexagram is part of the whole systemic symbolism, the changes implied by a pair of *cuòzōng* or *hùyì* or *jiāohù* hexagrams also symbolize the changes of situations or personnel according to these patterns.

---

42. Yú Xuětáng points out that there are three theories for this character *jǐ*. One is to read it as "*yǐ*" as in *yǐjīng* (already), another as "*sì*" as in *jìsì* (to venerate or worship) for "*yǐ*" and "*sì*" are interchangeable in the pre-Qín period. Her conclusion is that the third, i.e., to read it as *jǐ* is more conducive, quoting Dài Zhèng (AD 1072–1138) in the Sòng dynasty in support. The latter argues that "*jǐ* should be read according to the ten *tiāngān* ("heavenly branches" [Lynn] or heavenly "stems" [Rutt]) calculation as *jǐ* as in '*wù jǐ*' (the fifth and sixth in the sequence), for ten days after *jǐ* is *gēng*." *Gēng* means to *gé* (to change or to bring in revolution), see Yǔ, "Zhōuyì Gé guà 'Jǐ rì' Kǎoshì," 28–29.

43. For a discussion of some possible dates and scholars' debate, see Huáng, "Zhōuyì Gé guà zhōng dè Wǔ wáng fá Zhoù rì," 40–46. For related calculation recorded in other hexagrams, see H18 Gǔ which talks about "three days before *jiǎ* and three days after *jiǎ*" (*xiān jiǎ sān rì, hoù jiǎ sān rì*), H57 Shùn line five that mentions three days before *gēng* and three days after *gēng* (*xiān gēng sān rì, hoù gēng sān rì*). *Jiǎ* and *gēng* most probably indicate two of the *tiāngān* names for calculating dates. Huáng in his quotation of Xiè Xiàngróng has mistaken H57 for H59, see Huáng, 51. Lynn also holds the view that *jiǎ* in Gǔ and *gēng* in Shùn are the first and seventh characters in *tiāngān*, see 249. Rutt points out that *tiāngān* and *tìzhī* ("earthly branches") were already in use to form "a cycle of sixty bisyllabic number words (from *jiǎzǐ* to *guǐhài*)" from the second century BC onwards for numbering years, see Rutt, 19–20.

2. Changes, Timeliness, and the Subject

The significance of timeliness has been partly shown above. Potential changes imply a potential sequence of complex changes. As each hexagram implies a situation or particular timing,[44] every change thus implies the emergence or change of a new situation and timing. An interpretation from a hexagramic perspective shows the many angles from which one single event can be interpreted; and the complexity of changes which challenge one's ability in determining what is the best timing for taking any action. However, as shall be shown amidst the complexity, there are fundamental moral principles the *Yìzhuàn* is teaching its reader to follow. This can be illustrated by a case which occurred in a church which I know.

Around 2002, a vocational crisis was experienced by a Chinese pastor, Pastor Y, serving in a local Chinese church—a conflict that finally ended with his resignation. Before he became a pastor in that church, Pastor Y was a lay leader who served faithfully for more than ten years. Around the early 1990s, he started to serve as a pastor. Things went smoothly. To become better equipped for ministry, he proposed to the church leaders that he should pursue theological training in a seminary, with the aim of returning to serve. Upon his return four years later, full of vision and ideas for church growth, which he shared with other church leaders to motivate them towards change. Plans emerged and were implemented to bring changes.

Unfortunately, after half a year's effort, an older, influential member, who was also one of the founders of the church, objected to the pastor's innovative ideas and successfully lobbied key members who had originally been ready to follow the pastor's suggested plan under the pastor's leadership to change their minds. The disagreement eventually paralyzed the whole of the revolutionary programme.

Desperate and disappointed, Pastor Y resigned.[45] By then, having acquired a *Yìjīng* interpretive lens, and witnessing the whole course of events, I wondered whether or not he should have resigned? There was

---

44. See for example, Lǚ, *Zhoūyì chánweī*, 180–81.

45. Recent research (2001–2002) done by Dean R. Hoge and Jacquelline E. Wenger with a sample of about two hundred pastors from five denominations: Assemblies of God, the Evangelical Lutheran Church in America, the Lutheran Church-Missouri Synod, the Presbyterian Church (U.S.A), and the United Methodist Church shows one of the reasons pastors have left their congregations is due to conflict within the congregation. One particular example he gave (Pastor Frank) articulated that the root of the conflict lay with bringing changes to the church, see Hoge and Wenger, *Pastors in Transition*, 76–97, esp. 84–88.

A Double Vision Hermeneutic

no definite answer. Three hexagrams: H3 Zhūn ䷂ (Difficulty at the Beginning), H49 Gé ䷰ (Revolution), and H35 Jìn ䷢ (Progress) caught my attention at that time, as I tried to understand the scenario.

First of all, using the *Yìjīng* system to conceptualize what happened, it is understood that within the six lines in a hexagram, there is a beginning and an ending, the first and the sixth lines. When Pastor Y returned to the church after seminary training, although he was not entirely new to the church, he was deemed a relatively "new" member to the power structure after his years of absence. Thus, he needed to re-estimate his position within the structure—an invisible power structure.

With this in mind, my attention was caught by "*pánhuán*, tarry or difficulty in advancing," which appeared in the first line statement of H3 Zhūn (Difficulty at the Beginning).[46] It reads, "It will be advantageous for him to abide correct and firm" (*lì jū zhēn*). Meanwhile, I thought Pastor Y should not resign or make any move. As he did what was contrary to Zhūn's advice, I judged that he would not succeed in his next move. I thought he should instead stay in the same church and wait, as Wilhelm comments, one "must not try to force advance but must pause and take thought" and "hold back," for "any premature move might bring disaster."[47] Wilhelm's interpretation is based on a traditional understanding of *pánhuán* which he translates as "Hesitation and hindrance" or (*páihuái*).[48]

Meanwhile, I understood that Pastor Y's intention was to bring in a change, thus consulting H49 Gé ䷰ I found "Furthering through perseverance. Remorse disappears."[49] Wondering whether should he move ahead with his plan or not, I found H35 Jìn ䷢ (Progress) with its first *yīn* statement which says,

> Progressing, but turned back.
>
> Perseverance brings good fortune.
>
> If one meets with no confidence, one should remain calm.
>
> No mistake. (Wilhelm/Baynes, 147)

Should Pastor Y wait until the opposition moved away and more support came, he would see that *yīn* would not stay long as *yáng* was approaching. Although there might be difficulty at the beginning, he should press on

---

46. Lynn, 153 and Legge.

47. Wilhelm/Baynes, 16–17.

48. The modern Chinese translation also renders it as *paíhuaí liúlián*, *Book of Changes*, Chinese-English Interlinear, 24.

49. See Wilhelm's comment on *Tuànzhuàn* on Gé, Wilhelm/Baynes, 202.

with perseverance.⁵⁰ In short, if he were able to persevere and to prepare for people's hearts to become ready and things to be more in place, he would have been able to achieve his plan to bring revolution and change to the church.

Now if Pastor Y waited and made no radical movement, how might he readjust his plan and reposition himself? Firstly, he should learn from H38 Kuí ䷥ (Opposition or Contrariety). Kuí symbolizes the principle of ministering diversity and opposite forces for one single goal. Kǒng Yǐndá (574–648 AD) interprets it that a person who is able to appreciate the principle of Kuí and thus able to make use of the diverse powers within one organization must be one whose *dé*, moral excellence, is great.⁵¹

Kuí is formed with fire Huǒlí ☲ (Fire) above and Zhéduì ☱ (Lake) below. It is judged that it is a situation of opposition. There are at least two reasons to say why it thus symbolizes. First, fire and water (lake) symbolize contrary nature, and second, according to *Shuōguà*, Lí symbolizes the second daughter while Duì the third daughter. That is why *Tuànzhuàn* says, "*èr nǚ tóng jū, qí zhì bù tóng xíng*," meaning two sisters living together whose wills move in different directions, are like fire and water.⁵²

From another perspective, the corresponding fifth *yin* and second *yáng* are interpreted as "contrary entities," but having the same task; likewise, male and female are contrary entities and "do not pursue the same path" (*bù tóng xíng*) but "share the same goal" (*qì zhì tōng*). Here *Tuànzhuàn* teaches that situations that contain contradictory factors in fact implore one to look beneath the surface for deeper similarity that the contradictory parties share.⁵³

---

50. *Tuànzhuàn* on Zhūn, see Wilhelm/Baynes, 16. According to ministerial studies, pastors who stay more than five years have more the chance to bring changes and implement new visions. I attended a workshop run by International Natural Church Development (International NCD) in Hong Kong where Rev. David Chiu, the director of Chinese NCD and also now the Principal of On Track Institute as well as the director of CoachNet International Chinese department, who emphasized this time frame. See http://stayontrack.com/OLI/index.php?option=com_frontpage&Itemid=1; http://www.ncdchinese.com/index.php; and http://www.ncd-international.org/public/;jsessionid=3E82A642466D53C3D158AD85C3693614. Halverstadt also identifies that "church systems or church professionals with habitual relationships of from four to nine years may have abilities to deal constructively with conflicting differences," see *Managing*, 66.

51. Kǒng Yǐndá, 368–69. For more discussion of Kuí, see chapter 6.

52. See also Kǒng, *Zhōuyì zhèngyì*, 367–68.

53. Wilhelm/Baynes, 147–48; also Lynn, 368.

A Double Vision Hermeneutic

Pastor Y had returned to his church following his seminary education hoping to bring about a reformation. I have alluded to H49 Gé (Revolution) to interpret his relatively aggressive action. I judged: "Should Pastor Y wait until the opposition moved away and more support come, he would see that *yīn* would not stay long as *yáng* was approaching." *Yīn* could symbolize negative powers or factors or people who were against the reformation, while *yáng* could symbolize positive factors or those who were supportive of his agenda. What was crucial was timing. Pastor Y had to wait for proper timing. That meant waiting until things became clearer, situations less chaotic, or emotions more settled. Why should one wait for the proper time? Behind such a question is the implied answer: everything has its time.[54]

We have said that Pastor Y came back to his church after seminary training. Whether or not others considered him an able pastor, he himself believed that he had something to offer. Was it because he did not occupy "the right position" that he did not succeed in his reformation? As a pastor—a symbolic figure of power or leadership—he surely did occupy the right position? But perhaps he had not, at that moment, occupied the kingly position, symbolized by the fifth line, for which he needed to wait.[55]

Thus it is "time" which determines. It takes time to acquire the right position; it takes proper timeliness to see the effect of one's action in line with one's position. Once again the emphasis is on "timeliness," although the issue is power. Position and time are inseparable counter-partners in *Yìzhuàn*. Although it is important to know whether one is in a right position, it is more important to know the right time for one's action.

If Pastor Y should have waited, the question remains: for how long should he have waited? Before he could move to the kingly position, there were other interim moves. Pastor Y's situation can be interpreted by the use of another hexagram. H16 Yù ䷏ (Contentment) shows a *yáng* line among five *yīn* lines, symbolizing Pastor Y striving alone to change the external

---

54. As much as "one's examination of safety and danger should be focused on the positions of the lines (*cún hū wèi*)," as Wáng Bì indicates, "a line indicates that one can occupy a position is due to its having achieved the right moment to be there (*dé qí shí yě*)." As change may imply changes in position, a notion indicating a change of time may also implicitly imply a change of position. I shall not dedicate a whole a section to "position" as I did to "changes" as I shall to "time". See Wáng Bì, *Zhoūyì luèlì*; Lynn, 30.

55. Convention understands one, three, and five as *yáng* positions, two, four, and six as *yīn* positions out of the six positions of a hexagram. Out of the six, positions two and five are kingly and sublime positions. To be in the right position, *yáng* should also be in a *yáng* position, i.e. the fifth line in this case, or to be in the middle line of either of the two trigrams. See Zhū, *Yìxué*, 1:49.

situation so that the power relation could be conducive to carrying out his plan for a revolution in the church. The one *yáng* in the hexagram is Pastor Y and he occupies neither the second nor the fifth line.

As Wang asserts, in all the hexagrams where one finds only one *yáng* or one *yīn* line, the "lone ranger" is the determinant line.[56] He further explains,

> When what is focused on is the single act *yáo*, all the other *yáo* (lines) are responding to it to be united with it; what matters is not whether the positions (any of the lines) are resonant with each other,[57] for within such a case all would be resounding (to the sole *yáng*).[58]

Wilhelm also indicates that the lone ranger symbolizes "the ruler of the hexagram," is "the commander of the army," interpreting the bottom trigram Kūn ☷ as the army.[59] While convention interprets the second and the fifth lines as the kings, here there is a fourth that still symbolizes a ruler. The secret lies in it being a lone ranger.

If the lone ranger denotes the first secret of the success Yù ䷏ conveys, the second probably lies in the phrase *shùn yǐ dòng* in *Tuànzhuàn*, which Lynn translates as "acts only out of compliance,"[60] or obedience. As is found in the correlation of Kūn ☷ (the bottom trigram) to Zhèn ☳ (the upper trigram), the former symbolizes the obedience it has to the movement and dynamism symbolized by the latter.

This results in ambiguity regarding the subject-object of the 'compliance'. Does this imply the people complying with "the ancient kings"? Or "the ancient kings" complying with the time? If both sense are combined, in the phrase, "[it is advantageous] to establish a chief and send the army into action",[61] it is understood that "the ancient kings" comply with correct timing to lead and take action when people are complying. Timing implies a principle of heaven and earth. As the four seasons follow the natural course of time, so will the establishment of chiefs and the sending of the army.

56. See Wáng, *Nèizhuàn*, Book II A, 124.
57. In H31 Xián, it says, "*Xián, gǎn yě. Roú shàng ér gāng xià, èr qì xiāng yìng yǐ xiāng yǔ.*"
58. Wáng, *Nèizhuàn*, 124. Translation mine, *passim*.
59. Wilhelm/Baynes, 467.
60. Wilhelm/Baynes translates as "Enthusiasm (*yù*) shows devotion to movement."
61. Here I follow Lynn, 235. Wilhelm/Baynes' translation of "*jiàn hoú*" as "to install helpers" sounds vague.

A Double Vision Hermeneutic

When I referred to H49 Gé ䷰, I said Pastor Y needed to wait, in order that his revolution could succeed. While H16 Yù ䷏ does not say "wait," it still teaches timeliness as the key to encouraging people to comply. The 'lone ranger' in Yù is on the fourth line. In waiting, the 'lone ranger' *yáng* follows the course of heaven and earth until the fifth arrives. The passage from line four to line five is a natural course, a natural development. One has to wait, and take no action. To wait is to respond in obedience to the right time.[62]

Nevertheless, there remain two questions regarding the fitness of this 'sole *yáng*' to draw others to follow him, and the choice of this image to convey this implication. It has been explained earlier that the second and fifth positions are good, kingly positions. In Yù ䷏, it is seen that the sole *yáng* is neither in the second nor the fifth lines, but *Tuànzhuàn* declares that it has the attribute of *gāng* (firm and strong) it moves with "firm will" (*zhì*).[63] A "firm will" is therefore the determinant element for the situation symbolized by Yù ䷏. Not only should a sage move "with devotion" as Heaven and Earth does,[64] but he should also move with a firm will, as represented by *gāng*, so that his punishments and penalties will be just, and his people will be obedient to him.[65]

Although one sees that the position is not favorable to the sage, this *yáng* being neither on the second nor the fifth line, with his inner strength demonstrating a "firm will," even a time that seems unfavorable (with five *yīns* in a hexagram) he can become great. This, however, never denies the ever-present undertone of 'concern for timeliness'. Therefore, while "looking for proper timing and best propensity of situations" (*shěn shí chá shì*) is most certainly in the scenario here, an emphasis on inner strength as firmness and rectitude is also highlighted.

The above shows that if a subject appropriates a hexagramic lens to decipher changes of situation and timing, *Yìzhuàn* also advises him to build moral character. The tension between a mere fathoming of *shì* and moral capacity is never out of sight. The balance between these two

---

62. Wáng, *Neìzhuàn*, 125.

63. In pre-Qín old Chinese, *zhì* appears as 之 instead of *shì* (literati) with *xīn* (heart) signifying the intention and aspiration of the heart-mind. "之" is the phoneme, see *Shuōwén jiězì*. Lynn translates *zhì* as "ambition," which I consider too extravagant. See Lynn, 235.

64. Wilhelm/Baynes, 467. Here Lynn renders it as "acts only out of compliance," 235.

65. See *Tuànzhuàn* of Yù.

emphases can also be found in other hexagrams, for examples, H17 ䷐ Suí and H28 ䷛ Dàguò.

In H17 ䷐ Suí,[66] Wilhelm comments that the image of the hexagram itself informs us that "the firm (*gāng*) comes and places itself under the yielding (*roú*),"[67] meaning the first *yáng* comes under the second and third *yīn*. The first *yáng* here indicates that it is new and just emerging, so it says "come" (*lai*). This *yáng* has the attribute of strength and vigour, as in *gāngjiàn*;[68] and being *gāng* also implies it is firm and strong, which reminds us of the very nature of H1 ䷀ Qián, i.e., *zhìjiàn*, the strongest.[69] Wáng comments on Shuōguà, "Qián is (the symbol of) strength (*qián, jiàn yiě*),"[70] arguing that this moral attribute is incorporated into its hexagram statement to imply that it is the *human moral being* who is "strong."[71] Kǒng Yǐnda follows Wáng Bì's commentary and interprets *gāng* (firmness and strength) as referring to the Zhèn (thunder) at the bottom and *roú* (softness or yielding) as Zhé (water) at the top.[72] As Kǒng interprets it, because the Zhèn (the lower) trigram (that has a new *yáng*) is active (*dòng*), the Zhé (the upper trigram) is pleased; and as the latter is pleased, all things (*wù*) join in to follow the Zhèn.[73]

---

66. As for "*suíshí zhī yì* (the meaning of following the time)," none of the English translations got it right. I refer here to Legge, Wilhelm, and Lynn. What we have are the translations of *suí zhī shíyì* (the meaning of the time of following [Suí]). In Chinese *suí* and *shí* are put together forming a phrase which means "to follow the time," which means to keep in pace with timeliness, for such is the time everyone would follow a king. Kǒng explains *suíshí* as "what Suí is executing (*suí zhī shuǒ shī*) depends on the time" and "to talk about following the time for execution is to talk about securing the right time." See Kǒng, *Zhoūyì zhèngyì*, 209.

67. Wilhelm/Baynes, 472.

68. *Wényán*, Legge, 415

69. *Xici* II:12

70. This appears in *Shuōguà* section 7 as "Qian, strong," as in Wilhelm/Baynes, 275 or "Qian means strength and dynamism," as in Lynn, 122. Jiàn 健 is also called "Jiàn 鍵," the "key; linchpin" as it appears in Mawangdui text, see Shaughnessy, 39, 287.

71. Wáng, *Wàizhuàn*, 463; see also Wáng, *Nèizhuàn*, 9. Emphasis mine.

72. Kǒng, *Zhèngyì*, 208.

73. Thus it says, "By its action, delight occurs. This is Sui [Following]" (*dòng ér yuè, suí*)." See Lynn, 241. See *Xùguà* based on Wilhelm/Baynes is who says that the attribute of trigram Duì is "gladness" and that of Zhèn is "movement," see Wilhelm/Baynes, 71. Of course, Kǒng does not show how and neither does one know how he deduces from Zhé (☵ water) that which is now following Zhèn (Thunder or Quake) into saying all things (*wù*) would thus also follow Zhèn. Probably this is just one example of how through intuitive association traditional Chinese *Yìzhuàn* interpreters make similar interpretations.

A Double Vision Hermeneutic

If all things are drawn to follow the active *yáng*, in this way, "[B]y achieving great prevalence and through the practice of constancy, one stays free of blame (*dàhēng zhēn wú jiù*)."[74] Here *zhēn* is translated into English according to its moral sense: "constancy."[75] *Xiǎoxiàngzhuàn* states that there will be good fortune for one who follows what is *upright* ("*cóngzhèng jí*").[76]

Zhèn thus symbolizes a king (Thunder-Shock) who possesses the virtue of most *gāng* and *zhèng* (firm and upright) and holds the most sublime position. With humility he serves the people who are the *roú* (soft and yielding) in the upper trigram: Zhéduì ☱ (Lake-The Joyous). In return, the latter comes to serve the king joyously.[77] Therefore, the key phenomenon here is *tiān xià suíshí* (all under heaven follow the time). While the situation is never out of sight, the emphasis is on one's persistence in practicing a firm and upright attitude.

Other hexagrams have similar emphases on the concept of *zhēn* and *zhèng*, symbolizing uprightness. For example, *Tuànzhuàn* of H19 ䷒ Lín comments "*dàhēng yǐ zhèng*" (There is great progress and success, along with firm correctness)[78] or in H20 ䷓ Guān, *zhōngzhèng yǐ guān tiānxià*(Central and correct, he is something for the world to view)[79] where "the central and correct/upright" (*zhōngzhèng*) echo with "upright" and "constant" (*zhèng* and *zhēn*).[80] Therefore, it follows that what is correct, firm and upright is ultimately also auspicious (*zhèng jí*).[81]

---

74. Lynn, 241-42. For *zhēn*, Legge renders it as "firm correctness." Cf. The hexagram statement, *yuán hēng lì zhēn*, as found in the Qián statement.

75. The term "augury" is used by Rutt. Although *zhēn* in *Yìjīng* originally means augury or to divine, in its *zhuàn* (commentaries) e.g., *Wényán*, *zhēn* means *zhèng* 正 (upright or correct) or *zhōngzhèng* (central, undeflected and correct). Cf Lynn, 130; *Wényán*, 415. See also *Yǔléi*, Book 68, 1705–6.

76. Legge, 289. See also Kǒng, *Zhèngyì*, 211, of its line statement of the first *yáng*.

77. Cf. Huáng, *Zhoūyì dúběn*, 224–25.

78. English from Legge, cf. Lynn's who renders it as "Great prevalence is achieved through rectitude."

79. Wilhelm/Baynes, 486. Wáng annotates that *guān* means to show oneself and one's disposition for people to look upon, see *Nèizhuàn*, 146.

80. Also see H44 Goù discussed in the next subsection.

81. This correlates with the hexagram statement which says, "*yùan hēng, lì zhēn, wú jiū*" as Kǒng Yǐndá has commented *lìzhēn* here, saying : "*lì zhēn zhě, xiāng suí zhī tǐ, xū lì zaì dé zhèng. Suí´ér bù zhèng, zhé xié pì zhī daò, xū lì zhēn yě*," which can be paraphrased as "that which is advantageous and correct (*zhēn*) and firm is the object that one follows; the key is for getting the advantage lies in being upright (*zhèng*). To follow but yet not being upright is the way of treacherous; it is more advantageous (profitable) to follow what is correct and firm." Further evidence can be gathered from the line

Hence, for Pastor Y, if the time was not right for him to carry out any revolutionary action as symbolized by H49 Gé ䷰, and further if being a 'lone ranger' was too challenging, he could still learn from H17 Suí ䷐. With correct motivation, he could act vibrantly and enthusiastically (☳), not focusing only on his plan but on his people. With sufficient time, encouraged and touched (☱) by his sincere service, church members would join him.

However, sometimes waiting demands a total withdrawal. Withdrawal is not a passive waiting, and does not mean giving up. The *Xiàngzhuàn* of H28 Dàguò ䷛ teaches: "the noble man (*jūnzǐ*) is self-reliant and without fear, and if he has to withdraw (*dùn*) from the world, he does not feel dispirited (*wú mēn*)."[82]

The image of H28 ䷛ Dàguà itself is interpreted as a flooded house (symbolized with *dòng*, ridgepole),[83] which implies that the times (and circumstance) are bad or "chaotic."[84] The beginning (*běn*) and the ending (*mò*), i.e., the first and the last lines are both weak (*yīn*) compared to the middle which is over-strong (four *yáng* lines), symbolizing unfavorable circumstance on the outside.[85] In such a situation, against all odds, a *jūnzǐ* can persevere and prevail.[86] The sense of withdrawal is based upon the emphatic implication of an unfavorable situation for which a *jūnzǐ* can do nothing except sustain his own *dé* to wait (in retreat) for the time when *dào* would again prevail.[87]

---

statement of Suí itself where it says *zhēn jí* (it is auspicious to be firm and correct) with the *Xiaǒxiàng* commentary says *chóng zhèng jí* (to follow what is correct is auspicious). The translation taken from Legge, where *zhēn* and *zhèng* is but by one word difference: "firm." The divinational aspect of *zhēn* cannot be read from the English translation.

82. *Dàxiàngzhuàn*, my translation.

83. The word "ridgepole" borrowed from Lynn, 311.

84. Kǒng Yǐndá describes it as "*luànshì*" (a world in chaotic time), see Kǒng, *Zhèngyì* 289.

85. Chén, *Zhoūyì*, 261.

86. *Zhōngyōng*, 11 can echo this, saying, "There are superior men (*jūnzǐ*) who are in accord with the Mean, retire (*dùn*) from the world and are unknown to their age, but do not regret it (*bù hueǐ*)," Chan, *Source*, 100. This statement has almost the exact wording of the *Wényán* statement cited above. Confucius also says, "When Way prevails in the land, be bold in speech and bold in action. When the Way does not prevail, be bold in action but conciliatory in speech" (*Lúnyǔ* 14:4), see Waley, *The Analects*, 180.

87. Lǚ Shaògāng comments that it is commendable to have courage to advance, but nonetheless sometimes it is necessary to withdraw and bear with the times loneliness, isolation, and desertion, a strength of character that tests one's resilience, see Lǚ, *Zhoūyì chánweī*, 211.

A Double Vision Hermeneutic

The idea of withdrawal is consistent with *Lúnyǔ*, where Confucius says, "When the Way prevails under Heaven, then show yourself; when it does not prevail, then hide."[88] He commented on an officer called Qū Bóyù who being a true *jūnzǐ* knew when to withdraw.[89] However, the idea of withdrawal is more than simply knowing-how-and-when to retreat and advance; it is a way of life that teaches one to transcend time. It is the inner *dé* which enables one to be composed. In fact, in *Wényán* of Qián, where the idea of withdrawal is first mentioned, it is stated that,

> The submerged dragon does not take any action. What does this mean? The Master said: There he is who has the *dé* of the dragon, yet lying hid. He does not change because of the world; nor does he rely on fame to make success. If he needs to withdraw from the world, he does not feel dispirited; if he does not see rightness being practised, he does not feel dispirited. He takes action when things are conducive, but retires if things worry him.[90] He, indeed, does not project himself.[91] This is "the submerged dragon"[92]

Thus, the idea of withdrawal as a *dé* is pervasive; and is often based on one's judgment of time. Nevertheless, underlying such emphases, i.e. moral power and judging proper timing, the former carries more weigh than the latter. The withdrawal (always in accordance with time) being considered as *de*, moral power, is the most intriguing concept to wrestle here. While he may withdraw, retire, or retreat and take no action when the external circumstances are not ideal, what defines him is not success or fame but his *dé*.

Applying the above understanding of Dàguò, Pastor Y should have reconsidered his resignation. Perhaps a temporarily withdrawal would

---

88. *Lúnyǔ* 8:13, see Waley, *The Analects*, 135.

89. *Lúnyǔ* 15:6.

90. "*Bá*" in "*bù kě bá*" should be understood as in "*chū yú qí lèi, bá hū qí cuì*" in *Mèngzǐ* II:A or "*tǐng bá*", which means standing out. See Zhāng and Chén, *Gǔdài hànyǔ zìdiǎn*, 11.

91. This is my own translation based on Legge's, 409–10. I retain the transliterated form "*dé*" instead of translating it as "virtue." Legge misses the meaning of *bá* as I noted, his translation "he is not to be torn from his root (in himself)" is thus unacceptable. Rutt's translation with "unshaken" basically follow Legge's.

92. The problem with translation for *lè zhé xíng zhī* and *yōu zhé wéi zhī* is big. For Legge, *lè* is "rejoicing"; for Wilhelm, it is "lucky"; for Rutt, "happiness"; for Lynn, "takes delight (in the world)." For Legge, *yōu* is "sorrowing"; for Wilhelm, "unlucky"; for Rutt, "sadness"; for Lynn, i "finds (the world) distresses him." See Wilhelm, 379; Rutt, 435; Lynn, 132.

have been wise. Resignation denoted a complete withdrawal and a relinquishment of any further action. A temporary withdrawal would have allowed him enough time to cultivate moral influence, *dé*, within the church. With enough time, he could have secured and deepened the trust of those who were initially attracted to his plan and ideas. Perhaps, greater self confidence would have enabled him to see the incoming pastor not as a threat but a future colleague. With his supporters plus the new pastor, he could possibly have amassed the requisite number of positive factors to create a Dàguò situation, i.e., to find sufficient positive forces, *yáng* power, shown as the middle four *yáng* in the hexagram, ䷛. By this (simple) expedient, obstacles would become external negative factors as illustrated by the two *yīn* found in Dàguò.

Timeliness determines whether something is auspicious or not; time, however, is changing, as is situation. Therefore, there is neither an absolutely auspicious or inauspicious time, since a time which is auspicious now could be inauspicious later, and vice versa.[93] As Xúnzǐ's dictum states, "An expert in *Yì* (the changes) shall not seek recourse to divination (*shàn wéi yì zhě bù zhàn*)."[94] One who truly understands the way of Yì knows the Daò. Thus, the principle on which a *jūnzǐ* bases on his judgment whether or not to act is neither an external circumstance nor time, but the Daò, that which is firm, correct, and upright.

As was argued in chapter 3, Xúnzǐ placed a higher emphasis on moral excellence than his predecessors who deliberated the meaning of *shì*. As one who has appropriated Xúnzǐ's understanding of *shì* alongside his counter argument for moral excellence, I now also view *shì* in this manner. As I ponder over Pastor Y's situation, I see a power struggle scenario but I am also aware of the need for him to have paid more attention to cultivating moral character rather than focusing on *shì*. In other words, I am reading and applying not only the traditional texts into a current scenario, but have also appropriated Xúnzǐ's rhetorical argument against Hán Fēzīhǐ in his expositions of *shì*.

As has been elaborated on in the introduction, there were intertextuality between Xúnzǐ and Hán Fēīzhǐ's arguments of *shì*. However, *shì* as it appears in one and the other text as an intertext is not purely an intertext per se, but appears to be embodied in their rhetoric to serve their own argument. By interpreting Xúnzǐ, I not only appropriate his text but also

---

93. For the above, see Lǚ, *Zhoūyì chánwēi*, 179–81 for his elaboration. This idea already appeared in Wáng Bì, see *Zhoūyì luèlì*, in Lynn, 29.

94. Xúnzǐ, "Dàlué piān," see *Xúnzǐ dúběn*, 452.

his rhetoric. Hence, through intersubjective reading, I also perform an interpretation which serves my own rhetoric. Thus, as is shown in Xúnzǐ-Hán Fēizhǐ, hence Confucian-Legalist, debates in the pre-Qín period, on whether the emphasis should be on moral excellence or on *shì*; in contemporary scenarios where power struggles are at play and power relations considered, similar considerations emerge as I appropriate Xúnzǐ's rhetoric.

To sum up, there is paradoxically almost an equal emphasis on grasping proper time and disregarding of the notion of proper time, for there is no absolute proper time. To disregard it is to heighten the importance of cultivating moral excellence or *dé*. However, *Yìzhuàn* has no intention of throwing out the whole precept of grasping proper timing. The following will show how *Yìzhuàn* unified these two threads into one integrated philosophy.

3. Acquiring a Sage-like Wisdom: Plumbing the Utmost Profundity and Investigating the Pivotal

As was mentioned earlier, to know the proper timing is to know the patterns in nature and the timing of Heaven. As a popular Chinese proverb states, "*tiān jī bù kě xiè lòu* (the concealed knowledge of heaven should not be disclosed)." Thus, there is a belief that although Heaven does not speak, its principles are however readily manifested in the cosmos.[95] As Confucius himself said, "Does Heaven say anything? The four seasons run their course and all things are produced. Does Heaven say anything?"[96] Thus, man can fathom the deep and study the secret knowledge of the way of heaven if he tries hard enough.[97]

Yìzhuàn shows that the sages were able to fathom the Way of Heaven. There are several passages in *Xìcí*, which are of significant in knowing what 'fathoming the heaven' implies. The author of *Xìcí*, citing the Master states, "The *Changes* (*Yì*) deals with the way things start up and how matters reach completion and represents the *Daò* that envelops the entire world."[98]

---

95. The "cosmos" I use is different from κόσμος, a New Testament term which I will discuss later. I will use κόσμος particularly when I refer to its New Testament usage.
96. *Lúnyǔ* 17:19, see Chan, *Source*, 47.
97. *Xìcí* I:10.
98. *Xìcí* I:11, see Lynn, 63.

Interpreting Text A1

Having mastered the way of Yì, the sages would be able "to penetrate the aspirations (*zhì*) of all the people in the world, to settle the great affairs of the world, and to resolve all doubtful matters in the word."[99] How does *Yì* do that?

> It is by means of the *Changes* that the sages plumb the utmost profundity and "investigate the pivotal." It is profundity alone that thus allows one to penetrate the aspirations of all the people in the world; it is a grasp of "pivotal" alone that thus allows one to accomplish the great affairs of the world; and it is the numinous alone that thus allows one to make quick progress without hurrying to reach goals without forcing one's way.[100]

The three keys to the Daò are: "profundity," "pivot" and "the numinous." Let us first focus on "the numinous."

Lynn has here translated the Chinese word "*shén*", as "numinous." Legge however translates it as "spirit-like,"[101] while Wilhelm as "divine."[102] The meaning conveyed is of being untraceable and mysterious. It describes a magical-like power of coming and going without being known. The idiom "*shèn lóng jiàn shoŭ bú jiàn weĭ* (one might have a chance catching a glimpse of the coming [literally the head] of a *shén*-dragon, but can never possibly see its going [literally its tail])," exactly describes such luminous and divine character. It is probably taken from the description of the dragon in H1 Qián.

Adler summarizes from *Xìcí* XI, saying that the milfoil or yarrow stalks are "*shén* (spiritual/psychic) things"[103] through which the *Yì* responds "like an echo"[104] to the charge put by the diviner. In the relationship between divination (the milfoil stalks) and "*shén*" lies the implication that the diviner will be like the sages, who discern the incipience and change of things.

---

99. *Xìcí* I:11, see Lynn 64.

100. *Xìcí* I:10, the translation is Lynn's except "to investigate the pivotal" and "pivotal." I accept Puett's explanation of that a "[p]ivot is the point of the alteration of yin and yang." See Lynn, 63 and Puett, *To Become a God*, 180, and 89–90. Lynn contends that "incipience" *jī* connotes the "beginning" of a subtle change, see *Xìcí* II:5, Lynn, 84.

101. Legge, 370.

102. Wilhelm/Baynes, 316.

103. *Xìcí* I:11. For Adler, see Joseph A. Adler, "Chu Hsi and Divination," in Peter Bol et al., *Sung Dynasty Uses*, 235. Notice that Adler's interpretation should be understood from his analysis of Zhū Xī's (Chu Hsi) interpretation of *Yì*.

104. *Xìcí* I:10:2, 4.

Xìcí I:10 expands on this by suggesting that sages are experts in four different manifestations of *dào*: the use of words, understanding the changes of all things, capturing the images of myriad things, and divination. They can be experts in one, more than one, or indeed all four of these. Therefore, *Xìcí* acclaims, "[B]y their spirit-like ability they knew (the character of) coming events, and their wisdom had stored up (all experiences of) the past."[105]

As *Yìjīng* was originally born out of divination, only later were philosophies integrated into it. Thus among the four ways the sages were expert, there is no surprise that one was divination. Thus, as *Xìcí* teaches: "to penetrate through resonance" (*gǎntōng*), there is no need to exclude the possibility that it could really have been the gods with whom the ancients were communicating or consulting.

This leads to the notion of "the pivotal". Descriptions are applied to the *jūnzǐ* who, like the sages, must be a person who knows the incipiences of things. As stated in *Xìcí* I:10:

> To understand incipience [*jī*] (the pivot), is this not a matter of the numinous! The noble man is not fawning toward what is above and is not contemptuous of what is below. Is this not to understand incipience! As for incipience itself, it is the infinitesimally small beginning of action, the point at which the precognition of good fortune can occur. The noble man acts upon something as soon as he becomes aware of its incipience and does not wait for the day to run its course.[106]

> The noble man grasps the infinitesimally small and what is manifestly obvious. He understands the soft as well as the hard. So the myriad folk look to him.[107]

Puett contends that the "[p]ivot is the point of the alteration of *yin* and *yang*."[108] If Lynn is followed, to talk about "incipience" is to talk about the beginning, the very first moment of the whole process of things which end in their completion; but if we follow Puett, *jī* is the pivot of *yīn-yáng* alteration, meaning that every moment is a point of beginning and of

---

105. *Xìcí* I:11, see Legge, 372. Lynn's translation is misleading, which states, "[B]y virtue of its numinous power, it lets one know what is going to come, and by virtue of its wisdom, it becomes a repository of what has happened." The "it" and "its" are the results of his misreading. See Lynn, 64.

106. *Xìcí* II:5, see Lynn, 84.

107. *Xìcí* II:5, see Lynn, 85.

108. Puett, *To Become a God*, 190.

ending. Every *yīn* or *yáng* can grow from young to old or from old back to young, as symbolized in the Tàijí diagram. Thus, there are small changes in every moment of every process; the *jūnzǐ* therefore pays attention to all infinitesimal and obvious changes.

How should an experience of *rùshén*, entering into the luminous, be interpreted? It is believed that through his "*rùshén*," a *jūnzǐ*, as Wáng Bì (226–249 AD)[109] interprets it, "returns to the root of things," where "he will find quiescence" and "discover all the world's principles available to him."[110] This is sometimes achieved by fasting and meditation to purify the heart, so that in recluse the knowledge revealed through the *Yì* may be penetrated.[111]

A mind focusing on such an exercise is a mind in contemplation. In contemplation, one's mind is tranquil and differentiating, able to distill different powers that are working to create their effects. To return to the roots thus implies a return to what nature already shows, and to follow the pattern of coming and going according to its own timing.[112] By centering his mind, a *jūnzǐ* may gain confidence in repose, and thus not "overreach" or "exceed the proper limits (*kàng*)."[113] He can then capture "the soft" and "the hard", meaning the *yīn* (power) and the *yáng* (power). While there are *yīn* and *yáng* powers, being firm, a *jūnzǐ* need not fall sway to their influence but listen to the inner voice. Such a steadiness of mind enables him to respond to the externals, be it changes of power position, or the process and timing of things emerging and coming to pass.

As all changes start with a pivotal alteration, an incipient movement, the crucial element at that particular moment, is the exact timing. This helps us relate *jī*, the pivot of *yīn-yáng* (power) alteration, to our interpretation of *shì*. In the discussion of *shì* in chapter 3, there is a reference to the *Sūnzǐ* passage:

> The raging torrent can by its gushes float the boulders along its course; this is due to its *shì*; by one shot a swooping falcon breaks the back of its prey; this is due to its precision. Therefore, a good warrior makes good use of a risky *shì* (circumstance) and a blinking moment (*jié*); such a *shì* is liken to the bending

---

109. Wáng is one of the earliest and most prominent commentators of *Yìjīng*, who lived about two hundred years later than Paul.
110. Lynn, 82.
111. *Xìcí* I:11.
112. *Xìcí* I:11.
113. H1 Qían top *yáng*, *Wényán*.

crossbow, with such a timing (*jié*) in the releasing of the trigger (*shì rú zhāng nǔ, jié rú jī fā*).[114]

While *shì* as found in the raging torrent is more about power and force, the features are about force/power and timing. A swooping, an attack in a blinking moment, and a releasing of a trigger all take an exact timing into account. By appropriating a *Yìjīng* hexagramic lens, the timing in a sequence of at least six moments, as reflected in the six lines of a hexagram, can be seen. Moreover, each individual line (moment) is considered a potent for change as a *yīn* that can be changed to *yáng*, or vice versa.

Instead of making use of *shì* as Hán Fēihǐ suggests,[115] this interpretation focuses on a sensitivity to *shì* as a constellation of correlative powers (as within a hexagram). The demonstration of such sensitivity reflects an ability to see power relations within a structure, for example a church, as a dynamic one. There are different angles of interpretation of an event and different approaches to viewing how things are done. In accordance with the nature of such sensitivity time is understood as a series of moments. As one sees time with this mindset, the high regard for timeliness becomes a characteristic by which one's patience will be cultivated. Thus, the ability to comprehend the best *shì* and best timing is accompanied by an emphasis on moral character, as in Xúnzǐ who emphasizes not a domination by taking advantage provided by *shì*,[116] but ruling through moral excellence.

As has been shown thus far, the dynamic interpretation of power structure and relation through the lens of *shì* from the *Yìjīng* hexagramic perspective seems to prove effective. Used wisely, it helps a person to steer his life with bliss and without remorse. As the Master (Confucius) has counselled, a person should not be too settled, thinking his position is secure, lest he gets into danger. Neither should he think his continuance is always protected, lest he will be ruined, nor his order maintained, lest disorders arise. This is wisdom for living good life.

Having said this, there is a potential to become extreme as pointed out by Wáng Bì. According to him, the possibility of one's enslavement is due to one's preoccupation with securing one's position. Referring to the idea of *rùshén* in *Xìcí* II:5 which has earlier been referred to, he made the following comment regarding such a man:

---

114. "Bīngshì," *Sūnzǐ*, chapter 5.

115. See chapter 3.

116. Xúnzǐ, chapter 16: "Jiāngguó piān" (On Strengthening the State), see Knoblock, *Xunzi*, 241, 343 n. 26.

Interpreting Text A1

if he enslaves (*yì*) his capacity for thought and deliberation just so he can seek ways to put things to use and if he disregards the need to make his person secure just so he can sacrifice himself to achievement and fine reputation, then the more the spurious arises, the more principles will be lost, and the finer his reputations grows, the more obvious his entanglements (*lèi*) will become.[117]

Thus nothing that originates out of one's obsession for "achievement and fine reputation" should become one's motivation for action and speech, or a person will be enslaved (*yì*) by the thing which has become his master.

The interpretation of the idea of *rùshén* (luminous) and *zhījī* (investigating the pivotal), or *zhījī yòngshén* (to know what is the pivotal by entering into the luminous state) will prove meaningful when we come to chapter 7 where Corinthian Christians' obsession with esoteric and spiritual wisdom and knowledge are discussed.

The implication of this enslavement will be clearer when enslavement is understood from the perspective of Paul. Walter Wink, whose trilogy on powers which we shall discuss in the following chapter, has made a statement in his exposition of New Testament's, especially Paul's treatment of enslavement: "We become slaves of the elements by granting them an ultimacy they do not possess."[118] While Paul's treatment of "principalities and powers" vis-a-vis the whole κόσμος and αἰῶνος will be prominent in later chapters, this chapter was interpreted with all these in view.

4. Conclusion

With the above integrative interpretation of *Yìjīng* hexagramic system and *shì*, this chapter has demonstrated the intersubjective relationship of Texts A1 and A2. My interpretation of Pastor Y's situation reveals how such intersubjective understanding of Pastor Y's situation has worked out in the interpreting subject, myself, who has appropriated both texts into my very being.

While the intersubjective relationship between *Yìzhuàn* and Pauline texts has not been the main concern of this chapter. As are shown in some pointers and brief references to Pauline texts, the simultaneity is at play in the manner of what has been earlier referred to as "double awareness": focal and subsidiary awareness. While in this chapter I am *focusing* on the

117. For Wáng Bì, see Lynn, 82.
118. Wink, *Unmasking*, 134.

interpretation of *shì*, my awareness of the Pauline perspective, while acting as a *subsidiary*, has been ever-present in the background. As referred to in chapter 2, Polanyi says, "[w]hen focusing on a whole, we are subsidiarily aware of its parts, while there is no difference in the intensity of the two kinds of awareness."[119] Both Text A and Text B are parts of the whole and both are important; whereas Text A is the current focus, it will later be the subsidiarily awareness. Various parts are alternately focused on, while the whole is the undercurrent, being "managed" by the subsidiary awareness. In the final chapter of the thesis, however, the whole will be the focus. In the following two chapters, the focal awareness will be the fusion of Texts B1 and B2 as it appears first in the *notion of principalities and powers* (B1) and then through *Galatians and 1 & 2 Corinthians* (B2) where concrete manifestation of B1 can be examined. The implication and significance of the *Yìzhuàn* perspective will become prominent after B1 and B2 are interpreted.

---

119. Polanyi, *Personal Knowledge*, 57.

5

Text B1: Principalities and Powers: A Survey on Contemporary Discourse

In the previous two chapters, I have shown the intersubjectivity between Texts A1 and A2. On the one hand, they are intersubjectively related because they have both been appropriated by me, the interpreting subject; on the other, although appropriated by me they are self-subsistent. Here there are two layers of intersubjective relationship, one between the texts: Text A1 in or through Text A2 and vice versa, and the other between the texts and me. The texts and the meanings produced in the intersubjective interpretation help make sense of my initial experience of *shì* which was designated as Text 0 in chapter 2. As the interpreting subject, I am constantly and simultaneously holding two texts, two subjects (the texts and me), the texts embodied in me and the seminal experience of my double awareness.

The purpose of this and the following two chapters is to further analyze multilayered intersubjective relationships, as undertaken in the above example focusing on Texts B1 and B2. I have designated Text B1 as the Pauline notion of "principalities and powers." My experience and awareness of dominating principalities and powers in me has been expounded in the introduction: when I experienced the *shì*, I also experienced the power of sin dominating me. I shall attempt to interpret, in more detail, the power of sin as an aspect of "principalities and powers" in the next chapter.

In this chapter, I attempt to recapitulate the attention paid to this Pauline notion in recent scholarship. In contrast to *shì* where more attention was given to its root in antiquity, the Pauline notion in this chapter will be considered the context of its contemporary understanding. *Shì* came to me as the cultural-linguistic tradition in which I am rooted. However, the Pauline notion first came to me as part of my own subjective experience through the study of Pauline texts in personal devotion and in church. Where I have been introduced to insights on Paul and his idea of power, my relationship to these discourses is, using the Pauline metaphor of olive tree in Romans 11:17, of having lopped off the discourse from its Western "tree" and "grafted" it onto my Chinese "tree." Without reference to the long line of its development and influence in the Western tradition, I was led to it in its modern discourse. This exemplifies my historical limitation as a "historically effected consciousness" as Gadamer would put it. My purpose here is to show that although the Pauline notion originally entered into my awareness, as a traditionary text, it exists in its own history of effect independent of me. However, given the focus of this thesis, the discourse shown below will only occupy the attention of my subsidiary awareness as compared to the focal awareness of my initial experience of Paul's notion of principalities and powers, which led me to further readings of Pauline texts.

1. Earlier Treatment of Pauline Principalities and Powers

From the 1950s to the 1970s, before the sociological approach came to afore, New Testament ideas of power had taken the Pauline notion of "principalities and powers" into serious consideration.[1] For example, George Bradford Caird and Hendrik Berkhof paid particular attention to the Pauline texts while John Yoder, while not leaving the Pauline texts untouched, concentrated more on the Gospels.

In his study, *Principalities and Powers*, G. B. Caird has covered many key passages related to the Pauline notion of power.[2] As he points out, "[t]he idea of sinister world powers and their subjugation by Christ is built into the very fabric of Paul's thought, and some mention of them is found in every epistle except Philemon."[3] He argues that Paul was deeply "imbued

---

1. Earlier attempts in this direction include Berkhof, *Christ and the Powers*; Caird, *Principalities and Powers*; Yoder, *The Politics of Jesus*. Besides these, other important studies are Schlier, *Principalities and Powers in the New Testament*; Hengel, *Christ and Power* ; idem, *The Zealots*; idem, *Victory Over Violence*. Hengel and Yoder's work put more emphasis on Jesus and the gospels, which are not our concern here.

2. For examples, Rom 8:1–5; 1 Cor 2:6–8; Phil 2:10f.; Col 1:16, 20; Eph 3:30.

3. Caird, *Principalities and Powers*, vii.

with the Jewish idea of angelic powers behind the pagan order."[4] He summarizes the law, sin, and death in Romans as "a trio of evil forces," which should be "reckoned among the principalities and powers."[5] He makes the point, which later also appears in Wink's works, that the law although "a divine institution," is a derivative authority parallel to any other delegated authority from God, and "when men tried to make its authority absolute they made it demonic."[6] He states strongly that, "The demonic forces of legalism, then, both Jewish and Gentile, can be called 'principalities and powers' or 'elemental spirits of the world.'"[7] Thus the law is closely linked to demonic forces when it is made ultimate, and to "the god of this age" (2 Cor 4:4).[8] These motifs are hard to neglect as one enters Pauline texts.

Caird's work is seminal at least in terms of reintroducing Paul to modern attention in the 1950s. Although he covered many key ideas and vocabulary besides those mentioned above, for example the fall, to unmask and restore the powers, the powers' neutral nature, and the neutralization of the powers, these had already appeared in Berkhof's work several years earlier.[9]

Hendrik Berkhof in his *Christ and the Powers*, originally written in Dutch and published in 1953,[10] claims that, "In the last century little attention was devoted to this part of Paul's faith and thought."[11] Reinhold Niebuhr's *Moral Man and Immoral Society* has brought attention to the villainous nature of power, but is not a study which focuses on Paul.[12]

Berkhof sets the basic scope to which others more or less comply. He starts from a word study of *stoicheia* which he translates as the "world powers."[13] He addressed the lack of study of power in the New Testament, saying, "It is understandable but regrettable that the problem of the Powers was thus one-sidedly bound up with the political issue, which threatened

---

4. He especially refers to 1 Cor 2:6–8; 6:3; 11:10f.
5. Caird, *Principalities and Powers*, 44.
6. Caird, *Principalities and Powers*, 24, cf. 49.
7. Caird, *Principalities and Powers*, 51.
8. Caird, *Principalities and Powers*, 51.
9. Cf. Berkhof, *Powers*, passim.
10. In this regard, it is earlier than Caird's study.
11. Berkhof, *Powers*, 9.
12. See Niebuhr's *Moral Man and Immoral Society*. Nevertheless, *Moral Man* and other books of him should not be neglected if the study is focusing on political and public theology.
13. Berkhof, *Powers*, 15–16, also 17–18.

to lead the Biblical-theological investigation into an impasse."[14] He is not satisfied with limiting 'powers' in the New Testament to simply referring to "angels." He argues, "Whether they be conceived as persons or as impersonal structures of life and society, they form a category of their own."[15] He surveys post-Nazi theological literature on some key Pauline passages (e.g., Rom 8:38f.; 1 Cor 2:8, 15:24–26; Eph 1:20f.; 2:1f.; 3:10; 6:12; Col 1:16; 2:15) and concludes that Paul's understanding of "the relationship between the Powers and the world" should "be far broader" than talking about angelic powers.[16] In his study, the visible dimension of powers is addressed as "many earthly realities, through which the Powers manifest themselves."[17]

John Howard Yoder's discussion of power is found in his masterpiece, *The Politics of Jesus*, which aroused discussion in the area of theology and ethics. The book builds mainly upon Hendrik Berkhof, G. B. Caird and others.[18] Yoder in the chapter "Christ and Power" in *The Politics of Jesus* defines power as a network of people and agencies and as structure.[19] Similarly, the word power for him may encompass a larger semantic multivalent complexity, or "ambiguity."[20]

Referring to New Testament multivalent characteristics of power, he argues, "Something of the same stimulating confusion is present in the thought of the apostle Paul as he applies some of the same thought patterns to different challenges in different contexts."[21] On the one hand, he is aware of Paul's use of "principalities and powers" and "thrones and dominions," and thus argues Paul was also "using language of political color." On the other he points out Paul's use of "cosmological language like 'angels and archangels,' 'elements,' 'heights and depths'" with respect to power. Sometimes, for him the language referring to power "can be religious: 'law,' 'knowledge.'" He therefore concludes, in Paul "sometimes the reader perceives a parallelism in all these concepts, sometimes not."[22] Later in his

---

14. Berkhof, *Powers*, 58 n. 3.

15. Berkhof, *Powers*, 19.

16. Berkhof, *Powers*, 58 n. 3.

17. Berkhof, *Powers*, 58 n. 5.

18. Yoder, *The Politics of Jesus*, 137, 140, and footnote 5 and especially from 146–49 where more than two thirds are quotations at length from Berkhof.

19. Yoder, *The Politics*, 137–38, 143.

20. Yoder, *The Politics*, 136–38.

21. Yoder, *Politics*, 137.

22. Relying on Berkhof, Yoder points this out but reserves judgment as to whether Paul used these terms with exact precision as Berkhof suggests. What he wants to

revision, he became more convinced of this view, saying, "The Pauline perspective is far more clear about the intrinsic complexities of institutional and psycho-dynamic structures."[23] As we shall see below, Wink talks about the dual aspect of power which resembles what is described here.

However, Yoder's contribution to the discourse on power probably lies more in establishing a nuanced New Testament ethic of non-violent pacifism, challenging his readers to take Jesus' non-violence approach seriously, yet without neglecting the reality of the evil aspect of power. By "accepting powerlessness" as Jesus did, Yoder believes he had found the foundation for "Christian pacifism"[24] as the basis of political theology or ethics. Yoder calls Christians to be Jesus Christ's disciples by following the way of their Lord who rejects "the crown" but accepts "the cross,"[25] and renounces "the power offered to him by the tempter and by the Zealots."[26]

2. THE SOCIOLOGICAL TURN OF PAULINE STUDIES

The last thirty years have witnessed a sociological turn in New Testament studies. Stephen Sykes contends that the New Testament text and its first century ecclesiastical context, which reflect the exercise of power within the church and how church leaders interact within such a power system, can yield many insights for the study of power. Thus, the church is seen as an organization, a study of which, as a sociological phenomenon, will thus offer insights for one's study of power.[27] Sykes' work provides a concise review of the study of power and serves as a guidance to it's sociological turn, including that which is found in Pauline studies. My intention, in relation to this thesis, is to thus highlight recent Pauline studies which focus on power.

In terms of Pauline studies on power, among the first are Bengt Holmberg's *Paul and Power* and Wayne Meeks' *The First Urban Christians*.[28]

---

argue is that, "[t]o use several terms with roughly synonymous meaning or to use one term with different meanings and different contexts is not necessarily a sign of unclear thinking." See Yoder, *Politics*, 137.

23. Yoder, *Politics*, 161 in one of the epilogues added to the 2nd edition of his book.

24. Yoder, *Politics*, 234–39.

25. Yoder, *Politics*, 234.

26. Yoder, *Politics*, 234–39.

27. Sykes, *Power*, 56–57.

28. Sykes, *Power*, 109. For Meeks, see Meeks, *The First Urban Christians*, for his

A Double Vision Hermeneutic

As one of the pioneers, Meeks was one among the first to employ Peter Berger and Thomas Luckmann's sociological insights on his reconstruction of Pauline sociological context.[29] Examples from the nineties are Neil Elliott's *Liberating Paul*,[30] John Chow's *Patronage and Power*,[31] and Clinton E. Arnold's *Powers of Darkness*.[32] While Elliott focuses on vindicating Paul and rescuing him from accusation and misreading of his text as an instrument of the legitimization of various kinds of oppression such as slavery, the subordination of women, and political domination,[33] Chow's *Patronage and Power* focuses how the Corinthian Christian community's high regards on social status had influenced their view of power.[34] Arnold's study locates Paul's teaching on powers in the setting of its Graeco-Roman religio-social background, drawing attention to the practice of astrology, magic, and divination. His also differs from the aforementioned two categories: the one focusing on a socio-political reading using contemporary theory and the other on Paul's character, shaped through his relationship with Christ, not only in terms of the selection of text, but also of interest. Elizabeth A. Castelli's *Imitating Paul* and Sandra Hack Polaski, *Paul and the Discourse of Power*, as Stephen Sykes remarks,[35] relate Paul to the discourse of power, representing a cross-disciplinary approach to Paul and Michel Foucault.[36] A more recent study is Ehrensperger's *Paul and the Dynamics of Power*.[37] To briefly review Polaski and Ehrensperger: Polaski

---

citation of Berger and Luckman, see op.cit, index. For Peter Berger, especially his co-authored book, see Luckmann and Berger, *The Social Construction of Reality*. See also Horrell, *Solidarity and Difference*, 83–85. Sykes also marks a couple of earlier ones like Schutz's *Paul and the Anatomy of Apostolic Authority* and Holmberg's *Paul and Power* which appeared in 1970s. See Sykes, *Power*, 110. See endnote, 168 n. 103. For Holmberg, see Holmberg, *Paul and Power*.

29. Meeks, *The First Urban Christians*, 8. Italic mine.

30. Elliott, *Liberating Paul*.

31. Chow, *Patronage and Power*.

32. Arnold, *Powers of Darkness*. Clinton's study can be categorized after Caird, *Principalities and Powers*.

33. Elliott, *Liberating Paul*, 3–24.

34. Studies with similar concern include Savage, *Power Through Weakness*; Sze-kar Wan, *Power in Weakness*. Both Savage and Wan focus on studying 2 Corinthians.

35. Sykes, *Power*, 110. See Castelli, *Imitating Paul*; Polaski, *Paul and the Discourse of Power*.

36. Another work related to power is Pasework, *A Theology of Power*. See Sykes, *Power*, 14 and 155 n. 5, who regards Pasework's attempt as "heroic" but himself opts for a more humble "power and Christian theology" instead of "a theology of power."

37. Ehrensperger, *Paul and the Dynamics of Power*.

exemplifies the use of Foucault in biblical study; Ehrensperger shows how contemporary sociological perspectives integrated in the study of Paul can be enhanced by further exegetes of biblical, namely the Old Testament, ideas.

In the following, Polaski and Ehrensperger will be focused on. Polaski is chosen here due to her heavy reliance on Foucault for her study. Given that Foucault's influence in contemporary study of power in relation to Paul,[38] Polaski's work is worth taken as sample for review in this regard. While Polaski makes sociological insights relying on Foucault a major thrust of her thesis, Ehrensperger is more critical, who although also incorporates Foucault in her study,[39] and acknowledges that employing "contemporary sociological, philosophical and political theories" in the study of Pauline discourse could be fruitful, but does not want to follow these theories all through. She believes, given that Paul and his works were deeply rooted in the Old Testament theological and linguistic background, a study on key Old Testament theological motifs, e.g., God's righteousness and grace which appear in Pauline works, will be a justified supplement to the sociological approach. Moreover, God's grace through Jesus Christ is a significant counter-power that dissolves the power of sin (Rom 5:21). This is a theological thread that will prove indispensable in my double vision of power, which I will discuss in the final chapter. Because of this, Ehrensperger's study serves to show how my interpretation shares a similar theological reading of Paul but produces a distinctive theological construction.

Polaski follows the steps of others,[40] and borrows insights from "postmodern theorists," especially Foucault. She is interested in "the study of the mechanisms of power," and believes it can "offer an important point of entry" into Pauline texts,[41] and engages with two concepts related to power: discourse and ideology. The following briefly discusses her use of Foucault's idea of discourse.

Primarily, her intention is to "develop the category of *discourse* and apply the insights gained there to the Pauline texts."[42] According to her,

---

38. Castelli, *Imitating Paul*; Polaski, *Paul and the Discourse of Power*; Ehrensperger, *Paul and the Dynamics of Power* are three typical examples.

39. Ehrensperger, *Dynamics*, 21.

40. For example, she admits to following Castell's *Imitating Paul*; Moore, *Poststructuralism and the New Testament* in which a Foucauldian reading of Paul is highlighted, and Martin, *The Corinthian Body* in which the concepts of discourse and ideology are referred to.

41. Polaski, *Discourse of Power*, 20.

42. Polaski, *Discourse of Power*, 20. Italics hers.

a discourse is "a system for determining what gets said, a system for the production of knowledge and the transmission of that knowledge in language, either spoken language or texts."[43] Using the Foucauldian concept of discourse,[44] she acknowledges that "there is no separate, objective standard to which readers can turn for the 'facts' or the 'truth.'" What she means is that although it seems obvious that "Paul describes situations, outlines problems and recommends solutions, and articulates his fears and hopes for his congregations," and it seems that Paul has the authority to tell the congregation what to follow and how they should behave as if he holds the "truth" and they should thus listen to him, the reason they do respond to him is because both Paul and the congregation interact within a discourse.[45]

Polaski works on Pauline texts assuming Paul is involved in a "religious" discourse which she believes "works among the subjects who participate in it."[46] She distinguishes "power from conflict, and seeing power as 'transformative capacity' in which actors' interests may either conflict or coincide." Thus instead of focusing on the conflicts, her interest is to look into how Paul is "involved in *relations* of power."[47]

Having avoided regarding power relations in terms of conflict, she introduces the concept of discourse into her interpretation of Pauline texts. While it is correct to understand Paul's "response to opposition or challenge" within the context of power relation, Polaski contends that "it is appropriate to describe these power relations by speaking of them as discourse."[48]

However, one may argue that, although employing discourse theory does help to break new ground in interpreting Paul, it can also be a stumbling block. The reason she thinks Paul is not effective in aiding the understanding of power relations is that she reads Pauline texts and situations with a frame of reference originating from post-modern theory,[49] but excludes the mythological and spiritual dimension in Paul.[50] Her lens has

43. Polaski, *Discourse of Power*, 37.

44. She nevertheless acknowledges the Weberian approach to power which is adopted earlier by some scholars, for example, Holmberg, *Paul and Power*, in which Weber's notion of charisma and authority is linked with Paul.

45. Polaski, *Discourse of Power*, 20.

46. Polaski, *Discourse of Power*, 22.

47. Polaski, *Discourse of Power*, 37. Italics mine.

48. Polaski, *Discourse of Power*, 37. Italics hers.

49. Polaski, *Discourse of Power*, 104. Italics hers.

50. I will later refer to Wink for the "mythological and spiritual dimension" here

already determined what she could find in the texts, and her understanding of power in terms of discourse, has blinded her to other dimensions of power.

One work published later than Sykes' *Power* and thus not included in his review is Kathy Ehrensperger's *Paul and the Dynamics of Power*.[51] She sees grace as a motif meaningfully related to the discourse of power. She successfully incorporates into her discussion the Old Testament linguistic feature of 'grace' that indicates a relational aspect. She argues, "Power is involved in as much as the semantic field of נח/הסד (*charis/ḥesed*) indicates that the actions and attitudes which are exercised have a positive, favorable and life-supporting impact on the receivers."[52] She argues,

> Paul's scripturally rooted discourse of χάρις implies more than a mere reversal of the dominating imperial power discourse. A reversal of an existing structure does not change anything as structures of domination and subordination are merely turned upside down. This only leads to the establishment of new structures of domination and subordination, the only change effected is the exchange of the power in the dominating positions. Thus an interpretation of the Pauline discourse which views him simply as inverting existing power structures actually confirms that it inevitably contributed to the establishment of structures of domination and static hierarchies in church and society very much like those of the Roman Empire. The reading offered here perceives the Pauline discourse and the discourse of χάρις in particular, as clearly distinct from Roman imperial power but, rather than inverting structures of domination, Paul is seen as arguing for an alternative approach.[53]

Her concern is with hierarchies and in that setting χάρις reverses the play of power, contrary to the practice of Paul's own time. She argues that the whole discourse of χάρις in Paul is about power. It is about how one can have a positive effect on the other or reciprocally. Thus, rather than calling for "a reversal of existing power,"[54] her intention is to argue for a "mutual empowerment";[55] a reversal may change the power structures

---

stated. See especially Wink, *Naming*, 103–48.
51. Ehrensperger, *Dynamics*.
52. Ehrensperger, *Dynamics*, 76–77.
53. Ehrensperger, *Dynamics*, 78–79.
54. Ehrensperger, *Dynamics*, 78.
55. Ehrensperger, *Dynamics*, 78–80.

upside down, but does not change the structures being structures. These new structures will promote their own domination and subordination.[56]

She acknowledges that employing "contemporary sociological, philosophical and political theories" in the study of Pauline discourse could be fruitful but thinks that it should be used with caution. She does not want to rely on any particular theory,[57] but admits that Foucault is significant in her study.[58] For her, Foucault's emphasis is "on the all-pervasiveness of power and the differentiated perception of asymmetry and hierarchy in social relations deserves further consideration" in his reading of the Pauline discourse.[59] However, she thinks that Foucault's approach to power "does not help to analyze or explain power which arises from solidarity, or power arising from the consensus of a group of people to act together."[60] Pointing out the idea of solidarity is important for her reading of Paul, whose concern over solidarity within various churches was a key motif in his discourse of power.[61] She also thinks that Foucault does not include "transformative power" in his discussion.[62] This prepares her to incorporate grace as a "transformative power" into her discourse, particularly grace rooted in its Hebrew cultural-linguistic setting found in the Old Testament.[63] This unique theology of grace was further developed by Paul who as a Jew had inherited the Old Testament faith, and will prove significant in my final chapter. As I read, appropriate and embody Pauline texts, the grace of God as experienced and expounded by Paul will inevitably become my own experience and be integrated into my being.

The works of Polaski and Ehrensperger hence show examples of how sociological approaches could indeed help shed light, in the interpretation of biblical texts with regard to power relations. The question is not whether the insights could replace more theological ones, nor an either/or exclusive choice between the theological and sociological.[64] Appropriately used and integrated, the insights gained by using both theological and

---

56. Ehrensperger, *Dynamics*, 78–79.

57. Ehrensperger, *Dynamics*, 3.

58. Ehrensperger, *Dynamics*, 21. Other theorists on whom she relies include Hannah Arendt and Jacque Derrida, see *Dynamics*, 14.

59. Ehrensperger, *Dynamics*, 21.

60. Ehrensperger, *Dynamics*, 21.

61. Ehrensperger, *Dynamics*, especially 49, 60, 76, 79.

62. Ehrensperger, *Dynamics*, 22.

63. See especially Ehrensperger, *Dynamics*, 63–80.

64. Cf. Sykes, *Power*, xi, 83–84.

sociological lenses could enhance a fuller understanding of power more accessible to contemporary minds exposed to sociological studies.

3. Walter Wink: Returning to Principalities and Powers

3.1: Introduction

While adopting sociological approaches has yielded valuable insights for the study of power relations within the Pauline churches, to do so at the expense of the Pauline notion of "principalities and powers" is detrimental. It may only portray a partial picture and offers an insufficient interpretation of Paul's understanding of power. In the following I will focus on Walter Wink, whose approach I regard as representing a more thorough study of the theological motif of "principalities and powers."[65] As I will gradually show, while Wink may have learned from the sociological perspective in reframing the spiritual account of powers as social forces within the church and society and created order/nature, his contribution can be better acknowledged if his inclusion and further development of earlier theological studies on Pauline account of power are included into our review.

Wink's trilogy on power represents the most comprehensive study over the last three decades.[66] Despite crediting scholars like G. B. Caird, John Yoder, Hendrik Berkhof and others in a passing reference, he argues that most studies have ignored or overlooked "the pervasiveness of the language of power in the New Testament" and "tended to depend on word studies isolated from the entire language-field and on a thin selection of texts almost always only the 'disputed texts', and have thus been more impressionistic than exhaustive."[67] Although he affirms these earlier schol-

---

65. Wink's first study was motivated by his experience in Latin America where he saw much violence, human right violations, and hunger, concrete forms of evils. See Wink, *Naming the Powers*, xi. His second from continuing dialogs for fourteen years over biblical texts. My interest lies with the first two and part 1 of the third. Instead of following his analysis of these phenomena, I offer my own arena of Chinese pastor and his church where *shì* takes place.

66. Wink, *Naming the Powers*; idem, *Unmasking the Powers*; idem, *Engaging the Powers*. Yoder gives an updated remark in his epilogue to the chapter of "Christ and Power" recommending Wink's trilogy as "the most thorough review of the theme." See Yoder, *Politics*, 159.

67. Wink, *Naming*, 6. For Caird, see *Principalities and Powers*; for Berkhof, see

ars' roles as mapmakers for the study, he is unsatisfied with their "sweeps through the territory."[68]

3.2: Departing from Sociological Approach

Wink's argument has employed various sociological insights,[69] but the fundamental primary reference of his argument, or theoretical framework, is myth, and secondary, psychology.[70] As shown in volume one, anticipating a mythological rather than a sociological hermeneutical framework, he refers, in a passing comment in the footnote, to Holmberg's "critical use of Weber's sociological categories in analyzing Paul's use of power." He criticizes Holmberg's study for being "limited to the structure of the church."[71]

As Wink has pointed out, while the theme of power has been adopted by "recent studies in the sociology of the New Testament," the danger of making sociological theory "normative for New Testament reality," i.e. "imposing on New Testament data a framework that is foreign to it," should be heeded. A sociological approach could "be ill-suited," for it may miss "the most essential elements in the first-century understanding of power."[72] He names Peter Berger's *The Sacred Canopy* in particular as an example of the sociological approach. He praises Berger for his "analytical lucidity."[73] However, as Berger takes on a "methodological atheism,"[74] which has bracketed out "the most central aspect of reality: belief in the existence of God," Wink judges that sociological approaches as such "must not be permitted to guide the development of hypothesis" for New Testament reality. Rather, we should try to look into a New Testament text to find "its own categories for speaking of social reality."[75]

Christ and Powers; For Yoder, see Yoder, *The Politics of Jesus*; idem, *The Original Revolution*.

68. Wink, *Naming*, 35.
69. Wink, see *Naming*, 100 n. 1, 101 n. 2.
70. I will discuss these two aspects in following subsections.
71. Wink, *Naming*, 100.
72. Wink, *Naming*, 101. He is referring to Scroggs' article, "The Sociological Interpretation of the New Testament," 164–79. As is shown in the year of publication, the survey concludes in 1980.
73. Wink, *Naming*, 102.
74. For Berger, see *The Sacred Canopy*, 100.
75. Wink, *Naming*, 102.

3.3: Construing with New Emergent Spirituality

Wink's project reflects an intention to surpass a mere understanding of reality from a sociological perspective. Rooted in Western society, with its emergent spirituality, he sees beyond the visible society to the reality of an invisible dimension. He wrote the first of his trilogy in the 1980s when a new emergent spirituality was forming. According to him, the old framework, "the mechanistic, materialistic worldview," is considered "life-threatening." The emergent spirituality, in contrast, embraces "a more organic, life-enhancing worldview," which tries to restore a "participative relationship with nature."[76] He contends that this new spirituality perceives reality in a way that is more compatible with the world embedded in New Testament language in its reference to invisible powers, than with the old rational framework.[77] He thus attempts to draw from the New Testament language of power so that these powers which were once known as "spiritual realities"[78] can make sense to modern Western society.

He argues that the old physics focuses more on the parts than the whole, and neglects the interrelatedness of the parts. In contrast, the new science has corrected such a view. Instead of focusing on a substance itself, it sees into "the complex interactions that comprise events."[79] Referring to Birch and Cobb, Wink argues that an atom "is not a substantial entity out a multiplicity of events interconnected with each other and with other events in a describable pattern."[80] Thus what is determinant is the internal pattern of the interrelated relationship that marks the existence. Wink remarks, "Even the electron is characterized by its internal relations."

Seeing internal relations as the interiority of the existence of all things, he finds it somehow related to the "language of 'angels.'"[81] "An angel," he argues, "is both immanent within every member of its species and transcendent to it."[82] "Immanent" not in the sense of "a spirit" within a thing as "anthropologists and historians of religion" define it under the

---

76. Wink, *Unmasking*, 159.

77. See especially section "The Angels of Nature and the Emergent New Worldview" in *Unmasking*, 159–71. Noted that this book was published in 1986.

78. Wink, *Unmasking*, 1.

79. Wink, *Unmasking*, 160.

80. Wink, *Unmasking*, 160. He is referring to Birth and Cobb, *The Liberation of Life*, 84–91.

81. Wink, *Unmasking*, 160.

82. Wink, *Unmasking*, 160.

A Double Vision Hermeneutic

religious categories of "animism" and "pantheism" they invented.[83] Immanence implies withinness. Angels are transcendent, for they are heavenly beings. The idea of heaven indicates something 'up there', thus something transcendent.[84]

Thus, angels reflect a different level of reality. They are real, but exist in an imaginative realm. They belong to the transcendent dimension of reality, which exists in the "states of higher consciousness."[85] However, Wink argues that this transcendent dimension is also the inner dimension, which Carl Jung spoke of as "the collective unconscious," indicating "a realm of . . . spiritual reality linking everyone to everything."[86]

Therefore, instead of the old rational framework, the language of angel points to "a feeling-toned, intuitive relationship" of reality.[87] What is depicted as transcendent in the ancient cosmology is, in the language of the new emergent spirituality, the immanence, the interiority. Wink thus proposes a new worldview which he sees as compatible with emergent spirituality and the New Testament world.

> It sees everything as having an outer and an inner aspect. It attempts to take seriously the spiritual insights of the ancient or biblical worldview by affirming a withinness or interiority in all things, but sees this inner spiritual reality as inextricably related to an outer concretion or physical manifestation.[88]

He sees this as an "integral worldview" that "takes seriously all the aspects of the ancient worldview, but combines them in a different way."[89] The relation is depicted as below:

---

83. Wink, *Unmasking*, 160.
84. Wink, *Engaging*, 6.
85. Wink, *Unmasking*, 162.
86. Wink, *Engaging*, 6.
87. Wink, *Unmasking*, 162.
88. Wink, *Engaging*, 5. He claims that "[t]his new worldview is emerging from a confluence of sources: the reflections of Carl Jung, Teihard de Chardin, Morton Kelsey, Thomas Berry, Matthew Fox, process philosophy, and the new physics."
89. Wink, *Engaging*, 6.

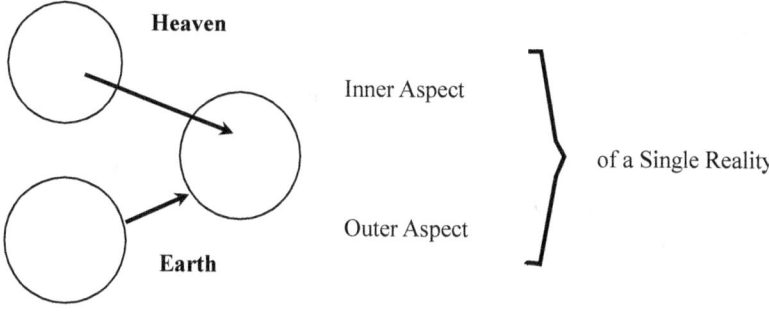

Diagram D

Thus, in this integral worldview, reality is not understood from a cosmological viewpoint that sees correlation between heaven and earth. While it is the same reality, that which is once called heaven is now addressed as the inner aspect, earth the outer aspect. In other words, heaven was once transcendent or invisible; in the new worldview, it is called the inner aspect.

3.4: The Mythic Perspective

In the first book of his trilogy, *Naming the Powers*, having identified key terms for power and surveyed passages that are related to power in the New Testament in the initial few chapters, he sets out to lay down the theoretical base for the later interpretation that will run through all three books, the mythic aspect. What is it? What is at play? Did the New Testament talk about these forms of powers? In what ways? These questions prompted him to write the trilogy beginning with a focus on New Testament texts exegetical studies of terms such as ἄρχων (*archon*), ἐξουσία (*exousia*), κοσμοκράτωρ (*kosmokrator*), κυριότης (*kuriotes*), and θρονοσ (*thronos*) which are directly power-related terminologies,[90] or also words which do not appear to be, but in reality are, power-related such as στοιχεῖα, sin and law in New Testament. His aim is to "attend carefully to the unique vocabulary and conceptions of the first century and try to grasp what the people of that time might have meant by power, within

---

90. For studies of power related terminologies, see Caird, *Powers and Principalities*, 1–30; Wink, *Naming*, 13–35; Dunn, *Theology of Paul*, 104–10 and Lee, "Interpreting the Demonic Powers," 54–56, 59–60. See also for my discussion in chapter 5.

the linguistic field of their own worldview and mythic systems."[91] Thus he endeavours to engage with the topic from a mythic rather than sociological perspective.

In the New Testament, powers are given names from mythic language. For example, powers "were called angels, gods, spirits, demons, devils."[92] However, they may be changed into other names. Wink argues that such a change has been found within Paul who "has already taken key steps toward" a demythologization of them by naming the powers with "categories of sin, law, the flesh, and death."[93] Whether in the former categories or in Paul's, the powers they represent still exist today,[94] although they may bear different names.

Wink thus proposes to interpret power with the new worldview, undertaking the step of demythologization and re-mythologization with modern myth and spirituality.[95] He does not remove the "mythic dimension" of the New Testament, but 'juxtapose[s] the ancient myth with the emerging postmodern (mythic) worldview."[96] His aim is to allow these two, mythical and postmodern, to "illumine each other"[97] and "to contribute toward a new, postmaterialist cosmology, drawing on biblical resources."[98] He sees a communicability between this postmaterialist cosmology and New Testament cosmology. While the message of the New Testament is not about first century cosmology, the message is conveyed within its context and language.[99]

Wink calls the mythic dimension "the atemporal, cosmic, supernatural aspect." He says, this dimension permeates "every statement made about the Powers" in his early chapters. The mythic "is the very framework of the entire notion of the Powers, the means by which they have been brought to language."[100] He thus cannot accept a reductionist explanation, for example a sociological one. He later disagrees with Peter Berger and Thomas Luckmann, arguing that they are half right in stating "human

91. Wink, *Naming*, 4.
92. Wink, *Naming*, 104.
93. Wink, *Naming*, 104.
94. Wink, *Unmasking*, 3.
95. I am indebted to Gilkey, *Naming the Whirlwind* for this use of "re-mythologization."
96. Wink, *Naming*, 104.
97. Wink, *Naming*, 104.
98. Wink, *Unmasking*, 6.
99. Wink, *Unmasking*, 5.
100. Wink, *Naming*, 103.

institutions are humanly formed," but adds, "These institutions are not simply subject to human fiat. They possess a spirituality, an inwardness. . . . The heavenly powers are not mere projections that mystify the real power relations. They are, quite the contrary, the real interiority of earth institutions, systems and forces."[101] Referring to New Testament times, he says, "people (at that time) did not read the spirituality of an institution straight off from its outer manifestations. Instead, they projected its felt or intuited spiritual qualities onto the screen of the universe, and perceived them as cosmic forces reigning from the sky."[102] Thus Wink is pulling down what used to be in *heaven up there*, demythologizing the language of heaven and angels, and clothing it with the language of spirituality of interiority, the inner aspect and the withinness. Wink points out that for the ancients, "spiritual Powers" were regarded as "non-material, invisible, heavenly entities with specific characteristics or qualities."[103] Earlier, Wink refers to these powers as forces of "physical, psychic, and social existence."[104] These powers were both heavenly and earthly, divine and human, spiritual and political, invisible and structural.[105]

In the first main section of chapter 5 of *Naming*, which is devoted to establishing his theses of the mythic dimension of power, Wink gives his first hypothesis: "The Powers Are the Inner Aspect of Material Reality."[106] This is probably the most important aspect, permeates all the others: an attempt to define anew what "spiritual" actually means, in the framework of his interpretation.

The "spiritual" or the "interiority", according to Wink, "means the inner dimension of the material, the 'withinness' of things, the subjectivity of objective entities in the world."[107] This inner dimension of power is *"the inner aspect of material or tangible manifestations of power."*[108] He redefines terms such as angels, principalities and powers, demons, gods, and Satan with new meanings according to this paradigm.[109] These are important

101. Wink, *Naming*, 135. He refers to Luckmann and Berger, *The Social Construction of Reality*, 90 and n. 63. He also describes the dual aspects of power: the "physical or institutional concretion" and "their inner essence or spirituality." See Wink, *Naming*, 107.

102. Wink, *Engaging*, 7.

103. Wink, *Naming*, 104.

104. Wink, *Unmasking*, 4.

105. Wink, *Naming*, 9–12, 99–100.

106. Wink, *Naming*, 104–13.

107. Wink, *Naming*, 107.

108. Wink, *Naming*, 104. Italics his.

109. Cf. Berkhof and Yoder above.

indicators for the understanding of his theological interpretation of power based on New Testament writings. He concisely summarizes the New Testament myths into a new worldview paradigm of inner aspect, saying,

> I suggest that the "angels of nature" are the patterning of physical things—rocks, trees, plants, the whole God-glorifying, dancing, visible universe; that the "principalities and powers" are the inner or spiritual essence, or gestalt, of an institution or state of system; that the "demons" are the psychic or spiritual power emanated by organizations or individuals or subaspects of individuals whose energies are bent on overpowering others; that "gods" are the very real archetypal or ideological structures that determine or govern reality and its mirror, the human brain; that the mysterious "elements of the universe" (*stoicheia tou kosmou*) are the invariances (formerly called "laws") which, though often idolized by humans, conserve the self-consistency of each level of reality in its harmonious interrelationship with every other level and the Whole; and that "Satan" is the actual power that congeals around collective idolatry, injustice, or inhumanity, a power that increases or decreases according to the degree of collective refusal to choose higher values.[110]

Elements of the above quote can be divided into two juxtaposing groups as shown in the following chart.

New Testament myths of powers	The Powers as The Inner Aspect of Material Reality
angels of nature	the patterning of physical things
the "principalities and powers"	the inner or spiritual essence, or gestalt
the "demons"	the psychic or spiritual power
the "gods"	the very real archetypal or ideological structures
the mysterious "elements of the universe" (*stoicheia tou kosmou*)	the invariances (formerly called "laws") which ...... conserve the self-consistency of each level of reality in its harmonious interrelationship with every other level and the Whole
"Satan"	the actual power that congeals around collective idolatry, injustice, or inhumanity

110. Wink, *Naming*, 104–5.

As earlier discussed, Wink incorporates new physics concept regarding the interiority in events, the parts within interrelated to the external whole. With this aspect in mind he discusses the patterning. Hence, angels speak of the transcendent aspect of the nature, while the internal patterning speaks of the inner aspect; likewise, "principalities and powers" speak of invisible powers *up there* in the air (Eph 2:2), while "inner or spiritual essence" speaks about what is found inside visible institutions, organizations, governments, and other bodies. Demons, gods, or elements of the universe referred to in the New Testament in mythical language are thus the psychic, spiritual or inner dimensions of realities or beings. Hence he turns the mythical into the inner, spiritual, or interior.

3.5: Angels, Demons, and Gods

Wink devotes almost the entire book two: *Unmasking the Powers* to defining and interpreting angels and gods as powers and principalities, stating that, the powers "were called angels, gods, spirits, demons, devils."[111] I will engage with Wink's discussion of Satan and demons in the conclusion of the thesis. At this point, the language of angels, referred to earlier, requires fitter explication.[112] In three separate chapters, Wink deals with "the angels of the churches," "the angels of the nations," and "the angels of nature."[113]

Wink first delineates the role of an angel vis-à-vis the church, as that of a heavenly messenger. He refers to early church documents, such as the *Ascension of Isaiah* which refer to "the angel of the Christian church" (3:15), and to Hermas who "designates Michael as 'the one who has power over this people [the church] and governs them' (*Sim.* 8.3.3)," and to the Book of Revelation where "Michael appears in some sense as the defender of the church," as well as to Heb 1:14 where angels are depicted as ones who are "watching over and serving the church.[114] Focusing on Revelation,[115] he tries to interpret the seven angels of the seven churches in terms of the inner/outer aspect and as collective entities. He says,

> It would appear that the angel is not something separate from the congregation, but must somehow represent it as a totality.

---

111. Wink, *Naming*, 104.
112. See section 3.3 above.
113. Wink, *Unmasking*, 69–86, 87–107, 153–71.
114. Wink, *Unmasking*, 70.
115. Wink, *Unmasking*, 70–74.

A Double Vision Hermeneutic

> Through the angel, the community seems to step forth as a single collective entity or Gestalt. But the fact that the angel is actually addressed suggests that it is more than a mere personification of the church, but the actual spirituality of the congregation as a single entity. The angel would then exist in, with, and under the material expressions of the church's life as its interiority. As a corporate personality or felt sense of the whole, the angel of the church would have no separate existence apart from the people. But the converse would be equally true: the people would have no unity apart from the angel. Angel and people are the inner and outer aspects of one and the same reality. The people incarnate or embody the angelic spirit; the angel distills the invisible essence of their totality as a group.[116]

Let me illustrate this with the following.

In a Chinese church preaching about church leadership in July 2008, I explained, "We have to ask God to elect a leader for our church. We should not leave it to fate. If our church is full of a spirit of 'leave it to fate,' it will continue to give birth to a spirit of fatalism. In other words, if our church is full of a spirit of distrust, it will give birth to an atmosphere of distrust; a spirit of indifference, to a look of indifference; a spirit of autocracy, to a lifestyle of unacceptance and narrowness." As I argue in an article:

> [And] whatever names the spirits may be given and whatever they are, they highly depend on the psychological and spiritual condition of the people they possess. A spirit of lust could possess one if he or she is indulging in the sin of lust, building a "house" for the spirit to live in and manifest itself as the spirit of lust. Our body is the house of the Spirit of God, and could also be the house for other spirits. But if the same spirit goes to another person who is bound by the sin of hatred, it will become the spirit of hatred.[117]

The different spirits described here manifest the potential spirituality that can be embodied in the church. My use of "spirit" is close to Wink's use of "angel" especially where it is applied to name the "spirit" of a church, or as

---

116. Wink, *Unmasking*, 70.

117. Cf. My expression of various spirits such as "the spirit of rage, spirit of [promiscuity], spirit of lust" in Ooi, "A Study of Strategic Level Spiritual Warfare," 59. Wink has pointed out that "traditional Christian pietism" also has the tendency to demonize one's inner aspect, i.e., one's "emotions." It can call various negative emotions as "a Spirit of Anger, a Spirit of Envy, or a Spirit of Lust." See Wink, *Unmasking*, 56.

Wink would call, the "gestalt" of the church.[118] However, the antithesis of "angel" could be "demon."

Wink tries to list some of the characteristics manifested by the angel of a church can manifest,[119] particularly pointing to is power structure. He says, "To a certain extent the way a congregation is organized is set by its denominational polity. Within that framework, however, there is tremendous latitude for leadership styles, theological orientations, and attitudes toward authority."[120] One can determine "what patterns of authority have predominated . . . just by the way people defer to us, withdraw, or regard us as peers."[121] However, pastoral leadership can be dominating with authoritarian style and paralyzing effect.[122] A pastor and the congregation can become cohorts, both contributing to the gestalt of the church. He gives an account of a personal experience to illustrate this.

Giving a session to a church exploring the biblical perspective on how a church should respond to its neighbor, Wink says,

> For the first hour I simply floundered. Everyone was perfectly nice. I encountered no overt resistance. Yet each question I asked seemed to be sucked down into a black hole. At the break I whispered to my colleague, "What's going on? Nothing is happening. Nothing!" "It's demons," she replied, half in jest. "You're right," I answered, shocked at our speaking this way.[123]

He was invited to assist his colleague in being a "change agent." However, change was resisted by a "demon," which prevented the church from reach out to "gays, blacks, Hispanics, and the elderly" in the community.[124] To know a church, one must therefore possess a spirit of discernment, not only to recognize the evil spirit, but also the spirit of man that dominates the church. In the above case, it was the collective consciousness, the "spirit" of the church manifesting its power. The session was set by "a new head" of the governing body of that church. He wanted to see change in the church. However, what was being arranged was "at odds" with the "spirit" and "at some level they all knew about it and responded with pas-

118. I had come to this use of "spirit" before I encountered Wink's books.
119. This is only the beginning of his analysis of the listed six characteristics, see Wink, *Unmasking*, 73–78.
120. Wink, *Unmasking*, 74.
121. Wink, *Unmasking*, 75.
122. Wink, *Unmasking*, 75.
123. Wink, *Unmasking*, 75.
124. Wink, *Unmasking*, 75.

A Double Vision Hermeneutic

sive resistance." Wink emphasizes, "They were doing exactly what they were 'supposed' to do."[125]

The formation of that "spirit" haunting the church took time. As Wink's colleague revealed to him after several weeks of investigation, due to the minister-in-charge's "physical ailment that would become aggravated under stress," over twenty years the minister had elected "a governing board that 'knew,' without it ever having been said explicitly, that their job was to keep their minister from being upset."[126] Because of this unspoken mutual consent, they allowed a "spirit" to grow within the church, which gained power, manifesting itself as a spirit of resistance to change, reaching out, and to growth. As Wink expresses it, "The angel of a church becomes demonic when the congregation turns its back on the specific tasks set before it by God and makes some other goal its idol."[127] The goal that has been made an idol in this church is "to keep their minister from being upset."

Addressed above is the collective consciousness of the church. It acts as if it had a personality, but in fact is the spirituality of the church, be it angelic or demonic. One would hesitate to call the spirit of that church an angel. It was a "demon" as Wink's colleague called it. Demon or angel, evil or good, it is a matter of psychic power. To understand this collective psychic dimension, it is better to start from the personal level, "the inner personal demonic," Wink discusses. He defines it as "a split-off or unintegrated aspect of the self which is not alien, but intrinsic to the personality, and which needs to be owned, embraced, loved, and transformed as part of the struggle for wholeness."[128] In other words, when these needs are not met, they turn into demonic beings injected with psychological impulses.

The personal psychological dimension is the foundation of the collective dimension. Institutions, organizations, or churches all have their collective consciousness. This is what has been addressed above as the spirit or the angel. As Wink further explicates, Jung calls these collectives "archetypes." He says, "The archetypes are the numinous, structural elements of the psyche that preform our experience in certain typical ways." By archetypes, Jung speaks "about what religions have called gods, spirits, angels, and demons."[129] To Wink, thus, the "gods," are "the 'within' of in-

125. Wink, *Unmasking*, 75.
126. Wink, *Unmasking*, 75.
127. Wink, *Unmasking*, 78.
128. Wink, *Unmasking*, 52.
129. Wink, *Unmasking*, 117.

stinctuality or as the collective spirituality of a society (including the gods or angels of nations and other corporate entities)."[130] The "'within' of instinctuality" are "the collective compulsions of society" that can "encounter us with such almighty power that we not only fail to resist but are awed into submission" which create a "false worship of the gods."[131] Here we see one key factor which leads to idolatry: the submission of the subject. Wink emphasizes, "We worship what enslaves us, forging our own chains."[132] He sees this as the reason Paul did not deny the existence of gods, for example saying, "Indeed there are many gods and many lords—yet for us there is one God" (1 Cor 8:5). Paul "knew their power to enslave."[133] If one submits to their power, they can become not only idols but gods. In this sense, gods are thus powers and powers are gods.

3.6: Power as a Domination System

Having defined "the language of power in the New Testament" in book one and "the invisible forces that determine human existence" in book two,[134] Wink engages in the discussion of power as a domination system in book three. In this book, he focuses on three aspects that he thinks have been greatly obscured, which could actually inform readers of the implication of a domination system: *kosmos* (world), *aeōn* (age), and *sarx* (flesh).[135] He points out, "The Greek word *kosmos* means, variously, world, universe, the creation, humanity, the planet earth, the theater of history."[136] As for the New Testament use of the word,[137] he asserts that it "refers to the human sociological realm that exists in estrangement from God."[138] He thinks cosmos (*kosmos*), as used in the New Testament, can be best translated as "system."[139] He bases his understanding of "system"

---

130. Wink, *Unmasking*, 119.
131. Wink, *Unmasking*, 125.
132. Wink, *Unmasking*, 125.
133. Wink, *Unmasking*, 125.
134. The subtitles of these two books.
135. Wink, *Engaging*, 51.
136. Wink, *Engaging*, 51.
137. He asserts that "[t]he use of *kosmos* in a negative or even evil sense is curiously absent from pre-Christian literature." See Wink, *Engaging*, 342 n. 3.
138. Wink, *Engaging*, 51.
139. Wink, *Engaging*, 51. For other sources for the definition of *kosmos*, see Wink, *Engaging*, 342 n. 3, 343 n. 7.

as defined by *Webster's Ninth New Collegiate Dictionary*: "a regularly interacting or interdependent group of items forming a unified whole." More importantly it is its newer meaning: "an organized society or social situation regarded as stultifying," Wink thinks is closer to the New Testament meaning of "world."[140]

One of the New Testament texts that most frequently uses *kosmos* is the Gospel of John, which Wink also cites on for his understanding of the word's meaning. Translating *kosmos* as system, John 7:7 would read: "The System (*kosmos*) cannot hate you . . . , but it hates me because I testify against it that its works are evil," and John 8:23: "You are of this System, I am not of this System."[141] Wink tries to convince that with *kosmos* translated as System, one would not perceive Jesus as "docetic" or "antiworldly." Hence, Jesus "was not 'of' the Domination System," but "belonged to God's system."[142] Thus rejection of the *kosmos* is a rejection of the establishment instead of the world itself, for the world was originally created good.[143]

Kosmos is primarily a spatial concept or as Wink constructs it, "systemic."[144] In the New Testament, one also finds *aiōn*, which is primarily a temporal concept. These two words are often interchangeable.[145] Through these two words, the New Testament conveys a spatial-temporal world in which humans live. Wink coins the two terms together calling them "the present world-period," which is "under the power of evil."[146]

The *kosmos* can also be called "the present evil epoch (*aiōn*)" (Gal. 1:4), "organized under Satan," who is "the god of this world-period (*aiōn*)."[147] As this spatial-temporal world is dominated by sin (Rom 5), human beings also live as "dominated existence," an expression Wink uses to translate Pauline phrase, *kata sarka*.[148] Wink asserts, the "most striking and theological weighty use" of this phrase is found "in reference to the self in its alienated mode."[149] A life that is *kata sarka* "denotes the [life] self externalized and subjugated to the opinions of others." He continues, "It is

---

140. Wink, *Engaging*, 343 n. 6.
141. Wink, *Engaging*, 52. For his citation of John, see 51–59 passim.
142. Wink, *Engaging*, 52.
143. Wink, *Engaging*, 51.
144. Wink, *Engaging*, 59.
145. Wink, *Engaging*, 59.
146. Wink, *Engaging*, 59.
147. Wink, *Engaging*, 59.
148. Wink, *Engaging*, 62.
149. Wink, *Engaging*, 61.

the self socialized into a world of inauthentic values, values that lead it away from its own centeredness in God." Thus, one who lives *kata sarka* lives a life dominated by the domination system and follows its values.[150] That is why Paul declares, writing to the Ephesians, "You were dead through the trespasses and sins in which you once lived, following the course of this *System*, following the ruler (*archonta*) of the power (*exousias*) of the air, the spirit that is now at work among those who are disobedient. All of us once lived among them in the passions of our *sarx*, following the desires of *sarx* and senses, and we were by nature children of wrath, like everyone else."[151] The externals as found in this passage are the *System* and *archonta*. They do not refer to opinions and values of others as Wink interprets it. Wink first demythologizes, then re-dresses these power symbols the values of the society where they exist, worldly standards, i.e., standards according to the System.

To use his language of System, the Ephesians are under the influence of the *System* and "the ruler of the power of the air" which are external. However, the latter, one of the externals, is also working in those who are disobedient (to God). The "in" indicates "in the passions" of the *sarx*, which together with the desires and passions collaborates in domination by "the spirit." Those who live in *sarx* therefore live a dominated existence.

4. Conclusion

Contemporary discourse on the Pauline understanding of power as delineated above is by necessity, selective. It aims to provide a context in which to anchor interpretation of the Pauline notion of principalities and powers. As stated at the beginning of this chapter, power discourse in the West is a branch "grafted" on a Chinese "tree" rooted in the Chinese cultural-linguistic tradition. Nevertheless, operating in the current climate of universal East/West interaction, while the emphasis of my rootedness in Chinese culture is indispensable, it must be admitted that once a hermeneutics is carried out, a fusion of Eastern and Western horizons must, to a certain extent, emerge.

While experiencing the power of sin, as described by Paul and the Pauline conscience working in me for many years, and with further readings of Pauline texts, my understanding of the Pauline notion of

---

150. Wink, *Engaging*, 61–62.
151. Eph 2:1–3, Greek transliteration and italics mine. The word *System* is Wink's.

principalities and powers has indeed grown. It is not possible to extract the later readings and understandings and separate them from the seminal one.

I have argued that Caird's and Berkhof's theological perspective of power is indispensable, in spite of movement towards sociological approaches from the 1980s onwards. A return to the New Testamental, theological-mythical understanding of power championed in Wink began almost simultaneously with sociological approaches. The argument that for Paul theological reasons in his critique of principalities and powers supersede sociological ones, i.e. for him the sociological was less of a concern to him than the theological, will be embraced in the discussion in the next two chapters.

6

Power in Text B2: Pauline Text I: Galatians

The aim of this and the following chapter is to interpret the Pauline notion of "principalities and powers" in Text B1 intermingling with Text B2—a reading of power relations in Galatians and 1 Corinthians. While chapters 3 and 4 prepared the "Chinese vision" for the execution of a double vision hermeneutics in the conclusion, this chapter and the next prepare the 'Christian vision'. Both Texts A and B are appropriated texts, embedded in the Chinese Christian double vision. To see the fusion of A and B, one has to first see the fusion within each vision, in other words the intersubjectivity of A1 and A2 as well of B1 and B2.

In chapter 4, the mechanism and philosophy of change in *Yìjīng* were explained. The basic elements indicating a change are the increase and decrease of *yīn-yáng* lines. Such *yīn-yáng* momentum forms the internal dynamism of a hexagram and therefore also creates the whole dynamism of the sixty-four hexagrams. A change in *yīn-yáng* proportion changes the power dynamic and thus the interrelated situations symbolized in the respective hexagrams.

In chapter 4 the use of symbolism of the hexagram to symbolize various situations was analyzed. The discussion was anchored in episodes encountered by two Chinese pastors and which were interpreted using several hexagrams. Inverted and counter-changed hexagrams were used to explained changes in perspective, when looking at different situations and power relations in terms of *shì*. The interpretation enhanced an understanding of *shì* as well as of power relations. Texts and contexts were brought fused and the intersubjective relationship between Text 0 and Texts A1 and A2 were shown.

A Double Vision Hermeneutic

In this and the following chapter, the multilayered meanings of *shì*, interpreted in chapters 3 and 4, will be presupposed, and the basic principles of the double vision hermeneutics will also be applied as the Pauline texts are interpreted. Thus the latter will be treated as traditional texts, objective and transcendent, but also be assumed as intersubjective texts, subjectively appropriated, which will be further deliberated on in the final chapter. My main interest of this and the following chapter is to identify power symbols in the Pauline texts and interpret them in the light of their primary historical and literary contexts.

It is important that the multi-layered and multi-textual understanding of *shì* presented so far be maintained as another layer of interpretation to be added on. *Shì* was first interpreted in the perspective of Text A1 and with Text A2. In other words, we can now see Text A1 through Text A2, and see Text 0 through Text A1 within Text A2.

In Text 0, the power relationship between myself, the deacons and the senior pastor was presented, and now understood as a constellation of powers. A subjective reflection, engaging statements as found in the H1 Qián hexagram in *Yìjīng* was also advanced. The way in which Text 0, Text A1, and Text A2 are intersubjectively related should now be clearer.

To show not only the Chinese traditional texts but also the Christian biblical texts effected in me, Texts B1 and B2 will be added to the interpretation in this chapter. Attention has been drawn to the Pauline notion of "principalities and powers" as referred to by Berkhof, Caird, and Wink. The aim is now to take this as Text B1. Texts A1 and A2 have been considered in separate chapters, and modern discourse on the Pauline notion of principalities and powers was discussed earlier, all of which will be woven into the discussion of Text B2 with its full result shown in chapter 8.

Galatians will be taken in this chapter, and 1 Corinthians in the next, as key Pauline texts for which sociological analysis and reconstruction of the community context of the two texts will be attempted. For the former, attention will be paid to the study of the στοιχεῖα and the law, taken as the key power symbols with which the Galatians were struggling. As to the latter, the concepts of wisdom and pneumatics, patronage and position are the power symbols reflected on.[1] Curbed within the above hermeneutical framework, the discussion below, regarding Galatians, will not be exhaustive.

---

1. Although the focus is on power or more precisely *shì*, it will not be a study on imperial and political power as delineated by Horsley and others. See Horsley, *Paul and Politics*; idem, *Paul and the Roman Imperial Order*; Elliott, *Liberating Paul*; idem, *The Arrogance of Nations*.

1. Galatian Church: A Brief Description of Its Birth

Every historical inquiry is an attempt at reconstruction. To enter into the text of Galatians and attempt to discover the context alluded to by Paul is to attempt a reconstruction to create a cohesive narrative based on the available traces. In the case of Galatians, primary sources available to us are Acts and Galatians.[2] The attempt here is to focus on the dynamic interaction between different parties that has caused the crisis, which prompted Paul to write such a desperate pastoral letter to "the churches of Galatia" (1:2).[3]

Where is Galatia? What groups of people had Paul in his mind when he wrote the letter? Why did he write such a letter? As our interpretation below is not historical per se, it will suffice to simply adopt one theory to proceed with our double vision hermeneutic by the reconstruction of a probable power struggle that might have been emerged before Paul wrote the letter.

Scholars have long debated the location of Galatia.[4] There is however no need for us to be involved into the debate. In this thesis the South Galatia theory in its "classical form" will be adopted, which entails the assumption that Paul had founded the churches there during his first missionary journey (Acts 13–14). It is simpler to reconstruct Galatians 2 and Acts 15 as compatible accounts of the same event.[5] There is no need to fix a date

---

2. I take these two texts as reliable even though the desired information is not available. One of the reasons for this discrepancy lies with the author's intention had not intended to write not for what currently interests us, but according to the felt needs of the time.

3. Hays believes that it is written to "a specific cluster of churches" (Hays, "Galatians—Introduction," 184).

4. Hays, "Galatians—Introduction," 191–93; Fung, *Galatians*, 1–2; Lightfoot, *Galatians*, 18–35; for more detailed discussion, see more updated discussion of Fung in *Galatians* (Chinese), 55–70; Longenecker, *Galatians*, lxiii–lxx. It is hard to be certain of whether the reference is to North Galatia, "the traditional territory of ethnic Galatians" or South Galatia "Romans provincial Galatia" (cf. Acts 14). See Hays, "Galatians—Introduction," 191. Moreover, the confirmation of an exact location has no full bearing on the interpretation of the text, as some scholars argue (Longenecker, *Galatians*, lxviii; also Fung, *Galatians* [Chinese], 55, who refers to Brown, *Galatians*, 475; Hays, "Galatians—Introduction," 191; Stanton, "Galatians," 1153a), although Fung contends that the discussion is still important in terms of historical study (*Galatians* [Chinese]), 55.

5. Hays, "Galatians—Introduction," 192–94. For the view of "classical form" that is represented by the (earlier) W. M. Ramsay, see Longenecker, *Galatians*, lxvii.

for Galatians in order to understand that there was a crisis that was caused by a group of people whom Paul addressed as the agitators.[6]

According to Acts 13:14, Paul and Barnabas reached South Galatia during their first missionary journey. After they left Antioch in Pisidia, they headed for Iconium, and then Lystra and Derby which were all located in South Galatia (13:51; 14:6). Jewish people there blasphemed them and their work, jealous of Paul and Barnabas' success in recruiting some followers in believing the gospel (13:42–45). There were also "unbelieving Jews" who stirred the Gentiles to hate those who believed (14:1-2). Because of this, "the residents of the city (Iconium) were divided; some sided with the Jews, and some with the apostles" (14:4). Both "Gentiles and Jews, with their rulers," attempted "to maltreat them and to stone them" (14:5). Not long after they reached Lystra and preached there, "Jews came there from Antioch and Iconium and won over the crowds. Then they stoned Paul and dragged him out of the city" (14:19). So they left there and moved south to Derby where they also managed to win some disciples (14:20).

From the narrative of Luke in Acts 13–14, assuming that Paul did establish churches there, or at least make a number of believers in various towns there, we may assume that from the outset there were trouble makers, the Jewish people who were against them and what they preached. While the new believers in South Galatia had just newly responded to the gospel (the Gentiles), there had long been converts in Antioch from where Paul and Barnabas were sent (11, 13:1). As Galatians 1:15—2:1 reveals, after his first visit to Jerusalem where he met Peter, he had spent some unknown years in Syria and Celicia before his second visit to Jerusalem where Paul probably had brought some to accept the gospel.

---

6. It has always been a challenge to date the Pauline letters, and Galatians is one of the most controversial. Murphy-O'Connor thinks that "Galatians could have been dispatched before the snows closed the high country in the autumn of AD 52." See Murphy-O'Connor, *Paul*, 181. Lightfoot contends that Galatians was quite probably written after 2 Corinthians and before Romans, which could place Galatians around AD 57 and 58, although he does not want to fix a date. As he dates Corinthians as "written at the close of the third missionary journey, in the years 57 and 58," if Galatians as he argues was written between 2 Corinthians and Romans, it probably would have been a few months before Romans was written (43). For Lightfoot, *Galatians*, 40–56. Lightfoot's view is still convincing in spite of Murphy-O'Connor's objection to Lightfoot's theory of Galatians having been written in Ephesus around the same period two Corinthians and Romans were written, based on their affinity and relatedness in style and content. See Murphy-O'Connor, *Paul*, 180–81.

2. The Emergence of Two Separate Groups

Moving to Acts 15 and Galatians 2, we see Galatians 2:7–8 where Paul says he "had been entrusted with the gospel for the uncircumcised, just as Peter had been entrusted with the gospel for the circumcised, for he who worked through Peter making him an apostle to the circumcised also worked through me in sending me to the Gentiles." Paul's claim suggests that there were two almost separate groups of Christians, the one Jewish and the other Gentiles, with Jerusalem and Antioch as their respective centres.

It should not be surprising that from these two groups, gathering around two separate centres, with two ethnic origins and under separate leaderships, could have grown different understandings of what the gospel of Christ truly meant to them. The meeting in Jerusalem (Acts 15; Gal 2) was a meeting of two interpretations and possibly two revelations. As Paul himself argued, he received his calling and the revelation of the gospel of Jesus Christ directly from God and did not need confirmation from any apostle in Jerusalem, for they, the "acknowledged leaders," had actually "contributed nothing" to him. Regarding leaders or apostles, Paul says, "what they actually were makes no difference to me;" for "God shows no partiality" (Gal 1:15–17; 2:6–8). What this implied was that he and the other apostles were on equal footing. We may for convenience's sake also call the Jerusalem leaders and Paul two separate power centers.[7]

I do not think that the Jerusalem and Antioch groups were consciously or intentionally building themselves up as centres of power; rather it was in the nature of *shì* that such prominent growth in Antioch became of equal power and a new equilibrium was called for. It was the *increase* in the Gentile Christian population surrounding Antioch as its centre that the original prominent status (*yáng*) of the progenitors of the Christian faith as represented by the first apostles of Christ became not the

---

7. It should be noted that I do not argue for an opposition of Pauline against Petrine Christianity as Tubingen school might have done so, which Beker has long argued no longer viable. I believe the problem of the relationship between the Jerusalem and Antioch churches was more subtle. To designate it as tension instead of "schism" or "separation" as Beker does not seem to be helpful enough. His argument is that the Antioch incident was in fact "an incident, not a split (Gal 2:11–14)." It is hard to judge how big was the gap. It is reasonable to think that whatever tension it might have been, the various traditions within early Christianity had to go through a gradual process of adjustment and clarification to reach its later form. Also, the above discussion has no intention to deal with the possibility of Mathean tradition which tradition says also located in Syria where Antioch was (Beker, *Paul the Apostle*, 130–31).

A Double Vision Hermeneutic

only power (*yáng*). It was a clash of two interpretations, which culminated in a head-to-head encounter. If both represented the true gospel, what did gospel actually mean? It could not be that both were correct.

The Galatians crisis is to be understood against such background. What actually happened to cause Paul to write such a letter reflecting his anxiety over the Galatians, was his understanding, described in Galatians 1:6 that the Galatians had deserted the gospel too "quickly." Paul was very shocked. But how "quickly" was that? It could be that it was not long after Paul brought them to Christ.[8] This problem is interwoven with the debate on the location of Galatia as referred to in Galatians. It could be the South Galatia referred to in Acts 14, as argued earlier, which will be referred to in the following.

3. Agitators or Just Another Interpretation of the Gospel?

The Galatians of course did not drift away simply because they were losing faith in what was brought to them by Paul. It was because there were people whom Paul described as "agitators" who came to disturb, confuse, upset, agitate and create perplexity (ταράσσω)[9] among them (1:7; 5:10; cf. Acts 15:24).

As J. Murphy-O'Connor contends, it is quite likely that "the Judaizers followed closely on the heels of Paul when he left Antioch, and so reached Galatia not long after he had left."[10] But who were these "Judaizers"?[11] Hays delicately defines them as 'missionaries." The term "Judaizers" has lost favor with scholars for it implies a Jewish and anti-Jewish faction which does not capture the real issue in Galatia for "Paul himself was a Jewish-Christian apostle, and the argument in Galatians is actually "between two different Jewish-Christian interpretations of the gospel." Second, there is a

---

8. Cf. Watson, *Paul, Judaism, and the Gentiles*, 111.

9. The antecedent are all possible meanings of ταράσσω. See Arichea and Nida, *A Handbook*, 13.

10. Murphy-O'Connor, *Paul*, 181.

11. There are different theories as to the identity of these people. For examples, Jewett's hypothesis is that they are "Jewish Christians who were stimulated by Zealot pressure into a nomistic campaign among their fellow Christians in the late forties and early fifties." See Jewett, "The Agitators and the Galatian Congregation," 198–212, cited from Longernecker, *Galatian*, xciii. Walter Schmithals thinks that they are Jewish-Christian Gnostics, and George Howard "Jewish Christian judaizers connected with Jerusalem." See Longenecker, *Galatians*, lxxxix–xcvi for detailed discussions.

Power in Text B2: Galatians

misunderstanding if the verb "Judaize" (2:14) is used. It appears to mean "to make someone else into a Jew," but the correct meaning is "to adopt Jewish practices." Hays thus remarks, "the label 'Judaizers' would aptly be applied to Gentiles who accepted the circumcision gospel, but it will not do to describe the rival missionaries themselves."[12]

As can be seen in Dunn's research, there had been different levels of assimilation of Gentiles into Jewish religious culture, whose status can be categorized as a) the proselyte, or full convert, b) the resident alien, and c) the God-fearer.[13] The need to go through circumcision as part of the gospel could have been regarded as a completion (Gal 3:3 ἐπιτελεῖσθε) of the rite of becoming a Jewish proselyte, a practice which was undergone at that time. As Jewett sees it, these Judaizers might have considered that they were bringing Gentile believers into "perfection."[14]

Thus, these "Missionaries" probably would not see themselves as "agitators," a word that reflects Paul's own "pejorative characterization of his opponents (1:7; 5:10, 12)," which quickly leads us to judge negatively what they do.[15] To them, it was Paul who had led the Galatians astray. What the "Missionaries" did was to try to bring them back onto the right track.

Thus, as Hays reconstructs, the "rival missionaries" were themselves, like Paul, Jewish by birth; but unlike him they had a different understanding of what the gospel implied. They "preached the necessity of circumcision as a means of entering covenant relationship with the God of Israel."[16] They probably "believed Jesus to be the Messiah of Israel and saw themselves as summoning Gentiles in the name of Jesus to come under obedience to the Law revealed to Moses at Mount Sinai," and "regarded Jesus as the authoritative interpreter of the Law."[17]

It is of interest to discovering these "Missionaries" had any direct relationship with Jerusalem, or with James, the leader of the Jerusalem churches. According to Murphy-O'Connor, James in Antioch was "strongly in favour of the maintenance of Jewish practices." Thus, he also infers, "The arguments used by those who insisted on the circumcision of all

---

12. For Hays above, see Hays, "Galatians—Introduction," 185; see also Dunn's study in "The Incident," 219–20.

13. Dunn, "The Incident," 212–19.

14. Jewett, he refers to his proposed Zealot theory in "The Agitators and the Galatian Congregation," cited in Longernecker, *Galatians*, xciii.

15. Hays, "Galatians—Introduction," 185.

16. Hays, "Galatians—Introduction," 185.

17. Hays, "Galatians—Introduction," 185.

converts must have appealed to James."[18] Hort is probably right to suggest that "the emissaries from James mistook his interests and turned his practical concerns into justification for their claim that Gentile Christians must be circumcised and take on a Jewish lifestyle."[19] However, it could be incorrect that James was simply concerned with a pastoral issue, i.e., "the Jewish-Gentile relations in the Christian communities found outside of Palestine."[20] It is quite possible that at that early stage, while Peter had a dramatic vision of unclean food which prepared him for the acceptance of unclean Gentiles, James was never recorded having experienced a similar incidence.

It is thus more convincing to think that while Paul was winning Gentile converts in Antioch and its surrounding region, most Jewish Christians in Jerusalem were still holding to the view that "circumcision was the traditional sign of belonging to the covenant people, which was seen as the divine channel of salvation,"[21] than that there was a fifty-fifty division in the Jerusalem church between the pro-libertine party (who thought of themselves as representing Paul's view) and the pro-tradition group.[22]

At some point the twin versions of the new faith through Jesus Christ were not allowed to develop independently. As Luke reports in Acts 15:1, "Then certain individuals came down from Judea and were teaching the brothers, 'Unless you are circumcised according to the custom of Moses, you cannot be saved.'" Here Luke could be talking about Christians from Jerusalem,[23] as he explains, "After Paul and Barnabas had no small dissension and debate with them, Paul and Barnabas and some of the others were appointed to go up to Jerusalem to discuss this question with the apostles and the elders" (15:2). Thus, the clash of two versions of Christianity had to be resolved through a more serious dialog.

---

18. Murphy-O'Connor, *Paul*, 138.

19. This is F. J. A. Hort's view, which is modified from J. B. Lightfoot, see Longenecker, *Galatians*, xci.

20. See Longenecker, *Galatians*, xci.

21. Murphy-O'Connor, *Paul*, 139.

22. Murphy-O'Connor, *Paul*, 138.

23. As has already been referred to, when Paul and Barnabas were preaching around the cities in South Galatia, already there were some Jews who objected to and disturbed their ministry (Acts 13:45, 50; 14:2, 19), although some Jews and proselytes accepted what they preached (13:43; 14:1). From the record of Act 13–14, there is no evidence to show that Jewish Christians caused the problem or even attacked them. Nevertheless, whether Jewish Christians were facing pressure from non-Christian Jews, Luke does not address clearly.

4. Jerusalem Conference: A Successful Attempt at Resolving the Galatian Problem?

One would expect that following the conference, consensus would have been reached and the problem settled. But it appears that meeting for discussion does not always solve more concrete problems in reality, at least not in a fortnight. The Jerusalem Conference was not directly about the situation in Galatia, but we can assume that even then, there were already people who had infiltrated the Galatian congregation to confuse them with "another gospel" (cf. Gal 1:6-9). Paul reminded the Galatians that those people "slipped in to spy on the freedom we have in Christ Jesus, so that they might enslave" them (2:4).

If we take the incident in Antioch where Peter avoided table fellowship with the Gentile Christians as happening after the conference,[24] it suggests that even after consensus had been reached in the conference, Peter could at times be ambivalent in relating to the Gentile believers. According to Paul, Peter "used to eat with the Gentiles," but after "certain people came from James . . . he drew back and kept himself separate for fear of the circumcision faction" (2:12).

Whether the Galatians had heard about the incident we cannot be sure, but Paul used it as a very strong example, for immediately after referring to it, he associates it with the Galatian situation, and admonishes them, "You foolish Galatians! Who has bewitched you? It was before your eyes that Jesus Christ was publicly exhibited as crucified! The only thing I want to learn from you is this: Did you receive the Spirit by doing the works of the law or by believing what you heard? Are you so foolish? Having started with the Spirit, are you now ending with the flesh?" (3:1-3).

This begs the question of why the Galatians were drawn towards the argument of whom Paul regarded as having agitated his congregation and dismantled the foundation he had laid. Paul mentions Peter in his letter to the Galatians. Does this imply that the way Peter acted had in some way influenced the Galatian community? Since Peter was among the significant figures in Jerusalem, a pillar of the church, together with James, it is possible that they naturally followed his way. As earlier stated, there were different

---

24. One view holds that the Antioch incident happened before the Jerusalem conference, which is supported by Ronald Fung, see Fung, *Galatians* (Chinese), 108. He provides one of the most detailed discussion of the issue (71-109). Even if it was after the conference, the word "ὅτε" (which either means "when" or "after") in Gal 2:11 does not help us much to ascertain how soon or how long after it Paul and Barnabas had gone back to Antioch and when Peter arrived.

A Double Vision Hermeneutic

levels of judaizing among Gentiles; these Gentile Christians might have assumed that receiving a more "complete" form of the gospel was not a major issue—i.e., being circumcised and following halakhic observance.[25] If the group from James (2:12) insisted that they needed to have both, as a younger church and at a time when Jerusalem still symbolized the authority of this emerging form of "Judaism," it would be entirely natural to follow the call of the power centre.

To think of Jerusalem as the orthodox, or symbol, of a stronger power centre would sound reasonable, for even Paul had a self-contradictory gesture toward the notional official centre of the Jesus faith. On the one hand, as Murphy-O'Connor points out, "The official tone of 'to submit something for consideration to somebody' (2:2)"[26] is an implicit recognition of the authority of the Jerusalem church.[27] On the other hand, the situation might have caused him to think that a stronger stance had to be insisted on. Thus, he emphasized his claim to an independent authority, received "through a revelation of Jesus Christ" (1:12) and that he "had been entrusted with the gospel for the uncircumcised, just as Peter had been entrusted with the gospel for the circumcised" (2:7).

We may argue that although he did not want to undermine the authority of Jerusalem, he was not willing to compromise, having seen the Galatians turning "to a different gospel" (1:6). He was compelled to argue against this other gospel. As a result, while Peter, Barnabas and other Jewish Christians (2:12–13), out of "pragmatic considerations, acted out as they would see it within the spirit of the Jerusalem agreement," to Paul, it was "an unprincipled compromise of the gospel (2:13–14)."[28]

It should be noted that by the time Paul wrote Galatians, some time had elapsed since the Jerusalem conference and it seemed that the interpretation of the gospel among the Gentile Christians had held sway. As Dunn infers, "the Antioch incident had a decisive effect in shaping Paul's future." He implies that, Paul "could no longer act as the Antioch church's delegate—the consequence, a breach with the church of Antioch." As a result he became an "independent missionary."[29]

---

25. Dunn, "The Incident," 227–29, 232.
26. Cf. Gal 1:6.
27. Murphy-O'Connor, *Paul*, 136. He is citing from Betz. For Betz, see Betz, *Galatians*, 86 n. 268.
28. Dunn, "The Incident," 227–29.
29. Dunn, "The Incident," 232.

If that is a correct estimation of Paul's situation, once Paul heard about what happened in Galatia, he could have felt an erosion of his power and authority over the Galatian churches, supposing these were in South Galatia, which he had established with Barnabas on their first mission trip sent by the Antioch church.[30]

However, what was more critical was that "covenantal nomism" was now threatening the heart of the gospel, although Peter might not have thought this, for he saw no contradiction between covenantal nomism and justification through faith.[31] For Paul, the danger of covenantal nomism was its emphasis on the Law as a condition of the covenant. If the Law was required, what was Christ's in justification through faith? Thus Paul posed a very serious statement to the Galatians: "for if justification comes through the law, then Christ died for nothing" (2:21). A purely theological reading will focus on finding in this statement an antithesis between justification (by faith) and the law and no reference to a power struggle. But could the law signify something other than serving as an antithesis to justification by faith? At this point, my interest lies in discovering if an interpretation of the text through the lens of power struggle can help shed light on our understanding of Paul's statement.

5. An Interpretation of Power Relations in the Galatian Church

I suggest that the Pauline notion of "principalities and powers" has to be brought into view to understand Paul's concern. It is a concern about power, but power that transcends the potential schism I underlined above. If Paul is only concerned with the power struggle on a sociological level, a sociological approach would best serve an interpretation of the text. As noted earlier, Sykes values employing sociological theories in the study of Christian theology and interpretation of biblical texts.[32] Polaski adopts this approach in relation to the Galatian church,[33] and will provide a useful example.

---

30. Cf. Dunn, "The Incident," 233–34. Dunn speculates that Paul's concern was that "his sphere of operations" were "being threatened and eroded," for what was decided to be an area marked by uncircumcised Christians would also become the circumcised one.

31. Dunn, "The Incident," 232.

32. Sykes, *Power*, 81–115.

33. She seems to rely heavily on Hans Dieter Betz's *Galatians* for her presupposition

A Double Vision Hermeneutic

According to Polaski, Paul's task "is to renegotiate power relations so as to re-establish his authority,"[34] for "he senses that his position of power is in jeopardy as the Galatians consider embracing a different conception of the gospel."[35] A purely sociological study of the above scenario would presumably focus on the power relationship first between Paul, and Peter and James, and secondly between the Jerusalem and Antioch churches, and probably also Galatian churches. Thus if the issue is one of power relations, i.e. the Galatians were facing Judaizers, and "exercising their ability to choose which beliefs to embrace,"[36] Paul was facing these "Judaizers" or probably the more challenging authority of Peter and James, to borrow Polaski, "[i]f Paul is to remain in a position of influence with them, he must negotiate this changing power relation in a way that fits with his own aims, redefining his role so that, he hopes, the Galatians will accept it and him."[37]

This slant has prompted Polaski to emphasize the autobiographical nature of Galatians and Paul's self-understanding as seen in Galatians 1–2,[38] and point out Paul's rhetoric in negotiating with the Galatians against "a complex relation of power." In other words, in order to persuade them that what he proclaimed was true, he had to refer to his authority by claiming a direct revelation from God.[39] Polaski's argument is as follows: as much as he obeyed the divine authority from which he received his authority, he wants his followers, the Galatians, to imitate him (4:11–12a) and be under his apostolic authority.[40] Thus, in Polaski's term, Galatians demonstrates how Paul dealt with power relations, casting his "disciplinary gaze" over the Galatians,[41] to demonstrate his power over them.

The sociological approach as such does indeed provide a perspective that helps capture the power dynamic of the Galatian situation. Sykes is correct in pointing out the dialectic between the real power of the gospel and its use as a medium to dominate. Moreover, it is a sound interpretation

---

of the nature of Paul's Letter to the Galatians. See Polaski, *Power*, 76. For an earlier review of Polaski, see chapter 5.

34. Polaski, *Power*, 75.
35. Polaski, *Power*, 101.
36. Polaski, Power, 76.
37. Polaski, *Power*, 77.
38. Polaski, *Power*, 77–83, 95–100.
39. Gal 1:1, 15–16; 2:7; see also Polaski, *Power*, 78.
40. Polaski, *Power*, 100–102.
41. Polaski argues this applying Foucault's insight, see Polaski, *Power*, 100.

of "the power of the gospel" rather than a naïve one, for which "an effort of imagination" is required to appreciate Paul's "rhetoric of power."[42]

Nevertheless, my conviction is that Paul's concern larger than simply power relations on personal level. Paul is concerned for a higher and deeper level: the invisible *shì* on a higher and more mythical level.[43] Paul judged "principalities and powers" to be of more concern. However, there is nothing in the text (Galatians) itself that allows us to bridge the Galatian situation and Paul's theology of "principalities and powers." For that, a more discursive path is required.

First, the situation had put Paul, an apostle-theologian and a profound thinker whom God had chosen to shoulder the burden of Gentile mission, on the brink of giving up and admitting his error or deriving a more profound theological reinterpretation of what the gospel really meant to Gentile Christians.

To use the language of *shì*, he preferred not to adopt the way of judging *shì*, the constellation of powers, i.e., to seek a balance of *yīn* and *yáng* power and adjust himself accordingly. His concern was not to manoeuver in the midst of "complex relationship of power" as Polaski puts it.[44] Rather than dealing with the tension between himself and those who had opposing ideas and interpretations of the gospel by engaging in a power struggle or liaising with them, he turned to a theological interpretation of the law vis-à-vis *stoicheia*.

I would argue against Polaski's application of Foucault in her estimation of the step Paul undertook to win back his position and influence over the Galatians.[45] It is more correct to believe that Paul did not try to reinforce his relationship with the Galatians and the true meaning of the gospel merely to bring them back within his disciplinary gaze. Such a motif cannot be derived from his calling by God, nor from his inner impetus to imitate Christ, because for him, Christ's work—dying on the cross for all—was not simply a political strategy, but a revelation of his and his Father's true being, one of mercy and righteousness. The work of Christ was to him a manifestation of God's profound knowledge and eternal plan to call Jews and Gentiles to be his people under the new covenant established through Christ.

42. Sykes, *Power*, 110–11.
43. I am using "mythical" or "myth" here following Wink's definition in Wink, *Naming*, 103–48.
44. Polaski, *Power*, 78.
45. Polaski, *Power*, 77, 100; see also above.

Thus, Paul may be depicted as "an architect *par excellence*" who discharged "pastoral power" in Foucault's terms with the ultimate aim of ensuring "individual salvation in the new world."[46] Such an interpretation of power may mislead one to think that Paul's concern was about pastoral power. However, although it was indeed pastoral power that was manifested, it was not Paul's aim to create such an influence. In the case of Galatian churches, the real concern for him was the Galatians' enslavement or captivation by the Law, as they had once been by the *stoicheia*.

It has earlier been stated that Paul could not entertain the imposition of circumcision on Gentile Christians and was furious about it, because it implied a return to enslavement by the cosmos of this age which the Galatians had previously been delivered from (Gal 4:8–10; Rom 5). In his mind, there was a fusion of implication between the *stoicheia* and the law. The following will focus on revealing how these converge in Paul's mind and their relationship to Paul's ideas on principalities and powers.

6. The Power of the στοιχεῖα and the Law

The στοιχεῖα and the law form a pair of power symbols in the Letter to the Galatians. While in Galatians 4:3, Paul refers to the στοιχεῖα (*stoicheia*), his concern is the Galatians' enslavement to the law. Ronald Fung contends that as "the servitude to the *stoicheia* in v.3 (*hypo ta stoicheia*) is described in v. 5 as subjection to law (*hypo nomon*), so that certainly what Paul has primarily in view here is the law, and that as an instrument of spiritual bondage."[47] He expressed his shock at the Galatians who were leading lives as if faith in Christ Jesus had had no effect at all. He thus challenges them with a series of questions: "You foolish Galatians! Who has bewitched you?" (v.4:1a) "Did you receive the Spirit by doing the *works of the law* or by believing what you heard? Are you so foolish? Having started with the Spirit, are you now ending with the flesh" (v.2–3)? "[D]oes God supply you with the Spirit and work miracles among you by your doing the *works of the law*, or by your believing what you heard (v.5)?"[48]

There is little doubt that Paul's interest was indeed in the law. However, it was probably due to the Galatians' pagan background that Paul referred to the *stoicheia* as he talked about the law's enslaving power on

---

46. Sykes, *Power*, 110.
47. Fung, *Galatians*, 181.
48. Italics mine.

them (4:8–10). The following will first focus on an exposition of στοιχεῖα followed by the law, and then interpret relationship between them, according to Paul.

6.1 What are the Στοιχεῖα?

What is the power of στοιχεῖα? Wink argues that the term στοιχεῖα "had no Hebrew antecedent, but was current in Greek from the time of Plato," and the use of it in Pauline letters "is uniquely Pauline."[49] The most significant characteristics of the στοιχεῖα, "elements," as Wink notes, refers to "the irreducible and basic principles or entities of a particular class of phenomena."[50] Dunn prefers to translate στοιχεῖα as "elemental forces" or "elemental spirits of the universe."[51] He defines στοιχεῖα as "heavenly beings (Gal 4:8–9—gods as popularly understood; Col 2:10—rulers and authorities)," pointing out that even within Judaism, there is a common belief in stars as living beings, and human beings as under the influence of these "cosmic forces."[52] Moreover, Dunn has pointed out that στοιχεῖα appears in Philo's *De aeternitate Mundi* (107–9) as "powers" and in Hermas's *Visions* (3.13.3) as the four στοιχεῖα that control the world.[53] These four elements are propounded as pairs of opposites, which include air versus earth and fire versus water, which "constitute the foundations of the cosmos."[54]

Furthermore, as Wink also argues, "When the ancients declared the four physical elements to be gods, they were in effect projecting into them the image of the quaternity, one of the oldest symbols of individuation,

---

49. For Wink's fuller discussion of στοιχεῖα, see Wink, *Naming*, 67–77; Wink, *Unmasking*, 128–52; Lee, "Interpreting the Demonic Powers in Pauline Thought," 61–63; also Longenecker, *Galatians*, 165.

50. Wink, *Unmasking*, 130–31.

51. Dunn, *Colossians and Philemon*, 150.

52. Dunn, *Colossians and Philemon*, 150. For evidences in Judaism, he lists Judg 5:20; Job 38:7; Dan. 8:10; 1 Enoch 86; Philo, *De opificio mundi* 73; *De plantatione* 12; Rev. 1:20; 9:1. Gerhard Delling has pointed out that the *stoicheia* that imply "the stars and other heavenly bodies, presumably because composed of the chief and finest of the elements, fire... did not appear in the literature until the middle of the second century A.D."; and that which imply "the stellar spirits, gods, demons, and angels" came only in the third and fourth century AD. See Longenecker, *Galatians*, 165.

53. Dunn, *The Epistles to the Colossians and to Philemon*, 149–50. Cf. Wink, *Unmasking*, 135 and Louis Martyn below.

54. Martyn, *Galatians*, 403–4.

wholeness, and the world-creating deity."⁵⁵ And that "we become slaves of the elements by granting them an ultimacy they do not possess."⁵⁶ These confirm our reading of στοιχεῖα in terms of power that can enslave.

6.2 The Στοιχεῖα of the Κόσμος

In Galatians 4:3 where στοιχεῖα appears, Paul forms a unique phrase combining στοιχεῖα with κόσμος as "τὰ στοιχεῖα τοῦ κόσμου (cf. Col 2:8; 2:20),"⁵⁷ i.e. "the elemental spirits (or the rudiments) of the world." Thus, there was according to Paul a connection between στοιχεῖα with κόσμος. In Paul's view, κόσμος—be it understood as the universe or the basic elements that exist and operate on certain principles—is not self-subsistent.⁵⁸

In Romans 5:12a Paul is announcing the entering of sin (ἁμαρτία) into the world or cosmos (τὸν κόσμον) with which came also the dominion of sin and death. Paul depicts this dominion of sin and death by referring to it as a kingdom (see ἐβασίλευσεν in 5:14, 21 and βασιλεύσῃ in 5:21), a collective power that exercises its dominion (βασιλεύω or κυριεύω) over us.⁵⁹ In other words, humans live in a power-dominated world. As humans we exist in the κόσμος of this αἰών which is "in estrangement from God" within a "system" alienated from God. ⁶⁰

From Paul's perspective, human beings are therefore not living in a neutral world but one that is infused with sin and the spirit of the dominating power. They are ruled by the ruler of the air of this aeon-cosmos (Eph 2:2).⁶¹ In Ephesians 2:1–2, Paul says, "You were dead through the

---

55. Wink, *Unmasking*, 135. For a fuller discussion of "the elements," see op. cit., 128–52 and Wink, *Naming*, 67–82.

56. Wink, *Unmasking*, 134.

57. Longenecker's contends that Paul's "use of τοῦ κόσμου ('of the world') seems also somewhat unique." See Longenecker, *Galatians*, 165.

58. Κόσμος (world) in its New Testament setting carries several layers of meaning. See Louw & Nida, 1.1; 9.2; 41.38.

59. For Paul's use of κυριεύω, see Rom 5:21; 6:9; 7:1; 14:9; 2 Cor 1:24; Eph 1:21; Col 1:16. See Wink, *Naming*, 20–21. I will not deal with verses in Eph and Col with respect to christological lordship and sovereignty over all other powers and principalities, as it is not the focus here. The focus is to show how these powers work than Christ's victory over them.

60. See Wink, *Engaging*, 51–52. For a fuller elaboration on the Domination System, see 51–63.

61. As Paul was speaking of αἰών in a Hellenistic context, he could have used it with "god of this age" in mind. See Markus Barth attests that at about 200 BC a god called Aion was being worship in Alexandria. See Barth, *Ephesians*, 214.

trespasses and sins in which you once lived, following the course of this world, following the ruler (ἄρχοντα) of the power (ἐξουσίας) of the air, the spirit that is now at work among those who are disobedient."[62] The two parallel clauses:

κατὰ τὸν αἰῶνα τοῦ κόσμου τούτου,
according to the age of this world,

κατὰ τὸν ἄρχοντα τῆς ἐξουσίας τοῦ ἀέρος
according to the ruler of the power of the air

could have been intended. Bruce, quite convinced of this reading believes that if ἄρχοντα means ruler then αἰῶνα should be read as a personified entity.[63] Markus Barth attests that around 200 BC a god called Aion was being worship in Alexandria and as Paul was speaking in a Hellenistic context, it is possible that he used it with the "god of this age" in mind.[64] However, it is not necessary to personify αἰῶνα in order to appreciate the parallelism of these two clauses.

Rendered together, αἰῶνα and κόσμου (genitive) in the first clause of Ephesians 2:1 carry enough weigh to imply a power at work in this κόσμος, which is against God. Paul uses ἄρχοντα (ruler) and ἐξουσίας (authority, power) to signify the influence of the invisible power that is "at work" (ἐνεργοῦντος).[65] While ἐξουσίας is often used to indicate "an authorization to exercise power," Bruce renders it as "dominion" or "domain". He provides a parallel reading in Colossians 1:13 where "the dominion of darkness" (τῆς ἐξουσίας τοῦ σκότους) is mentioned,[66] which in NRSV is translated as "the power of darkness." Thus "τῆς ἐξουσίας τοῦ ἀέρος" can be rendered as the *power (domain/dominion) of the air*. This power domain/dominion by implication is the "world-rulers of this darkness," which are also the "spiritual forces of wickedness" in the "heavenly realm," Bruce argues. Having deduced it as thus, he concludes that this "realm" is indeed what the "domain of the air" indicates.[67]

---

62. Also see Eph 6:12.

63. Bruce, *The Epistles*, 280–81. He gives 2 Cor 4:4 as one example of personification, which talks of "the god of this age."

64. Barth, *Ephesians*, 214.

65. The phrase "the sons of disobedience" (τοῖς υἱοῖς τῆς ἀπειθείας) will be discussed under the section "the power of sin."

66. Cf. NIV reads "the dominion of darkness."

67. Bruce, *Colossians, Philemon, and Ephesians*, 282.

A Double Vision Hermeneutic

To Paul "the rulers (ἀρχά)ς," "the authorities (ἐξουσίας)," "the cosmic powers (κοσμοκράτορας) of this present darkness", and "the spiritual (forces) of evil in the heavenly places" all belong to a category beyond the "enemies of blood and flesh" (v.12). While Wink argues that ἐξουσίας is often used in the NT to "refer to a structural dimension of its existence,"[68] he nevertheless acknowledges that Paul does use ἀρχῆς καὶ ἐξουσίας (καὶ δυνάμεως) (Eph 1:21; 3:10; 1 Cor 15:24) to denote spiritual entities.[69]

In talking about the στοιχεῖα which belong to the *aeon-cosmos* Paul wanted to emphasize that when the Galatians came to know God, they were "enslaved to beings that by nature are not gods" (Gal 4:8). Hays argues that, this shows that for Paul the στοιχεῖα were not merely "rudimentary religious principles," but rather "personified forces that once exercised hostile dominion over the lives of his readers," the Galatians."[70]

Such a religious-cultural background appears to have been an undercurrent that surfaced and found echo in the observance of "special days, and months, and seasons, and years" (4:10) though in this instance in accordance with the Jewish calendar. As Hays says, "The Galatians show themselves to be coming back under the sway of the *stoicheia* by adopting a pattern of life governed by fixed calendrical observances. The observances of the Jewish liturgical calendar were calibrated to the motions of the sun and moon (Sabbath, new-moon festivals)."[71] Thus, the Jewish liturgical calendar and the στοιχεῖα are indeed creating the same enslaving effect on the Galatians.

Paul's concern with enslavement to these elements through the Galatians' submission to a belief in them, or "granting them an ultimacy" as Wink remarks.[72] This idea will be woven into the following section for further deliberation.

---

68. Wink, *Naming*, 15–16.

69. Wink, *Naming*, 17. For its extrabiblical uses, see Wink, ibid, footnote 11.

70. Hays, "Galatians 4:8–11 Commentary," 287.

71. See Hays, "Galatians 4:8–11 Commentary," 288. He points out, "Jewish sources from the Second Temple period show that there was heated controversy between advocates of lunar and solar calendrical systems over the proper way of keeping times and seasons." Some examples of Second Temple sources Hays mentions are *Jubilees* and *I Enoch*.

72. Wink, *Unmasking*, 134.

6.3 Relating the στοιχεῖα to the Law

What kind of relationship exists between the law and the στοιχεῖα? Answering to his own query regarding "what relationship Paul envisaged between the law as a demonic agency and the principalities and powers,"[73] Caird concludes that "[e]ither Paul regarded the law itself as one of the powers, or behind the law he perceived the existence of angelic beings who were responsible for the law's enforcement."[74] This is not a satisfactory answer. Galatians needs to be examined for a possible linkage.

Paul had in mind certain practices the Galatians might adopt, which were in similar to τὰ στοιχεῖα τοῦ κόσμου. Following his criticism of στοιχεῖα as "weak and beggarly," he went on to admonish the Galatians for "observing special days, and months, and seasons, and years." Scholars have debated as to whether these refer to Jewish or Gentile practices,[75] but, in accordance with the incidence of Peter in Gal 2 and the continuing influence of the Judaizers in early Pauline ministry, I adhere to the view that these observances were probably the result of the absolutization of Judaism.[76]

Paul had a very clear idea that τὰ στοιχεῖα could not give life but rather enslave, thus by comparing the law to τὰ στοιχεῖα he prohibited it. For as Dunn says, "law" is a "quasi-power",[77] as much as it has become a binding power, it enslaves people, like sin and τὰ στοιχεῖα which work in this κοσμοσ. Like στοιχεῖα, it becomes itself a power "set in charge over Israel like a slave-custodian or guardian (Gal 3:23-25; 4:1-3, 9-10)."[78] Caird, in his study of the law, includes both Jew and Gentile as potential captives to the "régime of law" be it the régime of "elemental spirits" or "the Torah".[79] He asserts that "[t]he demonic forces of legalism . . . can be

---

73. Caird, *Principalities and Powers*, 43.

74. Caird, *Principalities and Powers*, 44.

75. See Longenecker, *Galatians*, for his discussion of this relating to the law (Torah), 165–66.

76. This is confirmed at least by Wink, Scott, Lee, Caird, and Martyn. Wink, *Naming*, 72, 77–82; Scott, *Adoption as Sons of God*, 157–61; Lee, "Interpreting the Demonic Powers in Pauline Thought," 62 where he also makes comparisons of Gal 2:19 with Col 2:20, Gal 3:23 with Gal 4:3, and Rom 8:3 with Gal 4:9 between the law and the στοιχεῖα; Caird, *Principalities and Powers*, 41–49; Martyn, *Galatians*, 412–15.

77. Dunn, *Romans 1–8*, 286.

78. Dunn, *Colossians and Philemon*, 150.

79. Caird, *Powers and Principalities*, 48–49, for a more complete discussion, see 39–51.

A Double Vision Hermeneutic

called 'principalities and powers' or 'elemental spirits of the world.'"[80] This is because the law had been "elevated to absolute validity,"[81] and granted "an ultimacy."[82]

Martyn hypothetically proposes that when Paul is speaking of στοιχεῖα in 4:3 and 4:9, he is not thinking about the four elements but expounding on opposites such as Jew versus Gentile, circumcision versus uncircumcision, male versus female, slave versus free, the law versus the no-law,[83] although to the Galatians' the στοιχεῖα would have been the four elements prior to their acceptance of the gospel. Martyn is probably correct, for from verses 1 to 7, Paul's refers to the power of the στοιχεῖα and the power of the law intermingled as if they both served as guardians and house managers with their respective powers, essentially the same but different in form, which tend to enslave.

It is assumed from comments in Paul's argument, that some teachers were introducing the Galatians to observe certain important dates. They were proposing that leaving their old religious way was not enough, or in Martyn's words, that there were certain holy times that were ordained by God himself in the law which should be observed. Moreover, as Martyn has particularly identified in chapter 4 verse 9 the notion of knowing God compared with being known by God, he suggests that those teachers "are enticing the Galatians by speaking of a state of perfection that can be achieved by ascent to true knowledge of God in the life of Law observance (3:3)."[84]

We do not know to what extent the Galatians had paid homage to the στοιχεῖα before they turned to Christ. In Paul's own words (Gal 4:8-9), "Formerly, when you did not know God, you were enslaved to beings that by nature are not gods. Now, however, that you have come to know God, or rather to be known by God, how can you turn back again to the weak and beggarly elemental spirits? How can you want to be enslaved to them again?" For Paul the fundamental nature of their current enslavement to the law is the same as once to the στοιχεῖα.

One fundamental question Paul could not avoid was the new status of the covenant and the law which God had established with his forefathers. Paul had possibly thought this through during his years in Arabia

---

80. Caird, *Powers and Principalities*, 51, cf. 43–44.
81. Caird, *Powers and Principalities*, 49.
82. Wink, *Unmasking*, 134.
83. Martyn, *Galatians*, 404.
84. Martyn, *Galatians*, 412–13.

(Gal 1:17) or throughout at least fourteen years of service, before he went up to meet the church leaders in Jerusalem (2:1-10). Galatians 3:24-26 is a key passage denoting Paul's resolution to this theological question: justification by faith rather than under the discipline of the law, and through faith becoming children of God. If this new foundation for admission into a covenantal relationship with God was crucial to Paul, his outrage and shock at the Galatians' captivity to the law is understandable.

While elaborating on the relationship between the principles of faith and law, and having reminded his audience of his unique relationship with them (Gal 4:11-20), he throws them a serious question: "Tell me, you who desire to be subject to the law, will you not listen to the law?" (4:21) He concludes by contrasting of two covenants (4:22-31), one under Mount Sinai which thus "corresponds to the present Jerusalem" (4:25a) and one under the "Jerusalem above"; one is of the law, the other through faith; one of the flesh, the other through the Holy Spirit (4:23, 29). The "present Jerusalem" may be important as a power centre, where Peter and other apostles are based; but it is not the earthly Jerusalem that determines one's status. It is in "faith" one finds one's status in the "Jerusalem above."

Paul's concern about the law is prominent—its influence over humans and its potential threat to the Galatians to lead them back into captivity by the στοιχεῖα. The allusion to στοιχεῖα in Gal 4 is entangled with Paul's concern over the law of circumcision being imposed on the Gentile Christians. Imagine now, Paul questioning the Galatians: Why allow yourselves to "submit again to a yoke of slavery" and "let yourselves be circumcised" (5:1-2)? After many years of preaching it, the profound implication of the gospel was now clearer to him. Paul understood the incompatibility of the two diverse ways: one through the perfection of the law, the other through faith in Jesus Christ. One cannot be intermingled with the other, not even a little. Thus he warned the Galatians: "Once again I testify to every man who lets himself be circumcised that he is obliged to obey the entire law" (5:3). A little "giving way," to the imposition of circumcision on Gentile Christians opened a broad way for the entire law to march in.

Nevertheless, Paul's view of the law is indeed subtle. In this reconstruction of the Galatian situation and interpretation of the relationship of στοιχεῖα and to the law, impression may have been given that for Paul everything about the law was negative. The law is an accomplice of sin (cf. Rom 7:8b-11), which arouses the flesh in slumber to wake up and sin. "For sin, seizing an opportunity in the commandment, deceived me and through it killed me" (Rom 7:11). As Caird pursues the relationship between the law, sin and death in Romans, he calls them "a trio of evil forces by which human life is held in bondage," which are "reckoned among the principalities and powers" Paul refers to again in Romans 8:38-39.[85]

However, "the law is holy, and the commandment is holy and just and good" (7:12). Rather than an accomplice of sin, the law is a guardian and trustee to whom God has entrusted His heirs to be under its care. Galatians 4:1-3 states, "My point is this: heirs, as long as they are minors, are no better than slaves, though they are the owners of all the property; but they remain under guardians and trustees until the date set by the father. So with us; while we were minors, we were enslaved to the elemental spirits (στοιχεῖα) of the world." Hence the law is also our "disciplinarian" (παιδαγωγός in 3:24-25).

Paul is here subtly weaving two strands of thought into one: relating to the law and to the στοιχεῖα. Those under the law should refer to the Jews who were given the law; those under the influence of the στοιχεῖα the Gentile Christians in the Galatian church.

First Paul defines those under the law as those under its guardianship and discipline who are heirs but lived as minors before Christ came. As minors, they were susceptible to the influence of the cosmos and thus "were enslaved to the στοιχεῖα" (Gal 4:3). In this sense, the Jews were not much different from the Gentiles who were directly under the enslaving power of the στοιχεῖα.

Paul thus interweaves two situations into an integrated argument, evident in verses 9 and 10: "Now, however, that you have come to know God, or rather to be known by God, how can you turn back again to the weak and beggarly στοιχεῖα? How can you want to be enslaved to them again? You are observing special days, and months, and seasons, and years." The convergence of these two groups of people is by way of the said observances. While in the past, the Gentiles might have paid their homage to the στοιχεῖα and gods (cf. verse 8) on special dates, the Jews were also giving special significance to particular laws, practices, and dates. If Paul used στοιχεῖα in parallel to the law, the τοῦ κόσμου might also be used to modify "the law." Although the law was meant for the good of the people, it could turn into a dominating power that could enslave. Thus, as Bruce remarks, as once τὰ στοιχεῖα τοῦ κόσμου had shown their power to enslave, the law now condemns those who do not do or have not done what the law requires.[86]

---

85. Caird, *Powers and Principalities*, 44.
86. Cf. Bruce's similar exposition in *Paul*, 182. Cf. Martyn, *Galatians*, 401.

No wonder Paul exclaims, "I am afraid that my work for you may have been wasted" (4:11). To Paul, both Gentiles and Jews, are children of God. For Jews, "born under the law," the requirements of the law were settled through Christ. They are now no longer "minors" (who were not much better than slaves, see 4:1) but are heirs, or indeed the children of God (4:4-8). Likewise, the Gentiles, formerly under the power of the στοιχεῖα, "have come to know God, or rather to be known by God" (4:9). Paul argues in Romans 9:25-26 citing the Book of Hosea,

> Those who were not my people I will call "my people," and she who was not beloved I will call "beloved." And in the very place where it was said to them, "You are not my people," there they shall be called children of the living God.

The new principle that unites these two groups is faith in Christ, not the law, for now faith has come and Christ has also come (3:23-26).

Paul was extremely angry and outraged by the effect the agitators had on the Galatian churches; having received their status based on faith the Galatian churches were deserting that gospel and accepting another (1:6).

Therefore, rejecting Polaski's sociological approach which depicts Paul's concern as his pastoral power over the Galatians and intention to win back his position and influence, I have argued that his concern was over their re-captive by the power of the cosmos through a false emphasis on the law. Thus, his most crucial and desperate need was not to deal with power relations. Instead, Paul's passion was to prevent the Galatians being drawn into emphasizing the law as the Judaizers saw it, or, by implication, believing in the necessity of abiding by rules and regulations to be regarded as a real Christian and then boasting about it (cf. 6:13).

Indeed, if Paul had lingered around the problem of power relations, it is doubtful that we would have his Letter to the Galatians as it stands today. Therefore, it is important to conclude from this discussion of Galatians that rather than focusing on the changing power relations, it is attention to Paul himself and his inner thought world that is the most crucial. Paul's inner thought life is a reflection of his inheritance of Jewish tradition, integrated with his calling by his Lord Jesus Christ. As Caird argues, "I would now suggest that his (Paul's) belief in the existence of demonic powers behind the law owed a very great deal to his own religious experience."[87] He elaborates,

---

87. Caird, *Powers and Principalities*, 52.

A Double Vision Hermeneutic

> He had been a Pharisee . . . His zeal for the law had led him to repudiate Jesus as a blasphemer who had died under the curse of the law . . . He who had thought to possesses in the law the complete and final revelation of God had failed to recognize God in the person of person of his Son. In defending the honour of God's law he had become the enemy of God.[88]

Caird has concluded that "Paul's treatment of the law bears at every point the indelible mark of that moment in his own spiritual history when he had realized that everything he had regarded as highest and best had combined to put Christ on the Cross."[89]

Paul's understanding of power cannot therefore be understood independently of his understanding of sin, for the latter had penetrated the cosmos of this age which is under the rule of principalities and powers not of this world, but of "the ruler of the power of the air" (Eph 2:2). All things within this cosmos are in need of liberation from bondage to this power, through faith in Jesus Christ (Gal 3:25). It is from this deeper level of his being that he saw what had happened in the Galatian churches. Paul, as a subject had appropriated a worldview that saw the invisible realm, which Wink has reinterpreted as the inner aspect of power; he thus saw what happened around him through this perspective on "principalities and powers."

This power is working from within the life of all humanity, judged to be "children of disobedience" (Eph 2:2). *It is a subjective power as if working from the inside, out of one's soul.* It is part of what it means to be human, a dominated existence locked within this aeon-cosmos. *Although the aeon-cosmos is first something "out there," it is also something that is at work in human flesh, reflecting an existential reality one yearns to be delivered from.*

Thus we have studied the two power symbols: the law and the *stoicheia* against the socio-historical context of Galatian church, from Paul's theological perspective of the principalities and powers, to demonstrate the intermingling of Text B2 and B1. The following chapter will assemble the other four from 1 Corinthians.

---

88. Caird, *Powers and Principalities*, 52-53
89. Caird, *Powers and Principalities*, 53.

7

Power in Text B2: Pauline Text II: Corinthians

This chapter, a continuation of chapter 6, serves as the second part of the discussion aimed at interpreting the Pauline account of "principalities and powers" as Text B1 intermingled with Text B2. While the last chapter focused on Galatians, this chapter will focus on 1 Corinthians. The purpose is to identify the power symbols that had a strong influence on the Corinthian church, attempt to consider them within the Corinthian social context and interpret them with an awareness of the Pauline critique of "principalities and powers." This intermingling of Texts B1 and B2 (as 1 Corinthians) will again serve to demonstrate the intersubjectivity of the two texts, each being appropriated into the other within me, the interpreting subject. The shift of focus between B1 and B2 exhibits a double awareness in the interpretation. Nevertheless, although "the same Paul" is the author, there are several years between the writing of Galatians and 1 Corinthians.[1] As the following discussion will serve the above purpose rather than be a study of 1 Corinthian on its own terms, engagement with 1 Corinthians is not exhaustive, but of necessity, selective.

1. An Introduction

Having discussed Acts 15 and Galatians, attention will now be focused on the Corinthian church, "the most exasperating church with which Paul had to deal," Murphy-Murphy-O'Connor comments.[2] Why? What hap-

---

1. See discussion in the introduction.
2. Murphy-O'Connor, *Paul*, 252.

A Double Vision Hermeneutic

pened there? What kind of problem was found in the Corinthian church? Meeks, in his classic sociological study of the Pauline letters, confirms the frequent appearance of terminology related to power and authority. He acknowledges that how the issue of authority is related to "the conflicts." In terms of who has power and authority, he points out that it also involves "who makes decisions and who has to obey" and "why."[3] This is particularly true when the focus is the power struggle between different groups.

This current study of power in 1 Corinthians will exploit two aspects: patronage and social network, or status, on the one hand, and wisdom and knowledge on the other. Andrew Clarke points out that patronage and social status in Roman Corinth is of particular importance.[4] Innumerable articles have been produced discussing the issues of wisdom and knowledge (gnosis) that have played a significant part in the Corinthian problem.[5] The intention here is to bring together these two aspects into a whole. Together with the law and the *stoicheia* explicated earlier, these will be used to construct a six-power constellation, based on the hexagramic system, to form a double vision hermeneutics of Texts A and B, which will be explained in the next chapter.

As asserted at the end of the previous section, Paul himself and his inner thought world are the true concern of the problem of power. Nevertheless, both the first and the second Corinthian letters, besides being revelatory of his soul,[6] also reflect the power relations he is a part of. If Paul and his inner thought world is the key hermeneutical lens through which the letters are understood, it can be assumed that his perspective would not have greatly altered over a short space of time, and therefore his experience in the Galatian and Corinthian churches formed a continuity that would become part of how he later regarded power. Such continuity could well have continued into the years during which situations prompted him to write Galatians and 1 Corinthians.[7] I would thus opt

---

3. Meeks, *The First Urban Christians*, 117.

4. Clarke, *Leadership*, 62. Clarke points out, "In Graeco-Roman times it was widely assumed that there was no equal standing before the law . . . All parties involved in litigation and were aware of their own status in relation to that of other parties."

5. For literature on this aspect, see discussion below.

6. Murphy-O'Connor thinks 2 Cor is "much-more self-revelatory" where "the Apostle unwittingly lays bare his soul." See idem, *Paul*, 252.

7. See Lightfoot, *Galatians*, 36–56 who dates 2 Cor and Romans to around AD 57–58; see also Fung, *Galatians* (Chinese), 79–109 for his critique of Lightfoot's view as well as Fung's own rationale for an earlier date and location of composition of Galatians to sometime before Jerusalem conference at Antioch in Syria. That would be a gap of around seven years between the two dates if we assume that the conference was held

for a wider time frame between his first visit to South Galatia and the appearances of Galatians and 1 Corinthians, which allows Paul enough time to reflect on various journeys and disturbances, and a more mature consideration practices that were not compatible with the gospel and the life and crucifixion of Jesus Christ. This view allows the Antioch incident to settle his mind in and the problem of agitators to further develop and ignite Paul's furious reaction to them in Galatians.

As Paul continued to preach the gospel, he was led by the Holy Spirit to visit Macedonia (Act 16–18). In the city of Thessalonica he (and Silas) once again faced the attack of Jewish people who were jealous of their work (17:1–9). As they moved to Beroea and preached in the synagogue, again those "Jews of Thessalonica" came "to stir up (ταράσσοντες) and incite the crowds" (17:13).[8] While there might be an undercurrent of Judaizers stirring up another faction in Corinthian church, it did not appear to be a main concern for Paul in 1 Corinthians. Nevertheless it may have been a problem, as seen in 2 Corinthians.[9]

---

around 51 according to Murphy-O'Connor's calculation. Since whatever the dating is, the issue is still unsettled. Murphy-O'Connor also criticizes Lightfoot's hypothesis in this regard as "without foundation." He argues, "It is not impossible that the Judaizers followed closely on the heels of Paul when he left Antioch, and so reached Galatia not long after he had left. If we further assume that their impact was immediate, and that Paul was warned soon enough, Galatians could have been dispatched before the snows closed the high country in the autumn of AD 52." See Murphy-O'Connor, *Paul*, 181. However, he dates Galatians to the spring (April or May) of 53. And following his argument, we will have a gap of around two years with his dating of 1 Cor to May 54. See *Paul*, 182–84. If that is the case, we still have between Galatians and 1 Corinthians a very close proximate time within which Paul's emotion and thought may remain focus on similar issues.

8. The same Greek word is used in Gal 1:7; 5:10.

9. Murphy-O'Connor hypothesizes a Judaizer's alliance with the free-thinking Hellenistic spirit-people. He reasons that, for the former group Moses was "the great Lawgiver, whose words had enduring value." For the latter, Moses who being described by Philo as "the perfect wise man" indeed "epitomized all Hellenistic virtues as 'king and lawgiver and high priest and prophet.'" For this reason, Murphy-O'Connor argues, "Moses was everything that the spirit-people aspired to be." Murphy-O'Connor, *Paul*, 302–3; for "spirit-people", see esp. idem, "*Pneumatikoi* in 2 Corinthians," 59–66; idem, "*Pneumatikoi* and Judaizers in 2 Cor 2:14—4:6," 42–58. Clues regarding spirit-people can be found embedded in 1 Cor 1–4, 13–16; see also idem, *Paul His Story*, 163–65. We shall talk about "spirit-people" later, but the problem of Judaizers will not occupy the attention in this discussion of 1 Corinthians.

2. Corinthian Situation

After Beroea, Paul arrived in Athens, and from Athens went to Corinth. As earlier stated regarding Galatians, dating composition of Paul's letters as well as their sequence is not as simple as it appears. Fortunately there is no necessity for meticulous reconstruction in this discussion.[10]

Paul stayed at Corinth for eighteen months (18:11). But something happened then between the time he left Corinth and the time he felt compelled to write 1 Corinthians. He reached Ephesus a few years after he had first planted the Corinth church. He may have written 1 Corinthians while in Ephesus,[11] but, as Paul himself says in the letter, he had already written a "previous letter" (1 Cor 5:9).[12]

According to Murphy-O'Connor's reconstruction, Paul left Ephesus in October 54, implying that he stayed there from summer 52 (July or August) to 54. However, most of the summer of 54 (probably from mid-June to early August) was spent in Corinth on a short visit to deal with an urgent issue. He possibly dispatched 1 Corinthians before his visit, which is dated to April or May 54. Then potentially he could have been in Macedonia in the spring of 55. Thus, 2 Corinthians could have been written during 55, before he visited Corinth again during that summer due to the crisis that triggered the writing of 2 Corinthians 10–13.[13] It is not necessary to regard 2 Corinthians 1–9 and 10–13 as two separate letters as Murphy-O'Connor does.[14] Between 1 and 2 Corinthians, there could have been an additional "painful letter."[15]

A reconstruction of the above time frame assumes possible problems and crises arising in the Corinthian church. It also helps identify the time span between the planting of the church and the dispatch of 1 Corinthians as around 4 to 5 years.[16] It is therefore quite shocking to see so many

---

10. For example, Murphy-O'Connor dates this to April 50, which means that Paul stayed in Corinth until September 51 (*Paul*, 28–29). Sampley dates it to around 50 as well, see Sampley et al., *Acts—First Corinthians*, 776; while Witherington to around 49-50 (*Conflict and Community*, 72).

11. Sampley, "1 Corinthians—Introduction," 776–77; Fee, *First Epistle*, 15; Lightfoot, *Galatians*, 38.

12. See also, Murphy-O'Connor, *Paul*, 182–83, 252, who dates it to the summer of 53; see also Fee, *First Epistle*, 6–7.

13. Murphy-O'Connor, *Paul*, 28–30, 180–82, 252–56.

14. For Murphy-O'Connor, see *Paul*, 254; for a recent supporter of the unity of 2 Corinthians, see Sampley, "1 Corinthians—Introduction," 776.

15. Murphy-O'Connor, *Paul*, 252.

16. This could extend to around five or six years if we include the writing of 2

problems emerging within just a few years. What happened in Corinth was no less striking than the crisis in the Galatian churches. It is therefore appropriate to project an understanding of the social background of the Corinthian community, back to its preexistence before the Christian community was formed.[17] I contend that the social background of the church members might have a bearing on the problems found in the Corinthian church.

A full scale survey of the composition of the Corinthian community and the subgroups within it that may have caused the problems to which Paul responded would be too broad for the purpose here.[18] It is not unreasonable to amalgamate the various problems of the Corinthian church by focusing on one issue: power. The following is an attempt to present the probable power symbols which existed within the church. Having said this, the immediate task is to reconstruct the *situation* Paul faced in the Corinthian church, revolved around the problem of power.

Our reconstruction is at first a sociological one. A theological interpretation will follow. While it is correct to say that the problems in the Corinthian church, as reflected in the first letter, "were social, not theological in origin," as Ben Witherington argues,[19] for Paul all the social issues in the Corinthian church arose from distorted theology, e.g., the Corinthian church members' view of authority and status compared to the crucified Christ, or their boasting of social background. The following will not be devoted so much to the reconstruction of what actually happened and who Paul's opponents were, but to identifying symbols of social power. The purpose of this approach is to uncover Paul's deeper concern: what these power symbols signified and in what way they contravened a true understanding of following Christ?

Corinthians. However, as the focus of this thesis is 1 Corinthians, the gap between the dates when 1 and 2 Corinthians were written is too to conceive of a major change in the atmosphere of the church.

17. For a good classic in this area of study, see Meeks, "The Social Level of Pauline Christians," in *The First Urban Christians*, 51–73; see also Theissen, *Social Setting*. Thiselton affirms that theirs should be perceived as "the accepted synthesis" of earlier reconstructions, see Thiselton, *First Epistle to the Corinthians*, 26.

18. Many scholars have done marvelous job in this regard, see literature on Corinthians referred to in this section.

19. Witherington III, *Conflict and Community in Corinth*, 74.

A Double Vision Hermeneutic

3. Church Members from Various Social Positions and Backgrounds

As scholars have pointed out, the Corinthian church resembles the make-up of the city itself (in terms of the socioeconomic and religious background of its members).[20] To begin with Paul's own remark: "not many of you were wise by human standards, not many were powerful, not many were of noble birth" (1 Cor 1:26). It is most likely that the majority of the congregation, mainly Gentiles, were from the middle to lower rather than the very top or bottom of the social stratum. If Theissen is correct, it was probably the lower end which made up the main church congregation.[21] The middle class could have been merchants and freemen who were not born into an élite or upper class background.[22] At the very top of Corinthian society were people such as great magnates while those at the very bottom were field slaves; both these groups were lacking in the congregation.[23] As for the élite they "were a minority in the city," let alone in the church.[24] The uneven proportion of upper class and privileged elite holding influential positions in the church to the make up of the church itself or was probably one of the main causes of disunity in the Corinthian church.[25] This people group had social ability which they could use to exert influence even in the church and they had no doubt dominated "the affairs of the church." As Murphy-O'Connor neatly puts it, they had taken "their authority for granted" and assumed their influence in the church by default, which made even the official positions in the church redundant.[26] Evidence for this view can be found in the text.

---

20. Sampley, "1 Corinthians—Introduction," 777.

21. Murphy-O'Connor, *Paul*, 273; also Meeks, *Urban Christians*, 73; Theissen, *Social Setting*, 69, cited from Thiselton, *First Epistle*, 26.

22. Murphy-O'Connor points out, "Among the unnamed members of the 'households' of Stephanas and Crispus, it is very probable that there were slaves (1 Cor 7:21). While legally disadvantaged, such house slaves often enjoyed a standard of living and education denied to those born free, and could look forward to exercising their trained talents in freedom. Only then would they have to provide for themselves; a slave was guaranteed food and lodging." See Murphy-O'Connor, *Paul*, 271. See also Barnett, *Second Epistle*, 5-9 for an analysis of these and the above mentioned figures.

23. Murphy-O'Connor, *Paul*, 273; also Meeks, *Urban Christians*, 73.

24. Murphy-O'Connor, *Paul*, 271.

25. Theissen, *Social Setting*, 69, cited from Thiselton, *First Epistle*, 26; Murphy-O'Connor, *Paul*, 271.

26. Murphy-O'Connor, *Paul*, 271.

There were two further categories of people in the Corinthian church. The first were the wealthy people of Corinth, possibly freemen, who had earned their social status by moving upwards using wealth and social connections. They represented a social strata similar to the modern middle or upper middle classes.[27] The others were slaves who, contrary to our conventional belief, enjoyed a certain freedom and social mobility.

There were also people such as Crispus (1 Cor 1:14) who "is identified by Acts 18:8 as an *archisynagogos*," probably "an honorific title awarded by a community in gratitude for a donation to their place of prayer." Such designation implies that Crispus may have been wealthy enough to have "sufficient superfluous wealth to become a patron" which had qualified for the title.[28]

Thus, those who were able to host Paul and his colleagues were probably more financially self-sufficient. A typical example is Chloe, 1 Cor 1:11, which refers to "Chloe's people" bringing Paul news about quarrels among the Corinthians. Those people, according to Meeks, were "slaves or freedmen or both."[29] Bruce suggests that Chloe "seems to have been head of the household or owner of the house," a reference to "Chloe's people" (1 Cor 1:11), implied "members of a well-to-do household or house-church, presumably."[30] In such a household we thus find both categories of people classified above.

Another example is Gaius (1 Cor 1:14) who was likely one of the people of wealth. He is mentioned in Romans 16:23 as "host to me and to the whole church."[31] Similarly, there were Prisca (Priscilla) and Aquila who were probably wealthy and had a relatively high social status. As merchants, they would have been freemen or even lower class, but definitely not from the bottom echelons. In other words, "[t]hey are artisans, but independent, and by ancient standards they operate on a fairly large scale."[32] Their affluence probably allowed movement from place to place and in turn, the establishment of a sizable house in three different cities. They

---

27. See Murphy-O'Connor, *Paul*, 271. See also Barnett, *Second Epistle*, 5–9.

28. Murphy-O'Connor, *Paul*, 267.

29. Meeks, *Urban Christians*, 59. While Meeks postulates that they "have brought news from Corinth to Ephesus," Murphy-O'Connor does not agree that they were from Corinth (*Paul*, 272).

30. Bruce, *Paul*, 258.

31. Murphy-O'Connor, *Paul*, 267. See Meeks, *Urban Christians*, 58 also for his evaluation of Gaius, Crispus, and Stephanas, Achaius, and Fortunatus' status in comparison to those Paul reprimanded.

32. Meeks, *Urban Christians*, 59.

had, according to Meeks, also "acted as patrons for Paul and for Christian congregations."[33] Nevertheless, not all members of the Corinthian church with such background were a support to Paul and his ministry. There were others who became the cause of various problems found in Corinthian church as will be discussed later.

Hence, wealth and pre-conversion social status were a natural precursor to becoming a church leader. Those who were wealthy enough to own a place enabled them to host a home, had the wherewithal to host an itinerant preacher such as Paul, or offer it as a place could be where a house church could meet, in which case, it was very probable that the social status of the new Christian household still functioned as it had done previously.

A master of a household turning to Christ in Paul's time may carry with it the implication of the whole household, including the slaves, following him.[34] This being the case, it is not hard to imagine that one's accepted social status may be in tension to the new status in Christ. A household-turned-house-church with its original household members, plus others who gathered there probably through previous social connections, may have formed one type of power centre and network, which may have been one of the causes of factions within the church.[35]

Paul had brought the gospel to Corinth only a few years earlier. Although there were some in the church who had come to Christ earlier than others, it is pertinent to question whether these new Christians had correctly understood the meaning of the gospel or if it had indeed transformed their hearts and lives.

Some might even have thought that the new community would provide a new opportunity to move up the social ladder. As Witherington infers, this kind of patronage relationship, which existed in the world Paul inhibited, is "a social arrangement that dominated relationships and shaped personality . . . outside one's family or circle of friends." It created struggle within a social system "where power and wealth were largely in the hands of the few," and "gaining honour and advancing up the ladder of society required help."[36] At its worst, this brand of patronage relationship existed "between persons of differing social status," or "between a superior

---

33. Meeks, *Urban Christians*, 59.

34. Such an implication can be found in texts like Philemon, Gal 3:28, and Eph 6:8.

35. Murphy-O'Connor, *Paul*, 271; see also Theissen, *Social Setting*, 69, cited from Thiselton, *First Epistle*, 26.

36. Witherington, *Paul Quest*, 47–48.

and an inferior" where "the elite accrued power and wealth at the expense of others."[37]

In the end, gaining a new identity and entering into a new community had not provided them a 'ladder' to heaven. The old power structure, through the social network and pattern of rule, still executed its power in the supposedly new community. Ultimately, "[t]he new group," as Meeks interprets it, "was thus inserted into or superimposed upon an existing network of relationships, both internal—kinship, *clientela*, and subordination—and external—ties of friendship and perhaps of occupation."[38] He continues, such a relationship had

> created the potential for the emergence of factions within the Christian body of a city. It may well be the case that the incipient factions addressed by Paul in 1 Cor. 1–4 were based in different households. The household context also set the stage for some conflicts in the allocation of power and in the understanding or roles in the community. The head of the household, by normal expectations of the society, would exercise some authority over the group and would have some legal responsibility for it.[39]

Besides, those who were attracted to the community may have come for a multiplicity of reasons. As Murphy-O'Connor postulates, "A number were attracted to the church because it seemed to offer them a new field of opportunity, in which the talents whose expression society frustrated could be exploited to the full. They were energetic and ambitious people, and there was little agreement among their various hidden agendas."[40] It seemed quite natural that those with good "educational" background, "financial resources," and "political" influence would not be content to simply be present in the community.[41] With or without the "hidden agenda," by virtue of social status and wealth, they continued to create influence. Indeed, they unabashedly exploited their power and status in the community.[42]

---

37. Witherington, *Paul Quest*, 48–49.
38. Meeks, *Urban Christians*, 76.
39. Meeks, *Urban Christians*, 76.
40. Murphy-O'Connor, *Paul*, 273.
41. Murphy-O'Connor, *Paul*, 273.
42. Use of the word "exploit" is intentional, to contrast with Jesus who did not regard his equality with God as some power he could exploit (Phil 2:6–8). I adopt this interpretation from Gorman, *Cruciformity*, 89.

Therefore, new converts who possessed significant social status, probably entered the church with their "hidden agenda." This may not have been intentional, but the social values they had assumed had effected in them over a lifetime and had not yet been cast aside. Others of a lower social status, or those who were slaves in the households, were equally unable to easily shake off a sense of identity socially engrained in their blood and body, to use Bourdieu's critique of power.[43] Thus while Murphy-O'Connor suggests that "[m]ost members had in common only their Christianity,"[44] and views their allegiance to the power symbols as following the value of "this age" (1 Cor 3:18), one wonders if they had a true understanding of what the gospel, and thus Christianity, meant.

As pointed out earlier, the early churches, such as in Corinth, were house churches whose members gathered in houses provided by wealthier members, who may also by default have become the natural leaders of the churches they hosted. As there were slaves within the household, the superior-inferior relationship would naturally extend to the new community. This aspect of power relations will be the focus of the following section.

4. The Power in the Patron-Client Relationship

The discussion above reflects scholars' identification of the presence of patron-client relationships and networking in Corinthian society and the church community. Again, sociological approaches to the study of New Testament texts help explain how power relations were at work. John Chow's *Patronage and Power* pays particular attention to the "relations and problems" of the Corinthian church and is convinced that patronage relationships had "become the background for understanding the relational ties in the church and some of the problems Paul discussed in 1 Corinthians."[45] He uses Weingrod's study of patronage,[46] and adopts an anthropological approach to consider "how persons of unequal powers seek to attain their goals through personal ties."[47] Chow employs concepts

---

43. Bourdieu, *The Logic of Practice*, 70.
44. Murphy-O'Connor, *Paul*, 273.
45. Chow, *Patronage and Power*, 82.
46. A. Weingrod, "Patrons, Patronage, and Political Parties," in Schmidt et al. eds., *Friends, Followers and Factions*, 323–25, from Chow, *Patronage and Power*, 33, n. 2
47. Chow, *Patronage and Power*, 33.

related to networking: ties, reciprocality, structures, clusters, boundaries, cross-linkages, asymmetricities, network collaborativity and competitivity.[48] These ideas are not abstract or philosophical ideas per se, but words which describe various formats of power relations. Meek has pointed out this phenomenon in *First Urban Christians*,[49] commenting, "[o]ne way of experiencing power in a group is to identify oneself with a figure regarded by the group as powerful."[50] Gordon Fee argues that by focusing on this patronage system for one's analysis of the Corinthian church, "many things" regarding 1 Corinthians "fall into place, including their dabbling in *sophia*" and "their 'examination' of Paul because he refused to accept patronage (9:1–19)."[51]

One example will be used to show how patronage relationships in the Corinthian church may have caused the issue with which Paul was very concerned—the litigation mentioned in 1 Corinthians 6. In the judicial system of any civil society, prosecutor and judge are usually both members of society. Likewise in Corinth, there were people who had connections with significant people of the city. Paul referred to the people involved in the disputes in 1 Corinthians 6 as leaders who had higher social status and therefore preferred to have their case dealt with in the court,[52] as they had social connections with those in charge of the law. As Clarke points out, high social status would gain the favor of the judge, who not only concerned with his own promotion but keen to protect the names of those in the upper classes; moreover, "the law insisted that certain people were protected from having a summons brought against them."[53] Meeks also contends, "The fact that some members of the Corinthian groups conduct lawsuits against other members also implies some financial or mercantile transactions (1 Cor 6:1–11),"[54] which only people of affluence and social status could afford or mobilize.

The power to mobilize could have been a backdrop to the scene of sexual immorality (incest) in 1 Corinthians 5 and its subsequent litigation,

---

48. Chow, *Patronage and Power*, 30–35.

49. A few years before Chow's work appeared, Gordon Fee adopted this position in his commentary, hypothesizing a rivalry between the patrons and Paul. Similarly, Witherington resorts to a more generic description of circle of friends and social system of patronage and of honor and shame: see Witherington, *Paul Quest*, 49–50.

50. Meeks, *Urban Christians*, 117.

51. Fee, *First Epistle*, 15.

52. Clarke, *Leadership*, 68.

53. Clarke, *Leadership*, 64.

54. Meeks, *Urban Christians*, 66.

mentioned by Paul in 1 Corinthians 6.[55] Having the power to mobilize, people involved may have been so "arrogant" (φυσιόω) (4:18, 19; 5:2) as to ignore what was obviously wrong and resort to the administrative mechanism within their power, to mobilize personnel who had a connection with them. This is similar to modern day corruption and nepotism.[56] They may have assumed they could rely on a patron, for support, or were themselves leaders who took position for granted due to their affluence and influence in society and probably also in the church community.

A patronage relationship usually affect both parties. It is not only in the superior position who is aware of this. The inferior is also very sensitive to and aware of the hidden rules of the bond. In the case of the Corinthians, Clarke argues, "If . . . the incestuous man was of high social standing he would in this instance be to some extent beyond reproach or criticism." At the same time, members within the community would refrain from confronting him with "the seriousness of his actions." This was possibly "a situation where clients have chosen to ignore the sinful actions of their benefactor rather than lose the favour of so prominent a person."[57] Together with this, an additional factor was probably at play, as Clarke further points out,

> Besides the matters of expediency and *gratia*, socially inferior people also faced legal obstacles against bringing those from the social élite to court. There was legal protection against those of the lower classes bringing *infamia* on a social superior. This was done by forbidding any person to enter into litigation with their superior.[58]

What he describes, whether regarding those inferior refraining from confrontation or ignoring the wrong of the superior to prevent losing the favor of the superior, is similar to Bourdieu's observation, i.e., the infiltration of power, in this case, into the blood and body of those who are considered inferior.[59] The system fortified legitimacy of the superior exert-

---

55. Clarke points out that here "a situation . . . where the honour of a leading figure is defended, rather than justice pursued," see *Leadership*, 79, also 86.

56. This refers to Karl Rennstich's first lecture in Eight Lectures on "Corruption: A Challenge to Society and the Church" given to a Christian ethics class in Sabah Theological Seminary in 2004.

57. Clarke, *Leadership*, 85–86.

58. Clarke, *Leadership*, 86. While this may be relevant in the Chinese society to which the pastors described in this thesis belong, it is not the aim to engage in a comparison from a sociological analysis of the two societies.

59. Bourdieu, *The Logic of Practice*, 70.

ing power over the inferior. Thus the influence of social status was so vast that despite sexual immorality,[60] some members of the Corinthian church could "remain 'puffed-up' over a man who is σοφός, δυνατός and εὐγενής, and yet also guilty of πορνεία."[61]

That is why Paul used the word "arrogant" to describe those people, for what mattered to them was no longer the teaching of the church, if they had someone to back them up, even if they had committed sin. Paul knew only too well what it meant to "[boasting] of social pride and status." As Wright comments, it is "a feature of what Paul knew from his own Jewish past which he sees, it now appears, as a reflection of standard pagan self-evaluation."[62] The Corinthians, to Paul "were not high up in the world's systems of social and cultural standing."[63] Wright argues that the gist of Paul's argument is that there is no point in boasting about one's social background other than the power and wisdom of God, and the new status freely given by God through Christ and his gospel of the cross.[64] The Corinthians overreached themselves, arrogantly executing social power over others and taking advantage of brothers and sisters in Christ with whom they shared the same status in Christ.

5. *Pneumatikos* and *Sophia*

Just as patronage represents social position and network, wisdom and knowledge represent new power symbols for the Corinthians. As mentioned earlier, some members of the church now had the possibility of expressing hitherto discounted aptitude through fresh opportunities afforded them in the new community.[65] If patronage was the power symbol of secular society, the patron-client relationship was given new expression, where holders of wisdom, knowledge, and probably also spiritual gifts (1 Cor 12–14) acted as patrons and their admirers and followers as clients.

---

60. Clarke, *Leadership*, 77–78. Such immorality as described was prohibited even according to Roman law.

61. Clarke, *Leadership*, 86.

62. Wright, *Justification*, 132. Although commenting on 1 Corinthians (130ff.), Wright makes a tangential reference to Romans and Gal 6:14 here.

63. Wright, *Justification*, 131.

64. Wright, *Justification*, 132.

65. See Murphy-O'Connor, *Paul*, 273.

5.1: The Problem and Cause of the Corinthians' Puffed Up or Boastful Attitude

Yeo has summarized six models proposed by scholars to address the problem of "radicalism" in the Corinthian church.[66] The first of these is the "normal Christian church model"; the second focuses on "Jewish-Gentile relations";[67] the third, the "philosophical schools model"; the fourth, the "mystery-religions model"; the fifth, the "Gnostic model"; the sixth, the "proto-gnostic model." The following will chiefly relate to proto-gnostic hypothesis and secondarily "philosophical schools" model. The latter can be helpful in demonstrating the wider, popular philosophical atmosphere in Corinth.[68]

While Yeo pays attention to the weak/strong language in 1 Corinthians, the focus of this section, is on the problem of "boasting" or being "puffed up."[69] In 1 Corinthians 1–4, Paul manifests a deep concern over some Corinthians boasting of excelling in wisdom and knowledge.[70] As has been referred to earlier, Paul describes the Corinthians as "puffed up" (φυσιόω, 4:6; 5:2). A similar indicator for "puffed up" is "boasting"

---

66. The problem of boasting or being puffed-up is related to radicalisms Yeo is addressing. See Yeo, *Rhetorical Interaction*, 120–30.

67. This is best represented by Karl Lugwig Bauer's "Jewish-Gentile Pauline-Apollonine and the Petrine-Christine hypothesis" as Yeo suggests. See Yeo, *Rhetorical Interaction*, 121.

68. For two examples that pay attention to philosophical schools of that period, see Engberg-Pedersen, *Paul and the Stoics*; Winter, *Philo and Paul*.

69. That boasting is a spiritual problem in Corinthians is without doubt, for some discussions on this, see Savage, *Power Through Weakness*, 54–62. The discussion here is based on 1 and 2 Corinthians, although in Rom 14 and 15 Paul also talks about the "weak" and the "strong." As Lo argues, the weak in Romans are the weak in faith (14:1), so Paul identifies himself with the "strong" in Rom 15:1 (see Lo, *Paul's Purpose*, 54), or with both "the strong and the weak" (Jewett, *Romans*, 878) while in 1 Cor 4:10 and 9:22 with the weak. The situations are different that an argument based on adjectives used on one occasion would necessarily imply a similar situation in another occasion would be a naive assumption. However, it is worth noting that Paul in Rom 15:1 is, as Jewett points out, "reversing the normal pattern of obligation in the patronage system," identified himself with the strong in the sense that the strong are obligated to please "our neighbour" instead of "ourselves." Jewett takes "neighbour" here as fellow members of the Roman house churches, see *Romans*, 878. With this reading, references in Romans are also congruent with those in 1 and 2 Corinthians. For detailed discussion of what "the weak" with regard to food-eating might imply in Greco-Roman background, see Jewett's commentary on Rom 14 in *Romans*, 834ff.

70. Yeo points out that 1 Cor 1–4 and 8 reflects a radicalism in terms of "the speculation of *logos-sophia* and *gnosis* spirituality," see Yeo, *Rhetorical Interaction*, 120.

(καυχάομαι, 1:31; 3:21; 4:7). One could trace main issues in 1 Corinthians by simply focusing on these key words.

As is shown in 4:6–7, which concludes Paul's earlier statement of the focus of their problems being their obsession with having wisdom, Paul first uses the word "puffed up" or "arrogant" then follow it with the word "boasting". They were puffed up because they thought they had something to boast of. Likewise, as has been said earlier, "Chloe's people" brought news about quarrels among the Corinthians (1 Cor 1:11). One of the causes was probably this "puffed up" attitude of certain members of the congregation. Social status may have been one of the reasons, but another could have been that they thought they were superior in spiritual wisdom, knowledge, and gifts.

As much as patronage and affiliation could have formed around those superior in secular social status, they could also have formed around those who were considered more knowledgeable and wise, or those who were thought to possess spiritual wisdom. Paul's notion of πνευματικός could have been a response to this latter group. People may have formed affiliations by dividing according to whom they belong, either to Paul, Apollos, Peter or Christ.[71]

Hence Paul reprimanded the Corinthians (3:21–22), and said, "So let no one boast about human leaders. For all things are yours, whether Paul or Apollos or Cephas or the world or life or death or the present or the future—all belong to you." Neither Paul nor Apollos nor Cephas owned anything which the Corinthians did not. Paul wanted to strip away their psychological projection of power onto himself, Apollos and Cephas.

Reading about Apollos in parallel to Paul, it is easy to understand why Apollos had become a symbol of knowledge and wisdom which the Corinthians admired:

> Now there came to Ephesus a Jew named Apollos, a native of Alexandria. He was an eloquent man, well-versed in the scriptures. He had been instructed in the Way of the Lord; and he spoke with burning enthusiasm and taught accurately the things concerning Jesus, though he knew only the baptism of John. (Acts 18:24–25)

---

71. Meeks contends that "according to Acts, through the good offices of Prisca. Despite a certain competitiveness among their partisans in Corinth (1 Cor 1:12; 3:1—4:6), there seem to have been good relations between Paul and Apollos." See Meeks, *Urban Christians*, 61.

The word translated as "eloquent" is *logios*, which Meeks suggests, "implies at least rhetorical ability, perhaps also rhetorical training."[72] Bruce explains that it "meant 'learned' or 'cultured' in classical Greek, but acquired the sense of 'eloquent' in Hellenistic and later Greek." Bruce argues that "the latter sense is probably what Luke intends, but the former need not be excluded."[73] Putting Apollo's eloquence in the context of the Corinthian congregation, Bruce reasons, "Evidently there was a quality about his ministry that made it more appealing to them than Paul's." Compared to Paul whose "bodily presence" was "weak, and his speech contemptible" (2 Cor 10:10), Apollos's eloquence was much more winsome to them and "his imaginative allegorization may have been preferred to Paul's deliberate eschewing of 'lofty words or wisdom' (1 Corinthians 2:1)."[74] In some way the difference between Paul and Apollos reflected the issue of boasting over knowledge and wisdom; therefore, an examination of the group associated with spiritual knowledge/wisdom (*pneumatikos*) and the group I call "sophist admirers" will help shed light on this attitude.

5.2: Pneumatikos

Scholars have attempted to identify some possible opponents of Paul in the Corinthian church and group them in four categories: Hellenistic Jewish propagandists, pneumatics, Gnostics, and Judaizers.[75] The possibility of the presence of Gnosticism in Pauline Corinth, advocated by W. Schmithals', has been refuted by some.[76] As the issue regarding Judaizers

---

72. Meeks, *Urban Christians*, 61.

73. Bruce, *Paul*, 255.

74. Bruce, *Paul*, 257.

75. See Harris, *Second Epistle*, 80 for these scholars' views. Based on Günther's review of 150 years identifying Paul's opponents in Corinthians, Harris adds to Günther's list: "conservative Hebrew pneumatics from Jerusalem" (by E. E. Ellis), "Jewish-Christian nationalists representing the Judaizing wing of Palestinian Christianity" (by C. Forbes), "educated Hellenists who were 'hybrists'" (by P. Marshall), "Hellenistic Jews propagating 'spiritual gnosticism'" (by D. Kee), "pneumatics who required and emphasized manifestations of the Spirit in apostles" (by J. L. Sumney), and "pneumatic Jewish Christian with an interest in 'sophia'" (B. Witherington).

76. Schmithals, *Gnosticism in Corinth*. Schmithals is refuted by scholars such as Hanzel Conzelmann, Gordon Fee, and Ralph P. Martin, see Winter, *Philo and Paul*, 236. For Schmithals' rejection of the view of sophistic background of 1 Cor 1–4, see Winter, op. cit., 148. See also Horrell and Adams, "Introduction," 19–20. For a list of scholars who adopted this approach, see also Yeo, *Rhetorical Interaction*, 123–24. Yeo agrees with Yamauchi's *Pre-Christian Gnosticism* arguing that the Gnostic hypothesis

will only be obvious in 2 Corinthians,⁷⁷ it will not be considered here. Thus there remain for discussion, the pneumatics and a group which scholars designate as "proto-gnostic," as Murray J. Harris explains below:

> Throughout his ministry at Corinth and therefore at the time of both 1 and 2 Corinthians, Paul encountered opposition from a sector of the Corinthian church that may be termed "proto-gnostic" in their denial of a future bodily resurrection, their libertinism or asceticism in morals, and their pride in γνῶσις.⁷⁸

Yeo argues that there existed among the Corinthian community a group who embraced the proto-Gnostic theology.⁷⁹ He assumes that they were probably "intellectual innovators, culturally assimilated urbanites with an ethos of individualism." They were also probably "those wealthy upper-class citizens who were denied social and legal recognition as Christians."⁸⁰

As Yeo points out, "words such as 'weak,' 'wise,' πνευματικός, and ψυχικός" that appear in 1 Corinthians 1–4 are clues to understanding the audience of 1 Corinthians and contends that "many of these words are gnostically related words."⁸¹ He believes that "the language of 'strong/weak' is related to the divisive language of the πνευματικός ψυχικός terminology found in major sections of 1 Corinthians."⁸² He argues for Philonic and Wisdom literature⁸³ as the possible source of the πνευματικός ψυχικός language and "the philosophy and theology of Philo and Gnostic mysteries"⁸⁴ as an influence on some of the Corinthian congregation.

However, finding traces that parallel to Philonic, Wisdom or Gnostic literature in passages of 1 Corinthians is not direct evidence of their influence. A very different conclusion can also be drawn, as Dale Martin

---

is invalid and there is "no 'hard evidence to prove the postulations" (127).

77. This is Harris' argument, see Harris, *Second Epistle*, 80. See also Witherington, *Conflict and Community*, 74.

78. Harris, *Second Epistle*, 80. See also, Yeo, *Rhetorical Interaction*, 124, 126.

79. Yeo, *Rhetorical Interaction*, 130–31.

80. Yeo, *Rhetorical Interaction*, 130–31.

81. Yeo, *Rhetorical Interaction*, 131. This was originally brought to attention by Horsley, see especially his articles, "Gnosis in Corinth," 32–51; idem, "Pneumatikos vs. Psychikos," 269–88.

82. Yeo, *Rhetorical Interaction*, 132.

83. He is referring to Horsley's reference to the Philonic and Wisdom exegesis of Gen 2:7a and 2:7b.

84. See Horsley, "Pneumatikos vs Psychikos," 275; Yeo, *Rhetorical Interaction*, 132.

argues: "one could say that anyone in the first century who held certain philosophical ideas (deprecation of the body, some form of anthropological dualism) was a proto-Gnostic, but this brings one no closer to a historical reconstruction of their social location."[85] Moreover, arguing against Horsley, Adams and Horrell criticize Horsley's citation of Philo as simply serving the purpose of his reconstruction of "Hellenistic Judaism," which is "problematic." Questioning Horsley's reliance on Philo as evidence, John Barclay contests, "Many of the purported parallels from Philo are from passages where Philo strives to interpret the biblical text in terms drawn from Stoic or Platonic philosophy." He reasons that the Corinthians "were engaged in a similar process, combining their Hellenistic theological culture with Jewish terms and traditions taught by Paul." They could indeed forge "a form of Judaized Hellenism" parallel to "Philo's Hellenized Judaism" yet "without any Platonic influence."[86] As Adams and Horrell conclude, "it is possible to assume that the Corinthians were making similar hermeneutical moves to Philo, interpreting 'Jewish' traditions as taught by Paul in terms of Greco-Roman cultural categories."[87] Therefore, there is no definite and direct link between the "πνευματικός ψυχικός language" and Philo's philosophy and theology.

Expanding the scope of the parallels, Adams and Horrell conclude, "[w]hen parallels are found in Gnosticism, Hellenistic Judaism, Stoicism, Cynicism, Epicureanism, and so on," there is no direct evidence that any of the movements had a "direct and specific influence" on the Corinthians.[88] Theirs was more of an "exposure to 'philosophical commonplaces,'" as Martin argues, what influenced by "'general principles or moral philosophy stemming from Cynic and Stoic traditions."[89] What is important is Heinz-Wolfgang Kahn's assertion that

> Paul is mixing both the rhetorical and gnosticizing elements with a Jewish apocalyptic Wisdom conception, thus splitting the σοφίας of his opponents into a Greek rhetorical wisdom, a wisdom of the world (corresponding to gnostic thinking) and of this bad age (corresponding to apocalyptic thinking) and

85. Martin, *Corinthian Body*, 71.
86. Barclay, "Thessalonica and Corinth," 190 n. 19.
87. Barclay, "Thessalonica and Corinth," 190 n. 19; also Adams and Horrell, "Scholarly Quest," 21 n. 112.
88. Adams and Horrell, "Scholarly Quest," 22.
89. Adams and Horrell, "Scholarly Quest," 22; for Martin, see *Corinthian Body*, 72. For a view of the permeation of popular Greco-Roman philosophy in Pauline world, see also Malherbe, *Paul and the Popular Philosophers*.

a wisdom of God. By taking over some of the terminology of his opponents, which seems to go into the direction of the later Gnosticism, Paul believes to overcome their theology.[90]

By employing contemporary terminology, Paul assimilated the appeal of his opponents' beliefs in his own writing. As scholars of Nag Hammadi may see in that, strands which developed in Gnosticism, but Paul uniquely appropriated and interpreted the term "aeon" to match his own theology of the "cosmos of this aeon" (Eph 2:2) that is dominated by sin.[91]

To return to the "proto-gnostic" hypothesis above, it is profitable to find a psychological link between it and pneumatics in the Corinthian church. The precise nature of the group shaping Corinthian thought cannot be ascertained, but Yeo's basic assumption "the language of 'strong/weak' is related to the divisive language of the πνευματικός ψυχικός terminology" in 1 Corinthians is still a workable hypothesis,[92] which will serve as the basis for an examination of those considered "spiritual" (πνευματικός) emerging as the symbolic "strong" ones.

The designation of this group as 'pneumatics', reveals, in its morphology, the assumed characteristics of its members. In Paul's list of spiritual gifts in 1 Corinthians 12, phrases such as λόγος σοφίας (utterance of wisdom) and λόγος γνώσεως (utterance of knowledge) call attention to an emphasis on utterance (λόγος), i.e., relating to the use of speech or words. The associated words σοφίας and γνώσεως also signify the importance of wisdom and knowledge. As has been shown earlier, Apollos was perceived as a person who had these gifts. Moreover, the spiritual gifts of "prophecy," "the discernment of spirits," "various kinds of tongues," and "the interpretation of tongues" imply the spirituality of the recipients and their possession of a certain not accessible to all.[93] To be in possession of these gifts may have symbolized a certain spiritual status in the congregation, where the possession of "faith," "gifts of healing," and the working of miracles perhaps symbolised holding divine power. It is interesting to note that

---

90. Kuhn, "The Wisdom Passage," 247, where he also states, "My point regarding Paul is that he nevertheless accuses his opponents of too much human rhetoric and 'sets the sophia of the cross against the sophia of rhetoric.' But he tries to win over the community by using some of the terminology of his opponents, which unlike the rhetorical elements appears to be gnosticizing." See also Adams and Horrel, "Scholarly Quest."

91. See discussion in the previous chapter.

92. Yeo, *Rhetorical Interaction*, 132.

93. Dale B. Martin made a similar argument, see "Tongues of Angels and Other Status Indicators," 547–89.

although these gifts are related to the "*pneuma*," they are also closely related to 'words' as found in λόγος σοφίας (utterance of wisdom) and λόγος γνώσεως (utterance of knowledge), which were associated with Graeco-Roman rhetoric practice in Paul's time.[94] This creates a bridge between 1 Corinthians 12–14 and 1–4 where there is intense discussion on σοφία and γνῶσις.[95] Thus, the pneumatics' boasting of their γνῶσις was not only an attitude which troubled Paul but a leitmotif running through the whole of 1 Corinthians. This suggests that there was *not only the immediate issue of patronage relationship, which had indirectly allowed incestuous sexual behavior (immorality) to be addressed, but also, on a deeper level, a certain belief or over-obsession with γνῶσις had evolved, which had become a more critical problem.*[96]

The "puffed up" Corinthians boasted of their spiritual gnosis. Having hitherto regarded themselves as "spiritual people," "many in Corinth saw themselves as 'judging everything' but 'being judged by no one.'" Johannes Weiss elaborates,

> The "spiritual" man knows and judges not only the being of God, but everything else, for the Spirit penetrates everything, even the deep things of God (1 Cor 2:15). These are the confessions of a spiritual ("pneumatic") mystic: his feeling of exaltation, his sense of superiority and unassailability are especially asserted in the statement (2:15), "but he himself is judged by no man."[97]

In other words, these puffed up people were arrogant, self-inflated, and so over-confident in their charismatic experience that they were, as earlier pointed out, even "unfazed by the most flagrant deviations from the community's—and the macrosociety's—sexual form."[98]

The "pneumatics" saw themselves as superior to others. As discussed previously, some in the congregation may have belonged to lower social strata before their conversion to Christianity and perhaps remained so after it. Some perhaps were of a socially higher status or, if not, at least affiliated to those who were. The congregation was a mixture of patrons,

---

94. Martin, *Corinthian Body*, 47–50. He claims that it is quite impossible to say that Paul had no rhetorical education (50).

95. For a recent review of current scholarship on 1 Corinthians 1–4 regarding wisdom, see Kwon, "A Critical Review of Recent Scholarship," 386–427.

96. Cf. Harris, *The Second Epistle*, 80.

97. For Weiss, see *Earliest Christianity*, 2:513, cited in Thiselton, *First Epistle*, 272.

98. Meeks, *Urban Christians*, 128–29.

freedmen and slaves gradually moving up the social ladder.[99] The new community had afforded an opportunity to discard their old identity and social status.

However, Paul appeared to introduce a different status, determined according to the possession of "esoteric knowledge communicated by the stuff of divine rationality" in contrast to those who claimed to possess true wisdom which ultimately was mere world wisdom.[100] According to Martin, Paul 'turned the table" by introducing a new kind of "high status indicator": "the pneumatic person judges everything but is judged by no one" (1 Cor 2:15).[101] Ironically, it was boasting induced by pneumatic esoteric knowledge that had become the congregation's problem, i.e., claiming to have the spiritual gifts listed in the previous paragraph. Attention now needs to be given to the question of the authority behind the true wisdom, which Paul designates to God himself.

5.3: Sophist Admirers

Bruce Winter argues for a sophist influence in the Corinthian church, affecting their perception of Paul and Apollos (Acts 18:24–28; 19:1–7; 1 Cor 3:1–10) in pointing out that "rhetorical terms and allusions appear in 1 Corinthians 2.1–5."[102] According to Winter, "[o]riginally the term σοφιστής described ancient wise man" and "[B]y the first century AD it was used to designate those rhetoricians whose ability in oratory was such that they could both secure a public following and attract students to their schools."[103] While Paul does not name them in his letter, it is reasonable to assume their influence in society at large that time. Winter points out that

> Parents expected the sophist to make public speakers of their sons, for they judged that this form of education was most useful in producing leaders accomplished in the great art of persuasion whether it be in the legal courts or the council or political assembly of their city.[104]

---

99. See in 1 Cor 12:13, it says, "For in the one Spirit we were all baptized into one body—Jews or Greeks, slaves or free—and we were all made to drink of one Spirit."
100. See Martin, *Corinthian Body*, 63.
101. See Martin, *Corinthian Body*, 63.
102. Winter, *Philo and Paul*, 145–202.
103. Winter, *Philo and Paul*, 3–4.
104. Winter, *Philo and Paul*, 5.

A Double Vision Hermeneutic

Hence, the ability to excel in public speaking and draw a large audience was a symbol of success in the profession, whose training included "rules on style, and the management of the voice and the body."[105] Moreover, parents who could afford to send their sons for this form of education predisposed a certain social status. Thus to be able to speak like a sophist was symbolic of high social status a fine education. As Winter remarks, "these sophists were among the well born and the powerful, and would have paraded their education as proof of wisdom."[106] Hence Paul's ironic comparison of 'puffed up' Corinthian church members with well educated sophists, remembering them that: "not many of you were wise (σοφοί) by human standards, not many were powerful (δυνατοί), not many were of noble birth (εὐγενεῖς)" (1 Cor 1:26)," not only alluded to their social background as less elevated than they estimated, but intentionally used language which did not present his argument with oratorical superiority, persuasiveness, confidence, eloquence, or the "power" of speech, thereby establishing on anti-sophist rhetoric which instead ascribed the highest regard to the power of the Holy Spirit and the wisdom of God.[107] Paul's discourse on wisdom and power, thus challenged the legitimacy of the Corinthians' assumption of wisdom and power and elevated social status as grounds for justification of their 'puffed up' attitude.

It is therefore proposed that the power dynamic of potential division in the congregation was illuminated by the rival parties' division into followers of Paul, i.e. the *pneumatikoi*, and of Apollos, i.e. the sophists. The strength of the sophist hypothesis was its ability to highlight the potential projection of some Corinthian members onto Apollos, the designation of a Christian sophist, an image transferred from contemporary secular society. The proposed hypothesis is not conclusive and relies on earlier scholars' theories; however, it creates cohesion in the text[108] and explicates the "I belong to" passages more clearly than any alternatives. Some scholars have argued that there was no rivalry between Paul and Apollos, at least from the point of view of the protagonists themselves.[109] However this does not preclude followers from creating such a division.

---

105. Winter, *Philo and Paul*, 5. Being eloquent, "well-versed in the scriptures" (Acts 18:24), some scholars have thought that Apollos could have been among the sophists.

106. Winter, *Philo and Paul*, 193.

107. Winter, *Philo and Paul*, 147–48, 153–55.

108. Cf. Fee, *First Epistle*, 15.

109. Clarke, *Leadership*, 89–93. But Clarke thinks Paul "conceived of no competition between himself and Apollos" and "no rivalry between himself and Apollos," see Clarke, *Serve the Community*, 216. As Martin argues, "Paul lumps . . . himself and

Power in Text B2: Corinthians

To advance the *pneumatikos* versus sophist hypothesis, Paul's minimalist gesture toward *logios* contrasted with Apollos' eloquence. However, it was probable that those who were proud of their special spiritual gifts, had projected onto Paul with their view of an ideal leader, i.e. one who excelled in speaking in tongues and performing miracles.

As previously stated, it is most probably that Paul did not view Apollos as a competitor, but rather presented him as a colleague. The church members themselves created the factions within the body of Christ (1 Cor 12), claiming affiliation with their preferred leader. Note Paul's emphasis in 1 Corinthians 1:12–13, "What I mean is that each of you says, 'I belong to Paul', or 'I belong to Apollos', or 'I belong to Cephas', or 'I belong to Christ'. Has Christ been *divided*? Was Paul crucified for you? Or were you baptized in the name of Paul?" Verse 13 does not mention Apollos nor Cephas; possibly Paul intended the rebuke particularly for those who considered they were under Paul's headship, as an affirmation that they belonged to Christ, and were baptized in His, and not Paul's name.

Paul could not permit any deviation from the gospel of Christ crucified which would endanger the faith of the Corinthian church members. To undermine the sophists, rather than boasting of his "speech (λόγος)" (1 Cor 2:4) Paul preached the λόγος of the cross (1:18), a contrast to λόγιος (cf. Acts 18:24). To Paul, the "kingdom of God depends not on talk (ἐν λόγῳ) but on power (δυνάμει)" (1 Cor 4:20), was not brought "with plausible (or persuasive) words of wisdom (πειθοῖς σοφίας λόγοις), but with a demonstration of the Spirit and of power (πνεύματος καὶ δυνάμεως)" (2:4), and was not of this world or man but of God. Likewise, to undermine the pneumatics, Paul counters, "Or did the word (λόγος) of God originate with you? Or are you the only ones it has reached? If anyone of you thinks that he or she is a prophet or a person 'of the Spirit' (πνευματικός) let them recognize that what I write to you is [a command] from the Lord" (1 Cor 14:36–37).[110] Fee acknowledges that this is "the third instance in this letter where Paul attacks" the position of the *pneumatikos* "head-on with the formula 'If anyone thinks he is . . .' (see on 3:18 and 8:2)." He continues, "the argument in each case indicates that by this formula Paul is zeroing

---

Apollos" into the category of "the lowest possible status," in contrast to those claimed a high status, see *Corinthian Body*, 65. Thiselton follows Bruce and sees that "Paul shows not disapproval of Apollos." For Bruce, see *Men and Movement*, 65, cited from Thiselton, *First Corinthians*, 124. Paul in fact always groups Apollos with himself, not with his opponents, see op. cit., 1332.

110. 1 Cor 14:36 taken from NRSV, while 14:37 from Anthony Thiselton in Thiselton, *First Corinthians*, 1131. Greek words in parentheses mine.

in on the Corinthians' perspective as to their own spirituality. They do indeed think of themselves as 'the wise' (3:18) and as 'having knowledge' (8:2), probably in both cases because they also think of themselves as being pneumatic."[111] In either case, some among them identified themselves with the sophists while others with the pneumatics, yet to Paul, those identified with sophist eloquence were only "wise in this age" (3:18) and had yet to obtain "the necessary knowledge." Addressing the pneumatics, Paul declared, "I could not speak to you as spiritual people, but rather as people of the flesh, as infants in Christ" (1 Cor 3:1b). In other words, with regard to the matters of spiritual things, they were babies; and by the standard of true wisdom, they were fools (8:2).

To sum up, the above argument attempted to contrast the *pneumatikos* and sophist-affected groups, and assumed that each made Paul and Apollos their respective leader. This hypothesis illustrated a possible division, aimed to highlight tension between two power factions, who perceived a schism between Paul and Apollos which neither leader had created or encouraged, as a precursor to the interpretation in section 6.

6. Relating Power Symbols in 1 Corinthians to the Principalities and Powers

It can be surmised that Paul was not interested in a sociological analysis of the situation in Corinth. His theology regarding the principalities and powers was his more direct interpreting framework. As argued earlier, Galatians and 1 Corinthians were written within a few years of each other, therefore, as "principalities and powers" had affected the Galatians, in the form of the *stoicheia* and the law, Paul possibly also attributed the Corinthian situation to them.

Thus, Corinthian obsession with λόγια, σόφια, γνῶσις and πνευματικός must also be discussed in relation to Paul's theology of "principalities and powers." While the focus of previous sections was on sociological aspects, the motif of principalities and powers, Text B1, as a subtext, had remained active as the focus of the "subsidiary awareness." Paul's theology of "principalities and powers" as the dynamic force behind the sociological aspects, i.e. the "puffed up" attitude of those who saw themselves as eloquent and possessing special wisdom, knowledge, and spiritual gifts, and patron-client relationship, requires considerations.

---

111. Fee, *First Epistle*, 711.

Power in Text B2: Corinthians

According to Paul, the realms of κόσμος and αἰῶνα are penetrated by sin and under "the ruler of the power of the air" (Eph 2:1-2) and "the cosmic powers of this present darkness" (τοὺς κοσμοκράτορας τοῦ σκότους τούτου, 6:12). While the study of *stoicheia* in the previous chapter focused mainly on Galatians, a cross reference to Colossians showed that the "*stoicheia*" (2:20) discussed within a discourse on the observation of festivals, worship of angels, dwelling of visions, puffed up attitude, etc (2:8–23). Thus when Paul warned the Galatians they had turned to the observation of "special days, and months, and seasons, and years" (4:10), he implied not only those from Jewish tradition, but those associated with pagan practice. The Colossians were considered pagans before they were reconciled to God, and as "following the course of this world, following the ruler of the power of the air" (Eph 2:2). Paul reminded them that such observation of particular feats etc "have indeed an appearance of wisdom in promoting self-imposed piety, humility, and severe treatment of the body, but they are of no value in checking self-indulgence" (Col 2:23). Paul thus linked his admonition of their practice to their false assessment of wisdom.

The Christological motif in the beginning of chapter 2, that Christ as "the head of every ruler and authority" (2:10) "in whom are hidden all the treasures of wisdom and knowledge," provides the impetus for Paul to bring all "principalities and powers", be it human tradition, Jewish law, worldly wisdom, the worship of intermediary deities such as "the ruler of the power of the air" (τὸν ἄρχοντα τῆς ἐξουσίας τοῦ ἀέρος) and "the cosmic powers of this present darkness" (τοὺς κοσμοκράτορας τοῦ σκότους τούτου, 6:12), under Christ's headship alone (2:15; cf. 1:16).[112] As head of all powers and the mystery of God's wisdom and knowledge, Christ will bring not only the powers at a cosmological level but also those on the level of human tradition, culture and religion into their proper position.

1 Corinthians advances the same premise, the Christological motif, providing an impetus for the discourse on power. Paul begins by affirming that, "(God) will also strengthen you to the end, so that you may be blameless on the day of our Lord Jesus Christ" (1:8), and reiterates this towards the conclusion of the letter:[113]

> Then comes the end, when he hands over the kingdom to God the Father, after he has destroyed every ruler and every authority

---

112. "He disarmed the rulers and authorities and made a public example of them, triumphing over them in it."

113. See Caird's argument that the discourse on wisdom in 1 Cor 2:6-8 "should be interpreted in the light of" 1 Cor 15:24, see Caird, *Principalities and Powers*, 16.

and power. For he must reign until he has put all his enemies under his feet. The last enemy to be destroyed is death. For "God has put all things in subjection under his feet." But when it says, "All things are put in subjection," it is plain that this does not include the one who put all things in subjection under him. When all things are subjected to him, then the Son himself will also be subjected to the one who put all things in subjection under him, so that God may be all in all. (15:24–28)

This suggests that a consistent theological power motif appears in Galatians, Colossians, Ephesians, and 1 Corinthians. As Paul's Christo-centric discussion in this regard is prominent, an intersubjective reading of Text B1, the motif of principalities and powers, with B2, Galatians and 1 Corinthians is a reasonable proposition, as the natural outcome of reading all the Pauline texts as a body.

For Paul, the Corinthians boasted in the wisdom of this age (αἰῶνος) and of this world (κόσμος) (1:20; 2:6, 8; 3:18, 19),[114] as were the spiritual gifts and knowledge boasted of by the pneumatics. Not all that claims to be spiritual is of God. It can be of the spirit of this world as much as of God (2:12). As discussed in the previous chapter, the overriding influence of the world and of this age is the dominating power of sin and death and of "the ruler of the power of the air, the spirit that is now at work among those who are disobedient" (Eph 2:2).[115]

As surveyed above, the wise, the spiritually gifted and the knowledgeable (pneumatics), and the eloquent had become power symbols in the Corinthian church. The role of these church members fused with the extant client-patron network based on social status. These people were the ἀρχόντα in the church, the heads, the principals, the leaders. As Wink comments, "We become slaves of the elements by granting them

---

114. Yeo has a footnote on the phrase "ἀρχόντων τοῦ αἰῶνος τούτου" in 1 Cor 2:6 that it "is not Gnostic but wisdom apocalyptic tradition, the ruler who 'did not know the wisdom because it was hidden by God throughout all the ages until now,' and this motif is common to wisdom-apocalyptic theology," citing Robin Scroggs. See Yeo, *Rhetorical Interaction*, 136. It is unsatisfactory that he states this in the footnote without arguing for or against it in the context of his argument for a gnostic or proto-gnostic Corinthian terminology, although he immediately goes to Hellenistic Jewish tradition to further his argument.

115. Here compare Dunn who also argues that "the spiritual powers he [Paul] focused his theological and pastoral concern on were not the 'rulers and authorities,' but the powers of sin and death." See Dunn, *Paul the Apostle*, 110. Compare also the difference with Wink's argument on "principalities and powers," see 110 n. 42–n. 44.

an ultimacy they do not possess."[116] To the ancient Greek philosophers, the "elements" (*stoicheia*) were the "first principles" (*archōn*)."[117] If "the Colossians were in danger of mistaking the basic elements of things for the ultimate reality,"[118] and the Galatians likewise offered the *stoicheia* and the law ultimate positions, the Corinthians had committed the same mistake, boasting of human wisdom, eloquence and spiritual gifts and knowledge. None of them, the elevated people who possessed these abilities as the ἀρχόντα in the Corinthian church, deserved the ultimate homage the church members paid to them.

Regarding ἐξουσίαι and ἀρχαί, as Werner Foerster has indicated, "it is not possible to distinguish between" them nor "to assign to them the different functions to two groups of powers." They are "different expressions for much the same thing."[119] Corinthian Christians who had the powers (ἐξουσίαι) naturally assumed the roles of leaders or rulers (ἀρχαί) within the power structure as reflected of the Corinthian church. However, as ἐξουσίαι and ἀρχαί, they were not exempt from the penetrating power of the air and of the darkness that operated within the κόσμος of this αἰῶνος. These powers, to borrow Bourdieu's metaphor, are running in their blood and body.[120]

According to Paul's reference to two levels of wisdom, one "of this age" which implies also the κόσμος, and the other "of the rulers of this age" (2:6), one belongs to the invisible and transcendent realm, the other to the institutional. Paul in Eph 2:2 treats the ruler of the power *of the air (the spirit)*,[121] the κόσμος, and the disobedient church members as partners. The transcendent ruler (of the air) is of the spiritual world and the power dominated realm, the κόσμος, in which it operates are correlational and they are accomplices. As part of the cosmic powers, they not only "represent the carnal side of fallen creation with the powers which seduce and

---

116. Wink, *Unmasking*, 134.

117. Wink, *Unmasking*, 135, who cites Clement of Alexandria.

118. Wink, *Unmasking*, 135.

119. Foerster, "ἐξουσία," 573.

120. See chapter 3.

121. Being in the air, this ruler is also of the realm "up there." This is correlated with Wink's reference to "[t]he idea of heaven" which points to things "up" there, which "is a natural, almost unavoidable way of indicating transcendence." See Wink, *Engaging*, 6. Also, Wink uses "transcendent" to refer to angels. "An angel," he argues, "is both immanent within every member of its species and transcendent to it." See Wink, *Unmasking*, 160. Demons and devils in this sense also belong to the "transcendent" level.

enslave men,"[122] but penetrate every area which has not yet been restored through Christ.

According to Paul, the Corinthians were "of the flesh" (3:1, σαρκίνοις and 3:3, σαρκικοί). He also hinted that some among them received "the spirit of the world (τὸ πνεῦμα τοῦ κόσμου) rather than that of God (2:12), and are of the ψυχικὸς instead of the Spirit (of God), contrary to their self-perception. They were proud of their wisdom, but it was "of this age" (αἰῶνος, 2:6), thus, while they claimed ability with words and speech or gave credit to those they considered possessed this, they were deaf and blind to the "words (λόγοις) not taught by human wisdom but taught by the Spirit" (3:13).

Hence, wisdom, eloquence, pneumatical gifts, knowledge, and the patronage relationship based on these or on previous social status all belonged to this κόσμος and this αἰῶνος. By promoting these, they had submitted to them and granted them "an ultimacy," and in turn were dominated by them.

Thus, the issue which concerned Paul in Corinthians had a similar basis those in Galatians. In the former the issue manifested itself as the social position, worldly wisdom, pneumatic experience and knowledge, while in the latter as the *stoicheia* and the law. He summed this up in 1 Corinthians 6:12, stating "'All things are lawful for me',[123] but not all things are beneficial. 'All things are lawful for me', but I will not be dominated (ἐξουσιασθήσομαι) by anything." By submitting oneself to that to which one grants ultimacy, one is by definition dominated by it.

7. Conclusion

The chapter above identified a range of powers which had become an obsession for Corinthian Christians. The discussion first described the sociological background then examined the situation in the Corinthian church. An interpretation of the intersubjective relationship of Texts B1 and B2 was assumed in the discussion of the sociological and ecclesiastical phenomena in relating the power struggle to Paul's theology of "principalities and powers." Thus, the situation of a particular church was interpreted through Paul's underlying theological concern, which formed a layer of the double vision hermeneutic.

---

122. Foerster, "ἐξουσία," 573.

123. It can be as Meeks does, translated as "Everything is permitted me," which is "the pneumatic' slogan." See Meeks, *Urban Christians*, 129.

Power in Text B2: Corinthians

As a hermeneutical task, the interpretation demonstrated in this and the previous chapter revealed that a double awareness is always present when two texts are present. An alternate focus on one and then the other text makes one the "focal" and the other the "subsidiary," but the awareness of both texts is never missing from the interpreting act.

Nevertheless, in this and the previous chapter, this doubleness was shown solely between Texts B1 and B2 as it had been between Texts A1 and A2 in chapter 4. A double vision hermeneutic that includes a fusion and intersubjective relationship between Texts A and B within me, the interpreting subject, will be the final thrust, bringing all aforementioned texts into an interpretation of the my intersubjective experience of *shì*, the intersubjective readings of Texts A1 + A2, Texts B1 + B2 and Pastor Y's experience.

With the law and the *stoicheia* explicated in the previous chapter, all six power symbols are now assembled to form a six-power constellation and ready for further interpretation in the light of the double vision hermeneutic in the next chapter.

8

The Double Vision Hermeneutics of a Chinese Pastor's Intersubjective Experience of Shì Engaging Yìzhuàn and Pauline Texts

This chapter aims to present the result and evaluate the claim of the double vision hermeneutic, i.e., its efficacy in interpreting the intersubjective experience of *shì* and the multilayered intersubjective relationships between Texts A1 + A2 and Texts B1 + B2 and between these texts and the subject. In this regard, an assessment of a double vision hermeneutics as a preferable interpretive framework for the simultaneous handling of both concerns alongside the intersubjective experience of *shì*, needs to be undertaken.

Additionally, this conclusion will answer how this thesis has responded to the call for an indigenous Chinese theology which highly valued an exegetical and expositional approach to the texts and engaged with the Chinese cultural-linguistic dimension.

Possible contribution of this endeavor to Chinese theological reflection will be articulated, and some suggestions for the potential direction of further research in this field, proffered.

1. Concluding the Fusion of Text A and Text B with the Subject

As stated previously, "a whole" is taken as a fusion of understandings, integrated within the subject. As a personal experience which stimulated

The Double Vision Hermeneutics

this research inquiry, I am postulated as "the subject." The "fusion" is the fusion between Texts A1 + A2 and Texts B1 + B2 and Text 0 (zero).

Chapter 3 explicated the various shades of meaning borne by *shì* in pre-Qín texts. Appropriated, it was a lens through which power relations were understood. As shown in chapter 4, the power dynamic conveyed in this word, rich in meanings in traditary texts, was explicated from various angles within the *Yìjīng* hexagramic paradigm. These two chapters created the fusion of Texts A1 and A2, through which power relations between Pastor Y and several other protagonists were interpreted. The dynamic aspect of *shì* was shown in terms of change and timeliness, as defined by *Yìzhuàn*. Moreover, the dynamic nature of the power relations was understood and explained as the increase and decrease of interlocking *yīn-yáng* relationships. *Yìjīng* was read through the lens of *shì*; *shì* was interpreted through the lens of *Yìjīng*.

Chapters 6 and 7 were devoted to reconstructing the causes of Paul's concern for the Galatian and Corinthian churches. The concern of enslavement to power, symbolized by the *stoicheia*, the law, patronage, wisdom, knowledge, eloquence, pneumatical experience and gifts was exploited. These power symbols and the problem of enslavement caused by them in the respective congregations were interpreted sociologically and theologically. Paul's theological view of the principalities and powers was intended as the underlying motif of the discussion. It was proposed that, as much as Christians in the Pauline churches were slaves to the *stoicheia*, they were also prey to enslavement by whatever they offered the seat of ultimacy to, i.e., wisdom, pneumatical experience et cetera. As Wink suggests, "We become slaves of the elements by granting them an ultimacy they do not possess."[1] By weaving a reconstruction of power relations in two respective churches with the Pauline concept of principalities and powers, the subject's suspicion of all power symbols, especially those became seen as an ultimate authority, was explained. Thus, the discussion of problems in the two churches was always overshadowed by an awareness of principalities and powers: Text B2 was read through Text B1.

The interpretation thus presented nevertheless was meaningful to the subject it caused for the hermeneutical processes to unfold. The interpretation thus had been aimed as preparation for their appropriation by the subject into his vision. The fusion of Text A and B required relevance to Text 0, the scenario which prompted the research, and success in analyzing how and why the experience of Pastor was interpreted as it was. While

---

1. Wink, *Unmasking*, 134.

A Double Vision Hermeneutic

the process of many re-readings of traditionary texts has complicated the hermeneutic relationship between texts and contexts, the primary context remains the subject, in whom all texts initial met, the original locus of my subjective experience of *shì* and the emergence of the double vision of *shì*.

The double vision using the "two texts" of *shì*/power had been with the subject since its emergence, at the beginning of the thesis, and during its process, as texts were interpreted from varying angles. New insights were gained which enriched the interpretation but never changed the basic concern of the double vision that sought an integrated self.

Having now reinstated the primary goal of unfolding the double vision hermeneutics of the intersubjective experience of *shì* following explication of its respective components, the current aim is to bring all interpretations exploited in individual chapters into one holistic view. The conclusion is thus a further deliberation on and unfolding of the double vision hermeneutics as revealed in chapter 2.

Hence, the double vision hermeneutics is a hermeneutical process that emerged from the real life context of a Chinese pastor with a subjective urge to integrate the two Texts—A and B through reflexive readings. The process had begun at an earlier stage, as narrated in Text 0. The interpretive acts presented in previous chapters were present throughout re-readings of the texts and reflection on the subject's experience.

These readings, understandings and appropriations of texts have been continuously formed into new modes of unity between the subject and the texts. As Gadamer asserts, our experience of art, by implication here as the reading of a literary text or reflection on a traditionary text, will always produce "a unity" between the person and that which is experienced" to form "a new mode of being one."[2] In chapter 2, a nuanced change of meaning was applied to Gadamer's notion of "new mode(s) of being one" into 'new modes of being'. It is now claimed that through many re-readings of traditionary texts, new modes of being have continuously been produced.

Re-readings of *Yìzhuàn* deepen the understanding of situatedness in Chinese culture and tradition in relation to the experience of *shì*, and have produced multifarious interpretations, through the *Yìjīng* hexagramic paradigm, as applied to the understanding of Pastor Y's experience. Re-readings of Pauline texts have produced new understandings which had not been perceived as the outset of the research. Initial feelings of guilt attributed to the influence of Paul epitomized in his expostulation,

---

2. Gadamer, *Truth and Method*, 53, 58.

The Double Vision Hermeneutics

"Wretched man that I am,"[3] led to the construction of a more complicated interpretation of *shì*/power. The result of readings of two texts have thus yielded a double vision hermeneutic of Texts A1 + A2 and Texts B1 + B2.[4]

Hence, an integration of the texts reveals a basic vision of powers in constellation as follows, while a more complicated construction will be explained later.

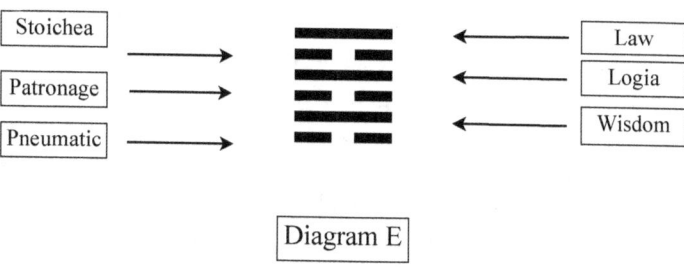

Diagram E

The hexagram above as an example is taken as the locus of a subject surrounded by different power symbols. The lines embody the possibility of increase or decrease in either *yīn* or *yáng* power.

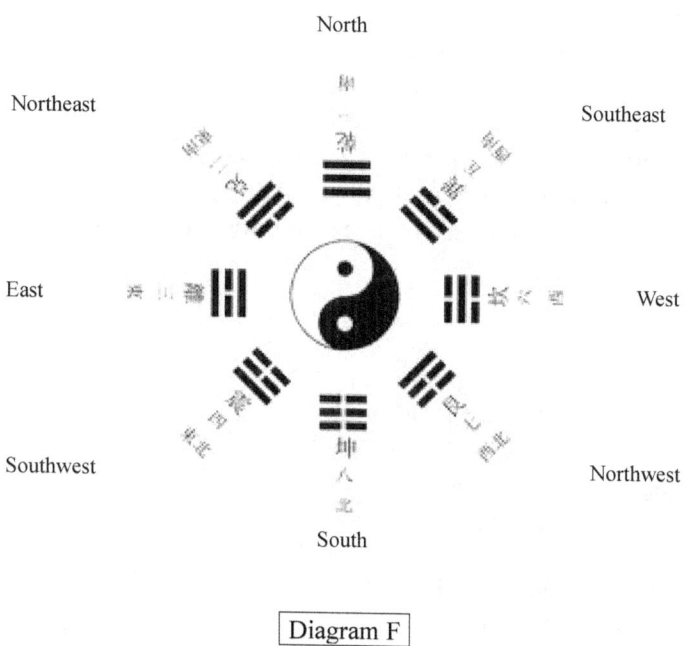

Diagram F

---

3. Rom 7:24.

4. For my initial construction of this model, see in more details in 95–98 of this thesis.

A Double Vision Hermeneutic

As I have presented in the introduction and in chapter 4, the initial inception of the eight trigrams, the primordial symbols that formed the sixty-four hexagrams, is attributed to Fúxī the legendary sage-king, who having observed natural and celestial phenomena created the eight symbols.[5] Although taken as a myth, the legend can still convey significant implications: man himself, as the centre, can give a subjective meaning to his surroundings. Although the eight trigrams are constelled in all eight direction, or *bāfāng*, as shown in the diagram of the Primordial Eight Trigrams above (Diagram F), the subject exists in the midst of all sixty-hexagrams. The sixty-four hexagrams symbolize all natural and human phenomena that correlate with one another as well as interrelate with the subject. Thus, six power symbols will be extracted from Pauline texts and integrated into the hexagramic symbol, to demonstrate that the vision of the subject is the fact which determines the movement of the constellation.

In a hexagram, the increase and decrease of each of the six lines is to be expected, whether it is a *yīn* or *yáng* line. Moreover, as was suggested in the interpretation of Pastor Y's situation, many hexagrams (see Diagram G on page 315), for examples, H3 Zhūn ䷂,[6] H4 Méng ䷃,[7] H16 Yù ䷏,[8] H17 Suí ䷐,[9] H28 Dàguò ䷛,[10] H35 Jìn ䷢,[11] H38 Kuí ䷥,[12] H49 Gé ䷰,[13] and H50 Dǐng ䷱,[14] can be used to ponder on potential changes and corresponding reaction to them.[15] The various projected situations are only possible since out of one hexagram many correlated hexagrams can be derived, thus signifying that out of one situation many different situations are possible. The subject situated in the position symbolized in the first hexagram, he is placed within all other possible permutations for a hexagram and within the system of many other hexagrams.

---

5. See the introduction for this in 144–46.
6. Tagged as "Difficulty at the Beginning."
7. Tagged as "Youth Folly/Juvenile Ignorance."
8. Tagged as "Contentment."
9. Tagged as "Following."
10. Tagged as "Excess."
11. Tagged as "Progress."
12. Tagged as "Opposition or Contrariety."
13. Tagged as "Revolution."
14. Tagged as "Caldrons."
15. See chapter 4.

The Double Vision Hermeneutics

The subject also discovered, through reading Galatians and 1 Corinthians, the potential for being enslaved or dominated by various powers. As Wink argues, we will be enslaved by anything that we grant an ultimacy to.[16] The Galatian and Corinthian Christians were dominated by granting ultimate position to the *stoicheia* and the law(Galatians), or to wisdom, *logia*, patronage, and pneumatics (Corinthians). From Paul's perspective, anything within this κόσμος and αἰῶνος not restored under the lordship of Christ is penetrated by sin and under "the power of the ruler of the air" (Eph 2:2).

Now the κόσμος and αἰῶνος can be understood as the whole universe of this age. As the sixty-four hexagrams symbolize every phenomenon and situation in heaven and earth, i.e., the whole universe, if the κόσμος and αἰῶνος are under the power of sin, everything symbolized by the sixty-four hexagrams is also under the power of sin. Sin, according to Paul, entered this world and penetrated everything. As Paul exclaimed, "the creation was subjected to futility" and "has been groaning in labour pains" waiting to be set free from its bondage to decay" (Rom 8:20–22). From the biblical perspective, the whole universe is God's creation. Thus, sin penetrated the whole creation which now awaits salvation through Christ.

According to the *Yìjīng* hexagramic paradigm, the dominant power of any of the six powers can vary according to its position within the six lines. If the law dominates, it creates a spirit of legalism; if pneumatics, a spirit of boasting, et cetera. Within the setting of a church, the dominant spirit can change, and the strength of its domination can vary depending on the degree of ultimacy granted to it, and the degree of power it gains from those who afford it ultimacy. Thus, a church may prevent a spirit of legalism, yet falling prey to a spirit of *pneumatikos*, and vice versa.

Employing the paradigm of six powers in a church setting during a period of change, before any decision is made or action undertaken, *would be a prudent exercise* since a weakening of one power could be a sign of the strengthening of another. A negative and dominating power which begins in the first line of the hexagram symbolizes its initial influence in the church. Yet this power, as it moves from the first, through the fourth, to the top indicates a reaching of its height and limit. The philosophy of *Yì* postulates that when *yīn* reaches its extreme, it reverts to *yáng* and thus when a thing reaches its extreme, it reverses its course.[17]

---

16. Wink, *Unmasking*, 134.

17. See for example the comments in *Wényán* on the top *yáng* line of Qían hexagram.

A Double Vision Hermeneutic

Nevertheless, a Chinese pastor informed by Pauline teachings will be able to identify all the aforementioned elements in the forms of power which had appeared in Paul's churches, and which can also arise in churches today. He himself should avoid becoming entangled in any of these forms of power, be it relying on patronage relationships, or overly respecting someone's social or professional status, academic degrees and titles, social background, or even their long standing influence in the church, and like Paul, should not permit worldly power to dominate. Chinese pastor should avoid being projected as a form of any of the stated power symbols. Learning from *Yìzhuàn* philosophy regarding the "waning and waxing" of all things. No power will remain strong forever: "A dragon that overreaches should have cause for regret" (H1 Qián top *yáng* statement).[18] Thus, a Chinese pastor in the midst of power relations, perceiving one dominant power, be it a leader who possesses pneumatical charisma, or one who promotes legalistic rules, should absorb from the *Yìjīng* a recognition, that all powers when pushed to the extreme will reverse their courses. Pastors should not be swayed too easily nor intimidated by any particular power party. While the *Yìzhuàn* teaches that a sage retires into solitary (contemplation),[19] through which he knows the comings and goings of things, a pastor acknowledges the power of God in Christ in tandem with his understanding of the rhythm of the increase and decrease of the *yīn* and *yáng*.

A Chinese pastor could be in the midst of the 'six powers' as shown in Diagram E (page 219). In reality, they do not usually all appear at the same time; but if they do, the pastor, being in the midst, can still recognize himself as one of the powers. A pastor in this situation, correctly handling the material as previously explicated, should be able to prevent the granting of any ultimacy to the said powers, including to himself as the assumed ultimate power.

However, he could also execute his own *yīnyáng* power. According to *Yìzhuàn*, *yáng* usually symbolizes firmness, strength and uprightness.[20] Rather than being swayed by the dominating power, the pastor should hold fast to these inner qualities; even when these inner qualities may appear contrary to strength, i.e. as gentleness (*róu*), firmness is still implied. As is said in the *Wényán* commentary regarding Qián hexagram: "(What

18. Lynn, 138.

19. See *Xìcí* I:11. I do not agree with Lynn's translation of *"tuì cháng yú mì"* as "When it is retired, it becomes hidden among its secrets." I believe it is the sage himself which indicated here, who "retires into seclusion." The above is a modified translation.

20. For these, see discussion in chapter 4.

The Double Vision Hermeneutics

is indicated by) Kūn is most gentle and weak (*zhìroú*), but, when put in motion, is hard and strong (*gāng*)."[21] While the emphasis is on the *zhìroú* nature, such a *roú* contains a *gāng* nature within it. Although it emphasizes compliance, it is to the course of Heaven one submits oneself to compliance. It is never a giving up of power nor a claim of powerlessness. It is remaining as a "submerged dragon" (*qiǎnlóng*), symbolizing a time for waiting. This does not imply passive aimlessness, or awaiting whatever falls on one's path, but a pro-active holding back of any action. Thus *Yìjīng* does not teach *yáng* as powerfulness, in contrast to *yīn* as powerlessness. Power, as implied here, does not necessarily signify domination as indicated by Lukes.[22] Nor is it like the *shì*, the propensity, a king may possess, for his convenience, to rule his people as Hán Feī Zǐ suggests but Xúnzǐ rejects.[23]

This having been said, viewed from the Pauline perspective, no one in this κόσμος and αἰῶνος is exempt from the influence of the power of sin. According to Paul, sin affects humanity on a far deeper leve and all are judged unrighteous (Rom 3:10). It may just be inferred all not only observe the world through the eyes of a sinner, but act as one. Humanity cannot escape from its domination by "principalities and powers" for they are not powers of "blood and flesh" but of "spiritual forces" (Eph 6:12). Wink interprets "Powers" as the "domination system" that is "beyond merely human control." One who experiences this domination system experiences "a total system operating" in his or her life.[24] He states, "No one person or group of people imposed the Domination System on us; it came wholly unbidden."[25] In other words, domination is in existence and has been experienced by humanity both externally and internally. Hence a pastor demonstrating attributes of firmness, strength and uprightness is not entirely free from the power of sin. Not only can the six power symbols dominate and enslave: the pastor himself can also fall prey to the domination system and become its accomplice, exploiting power and dominating the church members under his care, instead of advancing the restoration of power to its rightful place, under the lordship of Jesus Christ (Eph 1:20–22).

---

21. Legge, 418–19. Lynn translates *zhìroú* as "perfectly compliant" here (144); while Wilhelm/Bayne as "altogether yielding" (392).

22. For Lukes, see discussion in chapter 3.

23. See discussion in chapter 3.

24. Wink, *Engaging*, 41–42.

25. Wink, *Engaging*, 42.

The ethic of powers may perhaps have been internalized by society, dominated by "principalities and powers," and pride and strength used as the standard by which values and excellence in advancement are measured, resulting in an tendency to resort to power and violence when exploited by powers.[26] The rule of power is upheld and power fought with power. The "principalities and powers" are not 'out there' but have occupied the thrones in our lives.

The antidote for the Chinese pastor caught in the midst of the six powers and under the domination of sin is provided by Paul in his response to the problem of boasting in the Corinthian church, which is judged also to be applicable to the situation in Galatian church where knowledge of the *stoicheia* and the law were boasted of: grace alone, as found in 2 Corinthians.[27]

According to Paul, a life born of grace is a life liberated oneself the "powers" or the need to cling to these powers. Power, although appearing neutral and upheld by many, would no longer be relied on, as previously discussed, for example, with regard to the situation in Corinthian church society. Paul experienced the grace of God and taught Christ's example of self-emptying;[28] therefore the faith-praxis formed in his life requires examination.

Paul's autobiographical argument against the Corinthians epitomized a way of life based on boasting of one's weakness:

> [9] but he (Christ) said to me, "My grace is sufficient for you, for power is made perfect in weakness." So, I will boast all the more gladly of my weaknesses, so that the power of Christ may dwell in me. [10] Therefore I am content with weaknesses, insults,

---

26. See Wink's critique and analysis on American culture in this respect in chapter 1 and 2 of *Engaging* as in 13–49, especially regarding "the myth of redemptive violence."

27. It is presupposed in this argument that 2 Corinthians and 1 Corinthians were written to the same church, although the two texts differ in that Paul appeared more concerned, in 2 Corinthians, with the problem of superapostles. For example, although discussion of patronage-client relationship was based on an analysis of 1 Corinthians, the issue is equally found in 2 Corinthians, but plays out in a different fashion probably related to false apostles. But as Witherington alerts, one should not read too much of Galatians, "where the opponents were Judaizers," into 2 Corinthians (346). For more detailed discussion, see Witherington, *Conflict and Community*, 341–52.

28. It is appropriate to compare this with Paul's identification with the lowest possible status as he "ironically contrast[s] this to the high-status positions" claimed by the Corinthians in 1 Cor 4:1–21, see Martin's argument in *The Corinthian Body*, 65–68.

hardships, persecutions, and calamities for the sake of Christ; for whenever I am weak, then I am strong. (2 Cor 12:9–10)

This passage was the culmination of Paul's self-vindication contrasting boastfulness and weaknesses which began from 11:16. It might appear that in 2 Cor 11:16–30 Paul had been defending himself;[29] however, on closer inspection, it could also be read as a revealing demonstration of an apostle's spiritual life. Following a narration of his personal experiences of tribulation, suffering, and persecution, which he defined as external, he emphasized being "under daily pressure" because of his anxiety for all the churches"(11:28). This anxiety was an internal burden. The succeeding passage, "Who is weak, and I am not weak? Who is made to stumble, and I am not indignant? If I must boast, I will boast of the things that show my weakness" (2 Cor 11:28b–30; 12:5) sounds boastful, or as Harrris comments, "self-eulogizing;" however Paul employs an ironic twist, boasting not on what the world regard as honorable but on weakness.[30]

Paul indicated his right to boast of his supernatural experience (12:1–4), but rejected it, claiming instead a right to boast based on "a thorn" in his flesh (12:7). There is no need to speculate on the nature of the "thorn."[31] Of more importance was his reference to "power" (δύναμις)

---

29. Savage makes a similar remark: "At first sight it would appear that Paul is endeavouring to boost his self-esteem," but this leads him to an alternate line of argument. Others argue with reference to his rhetorical skills. For scholars who hold this view, see Savage, *Power*, 62–63. The precise nature of the false apostles Paul designated needs not affect our understanding of Paul's autobiographical narrative.

30. Harris, *Second Corinthians*, 730. Employing a rhetoric of persuasion that he is not like the super-apostle, the intruders (11:20–21), so that his audience would differentiate the sign a cruciform apostleship, as Harris remarks, he "judges that no other technique will be as effective in bringing the Corinthians to their senses."

31. Whether this "thorn" was used metaphorically or literally, to mean a sickness or a psychological state, and it's relation to "the messenger of Satan" have been the conjecture of many scholars with no satisfactory answer. Some suggestions include: physical a) illness, disfigurement, or disability, b) moral temptation, or c) relational as opposition or persecution, see Barnett, *Second Epistle*, 569. See also Lambrecht, *Second Corinthians*, 203, who notes the apposition of "thorn" and "the messenger of Satan" and identifies the former with the latter. He also notes that there is a double agent, as God uses Satan to bring this suffering to Paul. Harris is against the idea of double agency, who argues it should be explained "that Satan is active at the same time as God and by his permission." He thinks, "the deflation of pride" through this thorn "is God's distinctive work, while the infliction of suffering is Satan's distinctive work (Job 1:8–19; 2:3–7; Luke 13:16; 1 Cor 5:5)." See Harris, *Second Corinthians*, 856. It is worth noting that in the OT, there are several examples of a double agency (1 Sam 16:14; 1 Kgs 22:13–23), but the emphasis is on God's sovereignty. See also Wink's discussion of how Satan's evolving from God's servant to the evil one in *Unmasking*, 9–40.

in his acknowledgment of the Lord's promise: "My grace is sufficient for you, for power is made perfect in weakness," which was immediately followed by Paul's boasting in his weaknesses, the locus of his experience of the power of Christ (12:9). Ehrensperger provides an interpretation of the interplay between power and weakness as experienced by Paul:

> Power is not weakness, and weakness is not power, but power accomplishes, that is, has an effect through weakness. The boasting of Paul is a boasting of his weakness, nothing else. Paul boasts in his weakness, acknowledging it for what it is—a thorn in his flesh, and insults, hardships and persecutions are what they are, causing suffering and bringing Paul to the brink of death. He is at peace (12.10) with his weakness not because he realizes that weakness is actually not weakness but power, but because through weakness the power of God in Christ is manifested.[32]

Thus, the terminology of "weakness," "grace," and "power" for Paul, was not a rhetorical device to win an argument; it was his personal experience. Without a true experience of weakness, there would have been no experience of grace and power.

Grace created a paradox, a way of being, or self-perception, epitomized by 2 Corinthians 12:10: "Therefore I am content with weaknesses, insults, hardships, persecutions, and calamities for the sake of Christ; for whenever I am weak, then I am strong." On the basis of these verses, it appears that the strength (δύναμις) he found in Christ, through grace, was experienced concretely and substantially. This δύναμις had been expressed in 2 Corinthians 4:7, "But we have this treasure in clay jars, so that it may be made clear that this extraordinary power belongs to God and does not come from us." As much as grace was from God, the power he experienced was also from God, which was again grace.

Paul's mystical expression—"always carrying in the body the death of Jesus, so that the life of Jesus may also be made visible in our bodies"

---

32. Ehrensperger, *Dynamics*, 108. She bases her argument on the Greek preposition ἐν which she thinks should be understood as instrumental instead of modal. Nevertheless, her argument in fact finds echo in CU and NC versions which render as *zài (rén dè) ruǎn ruò shàng*. However, the possessive *rén dè* is added to Chinese. She also does not approve of the rendering of τελεῖται as "made perfect", arguing that "rather than referring to some perfection of power in weakness the intention here is to maintain that power only accomplishes what it set out to accomplish, i.e., to have an effect through weakness. Again, here in CU and NC, it is rendered as *xiǎn dé*, which does not emphasize the nuance "to manifest."

The Double Vision Hermeneutics

(4:10)—is as paradoxical as it is profound, reflected also in the following dialectic experience: "For while we live, we are always being given up to death for Jesus' sake, so that the life of Jesus may be made visible in our mortal flesh" (4:11). Paul described the life of Jesus in him as the power or the "treasure in clay jars." With this power in him, he proclaimed, he may have been "afflicted," "but [was] not crushed; perplexed, but not driven to despair; persecuted, but not forsaken; struck down, but not destroyed (4:8-9)." Thus, emerging from this life-death dialectic is a key to understanding the power that is given through grace.

The profound effect of the mystical experience, made effective through the life and death of Jesus, made possible Paul's argument that in death life was born.[33] In this way, the implication of Jesus conquering the powers through "taking the form of a slave" and "[becoming] obedient to the point of death—even death on a cross" in Philippians 2:7–8, and the mystery of exposing (or disarming, ἀπεκδυσάμενος) death and sin, powers and principalities and "[making] a public example of them, triumphing over them in him"[34] converge in Paul's own life. The juxtaposition and exchange of death and life which is in play here, is a dramatic recapitulation of Jesus' crucifixion and resurrection.

To conclude, the key to maturity of Christian character is claiming one's weakness in Christ rather than strength.[35] The "powers" cannot be conquered by securing and exercising more power over them, but through the experience of grace in suffering and weakness, the grace and δύναμις bestowed by God not according to merit or knowledge of God's way. As Sampley concludes, "The paradoxical (God's) power through (human) weakness frees, even compels, Paul to boast of his weaknesses."[36] For the captivating power of *shì*, to be stripped away, focus must be turned from striving to fathom the way of '*shì*', to following Christ, a way of life through which the grace of God is experienced.

---

33. The death that is "at work in us" can somehow activate a "life in you" (4:12).

34. See Wink's interpretation in *Naming the Power*, 57–58. Taking the principalities and powers as "the natural object of" ἀπεκδυσάμενος, he argues that "they would be the ones who have been stripped, disarmed, exposed, unmasked by the crucifixion of Jesus."

35. Samra's study has drawn attention to maturity and gives evidence of the lack of attention to this perspective in Pauline study, see *Being Conformed to Christ in Community*, 3–25. His argument is based on his review of Adolf Schlatter, Ernst Kasemann, Ed Parish Sanders, James G. Dunn, Wayne Meeks, Richard Hays, and Troels Engberg-Pedersen.

36. Sampley, "2 Corinthians 12:1–10 Commentary," 167.

A Double Vision Hermeneutic

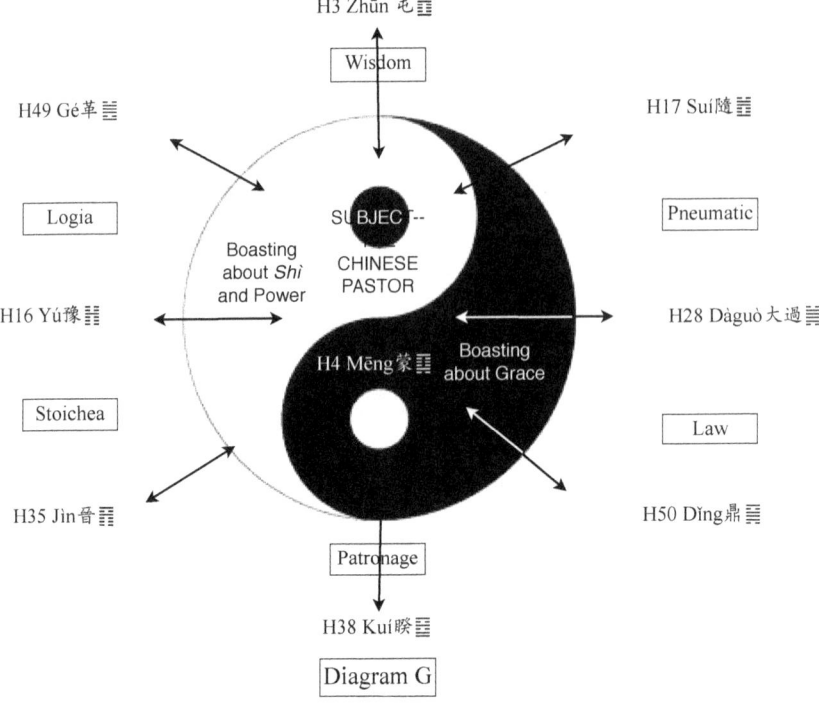

Diagram G

Diagram G, above, illustrates the demonstration of the double vision hermeneutics covered in chapters 3 to 7. It presents the subject, a Chinese pastor, concerned with *shì*, as it may be used in a church: to fathom *shì* is to judge the proper timing and the dynamism of the power constellations. As demonstrated in chapter 4, situated within a constellation of power in the church, Pastor Y was faced with the choice of several possible moves, symbolized in the diagram as circling around the subject. These moves are derived from one another and are mutually dependent, as shown by the different hexagrams. For example, H49 Gé can change to H50 Dǐng and vice versa. Likewise Pastor Y or the young Chinese pastor in the seminal example may witness various forms of power as exemplified in the Galatian and Corinthian church. All those forms of power can find new expression in today's churches, for example, different forms of patronage, boasting of spiritual gifts, or legalism. A Christian pastor, informed by a Pauline theology of power, recognizes the possibility of the emergence of various forms of power in a church, but does not allow these powers ultimacy nor permit or allow them to be made ultimate by others; neither should he be caught up with fathoming the perfect timing for a wise move in

The Double Vision Hermeneutics

bringing change to a church. Instead he should learn to imitate Paul who boasted only in the power of grace. An understanding that all situations will change may be learned from the *Yìjīng* hexagramic dynamism: Situations come and go, as *yīn* and *yáng* can increase and decrease all the time.

In the introduction the subject explained his experience of power struggle in the church: As a Chinese pastor, situated within a Chinese cultural context, who had learned and appropriated Chinese culture as transmitted through language and traditionary texts, his experience had been addressed as an experience of *shì*. He had also been convicted of temptation and ambition of power by his Christian conscience. The experience revealed the inheritance, or appropriation, of two traditions, Chinese and Christian, which led to the current hermeneutical venture. The hermeneutic evolved into a process of further inquiry into two traditionary texts: Texts A1 + A2 and Texts B1 + B2, which itself became a process of creating new modes of being,[37] thus the initial mode may now differ from the mode formed through the process of enquiry. The traditionary texts remains as a constant, however their effect in and through the subject may have changed. As traditionary texts, they are open to appropriation by others, either as standing alone or intertextually with others, as in this thesis.

To return to Diagram G (page 228), the subject's location in the centre of two paradigms of powers reveals the result of a double vision hermeneutics. To illustrate further using Text 0, the consequential births of new modes of being, in relation to the understanding of *shì* and power can be Text 1, Text 2, Text 3, Text 4 et cetera. Neither the multifaceted hexagramic interpretations, nor the six power symbols were initially present in the diagram, however they now appear in its present integrated form as understanding gained by the subject during his research.

2. Evaluating the Double Vision Hermeneutic

The primary principle the double vision hermeneutic has prescribed was a double awareness, functioning as defined in the introduction: 1) being aware of two visions or two texts at the same time or seeing them both in one vision at the same time, 2) seeing one vision or text in the foreground while being aware of another text or vision in the background, or 3) two visions or two texts appearing sequentially and alternately, implying an

---

37. For the notion of the "new mode of being," see Gadamer, *Truth and Method*, 53, 58.

interchangeable subsidiary and focal awareness between two texts, and more significantly between a Chinese eye and a Christian eye vis-à-vis a Chinese text and a Christian text.

The double vision hermeneutic has primarily been a *posteriori* hermeneutic, i.e., it explained a real life situation from the past, then, as a continuum continuously provided an ongoing hermeneutical experience between the subject and various texts. It was continuous because it was open to the emergence of "new modes of unity" between the texts and the subject as the experiences were appropriated by him.

Secondarily, the double vision hermeneutic aimed to address the deficiencies of previous hermeneutical attempts in this area by engaging with a more exegetical and expositional approach to the texts. Therefore, it highlighted as one of its principles an acknowledgement of the objective and transcendent nature of the texts. In chapters 3 to 7, the interpretation was controlled to first deal with the literary and historical contexts of the texts prior to further interpretation.

Further interpretations attempted to explain the intersubjective relationship between the texts, and between the texts and the subject. This fulfilled the principle of removing the objective-subjective dichotomy in order to address the intersubjectivity actually found between the entities. The strategy used to handle Texts A1 + A2 and Texts B1 + B2 separately allowed the first layer of intersubjectivity to be seen clearly. The convergent interpretation presented in this final chapter attempted to reveal a second and deeper layer of intersubjectivity between Texts A and B and the subject in Text 0, which had continued in the subject throughout the interpretative process until appearing in its penultimate form, as shown in Diagram G. It remained penultimate rather than ultimate since new modes of being would continue to emerge, as subsequent texts were integrated into the subject, the Chinese pastor, wrestling with his dual identity and the two texts. This process was demonstrated through the use of Text 1, Text 2, Text 3, Text 4, et cetera and did not preclude an ongoing process if further texts were addressed.

An assessment of the efficiency of the double vision hermeneutics in achieving what previous attempts did not, needed to be undertaken. Within its context of Chinese Christian indigenous theology, this thesis has argued that "two texts" approaches as proposed by Archie Lee's cross-textual hermeneutics and K. K. Yeo's cross-cultural hermeneutics could be further developed in a certain direction by incorporating a cultural-linguistic dimension. While scholars such as Peter K. H. Lee, C. S. Song, Liú

Xiǎofēng on one side, and Alister McGrath, Hendrik Kraemer, Anthony J. Gittens on another, had called for attention on the cultural-linguistic aspect, substantial work was lacking in the field. However, any engagement in serious reading and exposition of a text, by a Chinese Christian for the purpose of integrating his Chinese and Christian identity required the avoidance of any doctrinal approach that was susceptible to eisegesis. Consideration of the "rich reservoir of linguistic experiences,"[38] the "older philosophical and rhetorical tradition,"[39] and "the worlds-of-meanings"[40] embedded in the "deep structure"[41] of Chinese language was of equal importance.

These additional two concerns were integrated into the attempt to unfold the multilayered intersubjective relationships between the living texts[42] or what Gadamer calls "the traditionary texts," a "real life setting"[43] and the subject's intersubjective experience of *shì*. It is postulated that the work of the thesis offered the following contribution:

1. By its focus on *shì* as a cultural phenomenon, as described in the subjective vision of a Chinese pastor, it allowed the cultural-linguistic aspect to be studied in a focused way, and enabled the cultural-linguistic dimension implicit in Zhào Zǐchén's work,[44] to be an explicit resource for theological reflection.

2. It transcended the doctrinal and word study approach comparing a word, or a set of words, with other words conveying similar meaning in Christian scripture, and therefore avoided the mere comparison of texts aimed at the excavation of as many compatible, parallel ideas as possible.[45]

3. Although, at times it appeared complex, it allowed a concrete example of a fusion of horizons, by the use of one subjective real life experience as the locus of interpretation.

---

38. Liú, "Sino-Christian," 76–77.
39. McGrath, "Evangelical Theological Method," 36–37.
40. Gittens, *Gifts and Strangers*, 12.
41. Gittens, "Beyond Liturgical Inculturation," 51.
42. Yeo, "Culture and Intersubjectivity," 84.
43. Yeo, "Culture and Intersubjectivity," 85.
44. For Zhào, see chapter 1.
45. See for examples, Yao, *Confucianism and Christianity* and in some respects Yeo, *Musing*.

4. A model of Chinese Christian self-understanding of the intersubjective relationship between a subject and traditional texts was offered.

5. The very subjective nature of every hermeneutical act and process was demonstrated. Research undertaken using the same sources, for example *shì*, Paul and *shì* or Paul and *Yìjīng* by different people, or the same person at a different time, would not result in the same hermeneutical process and outcome.

Nonetheless, this thesis was not intended as a contribution to the field of Pauline, *Yìjīng*, or Gadamer research or the study of power and power discourse per se, but an attempt to respond to a lack of engagement with a cultural-linguistic dimension and as a more exegetical approach to the texts. It is suggested that study for the early chapters has given due prominence to *shì*, a significant word carrying heavy cultural implication, and that the double vision hermeneutic has successfully brought together the multifarious aspects entailed in the unfolding and explanation of the intersubjective experience of *shì*.

3. Implications for Future Research

Two possibilities for the direction of future research have emerged from this thesis: 1) engaging with *shì* for a theological study of history based on the concept of *shì* and the philosophy of *Yì*, and 2) the relationship between subjectivity and the Confucian notion of learning for oneself.[46]

3.1: A Theological Reflection on the Philosophy of History Based on the Philosophy of Shì

It has been found that, in spite of China's very rich and complex history and the use of *shì*, by historians and common people alike, to interpret its history and understand changes of dynasty in good times and bad,[47] no theologian has yet undertaken theological reflection whereby biblical theology engaged with Chinese history. A theology of history, in dialog with the notion of *shì* as it appears in the Chinese philosophy of history as formulated by Wáng Fūzhī for example, has yet to be attempted.

---

46. See De Bary, *Learning for One's Self*.
47. For example, see Hon, *The Yijing and Chinese Politics*.

The Double Vision Hermeneutics

Wáng Fūzhī saw history as the alternation of *zhì* (order) and *luàn* (disorder) and the *zhì* and *luán* understood in terms of *shì*. Wáng received Zhāng Zǎi's idea of *qì* (vital force) and inherited Zhū Xī's idea of *lǐ* (principle or pattern). He knew the idea of *lǐ*, but worked creatively toward the combination of *lǐ* and *qì*. He incorporated both aspects into his interpretation of *shì*. The latter was the crux of his whole philosophy of history and his understanding of *qì* and *shì* or *qìshì* (the power and disposition of *qì*) is prominent:[48] "All *shì* under heaven are but the (oscillating movement of) separation and unity, *líhé*, as well as the (manifestation of) either order or disorder, *zhìluàn*. The unity is but the separation being united; the order is but the disorder being ordered."[49]

A remnant of the Míng dynasty, having witnessed the fall of Míng, he was concerned with the propensities (*shì*) of history of his own time.[50] *Shì* was key to his understanding and interpretation of history and politics. By re-interpreting Sīmǎ Guāng's *Zīzhì Tōngjiàn* (Comprehensive Mirror to Aid in Government) which covers history from 403 BC to 959 AD, he reflected on the rise and fall of the dynasties before Míng. He was especially burdened to reflect on the fall of the Sòng dynasty into the hands of the Mongols who established the Yuán dynasty. He meditated on the similarity between the fall of Sòng and that of Míng, both had fallen to the hands of those he considered barbarians.

Fūzhī developed his philosophy of history from *Yìzhuàn*.[51] As mentioned in chapter 3, he interpreted *shì* using the concept of time, for example, "If the *moments* differ, the *shì* differ; and if the *shì* differs, the logics which govern the processes also differ." He proposed the idea of *lǐ-shì bú èr*, the non-duality of *lǐ* and *shì*, as his philosophy of history and politics, thus developing an application of *Yìzhuàn* philosophy to illustrate *shì*. The application of *shì* in this manner, as a key to interpret history, was not studied in this thesis but suggests a direction for future research.

---

48. For Wáng, see Táng Jūnyì, "Wáng Chuánshān zhī rénwén huàchéng lùn (xià)," 647-669; Liu, "Is History Predestined in Wang Fu-chih's Cosmology," 321-38.

49. Wáng Chuánshān, *Lǐjì zhāngjù*, 10:3.

50. His concern with this is evident in his works, especially *Dú Tōngjiàn lùn* and *Sònglùn*, which, to quote Ian Morran, are interpretations "of events" and critiques "of institutions and personalities according to a systematically intricate but coherent philosophy of history." See Morran, "Wang Fu-Chih and the Yung-li Court," 139.

51. Not only that he had written as many as six monographs directly on *Yìzhuàn*, namely, *Zhōuyì kǎoyì*, *Zhōuyì bàishū*, *Zhōuyì wàizhuàn*, *Zhōuyì dàxiàng jiě*, *Zhōuyì wàizhuàn*, *Zhōuyì nèizhuàn fālì*. His other works, for examples, *Zhāngzǐ zhèngméng zhù*.

3.2: The Learning for Oneself as a Research Objective

Another direction for future research is related to subjectivity. As is shown, subjectivity and intersubjectivity have been widely discussed in this thesis. Throughout the research, the position of self, i.e. the thoughts and feelings of the subject-researcher who undertakes the research, was noted. The researcher's subject and concern do not necessarily remain external, as topics for objective investigation: they may be of personal concern to the researcher, such as in this thesis, where the researcher aimed at integrative self-understanding, a concern which found echo in numerous sources, including his own Chinese cultural tradition.

Confucius, in the *Analects* (*Lúnyǔ*), declared that "learning among the ancients was for one's self (*wèijǐ*), but now it is for the sake of others' (meaning to impress others or gain their approval)."[52] "For one's self" (*wèijǐ*), de Bary remarked, it "tells us for what purpose it is to be pursued, namely to do something (*wèi*) for the self, to help make it or shape it into a person, rather than simply to have it take something in or put something on to satisfy others,"[53] suggesting that learning is not primarily undertaken to impress others or gain fame, but rather to become a *jūnzǐ*: "To be unsoured even if one is not recognized—is this not to be a noble man (*jūnzǐ*)?"[54] De Bary emphasized that, "for Confucius, unless such learning enabled him to stand on his own feet even when disappointed in his personal ambitions, it would not be true learning, nor would he be a truly noble man."[55]

Confucius' own epigraph, "learning for oneself" has become a tradition within Confucianism as an ideal for a *jūnzǐ*'s self-cultivation. Huáng Jùnjié commented, "Reading the classics is for the sake of the reader's self-cultivation in longing admiration of the ancient sages. Textual hermeneutics is a means to express 'learning for oneself' (*wei chi chih hsüeh*), weaving textual studies into one's personal existence, and one's life with the text's into a lived unity."[56] This is one of the ideals of a classic intellectual in the Chinese tradition.

---

52. Cited from De Bary, *Learning for One's Self*, x. I have changed the transliteration by de Bary here and the following from Wile-Giles to *pīnyīn* system.

53. De Bary, *Learning for One's Self*, x.

54. *Lúnyǔ*, cited from De Bary, *Learning for One's Self*, x. Transliteration added by me.

55. De Bary, *Learning for One's Self*, xi.

56. Huang, *Mencian Hermeneutics*, 258.

The Double Vision Hermeneutics

With regard to self-cultivation under this rubric, Huáng remarked that, traditionally, "the commentator" of Chinese classics did not aim for his commentary to be simply a scholar's achievement in terms of its scientific and objective accuracy as a piece of research. On the contrary, commentators unabashedly entrusted their "personal self-cultivation to the ancient Classics."[57] They did so in two ways:

> (a) Commentators read the classical texts in light of their personal experience, making the texts into their record of their "pilgrims' progress." Hermeneutics in China is experiential.
> (b) Hermeneutical exercises involve the entire exegete's life, in line with the existential character of the Chinese classics.[58]

The pilgrimage belonged to the exegete himself who involved his appropriation of the texts through reflexive reading in order to reach the land his innate moral being was imperatively called to.

Such a subjective concern, the continuing appropriation of meaning for oneself to achieve self-completion, echoed with Gadamder's idea of the experience of creating new modes of being, as discussed earlier. They point toward the direction of "learning for oneself."

Moustakas developed what he called a heuristic research,[59] which addressed the notion of "self-awareness" and "self knowledge," and resonated with the notion of learning for oneself. He described heuristic research as

> a process of internal search through which one discovers the nature and meaning of experience and develops methods and procedures for further investigation and analysis. The self of the researcher is present throughout the process and, while understanding the phenomenon with increasing depth, the researcher also experiences growing self-awareness and self-knowledge.[60]

Parallel to and along with this heuristic approach is Etherington's reflexive approach.[61] Etherington's innovation to this approach was through her

---

57. Huang, *Mencian Hermeneutics*, 257. The other two strands in Chinese hermeneutics Huang remarks are: hermeneutics for political operations and maneuvers, and hermeneutics as apologia, apologetics (256–57).

58. Huang, *Mencian Hermeneutics*, 258.

59. Moustakas, *Heuristic Research*, 14–27. Moustakas has derived the word "heuristic" from Polanyi, see for examples 124–31, 301–2, 382, 395, 397, 399 et cetera, and "incubation" in 121–22, 126, 129 et cetera, and "indwelling" in 59, 173, 195–202 et cetera in *Personal Knowledge*.

60. Moustakas, *Heuristic Research*, 9.

61. Etherington, *Becoming a Reflexive Researcher*.

personal journey from writing a master and then a PhD thesis, which came to fruition when she earned her PhD. She stated,

> Reflexivity is a skill that we develop as counsellors: an ability to notice our responses to the world around us, other people and events, and to use that knowledge to inform our actions, communications and understandings. To be reflexive we need to be aware of our personal responses and to be able to make choices about how to use them. We also need to be aware of the personal, social and cultural contexts in which we live and work and to understand how these impact on the ways we interpret our world.[62]

She further reflects that "reflexivity implies a difference in how we view the 'self': as a 'real' entity to be 'discovered' and 'actualized' or as a constantly changing sense of our selves within the context of our changing world."[63]

In other words, reflexivity is a movement of understanding within a hermeneutical circuit experienced and appropriated from outside that resounds in the researcher. It is a process of making sense of what is inside through what is read. In short, it is a process of understanding and self-understanding.[64]

Ricoeur also called attention not only to appropriation, as previously discussed, but also to subjectivity and reflexivity resonant with the above. Suggesting that "reflexive philosophy,"[65] Ricoeur says,

> considers the most radical philosophical problems to those that concern the possibility of self-understanding as the subject of the operation of knowing, willing, evaluating, and so on. Reflexion is that act of turning back upon itself by which a subject grasps, in a moment of intellectual clarity and moral responsibility, the unifying principle of the operations among which it is dispersed and forgets itself as subject.[66]

Reflexion as described above is a response to the deepest self inquiry into one's philosophy of life, one's being, and how one shoulder live. It aimed at profound self-understanding. Reflexion of this kind is never in isolation,

---

62. Etherington, *Becoming a Reflexive Researcher*, 19.

63. Etherington, *Becoming a Reflexive Researcher*, 30.

64. Cf. Etherington's discussion in *Reflexive Researcher*, 32–33.

65. See Ricoeur, "Appropriation." For a recent article on Ricoeur's hermeneutics as appropriation, see Suazo, "Hermeneutics as Appropriation."

66. Ricoeur, "On Interpretation," 12.

but demands and entails the study of all available resources whether internal, what has already been appropriated, or external towards what will be appropriated to facilitate self-understanding. Ricoeur explained,

> By "appropriation," I understand this: that the interpretation of a text culminates in the self-interpretation of a subject who thenceforth understands himself better, understands himself differently, or simply begins to understand himself. This culmination of the understanding of a text in self-understanding is characteristic of the kind of reflective philosophy which . . . I have called "concrete reflection."[67]

This is close to what has been argued in this thesis, and although a fuller discussion of Ricoeur would require a separate thesis, the above demonstrated the need for further research into subjectivity and "learning for oneself" or into research itself as a project for the learning of oneself.

It appeared that reflexivity, self-understanding, heuristic analysis, and appropriation, as articulated by Moustakas, Etherington and Ricoeur resonated with the tone and texture of this thesis, however, further development of the discussion of the Confucian tradition of *learning for oneself* would be meaningful. This strand was not developed in this thesis due to the constraints of focus and length.

Both research directions suggested above may be developed at a future date. This present thesis, having developed significantly from its inception as Text 0, could be designated as Text 5, or Text 6, or Text 7. This text could not be regarded as perfect; there will never be a 'perfect' Text since new modes of being will emerge and new Texts will constantly be appropriated. However, it is hoped that this thesis, by emphasizing and exploring the significance of a cultural-linguistic dimension to Chinese indigenous theology, may have served to fill the lacuna in the body of previously published research, and to have succeeded in combining the cross-cultural and cross-textual approaches, to help reduce the deficit in current textual exegesis. These concerns have been addressed by means of double vision hermeneutics which was intended to serve as an example of two texts integrated within a Chinese Christian. This thesis aimed to unfold and demonstrate the operation of double vision hermeneutics vis-a-vis the multilayered intersubjective relationships between the texts and the subject. An indigenous Chinese theology could express itself in many models. One which includes a Chinese cultural-linguistic dimension or one engages with multi-texts, may itself have different expressions. This thesis attempts to show only one of them.

67. Ricoeur, "What is a Text?," 158.

Appendix I: 64 Hexagrams

䷁ 坤 2 Kūn	䷖ 剝 23 Bó	䷇ 比 8 Bǐ	䷓ 觀 20 Guān	䷏ 豫 16 Yù	䷢ 晉 35 Jìn	䷬ 萃 45 Cuì	䷋ 否 12 Pǐ
䷎ 謙 15 Qiān	䷳ 艮 52 Gèn	䷦ 蹇 39 Jiǎn	䷴ 漸 53 Jiàn	䷽ 小過 62 Xiǎoguò	䷷ 旅 56 Lǚ	䷞ 咸 31 Xián	䷠ 遯 33 Dùn
䷆ 師 7 Shī	䷃ 蒙 4 Méng	䷜ 坎 29 Kǎn	䷺ 渙 59 Huàn	䷧ 解 40 Jiě	䷿ 未濟 64 Weìjì	䷮ 困 47 Kùn	䷅ 訟 6 Sòng
䷭ 升 46 Shēng	䷑ 蠱 18 Gǔ	䷯ 井 48 Jǐng	䷸ 巽 57 Sùn	䷟ 恆 32 Héng	䷱ 鼎 50 Dǐng	䷛ 大過 28 Dàguò	䷫ 姤 44 Goù
䷗ 復 24 Fù	䷚ 頤 27 Yí	䷂ 屯 3 Zhún	䷩ 益 42 Yì	䷲ 震 51 Zhèn	䷔ 噬嗑 21 Shìhé	䷐ 隨 17 Suí	䷘ 無妄 25 Wùwàng
䷣ 明夷 36 Míngyí	䷕ 賁 22 Bì	䷾ 既濟 63 Jìjì	䷤ 家人 37 Jiārén	䷶ 豐 55 Fēng	䷝ 離 30 Lí	䷰ 革 49 Gé	䷌ 同人 13 Tóngrén
䷒ 臨 19 Lín	䷨ 損 41 Sǔn	䷻ 節 60 Jié	䷼ 中孚 61 Zhōngfú	䷵ 歸妹 54 Guīmèi	䷥ 睽 38 Kuí	䷹ 兌 58 Duì	䷉ 履 10 Lǚ
䷊ 泰 11 Tài	䷙ 大畜 26 Dàxù	䷄ 需 5 Xū	䷈ 小畜 9 Xiǎoxù	䷡ 大壯 34 Dàzhuàng	䷍ 大有 14 Dàyoù	䷪ 夬 43 Guài	䷀ 乾 1 Qián

Appendix II: English Names of 64 Hexagrams

1. Creative	17. Following	33. Retreat	49. Revolution
2. Receptive	18. Arresting Decay	34. The Power of the Great	50. The Caldron
3. Initial Difficulty	19. Approach, Symbol of Advance	35. Progress	51. Thunder, Exciting Power
4. Youthful Inexperience	20. Contemplation	36. Darkening of the Light, Intelligence Wounded	52. Mountain, Arresting Movement
5. Waiting	21. Biting Through	37. The Family	53. Gradual Progress, Growth
6. Conflict	22. Adornment	38. Disunion, Mutual Alienation	54. The Marrying Maiden, Propriety
7. The Army, Group Action	23. Falling Apart	39. Arresting Movement	55. Abundance, Prosperity
8. Union	24. Returning	40. Removing Obstacles	56. Traveling Stranger
9. The Taming Force, Small Restraint	25. Correction, Innocence	41. Decrease	57. Gentle Penetration
10. Treading Carefully	26. The Great Taming Force	42. Increase	58. Joy, Pleasure
11. Peace	27. Nourishment	43. Removing Corruption, Breakthrough	59. Dispersion
12. Stagnation	28. Excess	44. Encountering	60. Regulation, Restraining
13. Union of Men	29. The Perilous Pit	45. Gathering Together	61. Inmost Sincerity
14. Great Possession, Abundance	30. The Clinging, [Brightness]	46. Ascending	62. Small Excesses
15. Modesty	31. Influence	47. Oppression	63. Completion
16. Harmony, Joy, Enthusiasm	32. Perseverance, Duration	48. A Well	64. Incompletion

Glossary of Chinese Expressions

This glossary lists characters and sentences that appear in the content. It runs in alphabetical order. For sentences, only the first alphabet of the first *pīnyīn* word of the sentence will be considered.

Bá	拔
bà dào	霸道
běn	本
bīngshì	兵勢
bīng wú cháng shì, shuǐ wú cháng xíng	兵無常勢，水無常形
bīng zhī guì zhě yì lì yě	兵之所貴者執利也
bù huǐ	不悔
bù kě bá	不可拔
caishì	財勢
Chǎo huì cóng shēng zhī wèi, hue yi ér wei yoǔ biàn yě	草卉叢生之謂，晦翳而未有辨也
chū yú qì leì, bá hū qí cuì	出於其類，拔乎其萃
chǔ shèng rén zhī yì	處勝人之執
cìyǔ	詞語
cóngzhèng jí	從正吉
cún hū weì	存乎位
cuò zòng fù zá	錯綜複雜
cuòguà	錯卦
dé qí shí yě	得其時也
dǐng	鼎
dìshì	地勢
dàhēng zhēn wú jiù	大亨貞無咎
Dàyān zhī shù	大衍之數
dòng	棟
dòng ér yuè, suí	動而悅，隨
dòng hū xiǎn zhōng	動乎險中
Dù Yù zhùan	杜預傳
èr nǚ tóng jū, qí zhì bù tóng xíng	二女同居，其志不同行
feīlóng zaì tīan	飛龍在天
gǎnyìng	感應
gāng	剛

241

Glossary of Chinese Expressions

gāngjiàn	剛健
gāngzhèng	剛正
gāngzhōng	剛中
gēng	更，庚
gù shàn zhàn zhě, qiú zīh yú shì, bù zhé yú rén	故善戰者，求之于勢，不責于人
guī	筮
Hán Fēizǐ, Hán Fēi	韓非子，韓非
Hétú	河圖
Huáinánzi	淮南子
hùyì guà	互易卦
jī	幾
Jì lì yǐ tīng, nǎi yǐ wéi shì, yǐ zǒu qí wài; shì zěh, yīn lì ér zhì quán yě	計利以聽，乃為之勢，以佐其外；勢者，因利而制權也。
jǐrì	己日
jiàn hoú	建侯
jiàn lóng zaì tián	見龍在田
Jiāngguó piān	疆國篇
jiaōhù guà	交互卦
jié rú jī fā	節如機發
Jīn bīng wēi yǐ zhèn, shì rú pò zhú, pì rú pò zhú, sex c c shù jié yǐ hoù, jiē yín rèn eŕ jiě	今兵威已振，譬如破竹，數節之後，皆迎刃而解
jìng	靜，境
jìngjiè	境界
jìnshì	進士
Jìxià	稷下
jūnzǐ	君子
jūnzǐ yǐ zhèng weì níng mìng	君子以正位凝命
jūzhēn	居貞
kàng	亢
kànglóng yoǔ huǐ	亢龍有悔
laǒ baǐxìng	老百姓
lè	樂
lè zhé xíng zhī	樂則行之
leì	累
Lì guī	利筮
lī-shì bú èr	理勢不二
lì zhēn zhě, xiāng suí zhī tǐ, xū lì zaì dé zhèng. Suí 'ér bù zhèng, zhé xié pì zhī daò, xū lì zhēn yě	利貞者，相隨之體，須利在得正。隨而不正，則邪僻之道，須利貞也

Glossary of Chinese Expressions

líhé	離合
liángzhī	良知
luàn	亂
Lùn liùjiā yàozhǐ	論六家要旨
páihuái	徘徊
páihuái liúlián	徘徊流連
pánhuán	磐桓
qìshì	氣勢
Qín	秦
qián, jiàn yiě	乾，健也
qíng	情
qíngjìng	情境
qiú zhī yú shì	求之于勢
Quánzhēn Daoist	全真道
qián lóng wù yòng	潛能勿用
qíngyì	情義
quán, quán shì, quánmoú, quányí	權，權勢，權謀，權宜
qūzhí	曲直
rén	仁，人
rényì	仁義
róu	柔
rùshén	入神
sāncái	三才
Sānjiào	三教
shàn wéi yì zhě bù zhàn	善為易者不占
Shèdiāo yīngxióng zhuàn	射鵰英雄傳
shén lóng jiàn shǒu bú jiàn wěi	神龍見首不見尾
shěn shí chá shì	審時察勢
Shèn Dào	慎到
Shèng Baǒluó zhuàn	聖保羅傳
Shuōwén jiězì	說文解字
shí	時
Shǐjì	始計
shì	勢，士
shì rú pòzhú	勢如破竹
shì rú zhāng nǔ	勢如張弩
Shí yì ér shì yì, shì yì ér lǐ yì	時異而勢異，勢異而理異
Shì yīn hū shì, lǐ yīn hū shì	勢因乎時，理因乎勢

243

Glossary of Chinese Expressions

shì zài bì xíng	勢在必行
shìlì	勢利
shìshì	時勢
Shíyì	十翼
shù	術
shùn yǐ dòng	順以動
Shuōguà	說卦
Sònglùn	宋論
suíshí zhī yì	隨時之義
suí zhī shuǒ shī	隨之所施
suí zhī shíyì	隨之時義
suí	歲
taìshǐ	太始
tiān jī bù kě xiè loù	天機不可洩漏
tiāngān	天干
tiān xià suíshí	天下隨時
tǐng bá	挺拔
tuì cháng yú mì	退藏於密
wáng daò	王道
Wàng Mǎng	王莽
weíjǐ	為己
wú cháng	無常
wù jǐ	戊己
wú mēn	無悶
wù shēngjī	悟生機
xiāngchuò	相錯
Xī Mín	西銘
Xián, gǎn yě. Roú shàng ér gāng xià, èr qì xiāng yìng yǐ xiāng yǔ	咸，感也。柔上而剛下，二氣相應以相與
xiān gēng sān rì, hoù gēng sān rì	先庚三日，後庚三日
xiān jiǎ sān rì, hoù jiǎ sān rì	先甲三日，後甲三日
xiǎn dé	顯得
xiǎn yǐn míng àn	顯隱明暗
xiàng	象
Xīn Dynaster	新朝
Xīshū	新書
xíngshì	形勢
xìnyì	信義

Glossary of Chinese Expressions

Xùguà	序卦
Xúnzǐ	荀子
Xūshí	虛實
yì	埶，義，役
yì tǐ liǎng tài	一體兩態
yǐ xìn chēng yì	以信稱義
yǐ xìn wéi zhí	以信為直
Yìjīng	易經
Yìzhuàn	易傳
yǒngshēng	永生
yoū	憂
yoū zhé wéi zhī	憂則違之
yuán, hēng, lì, zhēn	元、亨、利、貞
yùan hēng, lì zhēn, wú jiū	元亨、利貞、無咎
zaì (rén dè) ruǎn ruò shàng	在（人的）軟弱上
Zhī shí yǐ shěn shì, yīn shì ér qiú hé yú lǐ	知時以審事，因勢而求合於理
zhēn	貞
zhēn jí	貞吉
zhèng	正
zhèng jí	正吉
zhì	志，治
zhī guà	之卦
zhījī yòngshén	知幾用神
zhìluàn	治亂
zhìroú	至柔
zhōngzhèng yǐ guān tiānxià	中正以觀天下
zòngguà	綜卦

Selected Bibliography

Primary Sources

Chén Gǔ'yìn and Zhaò Jiànweǐ, eds. *Zhoūyì zhùshì yǔ yánjiū*. Translated by Chén Gǔ'yìn and Zhaò Jiànweǐ. Taipei: Taiwan Shangwu, 1999.
Giles, Lionel, trans. *The Art of War*, by Sun Tzu. Mineola, NY: Dover, 2002.
Griffith, Samuel B. trans. *The Art of War*, by Sun Tzu. Oxford University Press, 1971.
Hán Feī. *Hánfeīzǐ jiàoshì*. Edited by Chen Qitian. Shanghai: Zhonghua shuju, 1940.
Huáng Qìngxuān. *Zhoūyì dúběn*. Taíbeǐ [Taipei]: Sānmín shūjú, 1993.
Kǒng Yǐndá (576–648). *Zhoūyì zhèngyì*. BeǐjÍng: Jiǔzhoū chūbǎn shè, 2004.
Legge, James. *Book of Changes*. Vol. 1. 1st ed. Translated into Modern Chinese by Qín Yǐ. The Chinese=English Bilingual Series of Chinese Classics. Húnán: Húnán chūbǎn shè, 1993.
Mair, Victor H. *The Art of War: Sun Zi's Military Methods*, by Sun Tzu. New York: Columbia University Press, 2009.
Minford, John, trans. *The Art of War*, by Sun Tzu. London: Penguin, 2005.
Rutt, Richard. *The Book of Changes (Zhouyi): A Bronze Age Document*. Durham East-Asia 1. Richmond, UK: Curzon, 1996.
Shaughnessy, Edward. *I Ching*. New York: Ballantine, 1998.
Wáng Fūzhī. *Zhoōyì waìzhuàn*. Beijing: Jiǔzhoū, 2004.
———. *Zhoūyì neìzhuàn*. Beijing: Jiǔzhoū, 2004.
———. *Lǐjì zhāngjù*. In *Chuán Shān quán shū*. Húnán: Yuè lù shū shè, 2011.
———. *Dú Tōngjiàn lùn*. In *Chuán Shān quán shū*. Húnán: Yuè lù shū shè, 2011.
———. *Sònglùn*. In *Chuán Shān quán shū*. Húnán: Yuè lù shū shè, 2011.
———. *Zhoūyì kayǒi*. In *Zhoōyì waìzhuàn*, 525–34. Beijing: Jiǔzhoū, 2004.
———. *Zhoūyì baìshū*. In *Zhoōyì waìzhuàn*, 385–458. Beijing: Jiǔzhoū, 2004.
———. *Zhoūyì dàxiàng jiě*. In *Zhoōyì waìzhuàn*, 459–523. Beijing: Jiǔzhoū, 2004.
———. *Zhoūyì neìzhuàn fālì*. In *Zhoōyì waìzhuàn*. Beijing: Jiǔzhoū, 2004.
———. *Zhāngzǐ zhèngméng zhù*. In *Chuán Shān quán shū*. Húnán: Yuè lù shū shè, 2011.
Wang, Bi. *The Classic of Changes*. Translated by Richard John Lynn. New York: Columbia University Press, 1994.
Xunzi. *Xunzi: A Translation and Study of the Complete Works*. Translasted by John Knoblock. Stanford, CA: Stanford University Press, 1988.

Selected Bibliography

Zhū Xī朱熹. *Zhoūyì bényì*. Sìkù Quán Shū zhēnběn liù jí. Vol. 1. Edited by Wáng Yúnwǔ. Taiwan: shang wu [yin shu guan, 1976.

———. *Zhūzǐ yǔleì*. Edited by Lǐ Jìngdé. 8 vols. Lǐxué cóngshū. Beǐjīng: Zhōnghuá shūjú, 1994.

CHINESE SECONDARY SOURCES

Arnold Yeung (Yáng Mùgǔ). "Zhōngguó Shénxué." In *Dāngdaì Shénxué Cídiǎn*, edited by Arnold Yeung (Yáng Mùgǔ). Taíbeǐ [Taipei]: Xiàoyuàn chūbǎn shè, 1997.

Caì Rénhoù, Zhoū Liánhuá, and Liáng Yènchéng. *Huìtōng yǔ Zhuǎnhuà (Communication and Transformation)*. Taíbeǐ [Taipei]: Cosmic Light, 1985.

Chén Jiànhóng. "Zhōngjí guānhuái yǔ rújiā zhōngjiào xìng: yǔ Liú Shùxiān shāngquè." *Èrshí yī shìjì (21th Century) Bi-monthly* 58 (2004).

Chén Shoù. *Sān guó Hz*. Annotated by Pei Songzhi (Song Dynasty). Beijing: Zhonghua shuju, 1959.

Chuán Daòbīn. "Zhún guà gaǒ (An Investigation of Zhun Hexagram)." *Journal of Peking University (Philosophy and Social Sciences)* 42/4 (2005) 66-70.

Fù Jiànpíng. "Zhoūyì Xū guà lùnshì." *Huánán shīfàn Dixie xuébaò* 1 (1993) 30-37.

———. "Zhoūyì Xū guà tànyuán." *Zhōngguá wénhuà* 7 (1993) 102-107.

Fù Peìróng. *Rǔjiā yǔ xiàndaì rénshēng*. Taiwan: Yeìqiáng, 1989.

Gaō Hēng. *Zhoūyì gǔjīng jīnzhù*. Hong Kong: Zhōnghuá shūjú xiānggǎng fēnjú, 1963.

Gaō Huáimín. *Sòng Yuán Míng Yìxué shǐ (The History of Yi-Learning in Song, Yuan, and Ming Dynasty)*. Guìlín, China: Guǎngxī Shīfàn dàxué chūbǎn shè, 2007.

Hán, Feī. *Hán Feīzǐ Jiào Shì*. Edited by Chén Qǐtiān. 1st ed. Shanghai: Shanghai shu dian, 1996.

Ho Hing Cheong (Hé Qìngchāng). "Interpreting Christianity with Confucianism: A Study of Xu Songshi's Thought." MPhi thesis, Chung Chi Divinity School, Chinese University of Hong Kong, 2002.

———. *Zhoūyì zònghéng tán*. Taíbeǐ [Taipei]: Sānmín shūjú, 2007.

Huáng Hoùjī [Samuel Hio-Kee Ooi]. "Jǐjì yǔ weìjì—tatnaǒ Xiè Fúǎy wǎnqī sīxiǎng (1958-1991) hé shénxué daìmó ("Already But Not Yet: A Study of Hsieh Nai-zen's Late Thought (1958-1991) and His Theological Model"). MTheol thesis, SEAGTS Chung Chi Divinity School Branch, University of Hong Kong, 2002.

Huáng Róngwǔ. "Zhoūyì Gé guà zhōng dè Wǔ wáng fá Zhoù rì—Wù zǐ zíyí shuō." *Journal Beijing University of Chemical Technology* 3 (2004) 40-46.

Jì Xùshēn, ed. *Shànghaǐ bówù guǎn cháng Zhànguó Chǔ zhú shū (3) dúběn*. Taíbeǐ: Wàngjuàn loú, 2005.

Jīn Chūnfēng. *Zhoūyì jīngzhuàn shūlǐ yú guōdiàn chǔjiǎn sīxiǎng xīnshì*. Taíbeǐ: Taíwān gǔjí chūbǎn shè, 2003.

Jīn Jǐngfāng, and Lǚ Shaògāng. *Zhoūyì jiǎngzuò*. Taiwan: Taōluè, 2003.

Lam Wing Hung. *Qǔ gaō hé guà: Zhaò Zǐchén dè shēngpíng yǔ shénxué*. Hong Kong: CGST, 1994.

Lee, Archie. "Kuà yǔ wén běn yuè dú de fāng fǎ: yǐ Shīpiān yǔ Shījīng weí lì. In *Chōngtú yǔ hùbǔ: Jīdūjiào zhéxué zaì Zhōngguó*, edited by Xū Zhìweǐ and Zhaò Dūnhuá. Beǐjīng: Shèhuì kēxué chūbǎn shè, 2000.

———, ed. *Yàzhoū chǔjìng yǔ shèngjīng quánshì*. Hong Kong: Christian Literature, 2000.

Selected Bibliography

Lǐ Jìngchí. *Zhoūyì tànyuán*. 1st ed. Beijing: Zhonghua shu ju, 1978.
Lǐ Jǐngxióng [Peter K H Lee]. "Běnsè shénxué—Jiǔgēn yǔ xīnkěn" *Jǐng Fēng* (Chinese *Ching Feng*) 40 (1974) 7–15.
———. "Yērú duìhuà dè xīn lùxiàn." *Christian Times Weekly* 424 (December 15, 1995).
Lǐ Tiāngāng. *Kuà wénhuà quànshì: jīngxué yǔ shénxué dè xiāngyù*. Xīnxīng chūbǎn she, 2007.
Lǐ Xuéqín. *Zhoūyì suòyuán*. Bāshǔ shūshè, 2006.
Liào Míngchūn. *Zhoūyì jīngzhuàn yǔ yìxué shǐ xīnlùn*. Jǐnán: Qílǔ xuéshè, 2001.
———. "Cóng yǔyán dé bǐjiàn lùn Zhoūyì běnjīng dè chéngshū niándaì." In *Zhoūyì jīngzhuàn yǔ yìxué shǐ xīnlùn*. Jǐnán: Qílǔ xuéshè, 2001.
Liu Shu-hsien [Liú Shùxiàn]. "Xiàndaìhuà yǔ rújiā chuántǒng dè zhōngjiào yìhán." *Logos & Pneuma* 2 (Spring 1995) 127–51.
———. "Guānyú 'chaōyuè neìzaì' wèntí dè xíngshì." *Dāngdaì* 96 (April 1, 1993).
Liú Xiǎofēng. "Xiàndaì yǔjìng zhōng de hànyu Jīdū shénxué." In *Logos & Pneuma: Chinese Journal of Theology* 2 (1995) 9–48.
Lǜ Shaògāng. *Zhoūyì chánweī*. Taiwan: Taōluè, 2003.
Moú Zōngsān. "Dì sān pǎn xù." In *Lìshǐ zhéxué*. Taibei: xuéshēng shūjú, 1984.
———. *Zhōngguó zhéxué dè tèzhí*. Taíbeǐ: Taíwān xuéshēng shūjú, 1990.
Mun Kin-chok (Mǐn Jiànshǔ). *Yìjīng dè língdaǒ zhìhuì*. Hong Kong: Chinese University of Hong Kong, 2001.
Pān Yǔtíng. *Yìxué shǐ fāweī*. Shànghaī: Fùdàn University, 2001.
Sītú Zuózhèng (Paul C. C. Szeto). "Yǐ běntǔ wénhuà weí biāozhì dè bēnsè shénxué." In *Jìndaì shénxué qī dà lùxiàn*, 187–232. Hong Kong: Zhengdao, 1978.
Sūn Lóngjī. *Zhōngguó wénhuà dè shēnchéng jiégoù*. Taiwan: Huà qiàn shù chūbǎn shè, 2005.
Táng Jūnyì 唐君毅. *Shēngmìng chúnzaì yǔ xīnlíng jìngjiè*. Vol. 1. Rev. ed. Taíbeǐ [Taipei]: Xuéshēng shūjǔ, 1986.
———. "Wáng Chuánshān zhī rénwén huàchéng lùn (xià)." In *Zhōngguó zhéxué yuánlùn yuánjiào piān*, 647–69. Táng Jūnyì quánjí. Taíbeǐ [Taipei]: Taíwān Xuéshēng shūjú, 2004.
———. "Shìshì zhī lǐ zaì Zhōngguó sīxiǎng zhōng zhī dìweì jí sān baǐ nián laí zhī Zhōngguó zhéxué (shàng)." In *Zhōngguó zhéxué yuánlùn yuánjiào piān*, 670-687. Táng Jūnyì quánjí. Taíbeǐ [Taipei]: Taíwān Xuéshēng shūjú, 2004.
———. "Shìshì zhī lǐ zaì Zhōngguó sīxiǎng zhōng zhī dìweì jí sān baǐ nián laí zhī Zhōngguó zhéxué (xià)." In *Zhōngguó zhéxué yuánlùn yuánjiào piān*, 688–710. Táng Jūnyì quánjí. Taíbeǐ [Taipei]: Taíwān Xuéshēng shūjú, 2004.
Tu Wei-ming, ed. *Rújiā Fāzhǎn dè Hóngguān Toùshì*. Taíbeǐ [Taipei]: Zhèngzhōng, 1997.
Wáng Chéng, and Feī Zhí. "Yìzhuàn chéngxīn sīxiǎng dè xiàndaì jiěxī." *Dōng yuè lùncóng* 29/5 (September 2008) 70–73.
Wáng Xiǎobō. "Shèn Daò sīxiǎng zhī fēnīx." In *Xiān qín fǎjiā sīxiǎng shǐ luòn*, 231–65. Taíbeǐ [Taipei]: Lián jīng, 1991.
Weī Zhèngtōng. *Zhōngguó sī xiǎng shǐ*. 1st ed. Shanghai: Shànghaī shū diàn chū bǎn shè, 2003.
Wú, Lìmín. *Jīdūtú yǔ Zhōngguó shèhuì biànqiān*. Hong Kong: Christian Literature, 1981.
Xiè Bīngyíng. *Xīnyì sìshū dúběn*. Taipei: Sānmín shūjú, 2003.

Selected Bibliography

Xiè Fúyǎ. *Xiè Fúyǎ wǎnnián Jīdūjiào sīxiǎng lùnjí*. Hong Kong: Chinese Christian Literature, 1986.

———. "Píng xiāng gǎng shèngjīng gōnghuì xīnjìn biānyìn de 'lìshǐ dè gǎizaò zhě." In *Xiè Fúyǎ wǎnnián Jīdū jiào sīxiǎng lùnjí*. Hong Kong: Chinese Christian Literature, 1986.

———. "Zhoūyì xīntàn." In *Xiè Fúyǎ wǎnnián Jīdū jiào sīxiǎng lùnjí*. Hong Kong: Chinese Christian Literature, 1986.

———. *Baī'nián shīwén jí*. Hong Kong: Chinese Christian Literature, 1991.

———. *Beì yā pò zhě dè fúyī*. Hong Kong: Qīngnián Xiéhuì shūjú, 1938.

———. *Jù liú diǎn dī*. Hong Kong: Chinese Christian Literature Council, 1970.

———. *Nánhuá rén zhù shān fáng wénjí*, Vol.1. Hong Kong: Nántiān shūyè gōngsī, 1970.

———. *Xiè Fúyǎ wǎnnián wénlù*. Taíbeǐ [Taipei]: Zhuànjì wénxué chūbǎn, 1977.

———. "Zhoūyì dè zhōngjiào jiàzhí." In *Xiè Fúyǎ wǎnnián wénlù*. Taipei [Taipei]: Zhuànjì wénxué chūbǎn, 1977.

———. *Zhōngyōng yǔ daòlǐ—Zhōngxī lìdai zhéxué bǐ lùn*. Hong Kong: Hong Kong Baptist College Teaching and Learning Development Centre, 1986.

Xíng Fùzhēng. *Xúnqiú jīdūjiào dè dútèxìng: Zhaò Zǐchén shénxué lùnjí*. Hong Kong: Alliance Bible Seminary, 2003.

———. "Zhaò Zǐchén de zhōngjiào jīngyèn." Christian Study Centre on Chinese Religion and Culture, 2006. Online: http://csccrc.org/c4.htm.

Yeung, Arnold [Yáng Mùǔg]. *Fùhé shénxué yǔ jiàohuì gēngxīn*. Hong Kong: Seeds, 1987.

Yǔ Tùnkāng. *Hàn Sòng Yìxué jiědú*. Beijing: Huá xià, 2006.

Yǔ Xuětáng. "Zhoūyì Gé guà "Jǐ rì" Kaǒshì." *Gǔjí zhěnglǐ yánjiū shué kān* 2 (2001) 28–30.

Zhāng Lìwén. *Zhoūyì sīxiǎng yánjiū*. Húbeǐ, China: Rénmín chūbǎn shè, 1980.

Zhāng Shuāngtū, and Chén Taō, eds. *Gǔdai hànyǔ zìdiǎn*. Beǐjīng: Beǐjīng dàxué chūbǎn shè, 1998.

Zhaò Zǐchén [T. C. Chao]. *Shèng baoluó zhuàn*. Shanghai: Qīngnián xiéhuì shūjú, 1947.

Zhèng Shùnjiā. *Táng Jūnyì yǔ Bātè*. Hong Kong: Sānlián shūdiàn, 2002.

Zhū Bókūn. *Yìxué zhéxué shǐ*. 4 vols. Rev. ed. Beǐjīng: Kūnlún chūbǎn shè, 2005.

Zhu Xi. *Zhū Xī jiěyì*. Edited and translated by Yīn Meǐmān. Beijing: Dāngdai shìjiè chūbǎn shè, 2007.

English Secondary Sources in Chinese Studies

Ames, Roger T. *The Art of Rulership: A Study in Ancient Chinese Political Thought*. Honolulu: University of Hawaii Press, 1983.

———. "Yin and Yang." In *Encyclopedia of Chinese Philosophy*, edited by Antonio S. Cua, 846–47. New York: Routledge, 2012.

Ames, Roger T., and David L. Hall. *Focusing the Familiar: A Translation and Philosophical Interpretation of the Zhongyong*. Honolulu: University of Hawaii Press, 2001.

Angle, Stephen C. *Sagehood: The Contemporary Significance of Neo-Confucian Philosophy*. Oxford: Oxford University Press, 2009.

Selected Bibliography

Behuniak, James, Jr. "Symbolic Reference and Prognostication in the *Yijing*." *Journal of Chinese Philosophy* 32/2 (2005) 223–37. Online: http://dx.doi.org/10.1111/j.1540-6253.2005.00189.x.

Berthrong, John. *All Under Heaven: Transforming Paradigms in Confucian-Christian Dialogue*. New York: State University of New York Press, 1994.

———. "Boston Confucianism: The Third Wave of Global Confucianism." *Journal of Ecumenical Studies* 40/1–2 (January 2003) 38–47.

———. *Transformations of the Confucian Way*. Boulder, CO: Westview, 1998.

Blanc, Charles Le, and Huai-nan tzu. *Huai-nan Tzu: Philosophical Synthesis in Early Han Thought: The Idea of Resonance (kan-ying) with a Translation and Analysis of Chapter Six*. Hong Kong: Hong Kong University Press, 1985.

Bol, Peter, Joseph A. Adler, Don J. Wyatt, and Kidder Smith. *Sung Dynasty Uses of the I Ching*. Princeton, NJ: Princeton University Press, 1990.

Cao, Degui. "American Confucianism." *JCP* 32/1 (March 2005) 123–38.

Chan, Wing-tsit. *A Source Book in Chinese Philosophy*. 1st ed. Princeton, NJ: Princeton University Press, 1969.

Cheng, Chung-ying (Chéng Zhōngyīng). "Chinese Philosophy and Symbolic Reference." *Philosophy East and West* 27 (1977) 307–22. Online: http://www.jstor.org/stable/1398001.

———. "Confucian Onto-Hermeneutics: Morality and Ontology." *Journal of Chinese Philosophy* 27/1 (2000) 33–68. Online: http://dx.doi.org/10.1111/0301-8121.00003.

———. "Confucianism: Twentieth Century." In *Encyclopedia of Chinese Philosophy*, edited by Antonio S. Cua, 1020. New York: Routledge, 2002.

———. *Contemporary Chinese Philosophy*. Malden, MA: Blackwell, 2002.

———. "Inquiring into the Primary Model: Yi Jing and the Onto-Hermeneutical Tradition." *Journal of Chinese Philosophy* 30/3–4 (2003) 289–312. Online: http://dx.doi.org/10.1111/1540-6253.00121.

———. "Legalism versus Confucianism: A Philosophical Appraisal." In *New Dimensions of Confucian and Neo-Confucian Philosophy*, 311–38. Albany: State University of New York Press, 1991.

———. "An Onto-Hermeneutic Interpretation of Twentieth Century Chinese Philosophy: Identity and Vision." In *Contemporary Chinese Philosophy*, edited by Chung-ying Cheng and Nicholas Bunnin, 365–404. Oxford: Blackwell, 2002.

Ching, Julia. *Confucianism and Christianity: A Comparative Study*. Tokyo: Sophia University, 1977.

Chow, Kai-wing, On Cho Ng, and John B. Henderson, eds. *Imagining Boundaries: Changing Confucian Doctrines, Texts, and Hermeneutics*. SUNY series in Chinese Philosophy and Culture. Albany: State University of New York Press, 1999.

Chu Hsi. *Introduction to the Study of the Classic of Change*. Translated by Joseph A. Adler. Global Scholarly, 2002.

Chung, Chang-Soo. *The I Ching on Man and Society: An Exploration into Its Theoretical Implications in Social Sciences*. Lanham, MD: University Press of America, 2000.

Confucius. *The Analects of Confucius*. Translated by Arthur Waley. London: Allen & Unwin, 1938.

Cua, Antonio S. *Encyclopedia of Chinese Philosophy*. New York: Routledge, 2002.

De Bary, William Theodore. *Asian Values and Human Rights: A Confucian Communitarian Perspective*. Cambridge, MA: Harvard University Press, 1998.

Selected Bibliography

———. *Learning for One's Self: Essays on the Individual in Neo-Confucian Thought*. Neo-Confucian Studies. New York: Columbia University Press, 1991.

———. *The Trouble with Confucianism*. Cambridge, MA: Harvard University Press, 1991.

Elman, Benjamin A. *From Philosophy to Philology: Intellectual and Social Aspects of Change in Late Imperial China*. Cambridge, MA: Harvard University Press, 1984.

Gernet, Jacques. *A History of Chinese Civilization*. 2nd ed. Cambridge: Cambridge University Press, 1996.

———. "A Note on the Context of Xu Guangqi's Conversion." In *Statecraft and Intellectual Renewal in Late Ming China: The Cross-Cultural Synthesis of Xu Guangqi (1562–1633)*, edited by Catherine Jami, Peter M. Engelfriet, and Gregory Blue, 186–90. Sinica Leidensia 50. Leiden: Brill, 2001.

Graham, A. C. *Disputers of the Tao: Philosophical Argument in Ancient China*. La Salle, IL: Open Court, 1989.

Graham, A. C., and National University of Singapore. *Yin-Yang and the Nature of Correlative Thinking*. Singapore: National University of Singapore, 1986.

Guan, Zhong. *Guanzi: Political, Economic, and Philosophical Essays from Early China: A Study and Translation = [Guanzi]*. Rev. ed. Boston: Zheng & Zui, 2001.

Hall, David L. *Anticipating China: Thinking Through the Narratives of Chinese and Western Culture*. Albany: State University of New York Press, 1995.

———. *Thinking from the Han: Self, Truth, and Transcendence in Chinese and Western Culture*. Albany: State University of New York Press, 1998.

Hall, David L., and Roger T. Ames. *Thinking Through Confucius*. Albany: State University of New York Press, 1987.

Hamm, John Christopher. *Paper Swordsmen: Jin Yong and the Modern Chinese Martial Arts Novel*. Honolulu: University of Hawaii Press, 2005.

Hansen, Chad. *A Daoist Theory of Chinese Thought: A Philosophical Interpretation*. New York: Oxford University Press, 1992.

Harper, Donald. "Warring States Natural Philosophy and Occult Thought." In *The Cambridge History of Ancient China*, edited by Edward L Shaughnessy and Michael Loewe, 813–84. Cambridge: Cambridge University Press, 1999.

Höchsmann, Hyun. "Foreseeing a Fusion of Horizon—Gadamer, Quine, and Chung-ying Cheng." *Journal of Chinese Philosophy* 34/1 (2007) 127–49.

Hon, Tze-ki. "Human Agency and Change: A Reading of Wáng Bì's Yìjīng Commentary." *Journal of Chinese Philosophy* 30/2 (June 2003) 223–42.

———. *The Yijing and Chinese Politics: Classical Commentary and Literati Activism in the Northern Song Period, 960–1127*. Albany: State University of New York Press, 2004.

Huang, Junjie. *Mencian Hermeneutics: A History of Interpretations in China*. New Brunswick, NJ: Transaction, 2001.

Huang, Junjie, and E. Zurcher, eds. *Time and Space in Chinese Culture*. Sinica Leidensia. Leiden: Brill, 1999.

Huang, Paulos. "Confronting Confucian understandings of the Christian Doctrine of Salvation: A Systematic Theological Analysis of the Basic Problems in the Confucian-Christian Dialogue." PhD diss., University of Helsinki, 2006.

Inhoff, Albrecht W., Hsuan-Chih Chen, and Jian Wang, eds. *Reading Chinese Script: A Cognitive Analysis*. Mahwah, NJ: Lawrence Erlbaum, 1999.

Selected Bibliography

Jami, Catherine, Peter M Engelfriet, and Gregory Blue, eds. *Statecraft and Intellectual Renewal in Late Ming China: The Cross-Cultural Synthesis of Xu Guangqi, 1562-1633*. Sinica Leidensia 50. Leiden: Brill, 2001.

Jensen, Lionel M. *Manufacturing Confucianism: Chinese Traditions and Universal Civilization*. Durham, NC: Duke University Press, 1997.

Jullien, François. *The Propensity of Things: Toward a History of Efficacy in Chi*. New York: Zone, 1995.

———. *A Treatise on Efficacy: Between Western and Chinese Thinking*. Honolulu: University of Hawaii Press, 2004.

Keightley, David N. *Sources of Shang History: The Oracle-Bone Inscriptions of Bronze Age China*. Berkeley: University of California Press, 1985.

Kim, Heup Young. *Wang Yang-ming and Karl Barth: A Confucian-Christian Dialogue*. Lanham, MD: University Press of America, 1996.

Kwok, Benedict Hung-biu. "The Christological Doctrine of Reconciliation of Karl Barth and the Dialogue with the Self-Cultivation of Wang Yang-ming." *Ching Feng* 41 (1998) 83–114.

Küng, Hans, and Julia Ching. *Christianity and Chinese Religions*. New York: Doubleday, 1989.

Kunst, Richard Alan. *The Original Yijing: A Text, Phonetic Transcription, Translation, and Indexes, with Sample Glosses*. Ann Arbor: U.M.I. Dissertation Services, 1994.

Lai, Whalen. "Puritanism and Neo-Confucianism: A Mutual Challenge." *Ching Feng* 39/3 (September 1996) 149–72.

Lee, Peter K. H. "The I Ching's Cosmology of Changes in Christian Perspective: With Reference to Teihard de Chardin's Evolutionary Cosmology." *Ching Feng* 40/2 (June 1997) 92–127.

———. "Preparation for Christian-Confucian Encounter: The Protestant Story." In *Confucian-Christian Encounters in Historical and Contemporary Perspective*, edited by Peter K. H. Lee, 10–28. Lewiston, NY: Edwin Mellen, 1992.

Ling, Samuel D. "Christian Responses to the May Fourth Movement: 'The Christian Renaissance.'" *Chinese Theological Journal* (Huárén shénxué qíkàn) 2 (June 1987) 89–116.

Liu, Jeeloo. "Is History Predestined in Wang Fu-chih's Cosmology." *Journal of Chinese Philosophy* 28 (2001) 321–38.

Liu, Johanna. "Music [yue] in Classical Confucianism: On the Recently Discovered Xing Zi Ming Chu." In *Confucian Ethics in Retrospect and Prospect*, edited by Qingsong Shen and Kwong-loi Shun, 61–78. N.p: CRVP, 2007.

Liu, Lydia He. *Translingual Practice: Literature, National Culture, and Translated Modernity in China, 1900–1937*. Stanford, CA: Stanford University Press, 1995.

Liu, Shu-hsien. "From the Central to the Peripheral—the Historical Situation and Cultural Ideals of Contemporary Neo-Confucianism." *Hànxué yánjiū tōngxùn* (November 1990) 19/4: 555–63.

———. *Understanding Confucian Philosophy: Classical and Sung-Ming*. Contributions in Philosophy 61. Westport, CT: Praeger, 1998.

Liu, Xiaofeng. "Sino-Christian Theology in the Modern Context." In *Sino-Theology in China*, edited by Huilin Yang and Daniel H. N. Yeung, 52–89. Newcastle, UK: Cambridge University Press, 2006.

Selected Bibliography

Major, John S. *Heaven and Earth in Early Han Thought: Chapters Three, Four and Five of the Huainanzi*. SUNY series in Chinese Philosophy and Culture. Albany: State University of New York Press, 1993.

Makeham, John. "A New Hermeneutical Approach to Early Chinese Texts: The Case of the *Analects*." *JCP* 33, supp. s1 (2006) 95–108. Online: http://dx.doi.org/10.1111/j.1540-6253.2006.00393.x.

Marshall, S. J. *The Mandate of Heaven: Hidden History in the I Ching*. New York: Columbia University Press, 2001.

Minford, John. "Introduction." In *Sunzi, The Art of War*, edited by John Minford. London: Penguin, 2005.

Morran, Ian. "Wang Fu-Chih and the Yung-li Court." In *From Ming to Ch'ing: Conquest, Region, and Continuity in Seventeenth-Century China*, edited by Jonathan D. Spence and John E. Wills, 135–66. New Haven, CT: Yale University Press, 1993.

Neville, Robert Cummings. *Behind the Masks of God: An Essay Toward Comparative Theology*. Albany: State University of New York Press, 1991.

———. *Boston Confucianism: Portable Tradition in the Late-Modern World*. New York: State University of New York Press, 2000.

———. "Conscious and Unconscious Placing of Ritual (Li) and Humanity (Ren)." *Journal of Ecunemical Studies* 40/1–2 (2003) 48–58.

———. "The 'Puritan Ethic' in Confucianism and Christianity." *Ching Feng* 34/2 (June 1991) 100–103.

Ng, On Cho. *Cheng-Zhu Confucianism in the Early Qing*. New York: State University of New York Press, 2001.

———. "Chinese Philosophy, Hermeneutics, and Onto-Hermeneutics." *Journal of Chinese Philosophy* 30/3–4 (2003) 373–85. Online: http://dx.doi.org/10.1111/1540-6253.00126.

———. *Mirroring the Past: The Writing and Use of History in Imperial China*. Honolulu: University of Hawaii Press, 2005.

———. "Religious Hermeneutics: Text and Truth in Neo-Confucian Readings of the Yijing." *Journal of Chinese Philosophy* 34/4 (2007) 647–49. Online: http://dx.doi.org/10.1111/j.1540-6253.2007.00445.x.

Nylan, Michael. *The Five "Confucian" Classics*. New Haven, CT: Yale University Press, 2001.

Palmer, Richard E. "Gadamer and Confucius: Some Possible Affinities." *Journal of Chinese Philosophy* 33, supp. s1 (2006) 81–93. Online: http://dx.doi.org/10.1111/j.1540-6253.2006.00392.x.

Peng, Yan-qin, Chao-chuan Chen, and Xin-hui Yang. "Bridging Confucianism and Legalism: Xunzi's Philosophy of Sage-Kingship." In *Leadership and Management in China Philosophies, Theories, and Practices*, edited by Chao-chuan Chen and Yueh-ting Lee, 51-79. New York: Cambridge University Press, 2008.

Pfister, Lauren. "Re-Examing Whole Person Cultivation: Reconsidering the Significance of Master Kong's 'Knowing the Heavenly Decree' and Yeshuah's 'Beatitudes.'" In *Ching Feng* (New Series) 1/1 (Spring 2000) 69–96.

Puett, Michael J. *Ambivalence of Creation: Debates Concerning Innovation and Artifice in Early China*. Stanford, CA: Stanford University Press, 2002.

———. *To Become a God: Cosmology, Sacrifice, and Self-Divinization in Early China*. Cambridge, MA: Harvard University Asia Center, 2002.

Reldman, Laurie B., and Witina W. T. Siok. "Semantic Radicals in Phonetic Compounds: Implications for Visual Character Recognition in Chinese." In *Reading Chinese*

Script: A Cognitive Analysis, edited by Jain Wang, Albrecht Info, Hsuan-Chih Chen, 19-36. London: Lawrence Erlbaum, 1999.

Schaberg, David. *A Patterned Past: Form and Thought in Early Chinese Historiography*. Harvard East Asian Monographs 205. Cambridge, MA: Harvard University Asia Center, 2001.

Shaughnessy, Edward L. *Before Confucius: Studies in the Creation of the Chinese Classics*. SUNY Series in Chinese Philosophy and Culture. Albany, NY: State University of New York Press, 1997.

———. *Rewriting Early Chinese Texts*. Albany: State University of New York Press, 2006.

———. *Sources of Western Zhou History: Inscribed Bronze Vessels*. Berkeley: University of California Press, 1991.

Shaughnessy, Edward L., and Michael Loewe, eds. *The Cambridge History of Ancient China: From the Origins of Civilization to 221 B.C.* Cambridge: Cambridge University Press, 1999.

Shchutskii, Iulian Kostantinovich. *Researches on the I Ching*. London: Routledge & Kegan Paul, 1980.

Smith, Richard J. *China's Cultural Heritage: The Qing Dynasty, 1644-1912*. 2nd ed. Boulder, CO: Westview, 1994.

———. *Fathoming the Cosmos and Ordering the World: The Yijing (I-Ching, or Classic of Changes) and Its Evolution in China*. Charlottesville: University of Virginia Press, 2008.

Standaert, N. "Xu Guangqi's Conversion as a Multifaceted Process." In *Statecraft and Intellectual Renewal in Late Ming China: the Cross-Cultural Synthesis of Xu Guangqi (1562-1633)*, edited by Catherine Jami, Peter M. Engelfriet, Gregory Blue, 170-85. Sinica Leidensia 50. Leiden: Brill, 2001.

———. *Yang Tingyun, Confucian and Christian in Late Ming China: His Life and Thought*. Sinica Leidensia 19. Leiden: Brill, 1988.

Starr, Chloë. *Reading Christian Scriptures in China*. London: T. & T. Clark, 2008.

Sun, Lung-Kee. *The Chinese National Character: From Nationhood to Individuality*. Studies on Modern China. Armonk, NY: M. E. Sharpe, 2002.

Tan, Jonathan Y. "Father and Son in Confucianism and Christianity: A Comparative Study of Xunzi and Paul." *Theological Studies* 70/1 (March 2009) 205-6.

Tang, Andres S. K. "Confucianism and Bonhoeffer on Individualism and Community: From the Perspective of the Way of Humanization." In *Ching Feng* (New Series) 1/1 (Spring 2000) 97-103.

Tu Wei-ming. *Centrality and Commonality: An Essay on Confucian Religiousness*. SUNY series in Chinese Philosophy and Culture. Albany: State University of New York Press, 1989.

———. *Confucian Thought: Selfhood As Creative Transformation*. Albany: State University of New York Press, 1985.

———. *Confucian Traditions in East Asian Modernity: Moral Education and Economic Culture in Japan and the Four Mini-Dragons*. Cambridge, MA: Harvard University Press, 1996.

———. *Humanity and Self-Cultivation: Essays in Confucian Thought*. Boston: Cheng & Tsui, 1998.

———. "The Neo-Confucian Concept of Man." *Philosophy East and West* 21/1 (January 1971) 79-87.

Selected Bibliography

Tu Wei-ming, Milan Hejtmanek, and Alan Wachman, eds. *The Confucian World Observed: A Contemporary Discussion of Confucian Humanism in East Asia*. Honolulu: The East-West Center, 1992.
Waley, Arthur. *The Analects of Confucius*. London: Allen & Unwin, 1938.
———. *The Way and Its Power: A Study of the Tao Tê Ching and Its Place in Chinese Thought*. London: Allen & Unwin, 1934.
Wilhelm, Hellmut. *Heaven, Earth, and Man in the Book of Changes*. Reprint. Seattle: University of Washington Press, 1979.
Wilhelm, Hellmut, and Richard Wilhelm. *Understanding the I Ching*. Princeton, NJ: Princeton University Press, 1995.
Wilhelm, Richard. *The I Ching or Book of Changes*. Translated by Cary Baynes. 3rd ed. London: Penguin, 2003.
Yang, C. K. *Religion in Chinese Society: A Study of Contemporary Social Functions of Religion and Some of Their Historical Factors*. Berkeley: University of California Press, 1961.
Yao, Xinzhong. *Confucianism and Christianity: A Comparative Study of Jen and Agape*. Brighton: Sussex Academic Press, 1996.
Yearley, Lee H. *Mencius and Aquinas: Theories of Virtue and Conceptions of Courage*. New York: State University of New York Press, 1990.
Yu, Jiyuan. *The Ethics of Confucius and Aristotle: Mirrors of Virtue*. Loundon: Routledge, 2009.
Zhang, Longxi, *The Tao and the Logos: Literary Hermeneutics: East and West*. Durham, NC: Duke University Press, 1992.
Zhao, Yanxia. *Father and Son in Confucianism and Christianity: A Comparative Study of Xunzi and Paul*. Brighton: Sussex Academic Press, 2007.
Zhou, Xiaolin, and William Marslen-Wilson. "Sublexical Processing in Reading Chinese." In *Reading Chinese Script: A Cognitive Analysis*, edited by Jain Wang, Albrecht Info, and Hsuan-Chih Chen, 37–63. London: Lawrence Erlbaum, 1999.

English Secondary Sources in Pauline Studies, Theological, and Other Areas

Abasciano, Brian J. *Paul's Use of the Old Testament in Romans 9:1–9: An Intertextual and Theological Exegesis*. Journal for the Study of the New Testament 301. London: T. & T. Clark, 2005.
Adams, Edward, and David G. Horrell. *Christianity at Corinth*. Louisville: Westminster John Knox, 2004.
Anderson, Ray S. *The Shape of Practical Theology: Empowering Ministry with Theological Praxis*. Downers Grove, IL: InterVarsity, 2001.
Arichea, Daniel C., and Eugene A. Nida. *A Handbook on Paul's Letter to the Galatians*. New York: United Bible Societies, 1993.
Arnold, Clinton E. *Powers of Darkness: Principalities and Powers in Paul's Letters*. Downers Grove, IL: InterVarsity, 1992.
Barclay, John M. G. "Thessalonica and Corinth: Social Contrasts in Pauline Christianity." In *Christianity at Corinth*, edited by Edward Adams and David G. Horrell, 183–96. Louisville: Westminster John Knox, 2004.

Selected Bibliography

Barclay, John M. G., and Simon J. Gathercole, eds. *Divine and Human Agency in Paul and His Cultural Environment*. Early Christianity in Context 335. London: T. & T. Clark, 2006.

Barker, Paul A. *The Triumph of Grace in Deuteronomy: Faithless Israel, Faithful Yahweh in Deuteronomy*. Milton Keynes, UK: Paternoster, 2004.

Barnett, Paul. *The Second Epistle to the Corinthians*. The New International Commentary on the New Testament. Grand Rapids: Eerdmans, 1997.

Barrett, C. K. *A Commentary on the Epistle to the Romans*. 2nd ed. London: A. & C. Black, 1991.

———. *A Commentary on the First Epistle to the Corinthians*. 2nd ed. Black's New Testament Commentaries. London: A. & C. Black, 1971.

———. *Paul: An Introduction to His Thought*. 1st ed. Louisville, KY: Westminster John Knox, 1994.

Barth, Markus. *Ephesians*. Anchor Bible 34–34A. Garden City, NY: Doubleday, 1974.

Beale, G. K., and D. A. Carson, eds. *Commentary on the New Testament Use of the Old Testament*. Grand Rapids: Baker Academic, 2007.

Beker, Johan Christiaan. *Paul the Apostle: The Triumph of God in Life and Thought*. Edinburgh: T. & T. Clark, 1980.

Berger, Peter L. *The Sacred Canopy: Elements of a Sociological Theory of Religion*. Garden City, NY: Doubleday, 1967.

Berkhof, Hendrik. *Christ and the Powers*. Scottdale, PA: Herald, 1962.

Betz, Hans Dieter. *Galatians: A Commentary on Paul's Letter to the Churches in Galatia*. Minneapolis: Fortress, 1979.

Bevans, Stephen B. *Models of Contextual Theology*. Rev. and expanded ed. Faith and Cultures. Maryknoll, NY: Orbis, 2002.

Bhabha, Homi K. *Nation and Narration*. London: Routledge, 1990.

Bird, Michael F. *The Saving Righteousness of God*. Paternoster Biblical Monographs. Milton Keynes, UK: Paternoster, 2007.

Birth, Charles, and John B. Cobb Jr. *The Liberation of Life*. Cambridge: Cambridge University Press, 1981.

Boff, Leonardo. *Introducing Liberation Theology*. Theology and Liberation. Tunbridge Wells: Burns & Oates, 1987.

Bourdieu, Pierre. *The Logic of Practice*. Translated by Richard Nice. 1st ed. Stanford, CA: Stanford University Press, 1992.

———. *Masculine Domination*. Stanford, CA: Stanford University Press, 2001.

Browning, Don S. *A Fundamental Practical Theology: Descriptive and Strategic Proposals*. Minneapolis: Fortress, 1991.

Bruce, F. F. *The Book of the Acts*. Rev. ed. The New International Commentary on the New Testament. Grand Rapids: Eerdmans, 1988.

———. *The Epistles to the Colossians, to Philemon, and to the Ephesians*. The New International Commentary on the New Testament. Grand Rapids: Eerdmans, 1984.

———. *Men and Movements in the Primitive Church*. Exeter: Paternoster, 1979.

———. *The New Testament Documents*. Grand Rapids: Eerdmans, 2003.

———. *Paul, Apostle of the Heart Set Free*. Grand Rapids: Eerdmans, 2000.

Brueggemann, Walter. *Theology of the Old Testament: Testimony, Dispute, Advocacy*. Minneapolis: Fortress, 1997.

Selected Bibliography

Byron, John. *Slavery Metaphors in Early Judaism and Pauline Christianity: A Traditio-Historical and Exegetical Examination.* Tübingen: Mohr Siebeck, 2003.

Caird, G. B. *Principalities and Powers: A Study in Pauline Theology.* Oxford: Clarendon, 1956.

Campbell, Douglas A. *The Rhetoric of Righteousness in Romans 3.21–26.* Journal for the Study of the New Testament, supplement series 65. Sheffield, UK: JSOT, 1992.

Carlson, Richard P. "The Disputed Letters of Paul." In *The New Testament Today*, edited by Mark Allan Powell, 110–20. Louisville: Westminster John Knox, 1999.

Castelli, Elizabeth A. *Imitating Paul: A Discourse of Power.* 1st ed. Louisville: Westminster John Knox, 1991.

Chester, Stephen J. *Conversion at Corinth: Perspectives on Conversion in Paul's Theology and the Corinthian Church.* Studies of the New Testament and Its World. London: Continuum, 2005.

Chia, Philip P. "Differences and Difficulties: Biblical Interpretation in the Southeast Asian Context." In *Ways of Being, Ways of Reading: Asian American Biblical Interpretation*, edited by Mary F. Foskett and Jeffrey Kah-Jin Kuan, 45–59. St. Louis: Chalice, 2006.

Childs, Brevard S. *The Church's Guide for Reading Paul: The Canonical Shaping of the Pauline Corpus.* Grand Rapids: Eerdmans, 2008.

———. *Old Testament Theology in a Canonical Context.* London: SCM, 1985.

Chow, John K. *Patronage and Power: A Study of Social Networks in Corinth.* Journal for the Study of the New Testament, supplement series 75. Sheffield, UK: JSOT, 1992.

Clark, Gordon. *The Word "Hesed" in the Hebrew Bible.* Sheffield, UK: JSOT, 1993.

Clarke, Andrew D. *Secular and Christian Leadership in Corinth: A Socio-Historical and Exegetical Study of 1 Corinthians 1–6.* Arbeiten zur Geschichte des antiken Judentums und des Urchristentums 18. Leiden: Brill, 1993.

———. *Serve the Community of the Church: Christians as Leaders and Ministers.* First-Century Christians in the Graeco-Roman World. Grand Rapids: Eerdmans, 2000.

Coate, Mary Anne. *Clergy Stress: The Hidden Conflicts in Ministry.* New Library of Pastoral Care. London: SPCK, 1989.

Cohen, Paul A. *China Unbound: Evolving Perspectives on the Chinese Past.* Critical Asian Scholarship. London: Routledge, 2003.

Cosgrove, Charles H. *Cross-Cultural Paul: Journeys to Others, Journeys to Ourselves.* Grand Rapids: Eerdmans, 2005.

Douglass, Bruce G., and Clark Moustakas. "Heuristic Inquiry: The Internal Search to Know." *Journal of Humanistic Psychology* 25/3 (July 1985) 39–55. Online: http://jhp.sagepub.com/cgi/content/abstract/25/3/39.

Downing, Francis Gerald. *Cynics, Paul, and the Pauline Churches: Cynics and Christian Origins II.* London: Routledge, 1998.

Dreyfus, Hubert L. *Mind Over Machine: The Power of Human Intuition and Expertise in the Era of the Computer.* New York: Free Press, 1986.

Duffy, Stephen. *The Dynamics of Grace: Perspectives in Theological Anthropology.* New Theology Studies 3. Collegeville, MN: Liturgical, 1993.

Dunleavy, Patrick. *Authoring a PhD: How to Plan, Draft, Write and Finish a Doctoral Thesis or Dissertation.* Basingstoke, UK: Palgrave Macmillan, 2003.

Dunn, James D. G. *The Epistles to the Colossians and to Philemon: A Commentary on the Greek Text.* New International Greek Testament commentary. Grand Rapids: Eerdmans, 1996.

———. "The Incident at Antioch (Gal. 2:11-18)." *Journal for the Study of New Testament* 18 (1983) 3-57.

———. *The New Perspective on Paul*. Rev. ed. Grand Rapids: Eerdmans, 2008.

———. *Romans 1-8*. Word Biblical Commentary. Waco, TX: Word, 1988.

———. *Romans 9-16*. Word Biblical Commentary. Waco, TX: Word, 1988.

———. *The Theology of Paul the Apostle*. Grand Rapids: Eerdmans, 1998.

Eber, Irene, Sze-kar Wan, and Knut Walf, eds. *Bible in Modern China: The Literary and Intellectual Impact*. Monumenta Serica Monograph 43. Sankt Agustin, Ger.: Institut Monumenta Serica, 1999.

Ehrensperger, Kathy. *Paul and the Dynamics of Power: Communication and Interaction in the Early Christ-Movement*. Library of New Testament Studies 325. London: T. & T. Clark, 2007.

Elford, R. *The Pastoral Nature of Theology: An Upholding Presence*. London: Cassell, 1999.

Elias, Jacob. *Remember the Future: The Pastoral Theology of Paul the Apostle*. Scottdale. PA: Herald, 2006.

Elliott, Neil. *The Arrogance of Nations: Reading Romans in the Shadow of Empire*. Minneapolis: Fortress, 2010.

———. *Liberating Paul: The Justice of God and the Politics of the Apostle*. Biblical Seminar 27. Sheffield, UK: Sheffield Academic Press, 1995.

———. *The Rhetoric of Romans: Argumentative Constraint and Strategy and Paul's Dialogue with Judaism*. Journal for the Study of the New Testament, supplement series 45. Sheffield, UK: Sheffield Academic Press, 1990.

Ellis, E. Earle. *Paul's Use of the Old Testament*. Edinburgh: Oliver & Boyd, 1957.

Engberg-Pedersen, Troels. *Paul and the Stoics*. Edinburgh: T. & T. Clark, 2000.

Etherington, Kim. *Becoming a Reflexive Researcher: Using Our Selves in Research*. London: Jessica Kingsley, 2004.

———. "Writing Qualitative Research—A Gathering of Selves." *Counselling and Psychotherapy Research* 1/2 (2001) 119-25.

Fee, Gordon D. *The First Epistle to the Corinthians*. The New International Commentary on the New Testament. Grand Rapids: Eerdmans, 1987.

———. *Paul's Letter to the Philippians*. New International Commentary on the New Testament. Grand Rapids: Eerdmans, 1995.

Firet, Jacob. *Dynamics in Pastoring*. Grand Rapids: Eerdmans, 1986.

Flyvbjerg, Bent. *Making Social Science Matter: Why Social Inquiry Fails and How It Can Succeed Again*. Cambridge: Cambridge University Press, 2001.

Foucault, Michel. *Power/Knowledge: Selected Interviews and Other Writings, 1972-1977*. New York: Pantheon, 1980.

Foerster, Werner. "ἐξουσία." In *Theological Dictionary of the New Testament*, edited by Gerhard Kittel and Gerhard Friedrich, 2:560-75. Grand Rapids: Eerdmans, 1964.

Foster, Matthew Robert. *Gadamer and Practical Philosophy: The Hermeneutics of Moral Confidence*. Atlanta: Scholars, 1991.

Fung, Ronald Y. K. *A Commentary on the Epistle to the Galatians*, vol. 1 [Chinese]. Taipei: Campus Evangelical Fellowship, 2008.

———. *The Epistle to the Galatians*. 2nd ed. Grand Rapids: Eerdmans, 1988.

Furnish, Victor Paul. *The Moral Teaching of Paul*. Nashville: Abingdon, 1979.

———. *Theology and Ethics in Paul*. Nashville: Abingdon, 1968.

Selected Bibliography

Gadamer, Hans-Georg. "The Historicity of Understanding." In *Hermeneutics Reader: Texts of the German Tradition from the Enlightenment to the Present*, 256–92. London: Continuum, 1998.

———. "On the Problem of Self Understanding (1962)." In *Philosophical Hermeneutics*, edited by David E Linge, 44–58. Translated by G. B. Hess and R. E. Palmer. Berkeley: University of California Press, 1976.

———. "On the Scope and Function of Hermeneutical Reflection." In *Philosophical Hermeneutics*, edited by David E Linge, 18–43. Translated by G. B. Hess and R. E. Palmer. Berkeley: University of California Press, 1976.

———. *Truth and Method*. Translated by Joel Weinsheimer and Donald G. Marshall. London: Continuum, 2004.

Gaddy, C. Welton. *A Soul Under Siege: Surviving Clergy Depression*. Louisville: Westminster John Knox, 1991.

Gilkey, Langdon. *Naming the Whirlwind: The Renewal of God-Language*. Indianapolis: Bobbs-Merrill, 1969.

Gittens, Anthony J. "Beyond Liturgical Inculturation: Transforming the Deep Structures of Faith." *Irish Theological Quarterly* 69 (2004) 47–72.

———. *Gifts and Strangers: Meeting the Challenge of Inculturation*. Mahwah, NJ: Paulist, 1989.

Goldingay, John. *Israel's Faith*. Downers Grove, IL: InterVarsity, 2006.

Goldingay, John. *Old Testament Theology: Israel's Gospel*. Vol. 1. Downers Grove, IL: InterVarsity, 2003.

Gorman, Michael J. *Apostle of the Crucified Lord: A Theological Introduction to Paul and His Letters*. Grand Rapids: Eerdmans, 2004.

———. *Cruciformity: Paul's Narrative Spirituality of the Cross*. Grand Rapids: Eerdmans, 2001.

Greenman, Jeffrey P., and Timothy Larsen, eds. *Reading Romans through the Centuries: From the Early Church to Karl Barth*. Grand Rapids: Brazos, 2005.

Gregory. *The Book of Pastoral Rule*. Popular Patristics 34. Crestwood, NY: St. Vladimir's Seminary Press, 2007.

Grieb, A. *The Story of Romans: A Narrative Defense of God's Righteousness*. Louisville: Westminster John Knox, 2002.

Habermas, Jürgen. "On Hermeneutics' Claim to Universality." In *Hermeneutics Reader: Texts of the German Tradition from the Enlightenment to the Present*, edited by Kurt Mueller-Vollmer, 293–320. London: Continuum, 1998.

Hack-Polaski, Sandra. *Paul and the Discourse of Power*. Sheffield, UK: Sheffield Academic Press, 1999.

Halverstadt, Hugh F. *Managing Church Conflict*. Louisville: Westminster John Knox, 1991.

Harrington, Daniel, and James F. Keenan. *Jesus and Virtue Ethics: Building Bridges Between New Testament Studies and Moral Theology*. Lanham, MD: Sheed & Ward, 2002.

Harris, Murray J. *The Second Epistle to the Corinthians: A Commentary on the Greek Text*. Grand Rapids: Eerdmans, 2005.

Harvey, A. E. *Renewal Through Suffering: A Study of 2 Corinthians*. Studies of the New Testament and Its World. Edinburgh: T. & T. Clark, 1996.

Haugaard, Mark. *Power: A Reader*. Annotated edition. Manchester: Manchester University Press, 2002.

Selected Bibliography

Hays, Richard B. *The Conversion of the Imagination: Paul as Interpreter of Israel's Scripture.* Grand Rapids: Eerdmans, 2005.

———. *The Faith of Jesus Christ: An Investigation of the Narrative Substructure of Galatians 3:1—4:11.* Dissertation Series (Society of Biblical Literature) 56. Chico, CA: Scholars, 1983.

———. "Galatians—Introduction." In *The New Interpreter's Bible: Second Corinthians—Philemon*, edited by J. Paul Sampley et al. Nahsville: Abingdon, 2000.

———. *The Moral Vision of the New Testament: Community, Cross, New Creation: A Contemporary Introduction to New Testament Ethics.* San Francisco: HarperSanFrancisco, 1996.

Heil, John Paul. *Ephesians: Empowerment to Walk in Love for the Unity of All in Christ.* Atlanta: SBL, 2007.

Hengel, Martin. *Christ and Power.* Belfast: Christian Journals, 1977.

———. *Paul Between Damascus and Antioch: The Unknown Years.* London: SCM, 1997.

———. *Victory Over Violence.* London: SPCK, 1975.

———. *The Zealots: Investigations into the Jewish Freedom Movement in the Period from Herod I Until 70 A.D.* Edinburgh: T. & T. Clark, 1989.

Ho, Craig Y. S. "Biblical Scholarship in Hong Kong." *SBL Forum.* July 2004. Online:http://sbl-site.org/Article.aspx?ArticleID=290.

Hoge, Dean R., and Jacquelline E. Wenger. *Pastors in Transition: Why Clergy Leave Local Church Ministry.* Grand Rapids: Eerdmans, 2005.

Holmberg, Bengt. *Paul and Power: The Structure of Authority in the Primitive Church as Reflected in the Pauline Epistles.* Coniectanea biblica 11. Lund: LiberLäromedel/Gleerup, 1978.

Hornby, A. S. *Oxford Advanced Learner's Dictionary of Current English.* 7th ed. Oxford: Oxford University Press, 2005.

Horrell, David G. *An Introduction to the Study of Paul.* London: T. & T. Clark, 2000.

———. *Solidarity and Difference: A Contemporary Reading of Paul's Ethics.* London: T. & T. Clark, 2005.

Horrell, David G., and Edward Adams. "Introduction: The Scholarly Quest for Paul's Church at Corinth: A Critical Survey." In *Christianity at Corinth*, edited by Edward Adams and David G. Horrell, 1–50. Louisville: Westminster John Knox, 2004.

Horsley, Richard A. "Gnosis in Corinth: 1 Corinthians 8.1–6." *NTS* 27 (1980) 32–51.

———. *Paul and Politics: Ekklesia, Israel, Imperium, Interpretation.* Harrisburg, PA: Trinity, 2000.

———. *Paul and the Roman Imperial Order.* Harrisburg, PA: Trinity, 2004.

———. "Pneumatikos vs Psychikos: Distinction of Spiritual Status among the Corinthians." *HTR* 69 (1976) 269–88.

Jenkins, Philip. *The Next Christendom: The Coming of Global Christianity.* Oxford: Oxford University Press, 2002.

Jewett, Robert. "The Agitators and the Galatian Congregation." *NTS* 17 (1971) 198–212.

———. *Paul's Anthropological Terms: A Study of Their Use in Conflict Settings.* Arbeiten zur Geschichte des antiken Judentums und des Urchristentums Bd. 10. Leiden: Brill, 1971.

John Chrysostom. *Six Books on the Priesthood.* Translated by Graham Neville. London: SPCK, 1964.

Selected Bibliography

Johnson, Luke Timothy. *The First and Second Letters to Timothy: A New Translation with Introduction and Commentary.* New York: Anchor Bible, 2001.

———. *The Writings of the New Testament: An Interpretation.* London: SCM, 1986.

Keesmaat, Sylvia C. *Paul and His Story: (Re)-Interpreting the Exodus Tradition.* Journal for the Study of the New Testament 181. Sheffield, UK: Sheffield Academic Press, 1999.

Kim, Seyoon. *Paul and the New Perspective: Second Thoughts on The Origin of Paul's Gospel.* Grand Rapids: Eerdmans, 2002.

Knight, George W. *The Pastoral Epistles: A Commentary on the Greek Text.* New International Greek Testament Commentary. Grand Rapids: Eerdmans, 1992.

Koester, Helmut. *Paul and His World: Interpreting the New Testament in Its Context.* Minneapolis: Fortress, 2007.

Kraemer, Hendrik. *The Christian Message in a Non-Christian World.* London: Edinburgh House Press, 1938.

Kwan, Simon Shui-Man. "From Indigenization to Contextualization: A Change in Discursive Practice Rather than a Shift in Paradigm." *Studies in World Christianity* 11/2 (2005) 236–50. http://www.euppublishing.com/doi/abs/10.3366/swc.2005.11.2.236.

Kwok, Benedict Hung-biu. "The Christian Understanding of God as Transcendence and Immanence: A Response to Liu Shu-hsien's Understanding of the Pure Transcendence of God." *Ching Feng* 42/1–2 (June 1999) 35–58.

———. "The Christological Doctrine of Reconciliation of Karl Barth and the Dialogue with the Neo-Confucian Understanding of Self-Cultivation: A Response to Heup Yong Kim." *Ching Feng* 41/1 (March 1993) 233–48.

Kwon, Oh-Young. "A Critical Review of Recent Scholarship on the Pauline Opposition and the Nature of its Wisdom (Σοφία) in 1 Corinthians 1–4." *Currents in Biblical Research* 8/3 (June 2010) 386–427.

Lambrecht, Jan. *Second Corinthians.* Sacra pagina 8. Collegeville, MN: Liturgical, 1998.

Lee, Archie. "Cross-Textual Hermeneutics." In *Dictionary of Third World Theologies*, edited by Virginia Fabella and R. S. Sugirtharajah, 60–62. Maryknoll, NY: Orbis, 2000.

———. "Cross-Textual Interpretation and Its Implication for Biblical Studies." In *Teaching the Bible: The Discourses and Politics of Biblical Pedagogy*, edited by Fernando F. Segovia and Mary Ann Tolbert, 247–54. Maryknoll, NY: Orbis, 1998.

———. "Lamentations in the Hebrew Psalter and in the Chinese Shijing: A Cross-Textual Reading." *Ching Feng* 41/3–4 (1998) 249–73.

Lee, Jung Young. "Interpreting the Demonic Powers in Pauline Thought." *Novum Testamentum* 12, fasc. 1. (January 1970) 54–69.

———. *The Theology of Change: A Christian Concept of God in an Eastern Perspective.* Maryknoll, NY: Orbis, 1979.

———. *The Trinity in Asian Perspective.* Nashville: Abingdon, 1996.

Lee, Michelle V. *Paul, the Stoics and the Body of Christ.* Society for New Testament Studies. Cambridge: Cambridge University Press, 2006.

Lee, Peter K. H., ed. *Confucian-Christian Encounters in Historical and Contemporary Perspective.* Lewiston, NY: Edwin Mellen, 1992.

Lightfoot, Joseph Barber. *Saint Paul's Epistle to the Philippians: A Revised Text with Introduction, Notes and Dissertations.* 10th ed. London: Macmillan, 1890.

Selected Bibliography

———. *St. Paul's Epistle to the Galatians: A Revised Text with Introduction, Notes and Dissertations*. 10th ed. London: Macmillan, 1890.

Linge, David E. "Editor's Introduction." In *Philosophical Hermeneutics* by Hans-Georg Gadamer, x–lviii. Translated and edited by David E. Linger. Berkeley: University of California Press, 1977.

Lo, Lung-Kwong. *Paul's Purpose in Writing Romans: The Upbuilding of a Jewish and Gentile Christian Community in Rome*. Hong Kong: Alliance Bible Seminary, 1998.

Longenecker, Richard N. *Galatians*. Word Biblical Commentary. Dallas, TX: Word, 1990.

Luckmann, Thomas, and Peter L. Berger. *The Social Construction of Reality: A Treatise in the Sociology of Knowledge*. New York: Penguin, 1991.

Lukes, Steven. *Power: A Radical View*. 2nd ed. Basingstoke: Palgrave Macmillan, 2005.

Mabbett, I. W. *Writing History Essays: A Student's Guide*. Basingstoke: Palgrave Macmillan, 2006.

MacIntyre, Alasdair C. *After Virtue: A Study in Moral Theory*. 2nd ed. London: Duckworth, 1985.

———. *Whose Justice? Which Rationality?* London: Duckworth, 1988.

Mackey, James Patrick. *Power and Christian Ethics*. New Studies in Christian Ethics 3. Cambridge: Cambridge University Press, 1994.

Malherbe, Abraham J. *Moral Exhortation: A Greco-Roman Sourcebook*. 1st ed. Philadelphia: Westminster, 1986.

———. *Paul and the Popular Philosophers*. Minneapolis: Fortress, 1989.

———. *Social Aspects of Early Christianity*. 2nd ed. Philadelphia: Fortress, 1983.

Manning, Frank. "The Case of the Healthy Hindu." In *Symbols and Society: Essays on Belief Systems in Action*, edited by Carole E. Hill. Athens: University of Georgia Press, 1975.

Marshall, Peter. *Enmity in Corinth: Social Conventions in Paul's Relations with the Corinthians*. Wissenschaftliche Untersuchungen zum Neuen Testament 23. Tübingen: Mohr, 1987.

Martin, Dale B. *The Corinthian Body*. New Haven, CT: Yale University Press, 1995.

———. *Slavery as Salvation: The Metaphor of Slavery in Pauline Christianity*. New Haven, CT: Yale University Press, 1990.

———. "Tongues of Angels and Other Status Indicators." *Journal of the American Academy of Religion* 59/3 (Autumn 1991) 547–89.

Martin, Ralph P. *A Hymn of Christ: Philippians 2:5–11 in Recent Interpretation and in the Setting of Early Christian Worship*. 3rd ed. Downers Grove, IL: InterVarsity, 1997.

Martyn, J. Louis. *Galatians: A New Translation with Introduction and Commentary*. Anchor Bible 33A. New York: Doubleday, 1998.

McGinn, Sheila E., and Robert Jewett, eds. *Celebrating Romans: Template for Pauline Theology: Essays in Honor of Robert Jewett*. Grand Rapids: Eerdmans, 2004.

McGrath, Alister E. "Evangelical Theological Method: The State of the Art." In *Evangelical Futures: A Conversation on Theological Method*, edited by John G. Stackhouse Jr., 15–38. Grand Rapids: Baker Academic, 2000.

———. *Iustitia Dei: A History of the Christian Doctrine of Justification*. 2nd ed. Cambridge: Cambridge University Press, 1998.

Meeks, Wayne A. *The First Urban Christians: The Social World of the Apostle Paul*. New Haven, CT: Yale University Press, 1983.

Selected Bibliography

Meilaender, Gilbert, and William Werpehowski. *The Oxford Handbook of Theological Ethics*. Oxford: Oxford University Press, 2007.
Mitchell, Margaret Mary. *Paul and the Rhetoric of Reconciliation: An Exegetical Investigation of the Language and Composition of 1 Corinthians*. Hermeneutische Untersuchungen zur Theologie. Tübingen: Mohr, 1991.
Moore, Stephen D. *Poststructuralism and the New Testament: Derrida and Foucault at the Foot of the Cross*. Minneapolis: Fortress, 1994.
Mounce, William D. *Basics of Biblical Greek Grammar*. 2nd ed. Grand Rapids: Zondervan, 2003.
Moustakas, Clark. *Heuristic Research: Design, Methodology and Applications*. Newbury Park, CA: Sage, 1990.
Murphy-O'Connor, Jerome. *Becoming Human Together: The Pastoral Anthropology of St. Paul*. Good News Studies 2. Wilmington, DE: Glazier, 1982.
———. *Paul: A Critical Life*. Oxford: Clarendon, 1996.
———. *Paul: His Story*. Oxford: Oxford University Press, 2004.
———. "Pneumatikoi and Judaizers in 2 Cor 2:14—4:6." *AusBR* 34 (1986) 42–58.
———. "Pneumatikoi in 2 Corinthians." *PIBA* 11 (1988) 59–66.
———. *The Theology of the Second Letter to the Corinthians*. New Testament Theology. Cambridge: Cambridge University Press, 1991.
Negro, Teodor. "Gadamer-Habermas Debate and Universality of Hermeneutics." *Cultura International Journal of Philosophy of Culture and Axiology* 7 (2007) 113–19.
Niebuhr, Reinhold. *Moral Man and Immoral Society: A Study in Ethics and Politics*. New York: Scribner, 1932.
Niebuhr, H. Richard. *Christ and Culture*. New York: Harper, 1951.
O'Brien, Peter Thomas. *The Epistle to the Philippians: A Commentary on the Greek Text*. New International Greek Testament Commentary. Grand Rapids: Eerdmans, 1991.
Oden, Thomas C. *The Transforming Power of Grace*. Nashville: Abingdon, 1993.
O'Donovan, Oliver. *Common Objects of Love: Moral Reflection and the Shaping of Community: The 2001 Stob Lectures*. Grand Rapids: Eerdmans, 2002.
———. *Resurrection and Moral Order: An Outline for Evangelical Ethics*. 2nd ed. Leicester: Apollos, 1994.
Ooi, Samuel Hio-kee. "Already But Not Yet: A Study of Hsieh Nai-zen's Late Thought (1958–1991) and His Theological Model." MTheol thesis, SEAGTS, Chung Chi Divinity School Branch, Univeristy of Hong Kong, 2002.
———. Review of *Musing With Confucius and Paul: Toward a Chinese Christian Theology* by K. K. Yeo. *Mission Studies* 26/2 (2009) 276–77.
———. "A Study of Strategic Level Spiritual Warfare From a Chinese Perspective." *Asian Journal of Pentecostal Studies* 9/1 (2006) 143–61.
Osmer, Richard Robert. *Practical Theology: An Introduction*. Grand Rapids: Eerdmans, 2008.
Palmer, Richard E. *Hermeneutics*. Evanston, IL: Northwestern University Press, 1969.
Pan-Chiu Lai. "Sino-Theology, the Bible and the Christian Tradition." *Studies in World Christianity* 12 (2006) 266–81. Online: http://www.eupjournals.com/doi/abs/10.3366/swc.2006.0023#.
Pasewark, Kyle A. *A Theology of Power: Being Beyond Domination*. Minneapolis: Fortress, 1993.

Selected Bibliography

Percy, Martyn. *Power and the Church: Ecclesiology in an Age of Transition.* London: Cassell, 1998.

Pfister, Lauren. "From Western Studies to Global Order: Reflections on the Writings of Xie Fu-ya." *Ching Feng* 34/4 (December 1991) 245–62.

Phan, Peter C. "Betwixt and Between: Doing Theology with Memory and Imagination." In *Journeys at the Margin: Toward an Autobiographical Theology in American-Asian Perspective*, edited by Peter C. Phan and Jung Young Lee, 113–34. Collegevill, MN: Liturgical, 1999.

Piper, John. *The Future of Justification.* Wheaton, IL: Crossway, 2007.

Polanyi, Michael. *Personal Knowledge: Towards a Post-Critical Philosophy.* London: Routledge & Kegan Paul, 1958.

Polaski, Sandra Hack. *Paul and the Discourse of Power.* Sheffield, UK: Sheffield Academic Press, 1999.

Porter, Stanley E., ed. *The Pauline Canon.* Pauline Studies 1. Leiden: Brill, 2004.

Quarles, Charles L. "From Faith to Faith: A Fresh Examination of the Prepositional Series in Romans 1:17." *Koninklijke Brill NV, Leiden* 45/1 (2003) 1–21.

Rad, Gerhard von. *Old Testament Theology.* London: SCM, 1975.

Reasoner, Mark. *Romans in Full Circle: A History of Interpretation.* Louisville: Westminster John Knox, 2005.

Ricoeur, Paul. "Appropriation." In *Hermeneutics and the Human Sciences: Essays on Language, Action, and Interpretation*, edited by Paul Ricoeur and John B. Thompson, 182–96. Cambridge: Cambridge University Press, 1981.

———. *From Text to Action.* 1st ed. Translated by Kathleen Blamey and John B. Thompson. Evanston, IL: Northwestern University Press, 1991.

———. "Hermeneutical Function of Distanciation." In *Hermeneutics and the Human Sciences: Essays on Language, Action, and Interpretation*, edited by Paul Ricoeur and John B. Thompson, 131–44. Cambridge: Cambridge University Press, 1981.

———. *Interpretation Theory: Discourse and the Surplus of Meaning.* Fort Worth: Texas Christian University Press, 1976.

———. "On Interpretation." In *From Text to Action: Essays In Hermeneutics, II*, 1–24. Evanston, IL: Northwestern University Press, 1991.

———. "What is a Text? Explanation and Understanding." In *Hermeneutics and the Human Sciences: Essays on Language, Action, and Interpretation*, edited by Paul Ricoeur and John B. Thompson, 145–64. Cambridge: Cambridge University Press, 1981.

Ringgren, Helmer, G. Johannes Botterweck, and Heinz-Josef Fabry, eds. *Theological Dictionary of the Old Testament.* Grand Rapids: Eerdmans, 1974.

Sakenfeld, Katharine Doob, and the Harvard Semitic Museum. *The Meaning of Ḥesed in the Hebrew Bible: A New Inquiry.* Missoula, MT: Scholars Press for the Harvard Semitic Museum, 1978.

Sampley, J. Paul, Richard B. Hays, Judith Gundry-Volf, Morna Hooker, and Andrew T. Lincoln. *The New Interpreter's Bible: Second Corinthians—Philemon.* Nashville: Abingdon, 2000.

Samra, James George. *Being Conformed to Christ in Community: A Study of Maturity, Maturation and the Local Church in the Undisputed Pauline Epistles.* Library of New Testament Studies 320. London: T. & T. Clark, 2006.

Sanders, E. P. *Paul.* Oxford: Oxford University Press, 1991.

Selected Bibliography

———. *Paul and Palestinian Judaism: A Comparison of Patterns of Religion*. London: SCM, 1977.
———. *Paul, the Law, and the Jewish People*. Philadelphia: Fortress, 1983.
Sandmel, Samuel. "Parallelomania." *Journal of Biblical Literature* 81 (1962) 1–13.
Savage, Sara B., and Eolene M. Boyd-MacMillan. *The Human Face of Church: A Social Psychology and Pastoral Theology Resource for Pioneer and Traditional Ministry*. Norwich, UK: Canterbury, 2007.
Savage, Timothy B. *Power Through Weakness: Paul's Understanding of the Christian Ministry in 2 Corinthians*. Monograph series (Society for New Testament Studies) 86. Cambridge: Cambridge University Press, 1996.
Scheibler, Ingrid H. *Gadamer: Between Heidegger and Habermas*. Lanham, MD: Rowman & Littlefield, 2000.
Schlatter, Adolf von. *Romans: The Righteousness of God*. Peabody, MA: Hendrickson, 1995.
Schlier, Heinrich. *Principalities and Powers in the New Testament*. Quaestiones disputatae 3. Freiburg: Herder, 1961.
Schmidt, Steffen W., ed. *Friends, Followers, and Factions: A Reader in Political Clientelism*. Berkeley: University of California Press, 1977.
Schmithals, Walter. *Gnosticism in Corinth: An Investigation of the Letters to the Corinthians*. Nashville: Abingdon, 1971.
Schreiner, Thomas R. *Romans*. Baker Exegetical Commentary on the New Testament 6. Grand Rapids: Baker, 1998.
Schreiter, Robert J. *Constructing Local Theologies*. Maryknoll, NY: Orbis, 1985.
Schutz, John Howard. *Paul and the Anatomy of Apostolic Authority*. Louisville: Westminster John Knox, 2007.
Scott, James M. *Adoption as Sons of God: An Exegetical Investigation into the Background of [huiothesia] in the Pauline Corpus*. Wissenschaftliche Untersuchungen zum Neuen Testament 48. Tübingen: Mohr, 1992.
Scroggs, Robin. "The Sociological Interpretation of the New Testament: The Present State of Research." *NTS* 26 (1980) 164-79.
Smith, C. Ryder. *The Bible Doctrine of Grace and Related Doctrines*. London: Epworth, 1956.
Song, C. S. *Third-Eye Theology: Theology in Formation in Asian Settings*. Rev. ed. Maryknoll, NY: Orbis, 1992.
Stanton, Graham N. "Galatians." In *The Oxford Bible Commentary*, edited by John Barton and John Muddiman. Oxford: Oxford University Press, 2001.
Stegman, Thomas. *The Character of Jesus: The Linchpin to Paul's Argument in 2 Corinthians*. Analecta biblica 158. Rome: Pontificio Istituto Biblico, 2005.
Steinke, Peter L. *How Your Church Family Works: Understanding Congregations as Emotional Systems*. Herndon, VA: Alban, 2006.
Suazo, Ruby. "Hermeneutics as Appropriation: A Way of Understanding Oneself in Front of the Text." *PHAVISMINDA* 7 (May 2008) 109–21.
Sykes, Stephen. *Power and Christian Theology*. 1st ed. London: Continuum, 2006.
Tarazi, Paul Nadim. *The Old Testament: Psalms and Wisdom*. Crestwood, NY: St. Vladimir's Seminary Press, 1996.
Theissen, Gerd. *Psychological Aspects of Pauline Theology*. Edinburgh: T. & T. Clark, 1987.

Selected Bibliography

———. *The Social Setting of Pauline Christianity: Essays on Corinth.* Edinburgh: T. & T. Clark, 198.

Thiselton, Anthony C. *The First Epistle to the Corinthians: A Commentary on the Greek Text.* New International Greek Testament Commentary. Grand Rapids: Eerdmans, 2000.

Tillich, Paul. *Systematic Theology.* 3 vols. Chicago: University of Chicago Press, 1951, 1957, 1963.

Tracy, David. *Plurality and Ambiguity: Hermeneutics, Religion, Hope.* Chicago: University of Chicago Press, 1994.

Van Norden, Bryan W. *Virtue Ethics and Consequentialism in Early Chinese Philosophy.* Cambridge: Cambridge University Press, 2007.

Walls, Andrew F. "In Quest of the Father of Mission Studies." *IBMR* 23/3 (July 1999) 98–105.

———. "Structural Problems in Mission Studies." *IBMR* 15/4 (October 1991) 146–55.

Wall, Robert W., J. Paul Sampley, and N. T. Wright. *The New Interpreter's Bible: Acts–First Corinthians.* Nashville: Abingdon, 2002.

Wallace, Richard. *The Three Worlds of Paul of Tarsus.* New York: Routledge, 1998.

Wan, Sze-kar. "Betwixt and Between: Towards a Hermeneutics of Hyphenation." In *Ways of Being, Ways of Reading: Asian American Biblical Interpretation*, edited by Mary F. Foskett and Jeffrey Kah-Jin Kuan, 137–51. St. Louis: Chalice, 2006.

———. "The Emerging Hermeneutics of the Chinese Church: Debate between Wu Lichen and T. C. Chao and the Chinese Christian Problematic." In *The Bible in Modern China: The Literary and Intellectual Impact*, edited by Irene Eber, Sze-kar Wan, and Knut Walf, 351–82. Sankt Augustin, Ger.: Institute Monumenta Serica, 1999.

———. "Poised Between Grace and Moral Responsibility: T. C. Chao's Interrogation of the Ethics of Romans." In *Sino-Christian Studies: An International Journal of Bible, Theology and Philosophy* 4 (December 2007) 39–68.

———. *Power in Weakness: Conflict and Rhetoric in Paul's Second Letter to the Corinthians.* London: Continuum, 2000.

Watson, Francis. *Paul and the Hermeneutics of Faith.* London: T. & T. Clark, 2004.

———. *Paul, Judaism, and the Gentiles: Beyond the New Perspective.* Rev. and expanded ed. Grand Rapids: Eerdmans, 2007.

Weiss, Johann. *Earliest Christianity.* New York: Harper, 1937.

Wentz, Richard. *The Contemplation of Otherness: The Critical Vision of Religion.* Macon, GA: Mercer University Press, 1984.

Westerholm, Stephen. *Perspectives Old and New on Paul: The "Lutheran" Paul and His Critics.* Grand Rapids: Eerdmans, 2004.

Wheeler, Ray. "The Legacy of Shoki Coe." *International Bulletin of Missionary Research* 26 (April 2002) 77–80.

Wickeri, Philip. *Reconstructing Christianity in China : K. H. Ting and the Chinese Church.* Maryknoll, NY: Orbis, 2007.

Williams, David John. *Paul's Metaphors: Their Context and Character.* Peabody, MA: Hendrickson, 1999.

Wilson, Walter. *Love Without Pretense: Romans 12.9–21 and Hellenistic-Jewish Wisdom Literature.* Tübingen: Mohr, 1991.

Wink, Walter. *Engaging the Powers: Discernment and Resistance in a World of Domination.* Minneapolis: Fortress, 1992.

Selected Bibliography

———. *Naming the Powers: The Language of Power in the New Testament.* Philadelphia: Fortress, 1984.

———. *Unmasking the Powers: The Invisible Forces That Determine Human Existence.* Philadelphia: Fortress, 1986.

Winter, Bruce W. *Philo and Paul Among the Sophists.* Monograph series (Society for New Testament Studies) 96. Cambridge: Cambridge University Press, 1997.

———. *Seek the Welfare of the City: Christians as Benefactors and Citizens.* First Century Christians in the Graeco-Roman World. Grand Rapids: Eerdmans, 1994.

Witherington, Ben, III. *The Acts of the Apostles: A Socio-Rhetorical Commentary.* Grand Rapids: Eerdmans, 1998.

———. *Conflict and Community in Corinth: A Socio-Rhetorical Commentary on 1 and 2 Corinthians.* Grand Rapids: Eerdmans, 1995.

———. *1 and 2 Thessalonians: A Socio-Rhetorical Commentary.* Grand Rapids: Eerdmans, 2006.

———. *The Paul Quest: The Renewed Search for the Jew of Tarsus.* Downers Grove, IL: InterVarsity, 1998.

Wright, N. T. *The Climax of the Covenant: Christ and the Law in Pauline Theology.* Edinburgh: T. & T. Clark, 1991.

———. *Following Jesus.* Grand Rapids: Eerdmans, 1995.

———. *Justification: God's Plan and Paul's Vision.* London: SPCK, 2009.

———. *Paul: In Fresh Perspective.* 1st ed. Minneapolis: Fortress, 2005.

Yamauchi, Edwin M. *Pre-Christian Gnosticism: A Survey of the Proosed Evidences.* 2nd ed. Grand Rapids: Baker, 1983.

Yeo, Khiok-Khng. *Chairman Mao Meets the Apostle Paul: Christianity, Communism, and the Hope of China.* Grand Rapids: Brazos, 2002.

———. *Cross-Cultural Rhetorical Hermeneutics.* Jian Dao Supplement, Bible and Hermeneutics 1. Hong Kong: Alliance Bible Seminary, 1995.

———. "Culture and Intersubjectivity as Criteria of Negotiating Meanings in Cross-Cultural Interpretations." In *The Meanings We Choose: Hermeneutical Ethics, Indeterminacy and the Conflict of Interpretations,* edited by Charles H. Cosgrove, 81–100. Edinburgh: T. & T. Clark, 2004.

———. "The Debate in Galatians on Culture and Theology." (In Chinese.) *Journal for the Study of Christian Culture: Poetics and Theology* 18 (2007) 43–62.

———. "The Intertextual Reading of Pauline Theology and Confucian Political Ethics." (In Chinese.) In *God and Public Life: A Theological Vision of the Global Public,* edited by Philip Chia and Chin Ken-pa, 141–65. Hong Kong: Centre for Advanced Biblical Studies, 2009.

———. "The Law of Love According to Confucius and Paul: Cruciform Love and Ren Ren (Benevolent Persons) of Becoming Fully Human." In *Christ the One and Only: A Global Affirmation of the Uniqueness of Jesus Christ,* edited by Sung-Wook Chung, 203–22. Grand Rapids: Baker Academic, 2005.

———. "Li and Law in the Analects and Galatians: A Chinese Christian Understanding of Ritual and Propriety." *Asia Journal of Theology* 19 (October 2005) 309–32.

———. "Messianic Predestination in Romans 8 and Classical Confucianism." In *Sino-Christian Theology: A Theological qua Cultural Movement in Contemporary China,* edited by Pan-Chiu Lai and Jason Lam, 179–202. New York: Peter Lang, 2010.

———. "Musical Harmony According to Confucius and Paul." *Ching Feng* 5/2 (2004 [published in August 2006]) 163–89.

———. *Musing with Confucius and Paul: Toward a Chinese Christian Theology*. Eugene, OR: Cascade, 2008.

———. "On Confucian Xin and Pauline Pistis." In *Sino-Christian Studies: An International Journal of Bible, Theology and Philosophy* 2 (December 2006) 25–51.

———. "Paul's Theological Ethic and the Chinese Morality of Ren Ren." In *Cross-Cultural Paul: Journeys to Others, Journeys to Ourselves*, edited by Charles H. Cosgrove, Herold Weiss, and Khiok-Khng Yeo, 120–27. Grand Rapids: Eerdmans, 2005.

———. "Political Theology of Paul in a World of Violence: A Spirituality That Offers Peace." In *Cultivating Wisdom with the Heart: BCV Chinese Department's 10th Anniversary Anthology of Essays*, edited by Justin Tan, 99–127. Victoria, Australia: Bible College of Victoria Chinese Department, 2006.

———. *Rhetorical Interaction in 1 Corinthians 8 and 10: A Formal Analysis with Preliminary Suggestions for a Chinese, Cross-Cultural Hermeneutic*. Leiden: Brill, 1995.

———. "System of Harmony According to Confucius and Paul: Music, Goodness, Beauty." *Ching Feng* 6/1 (2005 [published in December 2006]) 37–51.

———. *What Has Jerusalem To Do with Beijing? Biblical Interpretation from a Chinese Perspective*. Harrisburg, PA: Trinity, 1998.

Yeung, Arnold M. K. "A Study of Tao in the Tao Te Ching: A Suggestion of an Alternative Model for the Chinese Theological Indigenization." Unpublished PhD diss., University of Cambridge, 1981.

Yoder, John Howard. *The Original Revolution: Essays on Christian Pacifism*. Eugene, OR: Wipf & Stock, 1998.

———. *The Politics of Jesus: Vicit Agnus Noster*. Grand Rapids: Eerdmans, 1972.

Yu, Zhenhua. "Tradition, Authority and Originality in a Post-Critical Perspective." In *Tradition and Discovery: The Polanyi Society Periodical* 32/3 (2005–2006) 40–56.

Index

Adler, Joseph, 107, 131
aiōn (αἰῶνος), 135, 160, 178, 179, 211–14, 221, 223
appropriate, appropriated, appropriates, appropriating, appropriation, xv, 8, 10, 14, 17, 18, 21, 35, 39–40, 44, 51–52, 58, 60–61, 69, 71, 77, 79–80, 83–86, 88, 96, 102, 104, 114, 124, 129, 130, 134–35, 137, 144, 146, 163–64, 186–87, 191, 205, 217–18, 224, 229–30, 235–37, 265–66
archon (ἄρχων), or archonta, 151, 161, 179, 180, 211, 213

being, xv, 6, 7, 11, 13, 17, 22, 29, 37–40, 42, 46, 49, 57, 61, 62, 67–72, 75, 77–80, 82–87, 90, 93–96, 98, 99, 100, 102, 106, 110, 111, 113, 115, 123–28, 131, 133, 135, 136, 146, 148, 150, 155, 157, 158, 160, 172, 173, 175, 177–83, 185–89, 194, 200, 201, 206, 208, 210, 213, 218, 221, 222, 225–27, 229–30, 233, 235–37
Berkhof, Hendrik, 138–40 147, 153, 162, 164

Caird, George Bradford, 138–49, 142, 147, 151, 162, 164, 181–86, 211
change, xiii, 12, 17, 23, 28, 31, 33, 53, 72, 75, 77, 79, 94, 96, 102, 104, 105, 108–22, 124, 128–34, 145, 146, 152, 157, 158, 163, 191, 217, 218, 220, 221, 227–29, 232, 234
Chinese, ix, x, xi, xiii, xiv, xv, 1–6, 8–9, 11–14, 16–18, 21–29, 31–32, 34, 36, 38, 43–61, 65, 68–71, 83–85, 87–93, 97, 102, 104, 106, 111–12, 115, 119–21, 124–25, 130–31, 138, 147, 156, 161, 163–167, 171, 188, 198, 216, 218, 222, 224, 226, 228–32, 234–35, 237
Ching, Julia, 22–25, 27, 30, 59
Chow, John, K. 142, 196, 197
circumstance, 1, 52, 66, 88, 90, 92–93, 97–98, 101, 127–29, 133
Confucian, Confucianism, xiii, 2–4, 12–14, 21–26, 28, 30–31, 33–35, 38, 45–46, 50, 54–55, 89–91, 94–96, 102, 130, 231–32, 234, 237
Confucian-Christian, 3–4, 23–25, 30
Confucius, 2, 14, 22, 38, 43–46, 91, 95, 104, 127, 128, 130, 134, 234
constellation, 18, 104, 105 115, 134, 164, 175, 188, 215, 219, 220, 228
Corinthian(s), xv, 8, 9, 15, 17, 18, 27, 38, 54, 84, 85, 135, 136, 142, 143, 163, 164, 166, 186–215, 217, 221, 224–28
cultivation, 14, 23
culture, ix, 2, 9, 14, 21, 24, 26, 35, 38–40, 42–45, 47–49, 53, 56–58, 69, 73–74, 102, 161, 169, 202, 204, 211, 218, 224, 229, 231
cultural-linguistic, xv, 2, 9, 17–18, 24, 46, 49, 51, 54–55, 57–58, 60–61, 65, 68, 70–71, 83–84, 86–88, 102–4, 138, 146, 161, 216, 230–32, 237

Dàguò, 111, 125, 127–29, 220, 228
diagram, 12, 13, 105, 107, 108, 133, 151, 219, 220, 222, 228–30

271

Index

Dǐng, 112, 115–18, 220, 228
divination, 13, 107, 111, 127, 129, 131, 132, 142
double vision, x, xv, 2, 4, 5, 6, 8–11, 17, 18, 21, 24, 34, 46, 51, 60–62, 65, 68, 81, 83–85, 88, 92, 102, 104, 143, 163–65, 188, 214–16, 218, 219, 228–30, 232, 237
dragon, 2, 7, 106, 107, 128, 131, 222, 223
Dunn, James, 151, 169, 172, 173, 177, 181, 212, 227
dynamic, 5, 7, 9, 17, 18, 31, 79, 86, 87, 89, 92–94, 105, 112–15, 134, 141–43, 145, 146, 163, 165, 174, 208, 210, 217, 226
dynamism, 7, 31, 96, 105, 110, 111, 113, 123, 125, 163, 228, 229

efficacy, 69, 89, 91, 93, 94, 96, 102, 105, 216
Ehrensperger, Kathy, 142, 143, 145, 146, 226
Elliott, Neil, 142, 164
embody, xv, 1, 9, 11, 17, 56, 67, 74, 76, 80, 99–100, 113, 129, 137, 146, 156
enslave, 134, 135, 159, 171, 176, 178–182, 184, 180, 214, 217, 221, 223
Etherington, Kim, 235–237
exegetical, xiv, xv, 30, 33, 60, 61, 82, 151, 216, 230, 232
exousia (ἐξουσία) 151, 161, 179, 180, 211, 213, 214, 228
experience, ix, x, xv, 1, 4, 5, 8, 9, 11, 12, 16, 17, 18, 19, 21, 24, 36, 37–39, 45, 49, 50–52, 55–58, 61, 63, 65, 69, 71–72, 76–80, 83–86, 88, 100, 102, 104, 115, 119, 132, 133, 137, 138, 146, 147, 157, 158, 170, 185, 188, 206, 214–18, 223–227, 229, 230, 231, 232, 235, 236

Fee, Gordon D. 190, 197, 202, 206, 208–10
Five Classics, 2, 111
Foucault, Michel, 142, 143, 146, 174–76

Fù, 32

Galatian(s), xv, 8, 9, 15, 17, 34, 44, 45, 84, 85, 136, 163–91, 210, 214, 217, 221, 224, 228
Gadamer, Hans-Georg, xv, 6, 8, 10, 36, 39, 40, 45, 46, 49–52, 57, 60, 62–70, 73–80, 82, 84–86, 88, 102, 104, 110, 138, 218
Gé, 112, 115–18, 120, 122, 124, 127, 220, 228, 229
Guān, 111, 126

Hán Fēi or Hán Fēizǐ, 14, 90, 94–96, 101, 129, 130, 134, 223
Hays, Richard, 16, 165, 168, 169, 180, 227
hermeneutic(s) xiv, xv, 2, 4, 8, 9, 10, 11, 12, 14, 16, 17, 18, 19, 21, 22, 24, 25, 26, 28, 30, 32, 34, 36, 37, 38, 39, 40, 42, 44, 45, 46, 48, 49, 50, 51, 52, 54, 56, 58, 59–86, 88, 90, 92, 96, 98, 100, 102, 104, 106, 108, 110, 112, 114, 115, 116, 117, 118, 120, 122, 124, 126, 128, 130, 132, 134, 136, 138, 140, 142, 144, 146, 148, 150, 152, 154, 156, 158, 160, 161, 162, 163–66, 168, 170, 172, 174, 176, 178, 180, 182, 184, 186, 188, 190, 192, 194, 196, 198, 200, 202, 204, 206, 208, 210, 212, 214, 215–237
heuristic, 235, 237
hexagram(s) xiv, 2, 7, 12, 17, 29–33, 83, 94, 104–6, 108–20, 122–26, 129, 134, 135, 163, 164, 188, 217–22, 228
history, 1, 9, 25, 30, 33, 35, 36, 47–49, 53, 63, 69, 70, 74, 75, 84, 96, 100, 102, 106, 118, 138, 159, 186, 232, 233

incipience, 131, 132
interpretation, 1, 5–9, 11, 14–18, 21, 25, 27–28, 30, 32–36, 38–39, 41–46, 51–55, 58, 60, 62–63, 65–66, 68, 72–75, 77, 80, 82, 85, 88, 94, 96, 105, 116–17, 119–20, 125,

272

Index

130–31, 133–37, 143–48, 151, 153–54, 161, 163–65, 167–68, 172–76, 183, 187, 191, 195, 205, 210, 214–15, 217–220, 226–27, 229–31, 233, 236–37
interpretative, 37, 230
intersubjective, xv, 1, 6–11, 17–19, 28, 34, 38, 42, 44, 51, 59–62, 65–66, 68–69, 71–72, 77, 80, 84–86, 88, 92, 102–5, 110, 130, 135, 137, 163–64, 212, 214–16, 218, 230–32, 237
intersubjectivity, 17, 39, 42–44, 46, 60, 71, 73–77, 83, 85, 102, 137, 163, 187, 230–31, 234
intertextual, 13–15, 36, 37, 39, 44, 45, 51, 88, 102, 103, 105, 129, 229

Jìjì, 32, 111
Jūnzǐ, 7, 32, 116, 117, 127–29, 132, 133, 234

Kǎn, 111, 113
kosmos (κόσμος) 212–14, 221,
Kuí, 121, 220, 228
Kūn, 29, 31, 32, 111, 115, 123, 223

Lee, Archie C. C. 18, 24, 25, 34–37, 48, 59–61, 230
Lee, Jung Young, 23, 28, 29, 48, 59, 90, 151, 177, 181
Lee, Peter K. H. 22, 23, 48, 49
legalist school, 12–14, 89–91, 95, 96, 130
Lí, 111
Lín, 111, 126
logia (logos) 36, 200, 219, 221, 228
Lúnyǔ, 14, 43–45, 52, 127, 128, 130, 234

Mair, Victor, H. 89–94
Minford, John, 91–93
multilayered, xv, 19, 65, 83, 137, 164, 216, 231, 237
Murphy-O'Connor, J. 15, 166, 168–70, 172, 187–90, 192–95, 199

narrative, 4, 25, 53, 54, 71, 84, 165, 166, 225
numinous, 131, 132, 158

pastor, x, xv, 4–5, 7, 15, 17, 61, 71, 84–85, 91, 97, 105, 112, 119–24, 127–29, 135, 147, 157, 163–65, 170, 176, 185, 198, 212, 215–18, 220, 222–24, 228–31
patronage, 17, 142, 164, 188, 193–94, 196–201, 206, 210, 212, 214, 217, 219, 221, 222, 224, 228
Paul, xiv, xv, 1, 5, 6, 8, 9, 11, 12, 15, 16, 17, 18, 22, 23, 25, 26, 30, 38, 43–46, 51, 53, 54, 55, 58, 59, 60, 61, 62, 65, 73, 74, 82–86, 88, 103, 133, 135–48, 151, 152, 159, 160–218, 220–29, 232, 235
Paul or Pauline, xiv, xv, 1, 5, 8, 9, 11, 12, 8, 15–18, 22, 23, 25–27, 30, 38, 43–46, 51, 53–55, 58–62, 65, 73, 74, 82–86, 88, 103, 133, 135–48, 151, 152, 159–229, 232
personal, 1–5, 8, 11, 18, 25, 45, 61–62, 64, 69, 71–73, 80–84, 89, 96, 136, 138, 140, 156–58, 175, 194, 196, 216, 225–26, 233–36
philosophical, 2, 13, 14 ,25, 48, 54, 64, 75, 89, 92, 96, 106, 143, 146, 197, 200, 204, 231, 236
philosophy, 2, 3, 7, 14, 17, 23, 31, 33, 54, 59, 63, 64, 67, 73, 88, 89, 93, 101, 106, 130, 150, 163, 203, 204, 221, 222, 232, 233, 236, 237
Pǐ, 111
pivot or pivotal, 16, 148, 130–33, 135
pneumatics, 17, 164, 202, 203, 205–7, 209, 210, 212, 214, 217, 219, 221, 222, 228
pneumatikos or pneumatikoi, 189, 199, 202, 203, 208–10, 221
Polanyi, Michael, xv, 62, 64, 65, 72, 73, 80–84, 136, 235
Polaski, Sandra Hack, 141–44, 146, 173–175, 185
power, 1, 4, 5, 7, 8–9, 11, 17–19, 29, 53, 71, 85–88, 90, 92–93, 95–101,

Index

104–5, 108, 110, 112–15, 120, 122–23, 128–34, 137–38,
principalities and powers, xv, 8–9, 17, 84–85, 103, 135–40, 142, 147, 153–55, 161–64, 173, 175–76, 181–82, 184, 186–87, 210–12, 214, 217, 223–24, 227, 256, 258, 266
profound, x, 175, 183, 227, 236
profundity, 130, 131
propensity, 87, 88, 90, 93, 94, 96, 101, 108, 115, 124, 223
Puett, Michael, 89, 106, 107, 131, 132
psychikos (ψυχικὸς) 203–5, 214

Qián, 2, 7, 29, 31–32, 51, 111, 115, 125, 126, 128, 131, 133, 164, 221, 222,
Qiǎn, 2, 223

reflexive, 218, 235–36
Ricoeur, Paul, 6, 9, 10, 21, 41, 43, 60, 77, 79, 80, 236, 237

sarx, 159, 161, 205, 214
self, xv, 5–11, 15, 17, 18, 21, 22, 24, 25, 28, 30, 31, 35- 37, 39, 41, 42, 44, 50, 51, 53–55, 57, 59, 60, 61, 63–65, 67, 69–72, 74–80, 83–87, 90–94, 100, 101, 104, 109, 116, 121, 122, 125–30, 132, 135, 137, 142, 149, 154, 156, 158, 160, 161, 164, 167, 168, 171, 172, 174, 175, 178, 181–83, 185, 188, 190, 192–93, 197, 199, 200, 201, 206–9, 211, 212, 214, 218, 220, 222–26, 232, 234
self-cultivation, 234, 235
Shaughnessy, Edward, 12, 13, 106, 116, 117, 125
shì, xv, 1, 5, 7–9, 11, 12 -15, 17, 18, 24, 51, 55, 61, 62, 65, 68, 71, 80, 82–98, 101–105, 110, 115
Shuōguà, 29, 113, 121, 125
slave or slavery, 135, 142, 178, 181–85, 192–94, 196, 207, 212, 217, 227
Song, C. S. 47, 48
stoicheia (στοιχεῖα) 17, 151, 164, 176–85, 219, 228

strength, 87, 94, 96, 114, 124, 125, 127, 134, 208, 211, 221–24, 226, 227
strong, vi, 5, 48, 55, 81, 90, 98, 106, 112, 116, 124, 125, 127, 139, 169, 171, 172, 187, 200, 203, 205, 222, 223, 225, 226
Sūn Wǔ, 87, 90–92, 94
subjective, xv, 8, 52, 58, 59, 66, 72, 76–78, 86, 92, 110, 138, 164, 186, 218, 220, 231–32, 235
Suí, 111, 125–27, 220, 228
Sykes, Stephen, 141, 142, 145, 146, 173–76

tendency, 1, 27, 53, 62, 87–89, 92, 156, 224
Theissen, Gerd, 191, 192, 194
Thiselton, Anthony C. 191, 192, 194, 206, 209
tradition, xv, 2–4, 6–7, 9, 11–12, 14, 17–18, 21–26, 33–34, 36–37, 39–42, 45–48, 50–52, 55–59, 61–71, 73–76, 78, 80, 83–88, 100, 102, 106, 138, 161, 167, 170, 185, 204, 211–12, 218, 229, 231, 234, 237
traditional texts, 18, 39, 50, 65–66, 68–69, 73–75, 78, 80, 83–88, 102–4, 129, 138, 164, 217–18, 229, 231–32
trigram, 29, 32, 33, 105, 107, 113, 118, 122, 123, 125, 126, 220
Tuànzhuàn, 31, 32, 112, 114, 117, 120, 121, 123, 124, 126

understanding, v, xv, 6–11, 16, 17, 24, 25, 26, 36, 39, 42, 43, 45, 48, 57, 61, 63, 64, 66, 67, 69–80, 82, 83, 86, 98, 103, 104, 105, 112, 117, 120, 128, 129, 132, 135, 137, 140, 144, 145, 147–149, 154, 159, 160–64, 167–69, 173, 174, 186, 191, 195, 196, 203, 216, 218, 222, 225, 227, 229, 232, 237

Xúnzǐ, 12, 14, 25–27, 90, 94–97, 101, 129, 130, 134, 223

Walls, Andrew F, 47, 48

Index

Watson, 16, 168, 205
weak or weakness, vi, 33, 53, 57, 90, 94, 112, 127, 142, 181, 182, 184, 200, 202, 203, 205, 221, 223–27
Wēijì, 32, 111, 234
Wényán, 29, 125–28, 133, 221, 222
Wink, Walter, 135, 139, 141, 144, 145, 147–162, 164, 175, 177, 178, 180–182, 186, 212, 213, 217, 221, 223–25, 227
Winter, Bruce, 200, 202, 207, 208
Witherington, Ben, 190, 192, 194, 195, 197, 202, 203, 224

Xìcí 31, 32, 104, 107, 109, 110, 114, 125, 130–34, 222
Xùguà, 112, 113, 125

Yeo, Khiok-Khng, ix, 18, 22, 24, 34, 38–46, 48, 59–61, 74, 102, 200, 202, 203, 205, 212, 230, 231

Yìjīng, 2, 3, 7–9, 12, 13, 22, 23, 28, 30–34, 53, 65, 74, 82–84, 86, 104–106, 111, 118–120, 126, 132–35, 163, 164, 217, 218, 221–23, 229, 232
Yìzhuàn, xiii, xv, 1, 2, 9, 12–15, 17, 18, 23, 27, 28, 30, 31, 33, 45, 51, 59–62, 73, 74, 84, 85, 88, 89, 91, 94, 103, 104, 106, 107, 118, 119, 122, 124, 125, 130, 135, 136, 216–18, 222, 233
Yoder, John, 138, 140, 141, 147, 148, 153
Yǔ, 122–24, 220, 228

zhēn, 29, 113, 120, 126–27
zhèn, 87, 113, 123, 125–26
zhèng, 116, 126–27
zhǔn, 111–16, 118, 120–21, 220, 228

www.ingramcontent.com/pod-product-compliance
Lightning Source LLC
Chambersburg PA
CBHW071240230426
43668CB00011B/1517